Myron D. Yeager

THE HUTTON STORY

THE HUTTON STORY

By
SIR ELDON GRIFFITHS
ROBERTA LESSOR
AND
MYRON YEAGER

CHAPMAN UNIVERSITY PRESS
Orange, California

Chapman University Press
Orange, California

Library of Congress Cataloging-in-Publication Data

Griffiths, Eldon.
    The Hutton Story / written by Sir Eldon Griffiths, Roberta Lessor, Myron
Yeager.
        p.   cm.
    ISBN 0-929765-61-3
    Includes index.
    1. Hutton, Betty, 1913–1995. 2. Hutton, Harold, 1904–1975.
3. Refining Associates, Inc. 4. Refican (Corporation) 5. Businesspeople--
United States--Biography. 6. Petroleum industry and trade--Asia.
7. Petroleum industry and trade--Indonesia. I. Lessor, Roberta, 1943–   .
II. Yeager, Myron, 1950–   .   III. Title.
CT275.H7965075   1998
338.7'6223382'09598--dc21
                                                              98-30805
                                                                 CIP

Manufactured in the United States of America

Distributed by Seven Locks Press
PO Box 25689
Santa Ana, CA 92799
(800) 354-5348

Book design by:
Sparrow Advertising & Design

DEDICATION

To the inspiring legacy of two great Americans, Harold and Betty Hutton.

CONTENTS

W hen the financial crisis of the late 1990s roiled across Southeast Asia, two women—one on a ranch in Montana, the other in southern California—watched from afar as a combination of depreciating currencies and irredeemable debt wreaked havoc in Malaysia, turned boom to bust in Thailand, and brought down the government of Japan. Each was especially moved by the chaos that erupted in the giant archipelago of Indonesia.

Barbara Chambers, one of these women, was raising llamas with her husband in the cool air of the Rocky Mountains. The other, Mary Struck, was a widow living close to her childhood home in the city of Orange. Yet both of these women shared a deep concern as the news of east Asia's meltdown exploded into the headlines in the summer of 1998. Both watched as day after day the media told the stories of a crowd of students forcing General Suharto, the once all-powerful president of Indonesia, to resign; of the riots that spread like wildfire across Java, Sumatra, and Bali; of the pillage, rape, and arson as racist mobs tortured and hacked to death thousands of Chinese merchants whose investments undergirded the economy of a nation that was fifth in size and population in the world.

Neither Barbara Chambers nor Mary Struck was surprised—though each shed a silent tear—when within weeks Indonesia's banks closed their doors and scores, then hundreds, of its factories ceased production, laying off millions of workers who earned less than $20 per week. Nor were they taken aback when the news stories described how deep and wide was the network of bribery and corruption that honeycombed the upper reaches of Indonesia and much of east Asia's government and business, while all around unemployment spread and hunger stalked a land that nature had equipped to become one of the world's greatest food producers. Both women had seen it all before. They had been there in the tumultuous 1950s when, in an uncannily look-alike preview of Southeast Asia's 1990s meltdown, an earlier president of Indonesia was forced out of office in a welter of bloodshed; when the rupiah, Indonesia's currency, previously had dropped like a stone; when other racist mobs slaughtered hundreds of thousands; and when the Indonesian army, then as now, turned out to be the only force that could hold this vast nation together.

Connecting Barbara Chambers in Montana and Mary Struck in California with these awesome events were the heroes of this book, Harold and Betty Hutton, whose adventures in the Pacific provide unique insight for anyone seeking to understand why and how the once-renowned Asian model economies fell to pieces in the latter years of the twentieth century. The Huttons pioneered the Pacific Rim over the decades that saw the rise—and sowed the seeds of the downfall—of these east Asian "tigers." They built up a trading empire that helped Japan recover from World War II, penetrated the forests of Thailand and jungles of north Sumatra, and in the process became multimillionaires and philanthropists. Barbara Chambers is Harold's only daughter, who joined him in Southeast Asia and made a name for herself as Singapore's ladies golf champion in the 1960s. Mary Struck is Betty Hutton's only sister, who worked alongside Betty as the Huttons' oil conglomerate expanded across the Pacific and later helped her become one of southern California's leading property tycoons. It is therefore fitting and natural that the authors turned to both these ladies as indispensable sources of the copious eyewitness material that provides the background to this intimate—yet globally wide reaching—biography of two American originals. Together with Tom Parker, chairman of the Hutton Foundation (and Betty Hutton's nephew by marriage), they and all the other living members of the very widely extended Hutton family gave generously of their time and memories, and their photo albums and scrapbooks. Among the treasures they made available were Harold's love letters to Betty and his own later correspondence and diaries.

Other indispensable sources on both sides of the Pacific included General Ibnu Sutowo, founder of the Indonesian oil industry, and his wife, Sally, and his colleague in north Sumatra, Brigadier General Johannes Pattiasina; Mrs. Edwin Chia and her daughters in Thailand; the Hiroshi Hirano family in Japan; and Madam Chin Ah Siew, now well over ninety years old, the Huttons' former *amah* (housekeeper) in Singapore. All these and many others made Sir Eldon Griffiths and Tom Parker welcome during their 1998 research visit to the Huttons' former haunts in Southeast Asia. Back in the United States, Charles and Miriam Clurman were a mine of information and photographs on Harold's work in China and the Philippines. Tom Chambers, Harold's son-in-law, along with Joe Gohier, Brad Hovey, Ralph Wathey, Willie Chapman, and Irene Anderson, provided valuable insights into the operations of the Huttons' companies, Refining Associates and Refican. *Pertamina*, the story of the Indonesian oil industry, edited by Professor Anderson G. Bartlett III, provided a wealth of historical scholarship from which we have quoted extensively. Richard Stegemeier also helped with the broad perspectives of a former chairman of Unocal.

Betty's high school friends Jean Hart Fairbairn and Iola Windolph Myracle offered vivid memories, as did Sylvia Law and Jerry Baker, two of the most perceptive—and affectionate—of the Huttons' employees and friends. Arlene Craig, president of The Betty L. Hutton Company, compiled and scrutinized facts, figures, and dates to ensure an accurate record of the Huttons' business activities, a testimony to her devotion to Betty Hutton as well as her loyalty to the company.

For genealogical research and analysis, the authors are indebted to Margaret Hoffman; their thanks are also due to Christi Broach Hendry, granddaughter of one of Betty Hutton's cousins, to Collen Caban of UCLA, and to Robert Myers, curator of the Berrien County, Michigan, Historical Association, for family history, and to Ann Cameron, assistant to the president of Chapman University who provided valuable assistance in the review of the book.

Last but not least, the authors' thanks go to the Hutton Foundation for its indispensable support for travel and research in Southeast Asia and to Chapman University for providing a generous share of the funding required to accumulate, write, and edit the many millions of words of research that went into *The Hutton Story*.

Sir Eldon Griffiths acted as overall editor as well as writer of the chapters dealing with Harold Hutton's early life and the Huttons' adventures in Asia. Much of the information on their oil business and the international context in which they operated reflects Sir Eldon's contemporary experience as a foreign correspondent and editor for *Time, Life,* and *Newsweek* and, later, as a Member of Parliament in Britain. Dr. Roberta Lessor, a sociologist at Chapman University, concentrated on Betty's family and her early life, as well as her courtship with Harold Hutton. Research and much of the writing on Betty's later business career and her contributions to Chapman University was undertaken by Dr. Myron Yeager.

The final assembly was done over close to two years by Sir Eldon and his indefatigable World Affairs Council aide, Patricia Fleeson, and by Lady Betty Griffiths, who cheerfully typed and retyped thousands of pages of drafts and edits of every chapter, more often than not three or four times. This she did in the former home of President Dwight David Eisenhower at the Eldorado Country Club in Indian Wells, California. Owned by the Hutton Foundation, this desert oasis was an appropriate location in which to complete *The Hutton Story,* for it was at a Palm Springs gas station that Harold Hutton and young Betty Spennetta first met on a blind date and in the Eisenhower house that Betty Hutton, in her later years, enjoyed her favorite pastime, entertaining friends and family in the California desert.

To all those others, too numerous to name, in many parts of east Asia and throughout the United States who contributed so willingly to this wide-ranging story, the authors express their thanks and appreciation. Only the mistakes, if there are any, are exclusively our own.

INTRODUCTION

The soldiers in their jungle camouflage fanned out on either side of the narrow, sagging pier that reached out from an area of weeds running alongside a muddy creek. To their left on a hill was an oil tank the size of a municipal gasometer; to their right was a shallow bayou with half a dozen rusting hulks protruding from the green water and a landing craft tied up to a dock pitted with bullet holes and shrapnel. A small oil tanker with a single funnel, peeling paint, and a woebegone air was berthed at a jetty at the end of the pier, along which a detachment of troops stood in line to greet and protect a small group of dignitaries approaching in an armored Land Rover and a Dodge power wagon.

The temperature at 10 A.M. was close to one hundred degrees Fahrenheit and the humidity was like the inside of a Chinese laundry as the two vehicles splashed to a halt in the mud at the entrance to the pier. Out of the armored Land Rover climbed two army officers in camouflage uniforms. One, the more senior, carried a swagger stick. The other, a major, opened the rear door of the truck for two American passengers.

The location could have been some faraway jungle creek on the Indian Ocean coast of Thailand or an inlet in the mangrove swamps of Luzon in the southern Philippines. It was actually Indonesia, on the shore of a muddy little estuary in the northeast of the still largely untracked volcanic island of Sumatra. The time could have been the late 1990s when the immense Indonesian archipelago was reeling from financial and political typhoons greater than any of those that had precipitated currency devaluations and political upheavals across the rest of east Asia. The actual date was May 24, 1958, in the bloody aftermath of World War II and Indonesia's untidy struggle for independence. The main actors, the two Americans who climbed out of the truck, were Harold and Betty Hutton—pioneers, merchant adventurers, and the heroes of this romantic "duography." Together they owned Refican, a small independent oil company whose activities spanned the Pacific. Refican's adventures in north Sumatra were to transform substantially the economy of Indonesia, change the way the world's oil industry did business with developing countries, and in the process, make the Huttons multimillionaires and philanthropists.

For the Huttons, it had been a long and dangerous journey from the orange groves of California to the jungles of north Sumatra. Along the way, they had transformed a love affair in the California desert into a lifelong business partnership in which Harold Hutton threw out ideas and made executive decisions while Betty provided backup and, when necessary, a word of caution or even a silent veto. Harold was a wildcatter by nature, a risktaker and a gambler, but he was also a fine judge of people, with a clear eye for an opportunity and more than enough of the drive and single-mindedness needed to grasp and exploit it. Betty Hutton was a good deal quieter, more reserved than her ebullient husband, but she, too, was shrewd in business. She inherited the pioneering spirit bequeathed to her by generations of her family who had crossed the American continent by covered wagon as fur traders, farmers, and merchants.

The Huttons in 1958 were pioneers in Pacific Asia. Already they had ventured to Moscow in an effort to trade oil for Kamchatka crab at the height of the Berlin airlift, which in 1948 brought the United States and the USSR perilously close to war. In the central Pacific, they had collected surplus U.S. Navy lubricants from the islands where they had been stockpiled in readiness for an invasion of Japan that never took place. The Huttons sold these lube oils to the Russians, the Japanese, and Chiang Kai-shek's Nationalist Chinese in Manchuria. The Huttons' oil products had made it possible for the Catholic churches of the Philippines and the Buddhist and Taoist shrines of the Asian mainland once again to illuminate religious services with the candles that had been denied to them during the Second World War. Most recently, in the high, densely vegetated mountains where Burmese rebels and the Thai army still fought a bloody war, Harold had rebuilt a secondhand refinery shipped from Bakersfield, California.

Indonesia in the mid-1950s was the Huttons' latest—and by far their most hazardous—adventure. All around them was a land with natural riches of timber, metals, oil, and the most fertile soil in Asia that cried out to be developed; yet then, as now, all but a few (nearly always the cronies of Indonesia's military rulers) lived in abject poverty, victims of their own country's history of home-grown and external oppression.

The Indonesian archipelago stretches across a sea area larger than the United States, its three thousand islands spanning the strategic sea routes that link the Indian Ocean to the Pacific and the China Sea. One day it would become the rice granary, mineral treasure house, and power plant of Southeast Asia, but when the Huttons first set foot there in the 1950s, Indonesia was in the same financial shambles and cockpit of civil war that it would be in in the 1990s.

Looking downstream from the pier at Pangkalan Susu, Betty Hutton noted the wrecks of half a dozen vessels lying on their sides in the channel. These offered a grim reminder of how the Dutch, who for three centuries had ruled Indonesia as the pearl of their east Indian empire, had destroyed Sumatra's oil fields to deny them to Imperial Japan, whose invasion of Indonesia followed soon after the 1941 attack on the U.S. fleet in Pearl Harbor.

Since then, Indonesia had known occupation by the Japanese, liberation by the British acting on behalf of the former Dutch colonizers, and a prolonged and messy struggle for independence. This struggle was interrupted by two shattering Dutch "police actions" as the Netherlands sought unsuccessfully to re-establish its prewar colonial authority. The Republic of Indonesia achieved its independence from Holland on November 28, 1949. Ever since, as the glory days faded, its people found themselves subject to the even greater tyrannies of hunger, civil strife, inflation, and disease that Dutch rule for the most part had forestalled. Rival chieftains in the outer islands struggled to assert their local supremacy in the face of the first nationalist government established in Jakarta by a silver-tongued revolutionary, Bung Sukarno.

Harold Hutton had met Sukarno in Los Angeles, California, soon after Sukarno became Indonesia's first president. Sukarno's fiery oratory instilled in his diverse people a sense of common identity and nationhood; but as happened in Castro's Cuba, Sukarno's penchant for Marxist "solutions" to economic problems was soon to infect the agriculture, industry, and commerce of the nation. Indonesia ceased to be able to grow enough rice or fruit to feed itself. Prices rocketed up by 200 percent per year. Cotton mills, sugar plants, even the crucial oil industry by 1958 were working at barely 20 percent of capacity. Nor was Jakarta in any position to borrow any more money from its creditors. In a poignant preview of the 1998 crash that was to bring Indonesia to its knees, foreign investment dried up in the face of triple-digit inflation, strong-arm tactics by militant trade unions, and massive corruption at all levels of government.

The parallels between the crisis of the late 1950s and that of the late 1990s are striking. Then, as now, there was no reliable legal system, no effective bank supervision, and little if any fiscal or monetary discipline. Looming over all this, too, was a fear on the part of the United States that President Sukarno was propelling Indonesia into an abyss that Washington deemed to be far worse than the financial collapse that the International Monetary Fund sought to stave off in the 1990s. Indonesia in 1958, when the Huttons first arrived there, was judged by the U.S. State Department to be on the brink of plunging into Sukarno's version of Marxist Leninism. Before long, the Central Intelligence Agency (CIA) forecast, Indonesia was destined to suffer the same fate as the former Nationalist China, enabling the power and influence of the Sino-Soviet bloc to extend across the crucial shipping lanes that join the Pacific to the Indian Ocean.

Harold Hutton was the first western oilman since the Dutch were driven out in 1942 to set foot in the remote provinces of north Sumatra that face Singapore and Malaya across the Strait of Malacca. Harold knew next to nothing and cared even less about Indonesian politics when he arrived in Medan, the main city of north Sumatra. What he did know was that the derelict oil fields left behind by the Dutch and Japanese had produced, when Shell Oil ran them, extremely high-quality, sulphur-free crude oil. He also knew that to obtain this oil he would have to formulate a deal with the only authority that could enforce its will in an immense and still primitive island—an island 900 miles long with mountain ranges reaching up to volcanos 14,000 feet high and swamps bigger than those of Louisiana, Mississippi, and Florida combined. That force was the Indonesian army, represented in north Sumatra by the officer with the swagger stick, Major Pattiasina, who escorted the Huttons to the port of Pangkalan Susu, and in Jakarta by "Patti's" boss, a physician-turned-brigadier general named Ibnu Sutowo. With General Ibnu, Harold had sealed with a handshake the shortest-ever contract in oil company history, two pages of amateurish type-script tapped out on a battered Remington machine in Ibnu's office. On that basis, the Huttons had agreed to provide and finance all the technical aid and equipment the Indonesians would require to re-open north Sumatra's oil wells, clear the pipelines through the jungle in the face of guerilla threats, and restore operations at the port of Susu.

Only then did they come face to face with potentially their greatest hazard—the risk that the world's greatest oil companies would take legal action to prevent any oil from north Sumatra from being sold on the global market. Backed by the governments of the United States and Britain, the Seven Sisters, as the major oil companies were known, had a strong case for intervention on grounds that Shell Oil, having opened up the Sumatran wells in the days before World War II, ought not to have been expropriated without compensation by Sukarno's government.

It was into this unpromising maelstrom that Harold and Betty Hutton had plunged every cent they owned. Their home, their business, their savings—all had been mortgaged to pay for this Sumatran adventure. The potential for profit was great but highly uncertain. When they arrived in Pangkalan Susu to watch the first small cargo of Indonesian oil being loaded at that shattered jetty, the Huttons and dozens of their employees had worked on the project for eighteen months without recompense. They had no guarantee clause in their contract. They could get no insurance on either the ship or its cargo since north Sumatra was an active war zone. Nor was safe passage to the open sea assured, since rebel troops occupied the island just two miles away from the jetty at Pangkalan Susu.

But the Huttons, especially Harold, were risktakers. Trailblazers and merchant adventurers, they were symbiotic partners in a lasting love match that brought them wealth, high living, and a lifetime of travel, adventure, and philanthropy. Like their forebears, especially Betty's, they were pioneers, but the frontiers they opened up were in the jungles of southern Asia. As they developed U.S. trade and new ways of doing business for the oil industry, they helped to carry the American dream way beyond the west coast of the continent. They also mirrored in their own lives and the ups and downs of their business the increasing engagement of the United States in the wars and political turbulence as well as in the titanic upsurge of the Pacific Asian economy.

The Huttons were to build a trans-Pacific oil kingdom, reaching from Manila to Tokyo, Hong Kong to Bangkok, Singapore to Jakarta, and back to California. The ambitions that impelled them to do this were unmistakably American. There were times in their early career when they might have been taken for babes in the wood, innocents abroad in a world that they only vaguely understood. Harold accepted, even gloried in, risks whose magnitude he and Betty only dimly apprehended. Turning a blind eye to the dangers, they took advantage when they could of the political and military convulsions that events threw in their path. And luck, more often than not, was on the side of this intrepid couple, enabling Harold to achieve his dreams of success as a Yankee trader and Betty to overcome the doubts that—along with the humidity, the flies, and the violence—assailed her at every turn in the road.

Harold was the first to burn out. Overstressed and overweight, he was a victim of the heavy smoking that he, like most men of his generation, had indulged in all his life. But death didn't come in the comfort of Villa Serena, which Harold had built for Betty in the hills of Orange County, California, or in the grand golf retreat the couple had purchased from Dwight D. Eisenhower when he left the Eldorado Country Club in the California desert at Indian Wells. Harold died, appropriately enough, on the other side of the great ocean where he and Betty had grasped the opportunities that brought them success. To the last, he was reaching out for one last wildcatter's adventure—to drill for oil in Russia's remotest waters, off Sakhalin island, north of Japan.

Betty Hutton was to survive her husband by twenty-three years but in no way as a grieving widow. The business skills she had honed as her husband's counselor and treasurer—and as the creator of the first woman-led business in the male-dominated oil industry—enabled her to build a second, though smaller, empire in the County of Orange where she grew up. Betty, as she aged, became an ever more private woman. She attracted the most intense loyalty, even love, from her subordinates, but lacking Harold's abilities to pick the best lieutenants, she came perilously close to losing the fortune the Huttons had earned. Yet Betty, true to her roots, discovered within herself the grit, perseverance, and good judgment to limit her losses, to fire some bad advisors, and to concentrate at the end on what painfully she learned to do best—invest selectively in southern California real estate at a time when the region came out of its 1980s recession and boomed.

Betty by then was happily remarried, but never would there be another Harold. Nor did they have any children to carry on his buccaneering legacy. Yet if Harold's song ended in Hong Kong, the melody lingered on, swelling into a crescendo as Betty, in the last chapter of her life, contrived an all-American happy ending to the Huttons' story. The charitable foundation that she and Harold had always dreamed of sprang into existence, allowing her before she died to share their wealth with hundreds, then thousands, who never otherwise would have tasted the riches the Huttons had earned.

Forty years later—as Indonesia teeters on the brink of economic chaos and civil strife and all the other Pacific lands where the Huttons traded and invested stagger in the face of the currency crises of the late 1990s—it is not easy to predict when and how east Asia will recover, though recover it will. A great deal depends on China and still more on the "global economy," a term that neither Harold nor Betty ever used. Yet the Huttons were among the progenitors and earliest individual practitioners of the global marketplace. They glimpsed, if only dimly, the now fast-developing possibilities of trade between West Coast America and the far east provinces of Russia. They saw first hand—and participated in—the titanic upsurge of east Asia that began in the late 1960s.

Harold Hutton died before the Cold War ended and the Soviet empire disintegrated. Betty Hutton, too, did not live long enough to see east Asia crash. Neither was therefore to know that Japan, where they first sold the tail-end oil (grease, as Harold called it) that laid the foundations of their fortune, would relive in the late 1990s the self-doubts that so many Japanese experienced when the Huttons first went to Tokyo. Nor could they have guessed that Jakarta, where Harold forged the strategic alliance with the founder of the Indonesian oil industry, would forty years later plunge back into the same state of political and economic chaos and near civil war that he and Betty lived and worked through during their middle years.

But the Huttons were movers and shakers in the early stages of these events. They understood, though they never shared in, Russia's midcentury ambitions for bilateral commerce with the United States. They were pioneers and active players in the explosion of trans-Pacific trade that transformed the east coast of Asia and the West Coast of North America in the 1980s and 1990s. They both were quick to recognize—and reject—those sly requests for bribes and under-the-table commissions that first greased, then undermined, the business culture of east Asia's miracle economies. Harold pulled back from Thailand and scaled back his activities in Indonesia in part because he and Betty were repelled by the corrupt practices that later were to contribute to the downfall of Suharto's "crony capitalism" in the late 1990s.

To understand the energies that drove the Huttons and the vision that inspired them, it is essential to know where they came from, to uncover their roots and to track the ambitions that enabled this venturesome pair to reach across the Pacific on the wings of luck and enterprise. The Huttons were quintessential Americans, forever reaching upward and outward, searching for the pot of gold beyond the horizon. Their qualities, which reflected their origins, made them two of the least known but, behind the scenes, most decisive Pacific pioneers of their times.

PART I   HAROLD'S STORY

The young Harold

THE BOY FROM ALBERT LEA, MINNESOTA

Harold Floyd Hutton was born on April 14, 1904, in Matoon, Illinois. He was the second of four children born to Albert and Caroline (Carrie) Hutton. Albert Hutton was a trim, good-looking man whose ancestors, he used to boast, came to America from England before the Declaration of Independence, though Albert never could find any documentary evidence of this.

Like tens of thousands of other young middle westerners in the late years of the nineteenth century, Albert started life on a farm but left home and the family acres as soon as he was able to buy a city suit and his first pair of patent leather shoes. Albert got a job as a salesman with John Deere, Inc., already a power in the land as the first farm equipment company to introduce the famous wave plow, which helped generations of American farmers to bust the sod and plough more deeply than any who had gone before. As a result, the Midwest by 1900 had become the food basket not only of America but of much of the world beyond. As a salesman for John Deere, Albert Hutton in his twenties spent many of his working days traveling from farm to farm across the corn and wheatlands of Illinois and Nebraska. During his early days with the company, he would arrive at the farm gate with his catalogues, samples, and price lists in the saddlebags of his horse; later, almost certainly, he drove a Model T Ford with John Deere logos on its doors.

Somewhere along the line, Albert Hutton met Caroline Floyd, the youngest of seven children born to a first-generation Irish-American immigrant who had moved from Jonesboro, Arkansas, to Matoon, Illinois. They fell in love and were married in Matoon. Their first child, Ivan, was born in 1901. Sadly, he lived only six years before dying of diphtheria, which, like scarlet fever and influenza, was an all-too-common illness among farm families in those years. Harold Hutton, born three years later, as a young child must have been aware of his parents' distress over his brother Ivan's death. The third child, Donald, born in 1907, lived and worked with Harold most of his life. The two boys were close companions until Donald died at age sixty on January 19, 1968. Harold's youngest sibling, Mary Lude, born in 1911, contracted food poisoning. Her death certificate describes the cause of death as "Moccasin poisoning," but it was the canned meat of that name, not the snake, that probably caused Mary Lude's death.

Not long after Donald was born, the Huttons packed their belongings and moved west to Albert Lea, a small town in the farm belt of southern Minnesota. All of America was on the move. With millions of new immigrants from Europe arriving in New York and Boston, the railroads were unloading tens of thousands of families in search of new lives and new jobs in middle America. Albert and Carrie Hutton responded to the mantra "Go west, young man." It was a time when the Middle West was booming. Optimism was the mood of the hour. The recession of the 1890s was forgotten. Agriculture, like steel, coal, and textiles, was doubling and redoubling production in response to the demands of a rapidly industrializing and urbanizing world that cried out for more of the American heartland's beef, pork, dairy products, and every kind of cereal and root crops.

Albert Lea in Harold's youth presented a microcosm of this buoyant national scene. Situated on the bank of a lake where in 1835 a young lieutenant with the First U.S. Dragoons, Albert Miller Lea, raised the Star-Spangled Banner in what then was wild Indian country, its adventurous history and robust growth imbued Albert and later his lusty son with the boisterous and happy-go-lucky convictions that clung to Harold for the rest of his life—that tomorrow will be better than today and that enterprise and risk-taking are the keys to growth and progress.

Lt. Albert Miller Lea described the city that bears his name as a "land of handsome lakes . . . beautiful prairies . . . surpassing any I have ever seen for beauty and fertility." But despite the area's fertile soil and abundant waters, the first permanent settler, Lorenzo Merry, did not arrive in Albert Lea until twenty years after the army got there. He was followed in 1856 by the town's first storekeeper, Julius Clark, who arrived in a covered wagon full of "trade goods" from Ohio. It was the railroads that made the difference in the town's population. By the turn of the century, six lines linked Albert Lea with Minneapolis, Minnesota; Milwaukee, Wisconsin; Chicago, Illinois; and St. Louis, Missouri. The trains picked up and deposited newly arriving settlers and freight in most every incorporated village surrounding Freeborn County, where homesteaders by the thousands arrived around the turn of the century. By 1910, when thirty-five passenger trains were arriving and departing every day, Albert Lea was the county seat and declared itself to be "the banner cream-ery and dairy center of Minnesota." The "big little city," as its boosters called it, was riding the crest of the wave of a farm boom that attracted more settlers, more investment, and not unimportantly, more boosters than any other city in Minnesota.

Harold Hutton's parents, Albert and Carrie, were among them. They arrived in a wagon with their two children in 1909. A slogan on the billboard at the edge of the town could hardly have failed to attract their attention: "Albert Lea grows every hour." The street scene underlined this: the dirt roads were being paved and public baths and a brand new fire department had just opened. Freeborn County's first street lights, switched on every evening, illuminated a fine new city hall, a federal post office, a court house, and a hospital. "The spirit of go-ahead and do things has accomplished highly desirable results," bragged the local newspaper. "If you are looking for a good town to live in or to do business in, Albert Lea is the answer."

The Huttons needed no persuading. Both had relatives with properties on the north side of the lake, who had written to offer the young couple help to get established. Finding a house proved difficult. Soon after the Huttons arrived, the local registry wrote, "Large numbers of new houses have been erected but there are no vacant places—everything is occupied as soon as it is built." Albert, thanks to his relatives and the references he could offer as an employee of John Deere, was fortunate to find a large clapboard house he could afford at 516 West Clark Street in a neighborhood of well-shaded boulevards with Norman Rockwell–style homes, nearly all with pointed roofs and ample porches. Skilled artisans, merchants, and traveling salesmen lived on Clark Street as they do today, but the house where Harold was brought up no longer is to be found. Almost certainly it was demolished to make room for a new wing added to Albert Lea's handsome Central School, which in those days combined elementary and high school classes in one building.

Harold was enrolled there as a first grader in 1910. He was an A pupil, a sturdy, good-looking blond child who fit in well with his predominantly Scandinavian, German, and Irish contemporaries. Later in life, Harold ceased to read anything more than his company accounts and paperback thrillers on airplanes, but long before he was ten he developed at Albert Lea Central School an abiding interest in early American and English history. His strong-minded mother made sure that he never failed to complete his homework under her watchful eye at the kitchen table.

By then their home was at 508 West William; the family moved in 1913. There, in a tall-ceilinged clapboard house that since has been subdivided into apartments, Harold grew from a chubby infant to a strapping teenager. From his bedroom window he could watch and listen to the rumble of freight and passenger trains pulling into or out of the main station and freight yards. His view to the north was blocked by a grain elevator beyond which West William ran out through a line of oaks and maples to the quiet place where the Huttons buried his brother Ivan and his sister, Mary Lude, in Graceland Cemetery.[1]

Not faraway from the Huttons' Albert Lea home on West William was a large grassy site where Barnum & Bailey's traveling circus pitched its big top

---

1. The cemetery is now marked by a floodlit Stars and Stripes that denotes the grave site of the Albert Lea men who died in uniform in two world wars.

every year. Harold and his brother Donald were regular attendees, gawking at the elephants and laughing themselves silly at the clowns. To the north, in the meadows running down to the lake, the city's better-off merchants were putting up smart, new homes, reflecting the prosperity that World War I brought to Albert Lea's packing plants, with gas-fired "Kitchen Kookers." One newly built home the Hutton boys visited was a Queen Anne–style shingle house owned by the cattleman Albert Wedge, who arrived in Albert Lea in 1856 and went on to become its state senator. Another big house, a self-described "idyllic country home," had been constructed between 1907 and 1910 for two sisters, Polly and Joy Horning McMillen, in a "wonderland of orchards, raspberry bushes, and strawberry patches." Harold sampled these fruits during midnight raids over the fence. Later in his life, when Harold and his wife Betty lived in a grand home in Singapore, Harold's ideas of residential style and comfort owed a lot to the impressions that Albert Lea's stately houses made on him during his teens.

Harold Hutton matured into a muscular and good-looking young fellow who easily won the hearts of the girls in his school. His grades were fairly good; his prowess on the football field attracted favorable attention; his popularity with his fellow students was said to be outstanding. Harold also played the piano, having been sent by his doting mother to learn at the hands of Albert Lea's most celebrated musician, a woman named Ida Bliss, whose daughter, Sadie, went on to become one of Minnesota's most admired singers and composers in the years after World War I. From Ida and Sadie Bliss and the hours he spent at his mother's insistence practicing scales on the upright piano in their living room, Harold inherited a lifelong love of sentimental ballads. One of his "pin-up girls" in Albert Lea was his mother's second cousin, Carrie Jacobs-Bond, who wrote a song that, corny as it sounds today, became a hit that was played far and wide on the phonographs that were as omnipresent in the homes of

America in the 1920s as television sets are today. Doris Christensen, his second cousin, recalls Harold's singing this song in a high tenor voice:

> I love you truly, truly dear,
>
> Life with its sorrow, life with its tear,
>
> Fades into dreams when I feel you are near,
>
> For I love you truly, truly dear.

Proud of his musical talents, Harold joined the Central School band, playing any instrument he could get his hands on but not very well according to Doris. The piano was the only instrument he ever mastered. He also played on Central High's football team and wore the colors of his home team and a triangle with the letter *H* (for Hoffman Cowlinge House) on his wide-collared "walking-out shirt."

In his preteens, Harold developed a concern that stayed with him all his life—to "look smart and dress well." He slicked down his hair and parted it in the middle in the manner of the young James Cagney. He was "forever fussing," to quote Doris (who evidently fell in love with the handsome young Hutton), to "make sure that all the buttons on his vest were neatly fastened." Harold's concern for appearances may well have reflected a certain Victorian primness in his mother Carrie's approach to life. Carrie liked to quote Shakespeare, "Manners maketh the man," and add her own codicil, "Modesty maketh ladies." Perhaps that is why Doris Christensen recalls, "Whenever I allowed my skirt to ride up above my knee, Harold would insist that this was unladylike and I must pull it down!"

Harold Hutton sowed his wild oats in abundance as a teenager, romancing his girl classmates, smoking behind the school fence, sneaking off on weekends to drive his father's car and ogle the girls on High Street. Visiting the Lea farm he would often gallop bareback across the stubble fields at breakneck speed on a horse named Nellie. In the winters he enjoyed skating and duck shooting; in the spring and summer Harold went fishing with his father in the nearby lakes.

Cousin Doris would often pick him up with his brother Don to go joyriding. "Harold always treated me as a perfect lady," she recalls. "Whenever there was anything on the road or in the fields that interested or worried us, he would stop the car, climb out, close the door, and tell me to sit tight: no way would he expose a lady to anything dangerous."

With his father, who evidently fancied himself as an engineer and inventor, Harold as a youngster tinkered about with the design for a cream dispenser that Albert Hutton dreamed might make the family's fortune. Albert had concocted a nondrip valve made of white metal and German silver to control the flow of cream or maple syrup out of pitchers, bottles, and jugs. This, he claimed, in advertisements that the Huttons pasted up on restaurant walls, "provided the means of serving with each cup of coffee just exactly the amount of cream you desire. No more—no less."

Alas for Albert, the Hutton cream dispenser worked well enough, as he promised, to produce "absolutely no dripping . . . saving cream . . . and increasing profit" but not for its inventor or his sons. The Hutton, as he called his invention, was beaten by cheaper rivals. As Harold was ruefully to comment when reminiscing about his father, "Albert Lea, as a dairy capital, was the right place to launch a creamer—but Dad just wasn't a hustler. His valve worked, but his marketing didn't. Maybe I learned something from that."

When Harold was fourteen, his family moved from Albert Lea to the big city, Minneapolis. The records do not show whether they made this major change in their own and their sons' lives because Albert lost his job at John Deere or because Carrie, always the stronger-minded partner, saw an opportunity to better the Huttons' fortunes by opening a hotel.

Carrie Hutton, a strong-featured woman whose photographs show her wearing dark dresses and a black toque, and nearly always holding at least one child in her arms, was an ambitious lady. She realized that the Huttons needed more income to raise their living standard than her easygoing husband, who

Harold (right, in tent) with father on camping trip

lacked his wife's drive and ambition, was likely to achieve. The family had to make a midlife change of location and occupation.

The Huttons therefore moved into the Grant Portland Hotel, a solid-looking, three-story hostelry built of stone, at 1025 Sixth Avenue South in what is now a historical district in downtown Minneapolis, where Carrie became the manager. During their time there as hotelkeepers, it was Carrie who did all the figuring and accounts. She turned the Grant Portland into a modestly successful business that catered to the growing number of commercial travelers, as salesmen were known in those days, who needed to stay overnight in Minneapolis.

The Huttons served big American breakfasts and four-course dinners in the main dining room. During the summer of 1921, Harold and his brother Donald waited on tables, cleaned shoes, and stoked the boiler. Weekends, when the hotel wasn't busy, they took off on fishing and hunting trips in the nearby hills and lakes.

Contemporary photos show Harold as a bronzed young fellow with laced-up boots and a fishing pole, perched on a fallen tree while his father sits in the entrance to their large tent rigged up with rough-hewn poles. All three Hutton males were avid smokers, Albert chomping on a pipe and Harold and Don with Camel cigarettes between their lips. Later in life, Harold forsook his fishing poles for golf clubs, but looking back, he would tell his friends that some of the best times of his life were those spent with his father among Minnesota's hills and waterfalls, fishing rod in one hand, Pabst Blue Ribbon beer in the other.

Transferring from the Albert Lea school, Harold went to Winona High School in Minneapolis. He was at best an average scholar, but he was a young lion on the football field and socially, it seems, a big success with the girls. When he graduated from Winona, June 14, 1921, Harold sent his mother, Carrie, an invitation to the commencement ceremonies written in a bold, firm hand with dramatic, teenage flourishes. A letter he sent to Doris Christensen asked her to

1920

Minnehaha Creek. Mpls.

Above: Romayne (left), sister, and friend (unknown) show a leg in Minnesota version of Ziegfield Follies.
Below from left to right: Harold at a fishing hole; with Romayne and his father's car

be his partner at the school dance that followed. But Doris was not to be his ladylove.

That fall, an attractive ash blond, whose parents, Bob and Edith Willey Bircher, lived in a duplex on Park Avenue, came to work as the Grant Portland's switchboard operator. Romayne Bircher, one year younger than Harold, had flashing blue eyes, wavy fair hair, and a magical laugh that captivated the hotel-keeper's son. She and her sister, Lorraine, had spent their early teenage years with their father in Long Beach and longed to return to California's beaches and sunshine. Romayne and Harold started dating. There are pictures of them sitting together, holding hands and laughing, on the grass outside the hotel. The young couple would disappear together to the movies, followed by milk shakes at the nearby soda fountain, and take night drives in Harold's father's car—with or without permission. When it snowed after Thanksgiving in the fall of 1921, they went sledding on frozen Lake Minatawa. The next spring they went with Lorraine to picnic by the woods at Minehaha creek. Photographs taken by Harold show the girls throwing up their skirts like the Ziegfield girls in the New York Broadway follies shows of the 1920s.

Carrie Hutton was not amused. She soon convinced herself that Romayne was not the right girl for her son and that Harold needed a dose of sterner discipline than she had time or her easygoing husband had inclination to administer. Carrie sent for prospectuses of a number of military academies. St. Johns in Delafield, Wisconsin, was strongly recommended by one of its former graduates who stayed at the Grant Portland Hotel.

Harold (center) at St. Johns Military Academy

St. Johns Military Academy

Dating back to 1854, St. Johns Academy was founded by Dr. James De Koven, a graduate of Columbia University who started work as a parish priest at a primitive little mission established on the banks of Lake Nagawicka not far from the Great Western Road that meandered from Milwaukee to Madison. De Koven could trace his family back to the original Governor Winthrop of Massachusetts. He opened St. Johns as a two-room, shed-like structure modeled on St. Peters College in Raleigh, England. Students dined at long tables, sitting on benches without backs, exactly as it was done at St. Peters; his students were also expected, as they were back in England, to row on the nearby lakes in Wisconsin's first six-oared boats.

In 1883, when Delafield boasted 115,587 residents, St. Johns Academy was taken over by the son of a British army officer, the Reverend Sidney Thomas Smythe. Smythe had no money, but with the assistance of a local physician he reroofed and repainted the building and got fifteen boys and girls to sign up as day students at an annual fee of $12. Smythe was a man with a mission. He envisioned St. Johns becoming the American equivalent of the great English boarding school, Rugby. Others saw only an uninviting little building with dingy ceilings and grubby windows, but the Reverend Smythe envisioned the imposing battlemented structure St. Johns was later to build. Right from the start, he insisted on discipline, school uniforms, and the classics. St. John's motto is "Work hard, play hard, pray hard." Its founder's educational philosophy was that "the best way to get the most out of a boy is to make him reach just a little farther than he had supposed his arms could reach."

That kind of life, not dallying with Romayne Bircher, was exactly what Carrie Hutton wanted for young Harold. She and Albert read every word of

St. Johns inch-thick brochure entitled "A School for Gentlemen's Sons." Under the heading "The Kind of Boys We Want" it stipulated, "We are desirous of welcoming young men who will delve during study time; who will play, and play heartily, during play time; boys who will all times be high-toned, courteous gentlemen. A boy who does not believe that he desires to be all this had better apply for admission elsewhere. We do not need him."

For Harold's parents the fees were expensive: $820 per year to cover tuition, board, lights, and fuel. Extra charges would also be made for laundry and for instruction in music, fencing, and boxing.

Jacob Reeds Sons Inc., military tailors of Philadelphia, were the specified academy tailors, who maintained a fitter with his assistant at the academy throughout the year. The careful cadet, said the catalog, "can make his uniform last from one and one-half years to two years."

Harold's parents took him to see St. Johns Academy in the spring of 1922. They traveled by train from Minneapolis, changing in Milwaukee and taking the electric car that carried them through the lake country to the school. They found the campus on a site sloping down to Lake Nagawicka nearby, as the catalog said, "a tall hill from which on a clear day 26 of southern Wisconsin's inland lakes can be seen." Carrie Hutton put a tick mark next to that item in her catalog. "The sight commends itself to parents . . . being removed from the temptations of large towns or cities." She made another tick at this item. "The school is noted for its health record." This item Carrie underlined.

St. Johns must have looked to Harold's eyes uncomfortably military. Its walls were crowned with battlements and octagonal towers. A twenty-foot archway through which the Huttons entered led to the offices of the aged but still redoubtable President Smythe. A cadet sprang to attention. He conducted the visitors on a tour of the students' mess with stained glass windows and backless benches (as in Oxford and Cambridge). Above was Welles, the barracks in which Harold was to spend the next year of his life. Next door was Smythe Hall, another gray limestone pile with octagonal towers at the corners. Inside was a six-foot-wide running track suspended ten feet above the polished floor. Below, in the basement, Harold visited the school armory packed with rifles and pistols.

The Huttons spent a whole day wandering across the campus at St. Johns. They saw the academy's muscular oarsmen pulling their shells across Lake Nagawicka and lingered at Harold's insistence at Knights Hall, another fortress-like building built of rough boulders from the surrounding hillsides, with ten immense windows providing light for the physics laboratory. It was there that Harold Hutton first tinkered with a bunsen burner, boiling and distilling liquids, including oil.

They completed their campus tour with a brief visit to Rosslynne Manse, President Smythe's colonial-style home near a grove of noble old trees. Then Harold and his parents returned to the administration offices to meet Major Roy Ferrand, commandant of the cadets, who wore on his uniform the diploma of the French Legion of Honor alongside the U.S. Victory Medal. Ferrand rattled out some of the requirements for new students, among them "a certificate of moral character from a clergyman in the town where the boy resides." Then, to Carrie's satisfaction, Ferrand formally welcomed Hutton, H. F., as St. John's newest cadet, adding for good measure that "at St. Johns, we train our boys to lead a Godly life."

That fall when Harold for the first time left home to go to college, he packed his trunk with care. The school's regulations were precise: each cadet must bring with him "6 face towels, 2 bath towels, hair brush and comb, toothbrush and water glass, whisk broom and shoe shine kit; 6 shirts, 3 night shirts or 3 sets of pajamas, 3 sets of underwear (medium weight), 12 handker-chiefs, one bathrobe . . . " What students must not bring, said the catalog, were "expensive rings and stick pins, watches, etc. These are no part of a cadet's kit." As for Harold's new quarters, his enrollment orders said, "We do not permit the exercise of the modern school boys' fad for the bizarre and the luxurious. Cadets should therefore be careful to leave at home all cushions and fancy pillows. Our rooms are furnished as befits the quarters of young gentlemen living the military life."

Cadet Hutton enlisted with ninety other first-year men in the class of 1922. He elected to study English literature, modern history, Spanish, and plane geometry in addition to St. Johns' standard courses in penmanship, spelling, declamation, military drills, and sports. His daily routine was strict. After a bugle call at 6:00 A.M., fifteen minutes were allotted for dressing and lavatory purposes before another bugler sounded breakfast call and the cadets fell in to march to the mess. After breakfast, the boys hurried back to "quarters" to tidy their rooms and make up their beds in time for inspection by the officer of the day, resplendent in white ducks, crimson sash, and gold braid. Harold soon got into the routine—shining his boots until he could see his face in them, lining up the sheets and blankets of his bed at exact right angles, hanging his clothes on proper hooks—that regulations directed.

Each morning at 8:30 A.M. he joined the school formation on the "gravel," a full order drill that ended with roll call. Next the cadets marched off to their section rooms for classes until 12:45 P.M. At 1:00 P.M. came dinner, the most important event in the life of healthy youngsters, and after that, battalion drill, with the long lines of gray-clad cadets breaking into "fours" and passing by the colonel. The rest of each afternoon was devoted to sport, in Harold's case, rowing and boxing. At age nineteen he was a husky fellow. The school magazine, *Cadet Days,* recorded him as rowing at 173 pounds and boxing at 158 pounds in the De Koven indoor meet of March 22–24, 1922. Harold was on the water daily, though there is no record of his being chosen to pull an oar for the "Wet Bobs," the academy crew. How well he fared in the boxing ring is also unrecorded, though later in life Harold would often playfully assume a pugilistic stance and pummel his brother Don with short jabs to the stomach and head.

St. Johns gave Harold Hutton a respect if not a taste for both the virtues and limitations of a military academy of the 1920s. Its ethos, as its founder intended, was masculine, muscular, and with Evensong in the chapel at 5:30 P.M. five afternoons of the week, staunchly Episcopalian and Anglican. The humor of its students and faculty, as recorded in *Cadet Days* magazine, was that of most upper middle class Americans of the time.

Winslow: Wouldn't she Rockerfellow?

Robbins: I never Astor.

Biron: At the Follies the other night my eyes felt like little birds.

Walker: How come?

Biron: Flitting from limb to limb, m'deah boy.

Harold Hutton seems to have been a round peg in a square hole at St. Johns. He enjoyed wearing the uniform. Pictures of him show a pushy young man leaning against the mantelpiece of the junior common room wearing a crimson military jersey and clutching a pipe between his teeth. Others show Harold and his roommates swaggering on a staircase wearing black leggings and German fencing-style hats. His military grades were good in "deportment, punctuality, cleanliness, smartness on parade." His academic performance was less impressive except in English and history, where nearly all his grades were in the high 70s and 80s. In Spanish, Cadet Hutton did worse, with monthly grades of 71, 66, 63, and a high one of 74. His plane geometry grades were better: 70, 65, 70, 75 for "an average of 74," according to his instructor (who plainly wasn't using a calculator).

By the end of his first year, Harold had had enough of St. Johns Academy. He found the routine tiresome, the discipline overbearing. Uncharacteristically, he failed to throw himself into the academy's extremely varied social activities: he wasn't in the orchestra and he did not sing in the choir, play in the band, or participate in the Boars Head Glee Club. He showed no inclination to seek promotion to corporal or sergeant.

More than likely, Harold was pining for his ladylove. Certainly, his sojourn at St. Johns did not lead him to forget Romayne as Carrie Hutton had hoped and intended. And no sooner did he return home than he took to going out again with Romayne. It was midsummer of 1923, the era of the golden '20s when the Charleston and the Black Bottom were all the rage among American teenagers. Harold and Romayne kicked up their heels at the local dance halls as well as, in all probability, some of the speakeasies that sprouted in the back streets of prohibitionist Minneapolis.

In modern parlance, the young couple was "doing their own thing," but in Carrie Hutton's eyes this behavior could not be tolerated. Carrie's determination that her son should have the best education she and Albert could afford never wavered. She was equally convinced that an early marriage or worse, premature fatherhood, would ruin Harold's chances in life. For Romayne, she showed little respect. She was determined to separate Harold from his first sweetheart.

Before Harold quit St. Johns, Carrie had written to a number of other boarding schools within a fifty-mile distance from Minneapolis, seeking their prospectuses. The one that impressed Carrie most was Carleton College in Northfield, Minnesota.

CHEMISTRY AND ASTRONOMY
AT CARLETON COLLEGE

Carleton in the '20s was one of the top ten Midwest schools. Located in Northfield, a pleasant little town of 4,000 located forty miles south of the Twin Cities, it was founded a year after the Civil War ended by a group of Minnesota Congregationalists whose stated purpose was to "maintain genuine Christian influences for the development of strong, well rounded characters." This mission statement appealed strongly to Carrie Hutton. Harold's father thought the fees were on the high side: tuition, $125.00 per semester; board, $120.00; rooms, $75.00; plus $12.50 for health and sports. But what Carrie Hutton wanted for her son, she made sure she—and Harold—got. Harold was enrolled in Carleton on September 10, 1923.

Arriving on campus, he was interviewed by the treasurer, F. J. Fairbanks, and the chairman of the Board of Deans, Dr. Edwin B. Dean, an emeritus graduate with doctorates in divinity from both Chicago Theological Seminary and Doane College. Fairbanks gave Harold a brief history of Carleton, starting with its first president, the Reverend James W. Strong. Pastor of the Congregational Church in Faribault City, Minnesota, Strong sought to model Carleton on Harvard and Yale. Returning home from a visit to New England in 1879, Rev. Strong was so badly injured in a railway accident that his family gave him up for dead. Miraculously, Strong survived. This so impressed one William Carleton, whose help he had sought for the college, that Mr. Carleton offered an endowment of $50,000, a huge sum in those days, to mark the pastor's recovery. Not surprisingly, Rev. Strong and a grateful board of trustees in 1871 renamed Northfield School for their benefactor.

It is not recorded how Harold Hutton reacted to his first interview at Carleton, but later in life he would share a few tidbits that stuck in his memory. Carleton's first degrees, for instance, went to James J. Dow and Myra A. Brown, whose commencement orations, respectively on "the attainment of true manhood" and "the intellectual culture of womanhood," led them six months later to be married on Christmas Day, 1874. Harold thought that story was "rich," as he put it.

On his first visit to the campus, Harold was handed a catalogue that continued Dr. Fairbanks's history lesson. Here he could have read that the school's first treasurer, Joseph Lee Haywood, was shot dead during the Jesse James gang's raid on the First National Bank of Northfield (1876) and that the college's first permanent building was destroyed by fire in the same year Edison invented the electric light bulb (1877).

As Harold took his first walk around the campus with his father, the leaves were turning red and gold. The two men strolled to a point on the college grounds where they overlooked a wooded valley filled with a series of artificial lakes. (These lakes were constructed in 1916 by Mr. and Mrs. George R. Lyman of Pasadena, California, as a memorial to their son, George Huntington Lyman, a Carleton graduate killed in the First World War.) Harold was to continue his rowing on these lakes, known as Lyman Lakes. He would also work out at Laird Athletic Park with its eight tennis courts, football field, baseball diamond, and pits for vaulting and jumping.

More interesting to Harold on his first tour of the campus was the astronomy building with its renowned Goodsell Observatory, which more than anything else had brought national recognition to Carleton. The Goodsell Observatory established the first U.S.-based time signals, setting the time for more than 12,000 miles of U.S. railroads. Harold was fascinated by the observatory's telescopes.

During his short and, it must be said, unremarkable career at Carleton, he was to acquire a lifelong fascination for stargazing. Later, when he met the girl who was to become the love of his life, Betty Spennetta, Harold would frequently romance her under the desert stars in Palm Springs by showing off his considerable (if amateurish) knowledge of the constellations. Many of the letters he wrote to Betty during their courting days contained references to the solar and stellar systems, many gleaned from the *Sidereal Messenger,* the world's only popular astronomical journal, published at Carleton since 1882. Subsequently, when Harold, searching for offshore oil, became a frequent voyager across the South Pacific, his letters written to Betty from his survey vessels contained other stellar references harking back to his exposure at Carleton to its student journal *Algol,* named for the variable star.

Despite his resistance to being separated by his parents from Romayne, Harold at first made more effort to fit into the Carleton milieu than he had at St. Johns. As a freshman, he was allotted room 126 in West Hall, a three-story brick structure. Many of his classmates were from Minneapolis. A 1920s catalog shows a total of 905 students of which 725 were from Minnesota, 69 from the Dakotas, 29 from Wisconsin, 15 from Iowa, and 12 from Montana. Ten others were classed as "foreigners": two from Canada, three from China, one each from France, Japan, Mexico, Persia, and South America.

Carleton, true to its Christian tradition, required all students to attend chapel services conducted by members of the faculty at 10:00 A.M. each week day, except Monday and Friday. Sunday evenings they were also expected to attend vespers in the college chapel. Harold was never religious, but he had a melodious tenor voice until excessive smoking made him hoarse, and it is probable that he took part in the college's choral activities.

At first, he also plunged into a wide range of athletic activities—rowing, boxing, and swimming. He easily completed the compulsory physical education class requiring three hours' marching and cross country running plus a "40-yard swim, a plain running dive to recover a small object in 8 feet of water, and towing an inert body." Those who played games for the college won their official C letters. A picture of Harold shows him wearing a crimson jersey with such a C, probably for boxing.

Another Carleton specialty was public speaking. Harold attended debates held during his first semester with Cornell, Colgate, and a visiting team from Oxford University in England. The Drama Club was no less active, putting on English classics such as *She Stoops to Conquer* by Goldsmith, *Twelfth Night* by Shakespeare, and *Arms and the Man* by George Bernard Shaw.

As a freshman, Harold took mandatory classes in English. His courses included English poetry and novels, news writing, and editorial writing with a brief study of the ethics of the press. His score in English was 101 for the first semester, but his final grade was Incomplete. He also tried his hand at Latin, supposedly spending four hours per week on works by Virgil and Cicero, but his grade was E (nonpass).

Harold's achievements at Carleton were unimpressive. As at St. Johns, he failed to take advantage of the broad curriculum and dedicated teaching force of a grand, if stern, institution whose strong faculty in the 1920s included twenty-four professors with doctorates from Yale, Chicago, and Michigan universities; one from the University of Wales, who lectured on political science; one from Oxford, who was a professor of history; and another from Naples, Italy, who taught music with a colleague from the Royal Academy of Music in London. Carleton's social life was no less distinguished. Dancing was permitted on the campus for the first time in 1919. The debating team regularly wore black ties and smart tuxedos. The school band, which traveled widely through the Middle West, attracted to its campus concerts celebrities like tenor Ecardo Martin, pianist Jan Giapusso, and baritone Walter Green. But Harold's mind was elsewhere. His academic performance in his first semester was mediocre to poor; it deteriorated further in his second semester. The only list of his grades that remains shows:

	First Semester	Second Semester
English	X	3C
Latin	E	E
Athletics	E	E
Public Speaking	3C	3B
Bible Studies	E	-
Art	-	-

Surprisingly, there is no record of Harold's grades in the only subject other than astronomy that stirred his imagination—chemistry. Carleton offered excellent training in both organic and inorganic chemistry under the guidance of Professors Lincoln and Bardwell, both Ivy League–trained chemists. "Inasmuch as chemistry is useful in the home, travel, and in business," intoned the college's catalog, "it is an essential part of all general education." Harold attended classes in the Leighton Laboratory. As at St. Johns, he dabbled in liquids and learned to break them down into their component parts in one of the special labs for quantitative and organic chemistry. There is no record of his achievements, but Harold undoubtedly built on the foundations he had acquired at his military academy to become proficient in laboratory work. "I got to know my way around a drop of oil," was how he put this in later years. He was to quit school without any formal training or qualifications as a chemist, but this did not stop Harold in later years from describing himself as having "graduated in chemistry" in the resumes he sent out when looking for work.

The biggest social event during Harold's time at Carleton was the 1923 May Fete, an elaborately orchestrated pageant showcasing a Greek costume drama that climaxed with the coronation of a May Queen. Thousands of spectators crowded onto the hillside overlooking a stage set up on an island in the lower Lyman Lake. Most of the women on campus took part, and a local reviewer described the fete as "the most beautiful impressive event of its kind in the northwest." But there is no record of Harold or his parents attending. More likely he slunk away from Carleton that weekend without permission.

Exactly what happened to bring about Harold Hutton's "withdrawal" from Carleton two weeks later is something of a mystery. According to Doris Christensen, his letters revealed no signs of unhappiness. They made no mention of any troubles he might have been experiencing with Dr. Dean, the school's disciplinary authority. So what kind of bad behavior led to Harold's expulsion? Had he skipped too many classes? Or were his grades simply not good enough to earn promotion from freshman to sophomore? One explanation of his sudden exit is that Harold all his life resisted and resented authority. As a teenager, he displayed the same lack of reverence for authority that later in life he was to feel for conventional wisdom and political correctness.

Perhaps, too, he was rebelling against his mother. When she loudly insisted on deciding what was "best" for him and his brother Don, the two boys often reacted by doing the opposite. Harold had strongly objected when he was packed off to boarding schools to "make a man of him," as Carrie put it. In his own estimation (and, it must be said, in that of his girlfriends) he needed no help to establish his masculinity.

But there was another far more immediate and more compulsive reason why Harold decided to leave Carleton. He was in love. No longer was he prepared to be separated from Romayne Bircher.

At every opportunity they had to be together in Minneapolis, the two youngsters talked of their future plans. Romayne yearned to return to California and the golden sunshine and beaches she had come to love as a child. Harold enthused about the subject that kept cropping up in the headlines—the California oil boom. His imagination had been stirred by stories from Los Angeles and Long Beach about "black gold." He had read about the giant gushers brought in during the early '20s by lucky strike drillers like Dry Hole Charlie and about the young farmer named Sam Mosher, who overnight had become a millionaire because he knew how to distill casinghead gasoline from heavy crude oil. Harold saw a future for himself in the refining part of the oil business. Romayne hated the bitter cold and darkness of Minnesota winters. In addition, like a million other young fans of the silent films of the 1920s, Romayne seems to have imagined that with her good looks, flashing smile, and svelte figure she might strike it lucky in the movies. Harold, the smitten lover, may well have thought so, too.

While Harold was still at Carleton, it is possible that he and Romayne were secretly engaged. He was twenty, and she nineteen, as they made plans to be married. Carrie Hutton suspected the worst. Once again, it seemed, Harold's waywardness had overcome his mother's determination that he should grow up a "Christian gentleman" and graduate with the good degree that none of her family had achieved.

"Whatever you do and wherever you go, when you matriculate at Carleton you become a part of the college for life and Carleton becomes a part of you," wrote one of Harold's contemporaries in the college's 125th year anniversary booklet, but there is little evidence of Harold's ever feeling that way. He valued Carleton for its football, though he played little, for its astronomy, and for its chemistry teachers to whose enthusiasm he paid tribute in his future career. But after the first semester, his mind was not on his work, his sentiments were otherwise engaged. The dean of students remonstrated. Harold was disciplined. His mother vigorously complained. But her son had made up his mind. Harold's university education ended prematurely and unsatisfactorily in June 1924. His final report at Carleton reads "Placed on probation by Board of Deans. No transcript to be issued without special note from Dr. Dean. Withdrew."

1920s sweethearts: Harold and Romayne, newly arrived in California

California, Here I Come

Harold Hutton and his sweetheart, Romayne Bircher, decided to elope when Harold's mother fired Romayne from her job on the switchboard at the Grant Portland Hotel. Then Harold and his parents got into a shouting match over the incident after Harold had had too much to drink. It was obviously time to leave.

The vehicle in which the young couple headed for California was a used 1921 Model T Ford, a convertible with large brown running boards and noninflatable tires. Details of their journey are scarce, but it was a long, uncomfortable drive south across the plains past Albert Lea, then west past Sioux City, Iowa, to the little city of Atlantic, Iowa, where Romayne was born. The Model T at best could reach fifty miles per hour as it rattled along the uneven and often unpaved roads to Kadoka, South Dakota, where they paused to look at the Badlands, and to Cody, Wyoming, where Romayne wanted to see the Buffalo Bill Historical Museum. They seem to have stayed at cheap hotels and in a cabin in the Yellowstone National Park, then headed south past Salt Lake City, Utah, to Reno, Nevada, where they were married. Harold took some pictures of his pretty young wife wearing a red-and-white checkered dress and clutching a small leather handbag. Romayne took a photo of Harold squatting in front of the Ford, a slightly sulky looking young man squinting into the sun in his thick Minnesota tweeds and waistcoat.

They were young, strong, and carefree, full of confidence and madly in love. En route, they sang in the car together, harmonizing their favorite songs, one of which was "School Days."

Ten days after leaving Minnesota, they reached Bakersfield, California. Harold stopped to look at the derricks in the Kern County oil fields where later in his life he was to become an oil tanker driver for Richfield.

As they headed south through the sprawl of Los Angeles, California, Romayne directed him past Griffith Park, where silent movies were being shot, west along Wilshire Boulevard with its forest of oil derricks, then south to Signal Hill. Harold's nostrils twitched as he sniffed the fumes from the oil stills. Farther on, there were row upon row of clanking oil pumps along the shores at Huntington Beach. There the couple shucked off their shoes and paddled in the Pacific. Romayne, greatly daring, wore one of the two-piece bathing costumes with bare midriff that were becoming fashionable in the mid-1920s in Hollywood. Harold looked long and hard at both the setting sun and the oil rigs. It was his first contact with the California oil industry in which he would spend the next half-century. It was also his first exposure to the Pacific Ocean on whose shores he would live a large part of his future and make most of his fortune.

When Harold and Romayne first arrived there, Los Angeles, not yet Houston, was the city most entitled to claim the name of Oiltown, USA. Stretching west and south from its civic center, hundreds of "donkey" pumps nodded up and down among fields of scarlet poinsettias. Along a four-mile stretch of Santa Monica and Wilshire Boulevards, more than 3,000 derricks had been in operation since 1893, when Edward L. Doheny had dug a 460-foot hole with his pick and shovel on a city lot just west of the downtown section. Doheny's gusher ignited a scramble for oil. Any Los Angeleno who could beg, borrow, or steal a few hundred dollars to buy or lease a lot was digging oil wells under the dusty streets.

Harold had studied the Los Angeles oil industry before he left Minneapolis. He told Romayne how a geologist named Bill Orcutt in 1901 had opened up the La Brea Tar Pits, a pool of asphalt containing a vast mosaic of bones from prehistoric creatures. Three years later on June 22, 1904, Old Maud, the biggest gusher the world had seen, sent up a column of oil and gas 150 feet in height, followed by a black river of 12,000 barrels of oil a day that spewed down the gullies and creek beds in the southwest section of Los Angeles.

Another of Harold's favorite stories concerned a driller who pulled the bailer from the bottom of a 2,200-foot hole in Lakeview. This was Dry Hole Charlie, who as another column of oil and gas roared up hundreds of feet, danced like an Indian, yelling, "My God! We've cut an artery down there."

Before he left Minneapolis, Harold Hutton would often tell anyone who would listen that the best place to head for in California was Long Beach. What had impressed him—"mesmerized him," said one of his girlfriends—were the headlines and reports in the *Minneapolis Tribune* about Alamitos No. 1, a gusher that blew near the summit of Signal Hill, halfway between Los Angeles and Long Beach, soon after Harold's sixteenth birthday. Alamitos No. 1 marked the opening in 1921 of the richest oil field ever known. As spectators and speculators thronged to Signal Hill to watch and smell the "black gold," fortunes were made—and lost—overnight.

As a teenager at Winona High, Harold loved to recount a story he had read in the press about a lot owner who had refused to accept a royalty rate of one-tenth, saying he knew he could get one-twentieth if he held out longer. Four years later, when Harold and his bride first arrived in southern California, Signal Hill had 642 derricks and 1,000 wells in operation. Its per capita wealth was the highest in America, far exceeding for several years that of Beverly Hills or Pasadena.

Signal Hill's hero in Harold Hutton's boyish eyes was Sam Mosher. Mosher, a red-haired young farmer, had been cultivating avocados on a seventeen-acre farm in Pico Rivera, not far from Long Beach. A neighbor had persuaded him to drive to the Signal Hill oil fields the morning after a freezing night when the young farmer had lost every orange, lemon, and avocado on his trees. Mosher parked his battered red Buick and walked up Signal Hill. He couldn't believe what he saw. Uncounted millions of cubic feet of gas were being vented into the air. The flares painted the night sky red. Mosher, like Harold Hutton when he arrived from Minneapolis, had no money. Instead, as Harold never tired of telling his young wife, he had a bright and simple idea: to turn this wasted gas into gasoline. With $4,000 borrowed from his skeptical father, Mosher built the world's first casinghead gasoline distilling plant using a dilapidated 1,000-gallon gasoline truck that was rusting away in a junkyard. Hooked into the crude-oil line at Shell Oil's No. 1 plant in Signal Hill, Mosher's truck tank became a workable still that produced whitewater gasoline. In May 1922, he set up his first company—Signal Oil and Gas. Sam Mosher went on to become one of California's and the world's most celebrated oilmen. For Harold Hutton, he became a source of inspiration as a wildcatter, risktaker, hustler, and later an international deal maker extraordinaire.

Romayne Hutton does not seem to have shared her husband's taste for oil fields or "messing about in labs." Unlike Harold, her dreams were focused on Hollywood. Her heartthrobs were John Barrymore and Douglas Fairbanks; her role models, Jean Harlow and later Norma Shearer. At first, Romayne had her way. She and Harold in early 1924 set up house in Hollywood in a ground-floor apartment that they christened "Harold's Hut."

Romayne, a good-looking bride with a flapper's bob hairdo, dark eyes, and a neat figure, hoped to find work in a movie studio. Although she tried hard, all the jobs seemed to be filled by other good-looking girls. Harold, however, was taken on at Howard Hughes's movie studios on Gower Street, first as a floor sweeper, then as an "assistant cutter." He told his wife and friends that he was on his way to the top in the brand new field of "Technicolor" though, in fact, this process did not become commercially viable until fifteen years later. Once they had an income, though not more than $20 a week, the young couple would spend their evenings and weekends soaking up the sun at the beach. A photo album shows Romayne in the surf and Harold in swim shorts and sweater outside the Sunbeam Buffet at Seal Beach.

The young couple would also spend long evenings with their friends in the bars and restaurants off Garfield Street and Golden West in Huntington Beach.

Harold could not get enough of the tall tales told by the "oilies" who had flocked from all over America to work in California's latest and richest oil field. Huntington Beach's first gusher had exploded with a roar on August 3, 1920, spewing 2,000 barrels a day over the coastal area. A young Standard Oil company driller, only a few years older than Harold, had persuaded his bosses to do what never had been done before—sink a well into a field of barley where previously real estate developers looking for water had produced bubbles of seawater and gas. Half a mile down, the young man's new rotary drill bit tapped into an undersea oil reservoir so large that six months after the strike there were 800 producing wells in the area, and a new town, Midway City, had sprung up to house its oilies.

Harold Hutton soaked up in the stories with which the hard-drinking roughnecks and the engineers, artisans, and bookkeepers who supported them regaled him over the whiskeys and beers he consumed with them on Saturday evenings. Harold listened and learned. They told him how 500 men with mules and shovels had worked for days to build a dike to hold back the tide of crude oil that flowed out of the giant oil pools left behind when the first gusher blew and how blowouts could lead to one 200-foot derrick being toppled onto another, setting off a domino effect of falling burning rigs. And they related how fires were put out—a roughneck would climb to the top of an endangered rig and attach a rope; others would then pull the rig in a safe direction to avoid the flames from the burning neighboring rigs, while firemen precariously balancing on top of the structure fought off the flames using high-pressure hoses.

Within a few months of the Huttons' arrival in California, Harold, though still working in Hollywood, was spending more and more time at his father-in-law's cottage not far from Huntington Beach. He wanted to be closer to the oil patch. The oil companies had decided that the biggest deposits were waiting to be tapped off shore and asked the city fathers to open the area for drilling. A hotly contested election in the fall of 1926 pitted the "oilies" against

From top: Oil rigs in Signal Hill in the 1920s; Harold's early cars

real estate and resort developers who wanted to preserve what was left of the city for vacationers, tourists, and retirees. Harold knew little of the issues. More than likely he and his father-in-law were on opposite sides of the debate.

The city fathers claimed that "oil means brothels, bootleggers, gambling dens, and crime," but when the vote came, the oilies won, leaving only eight blocks of downtown Huntington Beach legally off limits to drilling. Harold was triumphant. He joined a crowd of the victors in a boisterous celebration that sent him home to Romayne roaring drunk!

By spring 1926, Harold had earned enough working overtime at the studio to buy a used Stutz Bearcat. In this long, lean roadster, Romayne in a cloche hat and Harold in goggles and a long overcoat toured the sights of their new California home. They drove to Lone Pine and took photos of Mount Whitney, to Mammoth Lakes and the Owens Valley, and to Furnace Creek and the castle of Death Valley Scotty. On one memorable occasion, Harold took his bride to visit the Grand Canyon. Family pictures show him clowning about on an overlook, pretending that he might be about to fall over the rim to his death.

Shortly afterwards Harold's brother Don came out to California. He and Harold loved brawling and arm wrestling with one another. There are pictures of Don lying on the lawn in front of the Huttons' apartment with a golf ball in his mouth. Above him, Harold is swinging a golf club; it is unclear whether he will actually connect with the ball or his brother's head!

By late 1927, the first tremors of the Great Depression that was to hit the United States in 1929 were starting to make themselves felt. Back in Minneapolis, the Grant Portland Hotel lost business and went into decline. Carrie and Albert Hutton joined the massive migration to California. Over Harold Hutton's adult lifetime this migration grew from a steady trickle in the '20s into the flood that brought millions of hard-up but hard-working young families to the Golden State before, during, and after the Second World War.

It did not take Carrie Hutton long to find a new home and job for herself and Albert as resident managers of the Garden of Allah, a fashionable apartment

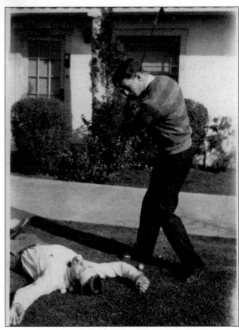

Above: Harold at Garden of Allah, Hollywood
Below: Don Hutton shows confidence in brother Harold's golf swing

complex near the Sunset Strip in Los Angeles where many of Hollywood's visiting celebrities stayed. Nearby, the Garden of Allah restaurant attracted well-to-do out-of-towners. Among them in later years were Betty Spennetta and her family, though Harold was not to know of this at the time. He and Romayne made an effort to be reconciled with his parents. When Romayne was expecting their first child, she and Harold moved into an apartment in the Garden of Allah. On June 12, 1927, their daughter, Barbara Lenore Hutton, was born at the Silver Lodge Hospital in Hollywood. Harold's contemporary photos show Romayne as a radiant young mother holding Barbara in swaddling clothes. Barbara was to be Harold's only child. He doted on her and spoiled her for the rest of his life. In later photographs, the Huttons' dog, Buster, is shown leaping off a sun dial over a pillow on which Barbara lies sucking her thumb in the sun. A year later, she appears peddling her tricycle under the adoring gaze of both parents.

Not long after Barbara was born, Harold gave up or lost his job in Hollywood. Instead, he moved into the business he cared most about—oil. Harold started driving a tanker truck carrying crude oil from the Richfield Oil Company's wells near Bakersfield to its refineries in Long Beach, California. On several occasions in the early '30s he took his daughter with him. Barbara remembers her father crooning hit songs in the cab. The bond between them was never broken. The fruit of Harold's first and most passionate, though not deepest, love, Barbara was also the surrogate son he never had. When she was a child, he showered her with presents. When later her first two marriages broke up, he fussed over her choice of a third husband, Tom Chambers. And when, as time went by, Barbara and Tom joined him in Singapore, Harold bought them a grand home. Tom Chambers became the Singapore representative of the Huttons' Asian oil company, Refining Associates (Canada) Ltd. "Refican" was the company's telex name, which became its intercompany nickname.

It was Harold's frequent absences on his trips to collect oil from Bakersfield that most likely caused the first strains on his marriage to Romayne. These started to make themselves felt in 1928 with the increasing fondness that both of them showed for hard liquor. There was nothing unusual about this. Millions of young Americans, especially in Los Angeles, New York, and Chicago, responded to Prohibition by drinking whenever they could. Harold developed the habit of "pub crawling" with his brother in Signal Hill and Long Beach.

Another cause of the couple's breakup may well have been money. The nationwide depression of 1929 was forcing thousands of companies to lay off millions of workers. Automobile production fell from a high of 5.3 million in 1929 to less than half that figure three years later. Oil companies' sales plummeted to levels far below the output of the nation's refineries, leading to price wars that had thousands of California gas stations selling gasoline at prices 20 percent lower than the cost of production. Richfield Oil's business contracted and along with it, Harold's pay packet. He and Romayne were soon finding it hard to make ends meet.

Nor was their marriage helped by what still was a deep-seated coldness between Harold's mother and Romayne. "Carrie wasn't very nice to her," said one close observer. "She was heavy-handed and may have well been the cause of their breakup."

By late 1930, with the depression shattering many young lives, Romayne had had enough. She and Harold parted early the following year when Harold lost his job with Richfield. Romayne took their daughter to live with her sister in Redondo Beach, California. Carrie Hutton tried and failed to win custody of the little girl, causing anguish for all concerned. Harold and Romayne, after the initial bitterness, remained on friendly terms. He paid frequent visits to Barbara. Once, as she vividly recalled, in the midst of the earthquake that rocked Long Beach in the spring of 1933, her house seemed to be shaking to pieces. The doorbell rang and in came her father, Harold, bearing a large box of chocolates. Harold's breakup with Romayne dealt both father and daughter a heavy blow.

Harold, deeply depressed at losing his wife and his job, moved from the beach to the desert. The only work he could find was parking cars at a hotel in Palm Springs, California, filling in part time as a gas station attendant. Age twenty-seven and broke, he was, as he said later, "a mess." But Harold had made an important decision. Henceforth, he would go all out to succeed in the business for which he believed he had a talent—oil refining. It was a resolution that had been formulating in the back of his mind ever since he first started "tinkering with oil" at St. Johns and Carleton College. There he had learned the rudiments of separating crude oil into kerosene, lube, and grease. Now, at a time when his self-confidence had been eroded and his natural ebullience badly bruised, he recalled the Leighton Lab's prescription: "Chemistry is the basis for all the principal world industries; geology is the chemistry of the earth; biologists are interested in the chemical changes of living organisms; agriculture is a special application of chemistry."

Harold fancied himself a chemist. It still took him several years and more than one false start to become established in the California oil business. What turned his aspirations into the drive and determination that eventually was to make him one of California's most redoubtable international wildcatters was a chance encounter. He met the woman who changed his character and redirected his life, a golden girl of the West, Betty Lee Spennetta.

PART II   BETTY'S STORY

Betty Spennetta as a teenager

Pioneers in the Black Hills

lizabeth Lee Spennetta, the golden girl whom Harold Hutton met in that Palm Springs gas station, was the first child of prosperous ranching parents J. D. Spennetta and Edna Chuning Spennetta. "Betty," as she would be known for the rest of her life, was born on February 20, 1913, in the bustling citrus town of Redlands, California, at a time when all things seemed possible in the West. J. D. and Edna, like other pioneers before them, had come to California in 1912 in search of gold, not the gold in the mines and streams of Northern California, but the gold in the citrus trees of southern California.

On the crisp February day that Betty Spennetta was born, the view from the hills around the town of Redlands seemed to stretch all the way to the ocean in one direction and back across the country in the other. Redlands Hospital was built in mission revival style, with a banistered stairway leading from the foyer to the upstairs rooms where Edna Spennetta rested with her first child. J. D., the proud father, could walk to the hospital to visit them, as the Spennetta's neat Victorian house at 618 East Fern was close to the corner of Nordina and East Clark Street where the hospital stood. It was a cheerful neighborhood with narrow streets lined by small Victorian homes with just a touch of gingerbread to decorate their eaves.

Redlands, however, was no sleepy little village but a center of agricultural commerce so thriving it had earlier warranted visits by President McKinley and Vice President Roosevelt, who came to speak about prosperity in the West from a second-story balcony in the middle of town. Eastern companies, such as National Life Insurance Company of Vermont and National Fire Insurance Company of Hartford, had established their western offices in Redlands. J. D. Spennetta was a cashier for Mutual Orange Distributors of Redlands.

Edna's and J. D.'s families had both moved west with the expansion of a new nation. Each came from a long line of pioneers. Edna Chuning Spennetta's great-grandfather, Thomas D. Pryor, fought in the Civil War. Tennessee born and raised, at eighteen he joined the Confederate Army along with his nineteen-year-old brother and served for the last four years of the war. Later, the two young men went west to seek their fortunes in Sidney, Iowa—then known to be the "last stop" on the way to the Black Hills of South Dakota, the reputed site of gold strikes.

Thomas brought his childhood sweetheart, Sarah Elizabeth (Lizzie) Preston Barr, to join him in Sidney where they married in 1868. A southern belle, she had never done cooking or washing, nor had she lived in a frontier town, but over the next few years she learned to do both. The couple settled in Lead, South Dakota, in 1877. Around that time, the Homestake Mine was reputed to be the largest gold mining company in the world. As the *Range Gazette,* Camp Crook, South Dakota's newspaper, would later report, Homestake was then "at the peak of its production when the typical gold field life prevailed with its saloons, dance hall girls, and periodic gun fights."

No sooner had Thomas opened a grocery store in Lead to supply prospectors for the Black Hills gold rush than he and Lizzie were forced to leave. The Pryor's store was boycotted by Homestake Mine when Thomas testified that he had "seen a young [independent] miner killed by a Homestake man."

Thomas struck out for Camp Crook, South Dakota, where he began a mercantile career that became the stuff of the Spennetta family's legend. By 1877, he was singlehandedly managing the Deadwood Grocers Trading Post, which served ranchers who drove cattle up from Texas, until Lizzie brought their sons, Hugh, Tom, and Paul, and their daughter, Sallie, to Camp Crook by covered wagon. Hugh Pryor's memoirs record the trip:

> Our heavy wagon crept across the sagebrush-covered hills of western
> South Dakota. Finally it reached the crest of a long ridge and the

travelers saw the trees along Indian Creek. [We] drove from day break to dark, sleeping under open skies [until] we could see a wide valley stretching away with more trees along it than we had seen on our entire journey. It was the valley of the Little Missouri River. Later we forded the river and could see a few houses. This was Camp Crook, which was to be our home for 17 years.

Thomas Pryor's Deadwood Grocers store was soon the center of trade among the Black Hills' early settlers, cowboys, and Indians. As Hugh went on to explain:

> The Indians would bring in their hides for sale or barter . . . Father would run his fingers through the hair . . . If the hair was thick, the hides were said to be prime and were of value commercially. The price for an antelope skin was usually about ten or fifteen cents, sometimes a little higher. Nearly all the Indians demanded money for the skins, but they always spent it, immediately, for tobacco, calico, muslin, and food.

When eighteen-year-old Sallie Pryor joined her father in Camp Crook, she was to meet her own frontiersman, Robert L. Chuning, Betty Hutton's grandfather. Chuning was one of nine children born to a prosperous merchant family in Bigelow, Missouri. At nineteen, Robert had come to the Black Hills driving a herd of cattle to start a ranch, the K-K, near the Redwater River five miles from Camp Crook. During the winter of 1886–87 a cold wind came out of the northwest and froze a hard crust over the snow. Robert Chuning lost his herd.

Nevertheless, he and Sallie Pryor were married in 1888. They started all over in a frontier land that continued to be dangerous and lonely. Sallie Pryor Chuning said of the 1890 winter:

> My brother Paul . . . was very sick. We sent our hired man . . . to Belle Fourche to get medicine. While there he heard the Sioux, under Sitting Bull, were on the war path . . . We hitched a horse to our buggy and

drove into Camp Crook. My son, Lynn, was three months old and my daughter not yet two . . . The men made ammunition and built some barricades. My husband and a number of men rode out scouting. They saw a party of Indians coming and got everyone inside the barricades. We had a company of troops camped near us for weeks. The army doctor took care of Paul but he died a few weeks later . . . Two young army officers [who] stayed overnight with us were both killed in the battle. Sitting Bull was also killed. That was the last of any Indian warfare in our country of South Dakota.[2]

A few years later, the Chunings bought Tom Pryor's interest in the Deadwood trading post. Robert Chuning in 1900 helped organize the Little Missouri Bank and served as vice president. Elected state senator for Butte County, he became, as author John Bye writes, "the mainstay of the Democratic Party in the Camp Crook area."[3]

Betty Hutton's mother, Edna Chuning, was one of the four children of Robert and Sallie. Her school was a one-room log cabin, donated to the town by her father, in which her cousin Bessie Pryor taught. The children's adventures took them into the range area and the surrounding hills running towards the Montana border. Edna remembered as many as eleven of them carrying their lunches and bottles of water as they ran through the pastures that fenced in fierce bulls and scrambling up steep slopes where the beasts could not follow. On one such excursion, peering through a hole down into a lower cave, Edna spotted what she thought was a bright tablecloth. Removing the cloth, she discovered to her horror a skeleton staring back at her. The cave turned out to be an Indian burial site; the skeleton, a woman's body that had been surrounded by spent cartridges and arrowheads. Strangely, the woman's feet were missing, but she had been buried with a bracelet, which Edna kept and passed down in the family.

---

2. John Bye, *Backtrailing in the Heart of Short Grass Country* (Everett, Wash., 1956).
3. Ibid.

On the range in the Black Hills, riding horses was a passion as well as a necessity for Betty Spennetta's mother. Dandy, an abandoned foal, was fed by the children using a large bottle with a nipple constructed by the town doctor and went on to became a race winner. Doc Lathram organized a race in the Chuning pasture, and Edna's brother Paul rode their pony to victory, winning the $25 prize. Edna used her share of the winnings to buy a camera with which she would record priceless memories of Camp Crook.

Shortly before her sixteenth birthday, Edna started to show symptoms of an illness that was to recur in the Chuning family. Diagnosed with tuberculosis, she needed a milder climate than occurred at Camp Crook. By good fortune, the Mulkay family of Baker, Montana, friends of the Chunings, were planning a trip to California for the winter. Edna's parents asked them if they would take her along. The Mulkays were delighted to do so since their daughter Violet was Edna's age.

The first leg of Edna's journey west from Camp Crook was traveled on Shorty Quinlan's stagecoach, which ran to the train station in Marmouth, South Dakota. After meeting the Mulkays and their daughter in Marmouth, young Edna set out on the same journey to California that was made by tens of thousands of other young Midwesterners, including her son-in-law to be, Harold Hutton. Her journey was to open up an entirely new chapter of her life.

Arriving in Long Beach after a jolting thirty-six-hour train journey, Edna described the town as "not much more than a village at that time." A month later, she and Violet Mulkay rented a room in the Los Angeles area. Their landlady, according to Edna's diary, was a Mrs. Harper, who "had lived in the Black Hills and knew the people that we did."

Los Angeles in those early days before World War I was well described as a hick town, though parts of it were starting to boom with the growth of movies and the oil business. Edna Spennetta had never seen anything like it. Every single day, she recorded in her diary, she and Violet ventured downtown where there were four different stock theater companies, each putting on a different afternoon show. In the mornings they browsed the stores. After lunch they attended a show and then had dinner downtown. To suggestions that she and her girlfriend shouldn't move around Los Angeles unaccompanied, Edna's retort was that she had, after all, been a pioneer most of her life!

It was soon after the two girls had settled in at the Harper home that a Mrs. Smith came to call. Her husband, Oscar Smith, was in the wine-making business in New York State and in Cucamonga, California, where he also had vineyards. Edna recounts that "Mrs. Smith took quite a fancy to us and invited us to come out to spend a weekend at the ranch." That Saturday night, to round out her dinner table, she had invited two eligible young men who worked at the Cucamonga Citrus Fruit Growers Association. One of them was Jesse Spennetta. Edna could not take her eyes off him. Jesse evidently felt the same about her. In the warm, arid air scented with citrus, Betty Spennetta's parents fell in love.

THE ANGLO-ITALIAN CONNECTION

Betty's father, Jesse Spennetta, was the son of an Anglo-Italian couple from the township of Buchanan in Berrien County, Michigan. His mother, Almetta Stevens, had her roots in an English family of three brothers, John, James, and William Stevens, who originally came to Massachusetts to make their living in the mercantile trade. Disguised as Indians, all three joined the Boston Tea Party raid against the British, but when the Revolutionary War broke out, John, the eldest brother, could not bring himself to fight against his homeland and returned to England. His younger brother William by contrast became a lieutenant in the Second Continental Artillery and fought against the British from Bunker Hill to Yorktown. Will was distinguished for his bravery in the battle of Morristown, New Jersey, during which, as an artillery commander, he received a citation and promotion on the field of battle.

After the Revolutionary War, one branch of the Stevens family headed west to become farmers. Property records suggest that they had settled in the Territory of Michigan just about the time it became a state in 1837. Will, the revolutionary war hero, lost his left arm in a threshing machine accident. Almetta Stevens' father, William R. Stevens, a cousin of Uncle Will, established himself as a farmer in Berrien county. Before he died at the age of thirty-eight, he sired six children, the third of which was Almetta.

Like her Stevens forebears, Betty Spennetta's Italian ancestors were also established in Michigan before the Civil War. Jefferson's father, Domanigo, was born in Italy. Married at the age of twenty-five to eighteen-year-old Suzannah Cruen on May 9, 1841, Domanigo, like William Stevens, became a farmer on a plot of Berrien County land. By 1860, he and Suzannah had four children, John, Franklin, Angeline, and Betty Hutton's grandfather Jefferson, running about in their log hut.

The social history of the Buchanan township shaped Domanigo Spennetta and his family into a typically Midwestern family. Town records of their property illustrate a problem that faced many nineteenth century immigrants—the misspelling of their family names. Domanigo, in various places, is recorded as "Domingo," "Domandigo," "Domango," "Domago," "Dominic," and even "Romargo." Spennetta appeared as "Spinetti," "Spinneto," "Spenette," "Spenetta," and "Spennette," with consonants sometimes doubled and sometimes not. Moreover, because Domanigo Spennetta signed the one extant legal document, his last will and testament, with an "X," it appears that he could not write, so there was no way to verify the correct spelling of his name. Perhaps out of frustration, along with pride in their newly adopted country, men like Domanigo Spennetta gave their children readily identifiable names such as "Franklin" and "Jefferson."

Jefferson Spennetta, the second son, was born in 1853. He too went to school in a log hut school similar to the one that his contemporary, Robert Chuning, Betty Hutton's maternal grandfather, attended in the same period in South Dakota. His parents' farm, just northeast of the creek flowing out of Wageners Lake, produced more than enough to sustain the family, with some extra wheat to sell for cash. Domanigo died with a personal estate assessed in June 1883 at $1,000, including several acres of wheat valued at $10 and one red cow worth $40.

By this time, Jefferson Spennetta and Almetta Stevens Spennetta had been married for seven years and had their first child, Eda Jane. Buchanan, Michigan, had grown into a substantial town, credited by the *History of Berrien and Van Buren Counties, Michigan, 1888,* with "463 private residences (11 of them brick), one hotel, (the Dunbar House), six churches, one public hall, four three-story brick business blocks . . . twenty two-story business frame buildings, two livery stables, three flouring mills (water power), four smithshops, one broom-handle factory, one machine-shop, three steam sawmills, one saw-mill, one coffin factory."

In this thriving city, Jefferson and Almetta named their second child and only son Jesse Domanigo. Jefferson felt secure enough in his American citizenship to give his own son this distinctly Italian second name, a name which that son would later again Americanize by using only the initials J. D.

J. D. turned out to be a restless, not to say adventurous, young man. In 1904, having finished only one year of his engineering course at the University of Michigan, he left for California and got a job in Redlands as a bookkeeper. His settling in Redlands was serendipitous. The lives of two pioneering families from the log hut frontier—the Spennettas and the Chunings—were about to converge.

J. D. Spennetta became the full-time bookkeeper at Mutual Orange Distributors (sometimes referred to as the "O.D. Company"), a clearinghouse for citrus growers, in 1906. Shortly before that, he met Edna Chuning and the two had fallen in love. Edna had not planned to stay in California but to return to South Dakota when she had regained her health. Instead she spent every weekend she could with J. D. and his friends. In spite of their proper chaperoning, they both felt "a bit of giddy freedom" to be young people, partly cut loose from family supervision, experiencing their first taste of courtship in the warmth of California.

It still took the couple two years—and numerous separations when Edna returned home to visit her family at Camp Crook—before the time came to be married. Once, when Edna was back in South Dakota driving her father's early automobile, a Pratt-Elkhart, she overturned the car and was literally scalped. At first, her family thought she was killed. When J. D. heard about the accident, he was "sick with grief and worry." But Edna survived. According to one of her daughters, Mary Struck, "she was stitched up so successfully that her hair covered her entire scar!"

J. D. by this time had carved out a career for himself in the citrus industry. Writing in December of 1910, he declared his love for Edna and asked her to marry him. The following year, on October 15, 1911, Jesse Domanigo Spennetta and Edna Chuning were married at Camp Crook, South Dakota, in a double ceremony with Edna's younger sister Ruth and Mr. Everett Baker of Baker, Montana. J. D. and Edna then set out for Redlands and the home where fourteen months later, their first child, Betty Spennetta, was born in the mission-style hospital.

A STAKE IN CALIFORNIA

The Spennetta family—J. D., Edna, and their first child, two-year-old Betty—moved early in 1915 to the charming little town of Orange, California, where J. D. had taken a new job as a fruit buyer for Red Fox Orchards. They bought land in nearby Villa Park, located on the corner of Lemon Street and Alice Lane, where the self-reliant Edna, already pregnant with her second child, Betty's brother Paul, threw herself into planning the family's new house. Known as "The Ranch" to family and friends, it was a single-story structure with a large family dining room, three bedrooms, and large back porch extending off the kitchen and rear of the house. Screened side porches served for summertime sitting, eating, and sleeping on warm nights. A small basement stored home-canned fruits and vegetables. Of sturdy board and bat construction, economical to build and suitably rustic in appearance, the house was painted a dark barn red and remained that way for decades. Maitie Bratsch, who lived on a nearby property for over sixty years, told friends that she "prayed that J. D. would some day paint the house anything but its somber dark red, but he never did."

The grounds of the ranch were initially planted with navel oranges and apricots by J. D.'s father, "Grandpa Jeff," who had moved from Cucamonga with Almetta to help out. Almetta and Jeff lived on a small, cheerful farm, catty-corner from the local school, within walking distance for the grandchildren. Betty and her brother and sister would always remember the farm's mules and the cows and chickens whose milk and fresh eggs Almetta would deliver each day to her customers around Orange. Nor would Betty ever forget playing underneath the tentlike quilts that Almetta made on her quilting frame or the shuttle that seemed to fly from her grandma's busy hands as she worked the loom with her feet. Betty, Paul, and Mary considered Almetta their "old-fashioned grandma," while Sallie Pryor Chuning, Edna's mother, was their "city grandmother."

J. D. Spennetta, Betty's father, worked hard. His day would begin at 4 A.M. and not finish until 6 P.M. According to Armor's *History of Orange County*, "The first year (at Red Fox) he shipped seventy-five cars, and now (1922) he dispatches 650." But true to the family formula for success, the Spennettas, like the Chunings, did not put all their economic eggs or fruit in one basket. Following the example of their pioneer forebears, they were involved in farming, banking, and politics. Orange County, with its virtually frost-free groves and orchards, was already describing itself in 1920 as "this Eden, the finest section of the Finest State in the United States."

The country was becoming the citrus capital of the West, and the fruit had to be carried to market and agricultural chemicals brought back to the ranches. J. D. recognized an opportunity and in 1916 established a trucking business, beginning with a Model T Ford. Less than seven years later, Armor's wrote of J. D.:

> He has a line of trucks engaged in a general trucking trade. He also
> handles fertilizer, about 10,000 tons per year. He is the largest dealer
> of barley and bean straw in Orange County . . . one of the original
> stockholders, directors, and a vice president of the First National
> Bank of Olive. In national politics he is a Republican, but allows no
> partisanship to deter him from lending a hand to boost both the city
> and county of Orange.

The Chuning side of the family by now were living on 51st Street in Los Angeles, where they had moved from Camp Crook in 1916. In the early 1930s they moved to San Diego, where they ran the Majestic Hotel, offering Betty another fine place to visit and spend weekends. The hotel was not far from the great naval base that Betty and her future husband were to supply with lubricating oil in World War II.

In 1920, after five years in Orange County, Edna Spennetta's long quiescent tuberculosis re-emerged. Edna was then pregnant with their third child, Mary, and while the pregnancy itself provided some "rest" to the lung by compressing it, her doctor advised convalescence in an even warmer and dryer climate. J. D. did not hesitate. Immediately after the delivery, Edna, along with her two older children, Betty and Paul, was moved to Palm Springs in the California desert, where sunshine is guaranteed 350 days each year. The family took a house on the "Street," in those days little more than a dirt road running through the town. Across the road was the desert home of actor Rudolph Valentino. Palm Springs in the early 1920s was little more than a dusty Indian oasis, still more agricultural than vacation-oriented in spite of the presence of its new Desert Inn. Paul Spennetta, who started school there at age five, remembers herds of donkeys and mules being driven through town. Once, when several of the animals strayed away from the herd, Paul drove them inside the Spennetta's large fenced yard. That evening, as the donkeys began braying, Edna discovered them, and a deflated Paul was ordered to "open the gate and get them out of here!"

Betty Spennetta attended third grade in a Palm Springs school. She and her brother remained with their mother throughout Edna's nearly two-year convalescence in the desert. Recovery took some time because antibiotics to fight the tubercle bacillus would not be introduced for another two decades, and the only treatment was rest in a mild climate. But the Palm Springs rest cure proved to be as effective for Edna as, twenty years later, it was for Betty. Edna never suffered another relapse.

Returning to Villa Park, both Spennettas threw themselves into the upbringing of their three children. Edna played with her children, read to them, chauffeured them about, and even before Mary began school, taught her to read. Later, much to the delight of Betty and her friends, Edna taught them to play bridge. J. D. because of his work was less accessible. But the family nearly always ate dinner together. Betty and Mary sat on one side of the table

Betty Spennetta: ready to ride at Palm Springs

with Paul on the other, where he could be the naughty one, dropping his vegetables to the waiting dog out of sight of their parents who sat at either end. Sunday breakfasts were a special family time, which as often as not included Grandma and Grandpa Spennetta. J. D. had a grill that he brought to the table to cook sausage and apples. Christmases were memorably cheerful, with the children awakening to the sound of sleigh bells merrily rung from an old harness as Grandma Almetta and Grandpa Jeff walked up the drive.

Betty Spennetta's family was not religious, and they did not belong to any church. Betty was married in a Methodist Church, Paul was sent to Sunday School at the Congregationalist Church in Villa Park, and Mary later attended the Presbyterian Church in Orange and was married in the Episcopal Church. The Spennettas were an ecumenical family indeed.

More fun than church, for Betty, was horseback riding. Throughout her college years she took lessons in English riding. A smart figure in her khaki jodhpurs and tan calf-high boots, a smiling Betty on her horse is a vision that remains with her sister, Mary, and brother, Paul, to this day. Betty also doted on cats, and at one point she and Mary had twenty-one cats in the orchard. Thereafter, over the fifty years in which she and her school friends exchanged Christmas cards, Betty's cards always had a cat on them.

Betty was a serious child. While her mischievous brother, Paul, earned a reputation for teasing their younger sister, Mary, he rarely tried his pranks on the older, more reserved Betty. While Paul and Mary went sliding down Villa Park's Onion Hill in the mud, using sleds made of pieces of old automobiles, Betty played more with her school friends than with her younger siblings. She was an honor student and a good writer, Paul recalls. "Even when I was a freshman at Stanford, I'd come home and she'd help me with term papers."

Betty's own formal education had begun at Villa Park Primary School. There was little traffic on the dirt roads of Orange County in those days and the community was judged to be safe.

Betty was an excellent student. Removed from school so that she could accompany her mother to Palm Springs during Edna's recovery from tuberculosis, she had no difficulty earning mostly "excellent" and "good" marks in all academic subjects and in "deportment." Betty graduated from her grammar school with thirteen other students in June 1927. An audience of family and friends heard her open the program with a piano solo, after which she appeared in a two-act play, "The Higher Education." Betty's casting as "Mrs. Randall, mother of the bride-to-be" is notable because, for all of her exuberance and love of fun, she already was recognized by her teachers and peers to be mature and serious for her age.

Betty entered high school in September 1927. School days started at eight o'clock and had six periods. Before a cafeteria was built on the campus, the school kids would walk two blocks south to get their lunch at Simon's Drug Store just north of the Orange Plaza. A milk shake and sandwich cost twenty-five cents. Another favorite diner was John and Carlotta Tiziani's luncheonette fronting the hockey field. For a nickel the girls could buy a huge salty pickle to go with their hot soup after finishing their hockey games.

During her high school days, Betty Spennetta's closest friend was Jean Hart, daughter of the editor and publisher of the local newspaper, the *Orange Daily News,* whose offices were only a few blocks from those of J. D.'s Inland Transportation Company. Betty Spennetta and Jean Hart soon found themselves at the center of Orange Union High School's social and sporting activities. Their group—"all classy girls" in Jean Hart's words—was known as the "Gang," a term that in later years was to take on more menacing overtones. For these girls at Orange High, it was to be their most beloved and long lasting association.

Binding the Gang together was the girls' love of sports. Betty excelled as an athlete, starting each year with basketball then moving on to hockey, volleyball, baseball, and tennis. It is hard to find a photo of any girls' athletic team at

Orange High that does not depict Betty as a team leader.[4] So proud was the team of its conquests that the girls would take their hockey sticks with them when they went to the beach. Years later, when Betty Spennetta Hutton was to dedicate the Harold Hutton Sports Center at Chapman College, there was a gala dinner for her former teammates. The highlight was the presentation to each woman of her own Orange Union High School hockey stick!

The girls' athletic curriculum included what was known then as "natural dancing." Betty and her friends loved performing these graceful free-form movements barefoot on the sunken lawn in front of the auditorium, stretching and leaping, arms flung wide, whirling in their short jagged-edge skirts. In 1927, Orange High's natural dancing class formed the Euterpeans Club, and Betty held office as treasurer. One of the class's performances was advertised in the local newspaper as a "Musical Comedy Review" with "10 Local Talented Singing and Dancing Girls—Clean, Classy, Clever." At that time the early movies were often accompanied by live entertainment, so when the motion picture *The Woman from Moscow* starring Pola Negri was shown in Orange, Betty and eight of her fellow Euterpeans performed in the double program. Betty was entranced with the film. Perhaps she dreamed of someday becoming a mysterious woman in Moscow, as in fact she later did.

For Betty Spennetta and her friends, their time at Orange Union High School in the late 1920s was happy and carefree. Off-campus, the high point of the year was their Girl Scout camp in the San Bernardino Mountains built by the Rotary Club, the Kiwanis Club, and the Lions Club and thus named Camp Ro-Ki-Li. Each year, the girls rode up the mountain trails in the back of one of J. D.'s trucks. Laughing and singing as they made their way out the back route from Redlands on Highway 38, they would stop at a place called Igo's for lunch. One of the Gang, Iola Myracle recounts:

---

4. Orange Union High School's lawn became the front "court" of Chapman University, of which Betty and her husband were trustees and generous benefactors.

Clockwise from top: With the Gang at Ro-Ki-Li camp (Betty, front row, second from left);
Ready for the ball . . . and a swim; dressed up for garden party;
with Paul and sister, Mary; front row in Model T Ford

Clockwise from top: Spennetta family portrait; Betty (center) dances at Orange Union High School (now Chapman University); on the beach with sister, Mary; Jean Fairbairn in Betty's car; ready for tennis

> Ro-ki-Li was right near the headwaters of the Santa Ana River and it was beautiful. There were cooks who prepared our meals. There was a rough rock swimming pool and we took lessons in lifesaving. We played ball a bit and hiked a lot! When we were older, they would let us hike to a little lake a mile and a half from camp. We went over there one evening and someone suggested we go skinny dipping. So we took our bathing suits off and went in. We thought we were really daring!

And what is camp without practical jokes? One night, the girls decided that they would have a little seance in their cabin and call up some spirits to see if they could "put one over on Betty." Says Iola:

> We had a flashlight with a red scarf over it. A girl named Evie from another troop was under the cabin with a long stick listening to the whole thing and ready to make the noises. One knock on the floor would be "yes" and two knocks would be "no." We thought we were going to scare Betty, but instead we scared the daylights out of Evie. I was looking at Betty who was listening to the whole thing and grinning.

The next day the girls "published" their first edition of the "Ro-Ki-Li Register," August 16, 1929, which announced in bold headlines: "EXTRA, EXTRA, YOUNG GIRL FRIGHTENED INTO HYSTERICS—ANOTHER INSANE—MAY LEAVE FOR HOME ANY DAY."

Betty Spennetta's self-confidence proved to be one of her abiding assets. Whether she was wearing a baseball uniform streaked with dirt from sliding into base or a nice dress, stockings, and her fur-trimmed coat, Betty all her life succeeded in giving the impression that she was cool, calm, and collected. She also became something of a legend as a perfectionist. "It has to be done right," was one of many precepts that she absorbed from her father, who always wanted things done "the proper way," whether at his trucking company or the bank.

From J. D. and her other trader forebears, Betty also inherited a strong instinct for enterprise. Trucking in the 1920s was a rough business. Betty's brother, Paul, who learned to drive semitrailers well before the legal driving age of fourteen and a half, remembers driving a truck down to the docks during a strike. "The strikers would throw rocks at you as you went by," he recalled. "Didn't make many hits . . . you were young and feeling invincible." Betty in her teens felt the same. But she also learned from her father the merits of treating her own employees decently. A. C. Myracle, who worked for J. D. for thirty-one years, says Betty's father once loaned him and his wife the Spennetta's beach house and even his charge card. Treating good employees well was an absolute for J. D., and Betty all her life continued the practice.

Growing up in comfort and style, Betty Spennetta, unlike her husband to be, never had to go without the good things that well-to-do families and caring parents can offer. The Spennettas always had large cars, usually Lincolns, in which, accompanied by Betty and Mary, Edna would drive to Los Angeles to shop in the downtown stores. J. D. would drive in later and take them to the Los Angeles Athletic Club where he could get a haircut and a manicure. Together they would attend plays and stage shows at the Shrine Auditorium and the Biltmore. Betty especially remembered a football game at the Rose Bowl, when her brother Paul played there for Stanford University.

Betty Spennetta, in short, was one of the "golden girls" of the '20s. She drove to school in a Lincoln Phaeton Roadster, a huge vehicle with a "turtle back," a rumble seat, a chrome-plated dash, and a two-gallon reserve fuel tank opened by a lever in the back. She never lacked for money or the care of a close-knit family that included both her maternal and paternal grandparents.

The Gang spent summers in their well-to-do families' beach homes at Newport Beach and Balboa Island. Bathing costumes were rapidly changing during the 1920s, and Betty's sister, Mary Struck, says, "my grandmother Chuning would nearly have a stroke every year from seeing the girls' bathing suits." Betty was a good swimmer and used to body-surf at Corona del Mar. For the upper-crust high school students of Orange County, Newport Beach was for staying with the family, but Corona del Mar was the "in" beach for meeting boyfriends.

Betty Spennetta is still remembered as the beautiful girl every young man secretly wanted to date but didn't. Her slight reserve, in spite of her fun-loving character, was her greatest attraction. She always had a full social calendar. Betty loved to dance and was fortunate to be living in the era of "Big Bands" with Artie Shaw and Tommy Dorsey at the Balboa Rendezvous Ballroom. Always adventurous, she was also the leader of the Gang when it came to trying new restaurants and new food. One exotic place she tried was the Garden of Allah in Los Angeles, whose menu she took home and saved in her scrapbook. Little did she know that not long afterwards the Garden was to become the home of the man of her dreams, Harold Hutton.

* * * * *

As the time came for Betty to go to a university, she was growing out of her small hometown of Orange. Like older teenagers everywhere, she was faced with two conflicting worlds and the task of somehow having to integrate them.

One world had the characteristics of Jay Gatsby's leisured class, a gilded domain into which her well-to-do family already had come close to propelling her. The other was far more challenging, a more modern world that included newly opening social space for independent young women who were active in sports and preparing for careers. Betty by instinct and experience had one foot in each of these worlds. She was secure in the bosom of her family. She also expected to drive herself to social functions in Los Angeles. She habitually deferred to her parents. She still relished the freedom to manage her own life during her sojourns in Palm Springs. Betty, in a word, was becoming accustomed to making her own decisions—but she still found this far from easy.

Perhaps nothing illustrates her dilemma better than her one-sided haircut. It was 1928, and nearly all the Gang at Orange Union High School had decided to have their hair "bobbed." Charlie Kester, the local barber, cut the girls' hair to just below their ears and left a little spit curl in front. He dubbed it "the Jean-Ola bob." Betty hesitated, then decided to follow the Gang and have her hair bobbed, too. Charlie began snipping. However, after he cut one side, she stopped him and wouldn't let him touch the other. So until her wavy hair grew out again, Betty was on one side a traditional girl and on the other a new woman of the twenties.

The University of California at Los Angeles (UCLA) was only twelve years old when Betty Spennetta arrived there in the late summer of 1931. Its academic reputation was yet to be firmly established, but its football team, the Bruins, was already a power in the western states, and its social life, based on Ivy League–style fraternity houses, was starting to compete with that of its older— and more expensive—private rival, the University of Southern California (USC).

Betty, with her excellent grades and top-level social connections, was "rushed" at UCLA by several of the most sought-after sororities. From early August until mid-September of 1931, she attended countless football luncheons, lavender and lace teas, and "formals," offered by Sigma Kappa, Alpha Gamma Delta, Kappa Delta, and Zeta Tau Alpha. She rarely missed the Bruins' fall football matches, saving the program and news clippings of their 1931 homecoming.

This event began on a Friday night with the traditional "Pajamarino," in which students and alumni paraded through Westwood Village wearing pajamas. More than 10,000 students then attended the lighting of a huge bon-fire of "boxes, boards and combustibles" which, according to the *Los Angeles Times*, "for the last three days, the freshman toiled unceasingly to construct."

Betty's first residence at UCLA was the Winslow Arms at 945 Hilgard, the nicest and smallest of the women's residence halls. Its twenty-four women lived in housekeeping apartments for two that rented for $50 to $75 per month. Later, she accepted Alpha Omicron Pi's invitation to join its UCLA chapter, known as Kappa Theta. She moved into its Edwardian-style mansion with its formal rooms on the first floor, bedrooms on the second, and a basement study room known to one and all as "The Pit." To stay at Kappa Theta, all members of the sorority were expected to maintain grades of not less than B-. Betty, who declared a major in "Pre–Commercial Studies," surprisingly found it a struggle to keep up. She was experiencing a troubling fatigue. Like her mother, Edna, at the same age, Betty was diagnosed with tuberculosis.

And so it was that Betty Spennetta in the spring of 1932 was packed off by her father to recuperate in Palm Springs. His wife had recovered from the same affliction in the dry heat of the desert so to Palm Springs, said J. D., his daughter must go, too. Betty withdrew from UCLA on the understanding that she would finish college when she was better, but fate was to rule otherwise. Her move to Palm Springs, like Harold Hutton's when he left Minnesota, was to change the direction, enrich the quality, and globalize the scope of her life.

PART III   A LOVE AFFAIR BY MAIL

A glamorous Betty

A BLIND DATE IN A PALM SPRINGS GAS STATION

I t was a blisteringly hot afternoon when the tan convertible drove into the only gas station that Palm Springs could boast in 1931. At the wheel was eighteen-year-old Levora Raney, a brunette girl from Orange, California. She was staying at the cottage of a friend taking a year out from her studies at the University of California at Los Angeles to recuperate from a mild case of tuberculosis. The brunette asked the gas station attendant, a thick-set young fellow in stained overalls, to fill the tank and wash the windscreen. As Harold Hutton did this he fell into conversation with Levora Raney, and as she paid for her gas, he cheekily asked for a date.

Levora was flattered, though by no means surprised. Half the young men in Palm Springs, of whom there probably were not more than a few score in the early '30s, were only too well aware of her and her companion, Betty Spennetta. The two girls often rode into town from the Spennetta family's cottage on bicycles, causing quite a stir with their short-shorts above long tan legs. Pedaling down the grade at high speed, they would often hear people screaming, but "when we stopped to see what all the fuss was about," said Levora, "Betty and I realized that the crowd was screaming about us."

Levora's response to Harold Hutton's request for a date was to tantalize him. When he pressed her to let him take her out "tonight, tomorrow, or anytime next week," she told him no. Instead, Levora told him, she'd introduce Harold to a friend who "all the boys are after—they practically line up at her door."

The next day Levora brought her tall, blue-eyed girlfriend, twenty-year-old Betty, to meet the young man at the gas station. Out of that blind date stemmed a lifelong romance, a rewarding partnership, and a globe-girdling business alliance that made both of them multimillionaires and philanthropists. Their relationship took some time to root, but once it blossomed, Harold and Betty were to enjoy a companionship of rare trust and affection that lasted for the next forty-two years. Their man-and-wife business was to span three oceans and five continents. Their comradeship rewarded each with joys and heartaches, shared adventures, and a sizable fortune that would go on after their deaths, benefiting tens of thousands who had never met Harold and Betty as well as hundreds who had.

None of this was predictable at their first meeting at the gas station. Far more obvious was the wide gap in their backgrounds and circumstances. Betty Spennetta, vivacious but cool, was the darling daughter of established Orange County parents who had brought her up to be well-mannered, well-dressed, well-spoken, and reserved in her contacts with men. Harold Hutton was gregarious and rugged with deep blue eyes and an infectious grin, but his build was more stocky than lithe, his clothes rough, his fingers thick, his hands calloused from driving an oil truck. Harold was also ten years older than his well-bred, good-looking young date, and he was a divorced man with alimony payments and a baby daughter to support. Betty had three homes, all of them spacious and comfortable, in Villa Park, Balboa Island, and Palm Springs. Harold had no home of his own, no money, no regular job, and at the time he and Betty met, precious few prospects of getting one. Betty was supposed to be "resting" in her family's vacation villa, taking time out from a university where she was a member of one of the smartest sororities and to which she was planning to return. Harold's school record was poor and he had all but been expelled from his college. Still suffering the pangs of a broken marriage and the loss of his child and his job, Harold, unlike Betty, could not turn to his parents for help.

Harold, in short, was alone and lonely. Betty, by contrast, was surrounded by a warm circle of relatives and friends. The girls from her gang at Orange Union High School were frequent visitors to her Palm Springs cottage, where they joined her in horseback riding and tennis. J. D. and Edna, her parents, came to see her most weekends, organizing picnics with her brother, Paul, and sister, Mary, to pick cherries in the high desert foothills.

It was never in his nature for Harold Hutton to feel sorry for himself. Deep down, he retained a boundless—and strangely magnetic—self-assurance that kept him sweet tempered, generally resilient, and nearly always self-deprecatingly humorous. But when Levora Raney first introduced him to the woman who was to brighten up his life, Harold was undergoing a crisis of confidence. That day in the Palm Springs gas station the brashness of his "Hi, toots" greeting disguised much more than his lack of funds to take Betty anywhere grander than the nearest hamburger stand. Harold was down and out. For the first and, as it turned out, the last time in his life, he had tasted the bitter fruit of failure and felt a twinge, though only a small one, of self-doubt.

Whether Betty Spennetta sensed this on their first date is hard to estimate. But she quickly recognized in the charming man who climbed into her car beside her—because his own, he said, was "being repaired"—an individual with talents and ambitions very different from those she had expected to find in "the guy with the greasy overalls" to whom Levora had introduced her. It was Harold, however, who asked most of the questions as they drove out along the dusty road that led across the sandy sage and cactus-speckled desert to Palm Canyon. There, under the cool green palms that surround an ancient Indian watering hole, he asked Betty why she was living in the desert. To her surprise, Betty found herself confiding, as she rarely did with her other boyfriends, that appearances can be deceptive, that despite her good looks and energy, she was suffering, as her mother had, from a weakness in her lungs that the doctors thought might be tuberculosis.

That said, she accepted when Harold offered her the first cigarette in a fresh pack of Camels. As they sat in her car that evening, they smoked nearly the whole pack. It was thirty years prior to the U.S. Surgeon General's report on the dangers of nicotine. Smoking was not only popular, but it was regarded by most

Americans as a mark of sophistication and maturity. Betty confided in Harold that she and Levora, in fact, were trying to "learn" to smoke. With their independence from their families that winter and plenty of leisure time while Betty was "recuperating," they had smoked and smoked in Palm Springs, trying their best—but so far failing—to acquire the habit.

"Why do that?" asked Harold, who had been smoking Camels off and on since he was twelve and regularly since he was sixteen.

"So we can go back home looking grown up and fashionable," said the girl diagnosed with tuberculosis!

Over the half-century that followed, Betty seldom saw Harold go more than a few hours without a cigarette, even though as the years went by Harold's breathing became more difficult and his voice took on a telltale smoker's rasp.

All that, however, was in the future. For now, it was enough that during their desert trysts·they came to know and like and understand one other. Betty found deep satisfaction in sharing Harold's very different experiences. Within a week, she had his heart. They fell in love under the huge starlit desert sky, where Harold pointed out the constellations he had learned to recognize at Carleton College—the Big Dipper, the square of Pegasus, and the giant constellation Orion. Betty, for her part, told Harold about her gang at Orange High, her sorority at UCLA, and her love of sports, which he shared.

Harold's stories fascinated Betty. Her sheltered life had provided her with little inkling of the harsh realities he recounted of the bitter cold of Middle West winters, the inanities of military colleges, the opportunities and romance of the oil industry. Ten years older and vastly more worldly wise, the gas station attendant brought out in his new girlfriend deeper and more complex feelings than Betty ever previously had experienced. One was a desire to repair a heart broken by a marriage gone wrong. Another was an urge to hug and to hold a strong man whose rugged exterior could not disguise the hurt little boy trying to overcome his discouragement. Above all, Betty started identifying herself with

Harold's dreams of a bright future. Oil was America's gift to the world, he kept telling her. It would bring fame and fortune for them both, if only she would agree to join and share in his quest.

Early in 1933, Harold took Betty for a long drive in her car to Mexicali and the Bay of Cortes, south of the U.S.-Mexican border. It was her first exposure to Mexico—the garish lights, mariachi bands, and seedy gaming parlors of a frontier city. Betty was thrilled. But somehow, the trip went wrong. They claimed to have met a certain Señor Vascos, possibly a fortune teller. More likely it was a fictitious name for the keeper of a saloon where, unwisely, Harold "fell off the wagon" and upset Betty by drinking too much. It may be that in a moment of passion, the couple had driven across the border to be married in Mexico. But something stopped them. Harold in a letter he wrote several months later, hints that it may have been his behavior that night that did it:

> I have been doing a great deal of thinking since I have been home. I was a great fool for drinking the way I did. I never did a thing like that before in my life and I am sure [I] shall never again. My only excuse is that I had met you under adverse conditions [at least I thought them so], I was broke, without clothes, and ashamed of my job. In other words, sailing under false pride caused me a bit of an inferiority complex. Liquor seemed to give me courage.

Whatever happened between them in Mexicali, only one item lasted—Señor Vascos. Time and again, when Betty and Harold would talk and laugh about Prohibition or about the decision they soon were to make to postpone getting married for a year, the code word they used was "Vascos"; he stood for "mañana" (tomorrow).

When spring came in 1933, Harold and Betty were thinking seriously about how, when, and where to start a new life together. But it didn't prove easy for Harold to "getta Spennetta," as he once remarked with the boyish humor that Betty found so endearing.

Neither J. D. nor Edna was amused when the Spennetta family became aware of their daughter's "serious intentions" toward a divorced man with a former wife and child to look after. Harold, when they first met him, impressed them as "a good looking guy with lots of drive and intelligence, though at times inclined to be surly and use bad language," as Edna described him.

His enthusiasm, now recovered, was infectious. His love of life and reviving self-confidence, though still scarred by the loss of his first job and his child, were hard to resist for a girl who, for all Betty's self-assurance, had grown up in an environment far more limited and conservative than that of the tough-talking Minnesotan. Divorces and broken homes were foreign to the Spennettas. Harold's liking for strong drink, though he only rarely indulged it, was also an anathema to Betty's parents, who originally had supported Prohibition and had brought up their family on the precept of "moderation in all things." Harold, in his first letter to Betty, asked, "What did your mother think?" and then answered his own question, "probably that we are crazy."

Neither J. D. nor Edna was inclined to browbeat or pressure their daughter, but it is not difficult to imagine some of the comments that they must have left hanging in the air. "You met him at a gas station?" "How does he propose to support you?" J. D.'s questions in all likelihood were more searching: "What does he do for a living, apart from mucking around with those film people and telling tall tales about oil?" Grandma Spennetta could well have added, "Is he after your father's money?"

For a while, her parents' concerns seem to have reinforced Betty's own natural caution. Harold, after all, had been homeless and jobless when she met him; maybe he was just on the rebound from his divorce and looking for a shoulder to cry on. Perhaps too, Betty conceded, she herself, feeling jaded after months away from home and wrestling with her suspected tuberculosis, had succumbed too easily to the charm of an older man who had talked so learnedly about the stars. Whatever the reason, Betty resolved and Harold agreed that they should wait a little longer before moving onto the next stage—marriage.

J. D. and Edna breathed a sigh of relief when Betty moved back to Orange in May of 1933 as the summer desert heat began to increase. Harold struck out for Los Angeles "to find my place in the oil industry, where I belong," as he told her.

Harold and Betty pledged their troth on the coast of Mexico

"COURTIN' BETTY"

It was May of 1933, the depths of the depression, when Harold Hutton went to Los Angeles to look for work and to figure out how to marry Betty Spennetta. In his first letter to her on May 7, 1933, he wrote:

> Dearest Betty,
>
> I arrived in Los Angeles yesterday and the depression is really on. It is undoubtedly [for] the best that . . . the Doctor feels you best wait a year. A year at least is going to be needed to even find a job in this town.
>
> Dear, you must forget seeing me for some time now. I would love to visit you but conditions make it impossible. You can depend that I will see you the first decent opportunity that presents itself. In the meantime, believe me, you have all my love, always.

So began Harold Hutton's double struggle, to make his breakthrough into the oil industry and to hang onto the young woman he had come to idolize. The way ahead seemed hard. Harold wrote in late May:

> If I can only get to working I will probably feel better about everything. As it is now the whole town and everybody in it reminds me of a large insane asylum.

His letter of May 25 brought better news:

> I am holding down the one job now—the garage. Have looked every day for something else and have several good things lined up.

But in the face of discouragement after discouragement, Harold's optimism flagged. His next letter said,

> Pray for me, Dear, pray that I will find the means of supporting us both—and soon.

Harold in his off hours took to studying physics. Even this led him back to Betty:

> In contemplating the intricate scheme of atoms and electrons I could not help but thank some power for swinging my orbit near yours (also cursed him for swinging it away again). . . . I, personally, would rather hold you than the secret of the universe.

June brought a useful step forward. Harold got a temporary job as a junior chemist at the British-owned St. Helens Petroleum Corporation, a job that eventually led to steady work. Of his first day at St. Helens, whose plant was in Montebello, California, he wrote:

> I got up at 5 A.M. this morning after driving for Abe Lyman last nite until 2 A.M. When I got out to the end of the bus line I had to walk 3 miles to the Plant.

But Harold was looking on the bright side:

> Gee, Honey, just think—if I could only keep this one we could be married in about three months. I am making $175.00 a month, maybe you don't think that seems like a lot of money but it would be enough.

It would be enough to fulfill his dream of a small studio apartment where they could live together and "send out the laundry."

Harold's hours of work and travel to the St. Helens lab left him little time for leisure, except occasional movies and visits to a bowling alley. At work he was rapidly picking up the rudiments of the trade that was to become the foundation of his future business and fortune, separating crude oil into specific grades and weights of kerosene, lubes, and heavy grease. Yet often when the drudgery and his shortage of money bothered Harold, he found himself starting to worry that Betty might be out of his reach, that he would never be able to provide her with the lifestyle to which she was accustomed, that she herself might be having second thoughts. His anxieties overflowed when Betty wrote to him about the parties and dances she was attending with her well-to-do friends in Newport Beach. He grew jealous, wondering if she was attracting the attention of young men, and more importantly if it was she, rather than her mother or doctor, who wanted to put off their marriage. In one pained letter he pleaded:

> You will keep on loving me, won't you? Please wait the year, anyway.

Harold's nagging insecurity over Betty's affections led him in several letters to hark back to a notion he had had in the dark days after his break with Romayne, namely, to take a job in faraway Brazil. He kept referring to the jarring trip to Mexicali that he and Betty had made together:

> We wanted each other so much at the time and it seemed as though we were going to be separated by thousands of miles. God how disappointed I was when we left Mexicali that night.

Adding to his dilemma was his anxiety that Betty's parents might put an end to their dream of marriage on the grounds that Harold had been married before and had a young daughter to support. But Harold would not dissemble or make light of his commitment to Barbara. Proudly, he told Betty that the little girl had visited him at his parents' flat at the Garden of Allah and had beaten him playing jacks:

> She had more disqualifying angles for me. I think a lot of them were phonies but not being very familiar with the game I wasn't sure—anyway she has two new teeth.

One of the low points of Harold's first three months of separation from Betty came when, greatly embarrassed, he had to ask her to lend him some money. Writing in late June, after his job at St. Helens looked secure, he said,

> Will be able to pay you that money I borrowed by the end of the month—then you can come to Los Angeles and buy something and I will be able to see you again.

And so it transpired. Once Harold's job at St. Helens became more or less permanent, it proved easier for him to meet and feel at ease with Betty's parents. When they visited Los Angeles to go to dinner or a show, he was invited. Betty also took to dropping in on Harold and his brother Don on her way home to Orange County after she resumed her classes at UCLA. These visits and her telephone calls to his lab or the public phone box outside his apartment were the moments Harold lived for. Through his struggles, it was the thought of finally winning Betty that kept him going. Once, having recently read a novel about Leonardo da Vinci, he likened her to the *Mona Lisa,* saying that there was a similar "quality of constancy" in both.

Psychologists may surmise that it was Harold's preoccupation with Betty's "hard-to-get" qualities and his concern for her constancy that he saw reflected in the *Mona Lisa*'s face. What is certain is that the longer the period—and distance—of separation between them, the greater was Harold's feeling of both enchantment and unreality. In his letter of June 5, 1933, he told her the following:

> You seem like a dream to me—a beautiful dream—I am afraid you
> are fast becoming an ideal—something I want more than life itself
> and [I'm] oh so afraid I won't get it.

Betty's response to this outpouring was to invite Harold to Orange for the weekend, an invitation he found hard to accept. After arguing about it by telephone, he wrote the following:

> After talking to you tonight I am feeling as tho I have done something
> bad. Dear, if you only knew how much I want to go to Orange
> Saturday you would realize how much I care for you. I just sort of
> have a silly pride and I am so afraid of something, I don't know how
> to explain it, exactly. Afraid of some impression you might get of me
> that would make you stop loving me. Let's just forget it for this time,
> I would be uncomfortable and I just can't help it.

Standing in the way was Harold's continuing disquiet over the difference in their circumstances, which Betty, for her part, wanted to ignore. While she was weathering the depression in the comfort of her life in Villa Park, Harold was scrambling to survive. His only relaxation was odd nights out with his work-mates at company boxing matches. But Betty had her way and Harold ended up in Orange for that weekend. He wrote to her the following Monday:

> Here I am back to stark realism after the most wonderful weekend with the most wonderful girl, I have ever known . . . All day long, scenes have been running thru my mind. Star Pine tree, Orange groves, Bobby [Betty's dog], steaks without salt, Bunny [a pet name for Betty's sister, Mary], so delightfully adolescent one minute, so chic and grown up the next . . . bikes, the beach and boats, all these things with Betty's placid and serene smile in every new picture.

And so began a pattern of Betty's introducing Harold to the comforts and relaxations of a world he had never known. His increasingly frequent visits to Orange County eased the hesitation of Betty's parents toward the mar-riage. Perhaps, too, they gave Harold a model for the high standards and quality of life that in years to come he would go on to acquire and surpass for himself and his wife.

By midsummer Harold saw better prospects in the refinery at St. Helens:

> They just closed a contract for 10,000 Bls of orchard spray oil and it probably will necessitate putting on a chemist at night.

Harold got the job and once again felt more optimistic:

> This depression is clearing itself up and soon there will be an entirely new era of good times. My plans are to somehow, some way, get myself lined out so that you and I can enjoy our share of it . . . There has been a disagreeable part in my past life but, really, there is nothing I have done I am ashamed of. With the possible excep-tion of my obligations to Barbara, my whole interest is centered on you and your happiness . . . I am openly declaring myself—I want to marry you in at least three months.

Unfortunately, Harold's prediction, like his proposal, was premature. The depression in fact was worsening. It was closer to three years before he and Betty were united. Yet as the months went by, Harold's self-esteem recovered. The tone of his letters subtly changed. Harold was getting back onto his feet. He felt a growing competence and confidence in his work. He and Betty were also developing something deeper and more enduring than they had experienced during that single winter in the desert. They shared an ever-wider array of interests in business and culture as well as in friends and family that is the best foundation of an enduring marriage.

Harold did a lot of reading, went to the movies, played a little golf or bridge, took the streetcar out to Santa Monica to go to the beach. He even did some boxing. But everything he did, Harold described to Betty; she, in turn, did the same with him. They listened to the same radio programs on stations KHJ and KFI. She asked whether he had heard the broadcast of a certain song, "After Tonight, Tomorrow." (He had.) Harold, in turn, wondered if Betty heard Donald Novis singing "Trees" or the "divine Richard Crooks" singing "One Alone." (She did.) He wanted to know if she liked Burns and Allen. ("They're just terrific," she replied.)

One day, Harold wrote that he was reading *Magic Island,* a travel book about Haitian voodoo practices and zombies, saying that he felt about as animated as the "plodding dumb brutes" in the book. Curiously, he also quoted the French philosopher Montaigne, firing off the observation that "we find out more about ourselves in five minutes of self-disgust than in weeks of self-satisfaction." Though they were separated by many miles and a still wider gap in their standards of living, Betty and Harold were creating a kind of synchronous experience through their daily correspondence, listening to the same radio, gazing up at the same California moon. At times, it seemed as if they already were married. Harold worried about Betty's sprained ankle, her sunburnt lips, and the chance that she might get stung by "stingerees," or jellyfish, while swimming at Balboa beach. But mostly he was anxious, although he never mentioned the word, that her tuberculosis might be worsening:

> You mustn't work too hard with all this company and parties. Remember I have a first mortgage and I don't want you abusing my property.

Shortly afterward, Harold paid another visit to Orange. He talked to J. D. about President Franklin D. Roosevelt's New Deal (about which they both were skeptical). Of Betty's work in the office at Inland Transportation, he told her:

> I am hoping you will be working for me before many months pass. I will put you on an easier schedule than Franklin's NRA. All you will have to do is burn paper plates and give me a kiss.

By now Harold was feeling easier about discussing with the Spennettas his earlier life and the daughter he had with Romayne. A late August letter read:

> Barbara was here for the night. She is like a wild cyclone hitting the place. Right now she has my bed all torn apart and it looks as tho we are going to sleep under a tent tonight. I put up the argument that it is too hot for it but she showed me all the places air can get in. She says this is keeno (whatever that is).

Then he went on to say:

> I have been listening to all the orchestras tonight and it seems so long since I have been out, I doubt if I would know how to act. The bright lights would probably blind me. I really can't see how you can love me at all, I have done such a weak amount of "courtin." I am sure of one thing tho—you are not a gold digger (isn't that funny?). Good night, Dear. Like the Arabs I shall fold up the tent and steal away (sometime after Barbara is asleep).

As the depression ground on, Harold's company managed to expand, with plans to drill a new well near Richfield in Fullerton, California. But the lines outside the soup kitchen and government employment offices still wound around the blocks of downtown Los Angeles, and employers did not worry about their men not working hard. Harold kept Betty apprised of his progress on work:

I have worked 34 hours out of the past 48 and 8 more for street cars . . . We are running some road oil and I have had to work double shifts for the past 2 days . . . But, they pay me overtime, so I really am not kicking. If they were robbing me of hours with you then it would be different—but I only just go home and go to bed so I am glad to get the extra work.

Slowly and painfully, Harold Hutton proved his worth at St. Helens Petroleum. He wrote of his progress to Betty in a letter:

I'm not in the Laboratory anymore. I am in the long wooden building you pass [on the way] to the lab . . . I blend the lube oil and greases, put them in drums and cans, take inventory twice a month, help load it out, unload the full cans of oil that come in and in general get myself about as dirty as a coal shoveler. It is hard work but I like it—it is bringing Betty closer.

By the fall of 1933, the situation was brightening still further:

I am getting the spray-oil pushed into my dept. and after it gets nicely going I will ask for a raise. I also have a few ideas I think will help in the handling of it.

He went on to confide that St. Helens was about to set up a canning operation so as to be able to ship its own products. Harold's involvement in this equipped him to set up and manage his own canning plant in Indonesia in the mid-1950s. But the depression was still far from over. Commenting on one of President Roosevelt's fireside chats, he wrote this one October day:

Sunday night I listened to Franklin Delano cheer up the depression-depressed. Last night Charlie Chaplin tried to do the same thing . . . he has a splendid voice—slightly English. It strikes me rather funny that the powers that be who arrange these radio N.R.A. broadcasts think the world's greatest clown would have something serious to say.

Several times Harold wrote that "having enough to eat is an accomplishment in itself during this Depression." Because his wages still barely met the cost of his food and rent and Harold still had no car of his own, he was reluctant to accept any more of Betty's family's generosity, which he was in no position to repay.

He was constantly embarrassed that he had to take Betty out in her father's car. Betty too was uneasy. Along with the depression, there was another dark subject that recurred from time to time throughout their correspondence— Harold's drinking.

On October 30, 1933, Harold wrote to explain to Betty why he sounded a little tight on the telephone. He said that he had been to dinner at his boss's house to further discuss their plans (most probably for the canning endeavor) and that he had a few "refreshments" on the urging of his boss. He wrote,

> This was the only time, Dear, and as Mr. Webb is manager of the refinery, I have just a little excuse, eh?

But Betty was not reassured. After the trip to Mexicali, Harold had promised that he would never drink to excess again. Now on December 4, 1933, with Prohibition about to be repealed, he closed his letter with the joking caution:

> Tomorrow is repeal. Stay sober—tonight is the rejuvenation of John Barlycorn but it doesn't mean a thing to me. I haven't even had a little nip for my cold.

The year 1934 started out with continued rain and flooding in southern California. Betty went to ski in the mountains and came home with a hurt knee. Harold had a lingering cold and could not go to work. He complained,

> If it wasn't for books, I fear I would be terribly bored with life— especially the present one.

But in spring things brightened up for them both. Harold spent more time in Orange, and he and Betty shared some very late nights, which ended with

Harold coming back to Los Angeles bleary-eyed but very happy as he listened to "You Are My Everything" on the radio. St. Helens also opened a new operation in Santa Maria and Harold's plant got a big order. During the inventory, he stepped onto the top of a drum of transmission grease but the lid was not securely battened down. Harold good humoredly wrote that he

> fell in and got mired waist high in goop . . . It took about half the personnel to clean me up.

There was also a fire at the plant, so Harold hastily closed a letter he was writing in the office:

> I may have to quit this letter as the fire trucks are pulling up to the building. If this letter is scorched you will know I waited too long (of course thinking of you could scorch it too).

By June 1934, Harold seemed to be burning the candle at both ends. He started one of his letters that month saying:

> I had cross eyes today—but it was worth it. I am sorry I went to sleep in the car while we were parked at the Palisades [near the ocean at Santa Monica, California], but it was wonderful seeing you and getting that goodbye kiss as I left.

Harold now had a car that Betty named "Essy." It turned out to be an unreliable old heap, and Harold never knew whether it would last out the one-and-a-half-hour journeys he now tried to make each weekend to Orange County. But that and his financial situation did not deter him. In August, he wrote the following:

> I received a sweet letter from you today and I am debating whether to come to Orange tomorrow or not. My financial condition is such as to make me hesitant to even venture out of the front door; but, hell, it has been that way for so long, I am beginning to gain a fortitude that would be the envy of a professional hitch-hiker, so you may see my driving up in all my broken-down splendor.

Fortunately for Harold, the tractor operator at his plant said that he could fix "Essy" up in minutes, and a skeptical Harold was very impressed when he did just that by adjusting the distributor.

So the summer of 1934 drew to a close and the couple made plans for Labor Day. Harold was able to stay over in Orange County. Betty woke him up to come outside and look at the moon. In the morning he could barely remember what it looked like. Having caught another heavy cold, he was confined to bed. His post–Labor Day letter began:

> Darling, I can't remember anything I have ever hated to do more than leave you Tuesday morning. I am still a little ill and think maybe my cold has something to do with it.

By early 1935, events in Europe had started to stimulate the California oil industry. In Germany, the Nazi party was trying to snap the Third Reich out of massive unemployment and the runaway inflation that had turned the mark into "confetti money" by launching pogroms against the Jews and a crash program of all-out re-armament. Out of the blue, Harold wrote to Betty in early June 1934,

> Hitler is kind of raising Hell in Germany, isn't he?

One side effect of the rise of Nazism in Europe was a huge increase in German and Italian imports of oil to feed these countries' growing war machines. Britain and France, despite their attempts at appeasement, also started ordering warships and guns, and the United States joined them in building up huge stockpiles of oil. Harold's company, St. Helens Petroleum, along with all other U.S. oil companies, received first a trickle then eventually a massive flood of new orders as the drums of war in Europe beat louder following Hitler's reoccupation of the Rhineland.

Harold, as he was to discover time and again during his business career, noted how events in far-off countries could influence, sometimes transform, the lives of ordinary Americans who knew nothing and cared less about the quarrels of the rest of the world. It was re-armament in Europe that eased the depression in America. Harold's workload at the refinery doubled and redoubled.

For Betty, the irony was that her fiancé's success in his business widened the physical distance between them, even though Harold was now starting to earn enough money to begin looking for a home of their own. Promoted to area salesman, he moved up from a junior sales post in the Long Beach area to head up the refinery's office in San Bernardino. He told Betty that he liked his new position because

> so much of the time I spend just riding around—and thinking of you know whom.

Betty, however, was now back at UCLA and they saw less, not more, of one another after the Christmas they spent together in Villa Park. Harold wrote:

> There is so much we are missing, but, Darling, we are making progress. A little while ago we didn't even have a car—we'll wait some more . . . and have loads of fun—soon too.

That fall, Harold reported that he had won several new large accounts. His knowledge of the oil industry was widening and deepening. Everywhere in southern California, he was building up his contacts in oil field management and learning about the procurement of all kinds of equipment as well as refining and sales. He was just past his thirty-second birthday, and Harold's capacity for hard work expanded as the pressures increased:

> Darling,
>
> I have been working so late and early it is almost impossible to find time to do anything except sleep and work. If I don't write you know it is not because I am not thinking of you . . . Certain things are shaping up in the oil industry—if they break right it is sure to be better. Anyway, I love you and think of you all the time . . . You keep loving me—and I'll keep working. Something will break—All my love.

And that is where, in February 1936, this series of Harold's letters, each lovingly kept in Betty's files, trails off. Betty's replies have never been found. Harold either mislaid or did not keep them. But Betty was now utterly convinced that the shape of her future with Harold was clear enough for them to grasp it with both hands. Harold had proved himself by hard work and flair. His feet were on the ladder of the business where he wanted to be and from which, as Betty now believed, he and she could earn a rich reward. Hence she decided to create their "start-up fund." Already, she had contributed a windfall $300 she had inherited from her grandfather Chuning. Harold, too, was saving as much as he could to make a down payment on a home or a business. The couple was beginning the financial partnership that over the next half-century was to supplement and underpin their romance. The waiting had gone on long enough. It was time to get married.

In the fall of 1936, Harold bought Betty a ring. They set a date and then told, not asked, their families about their plans—first the Spennettas in Orange, then Harold's brother Don, and Carrie and Albert Hutton in the Garden of Allah apartments. It was to be a simple ceremony. In keeping with the spirit of the times, when millions of Americans were still out of a job and conspicuous consumption was frowned on, Betty wanted no elaborate bridal gown, no lavish floral decorations of the kind her girlfriends had enjoyed. A frugal wedding, in any case, was considered in the best taste when one of the partners had been married before and could not, under the rules of many Christian denominations, be married a second time in church.

Happily, the Reverend Willsie Martin of the Wilshire Methodist Church in Los Angeles entertained no such inhibitions. Harold Floyd Hutton and Elizabeth Lee Spenetta were therefore pronounced man and wife at a modest ceremony in the presence of their parents and siblings and virtually no one else on December 19, 1936, at 10 A.M. Betty was two months shy of her twenty-third birthday. Harold was thirty-two.

PART IV   BUILDING A BUSINESS

Harold (middle) with brother Don (right) and unknown companion

Setting Up Their Own Enterprise

Despite their long courtship, the Huttons' marriage profoundly changed the shape and direction of both their lives professionally as well as personally. Betty's quiet support quickly restored the natural ebullience and self-assurance of her husband that had been shaken by his breakup with Romayne and the difficulties that he had experienced in finding worthwhile employment. From time to time, Harold still had too much to drink, but when he did, Betty locked him out of the small apartment they moved into at 544 South New Hampshire Street in downtown Los Angeles. Whenever this happened, he would stay the night with his brother, Don, in his room at the Garden of Allah. Once, after a hard day's work, too much whiskey, and a heavy dinner, Harold took Betty to see a movie and fell asleep during the performance. When he woke up, she had left. Harold soon got the message. He, if not Don, cut down his consumption of alcohol—and started to eat more as compensation.

Betty meanwhile got a job in the accounting office at St. Helens Petroleum. The references she had been given by the senior partner of Winans & Henry, Accountants, Auditors & Tax Consultants of Anaheim testified to her diligence and competence:

> Miss Spennetta has been associated with my office for the past six
> months. She is of high character, conscientious and a willing worker.
> She is a capable stenographer and meets the public well.

For a while, the couple was able to drive to work at St. Helens together, but not for long. Company policy, reflecting a time when jobs still were scarce, was changed under pressure from Washington. Husbands and wives no longer could be employed by the same company at the same time. Betty had to resign. Before quitting, she showed Harold an application form that her boss had told her to fill out. Issued by the Fidelity & Deposit Company, St. Helens' insurers, this application would have provided a bond in Betty's name enabling her to move into a more senior position, with authority to write checks on the oil company's account. To ease her disappointment at having to give up this promotion, Harold filled out the form in Betty's name: "Age 24; Height, 5'4"; Weight, 125; Color eyes, Blue. Other distinguishing features: Beautiful red lips, soft luscious eyes, loving arms. Agent: Harold!"

On leaving St. Helens, the new Mrs. Hutton went to work at the American Fruit Growers Exchange. Her father, J. D. Spennetta, and his Orange County rancher friends, had all the influence required to make sure that his red-lipped daughter with those soft luscious eyes—plus a glowing reference from St. Helens—quickly obtained a position in the accounts department. Harold remained at the oil company, where his feet were now firmly on the ladder for promotion. He had served his apprenticeship in the two fields that were to be crucial to his future success—as a hard-driving salesman of oil products of all kinds and as an accomplished blender of different types and grades of crude oil to meet the discrete needs of his customers.

Both Harold and Betty worked long hours in the mid-1930s. Their combined income left little to spare after paying the rent, Harold's alimony to Romayne, and monthly installments on yet another Stutz Bearcat Roadster that was Harold's pride and joy after he bought it as a wedding present for them both. The young couple made a point of keeping up the high standards of clothing and footwear to which both, by choice as well as upbringing, had become accustomed; but Betty frequently worried about bills that went too long unpaid. When their phone was disconnected, she wrote three anxious letters to Harold who was on a business trip to Portland, Oregon. Characteristically, he replied, "Quit worrying about the money—I am going to love you so much when I get home you won't need any."

In later life, Betty liked to recall that on the first Christmas after their marriage, the Huttons, in common with millions of other young Americans, couldn't afford a Christmas tree. That story was a bit of an exaggeration, since at all times she could count on help, including a Christmas tree if she'd asked for one, from J. D. and Edna. More likely, the two young people were saving every penny they could lay their hands on, planning for the day when they could cease working for other people and launch a new business of their own.

Harold never had any doubt that one day he would make a fortune in the industry he knew best—processing and marketing oil. He was encouraged by the example of his hero, Sam Mosher, whose reaction to the gloom and doom of the depression in which California still floundered was not to cut back but massively to step up promotion of his Signal Oil products. Most other U.S. companies had scaled down their advertising, on the grounds that with incomes falling it made no sense to encourage people to purchase what they lacked the money to buy. Mosher, by contrast, flooded California in the early '30s with new Signal promotions like the Huttons' favorite radio program, the *Signal Carnival,* which ran every Sunday night from 1932 until the Japanese attack on Pearl Harbor. Signal advertisements featuring Ann Sheridan, the original "Oomph Girl," appeared on billboards that proclaimed, "Signal is the gasoline with more oomph to the mile!" Following the first Tarzan movie with Buster Crabbe in the title role, a 52-piece Tarzan band, each player wearing a duplicate of Tarzan's leopard-skin costume, led a Signal caravan to Los Angeles City Hall, where the mayor gave them his greetings, and then proceeded down Broadway to the Paramount Theater where a special matinee show of *Tarzan the Fearless* was open for all Tarzan club members.

Harold was impressed and fascinated. Like millions of his fellow countrymen, he tried out in the shower the ape-man's victory yell, "E-eee-ough-yough." Whether Betty played the part of Jane in response is not recorded—but years later, when she and Harold met Sam Mosher and got to know Sam's sister-in-law, Laura Scudder, founder of the American potato chip business, both Huttons are said to have teased her with a genteel version of "E-eee-ough-yough!"

Most weekends when Harold wasn't working, the young couple drove down to the Spennetta's home in Orange. In the summer they went to J. D.'s beach home on Balboa Island. Harold was a lusty though not a stylish swimmer. Betty loved to sit in the sun, reading and writing letters, a habit she was to pursue throughout their later life in the Pacific islands and Singapore.

Paul Spennetta, Betty's brother, recalled Harold in his early thirties as a "physically tough guy with lots of muscles, a good swimmer and golfer, always nicely dressed and full of fun." Harold as well as Don Hutton habitually drank a lot, as did most young men during Prohibition, but the bad habit Paul most vividly remembered was Harold's snoring. Before he and Betty were married, Harold would share a room and sleep in the same double bed as Paul when he visited the Spennetta's beach house. "His snoring was so terrible," said Paul, "that in the middle of the night, I would get up and drive home from the beach to Orange so as to get a night's sleep."

On these weekend visits to Orange and the beach house, Harold would take time out to visit his daughter, Barbara, who was living with her mother near Long Beach. Betty rarely went with him. She felt uncomfortable about meeting Romayne. The divorce had been a messy one largely because Harold's mother, the redoubtable Carrie, had tried but failed to get custody of their daughter, Barbara. Looking back on her childhood, Barbara says that she "adored Daddy" but for many years "resented Betty as the woman who had taken him away from her."

In later life, the two women became fast friends when they lived and worked together in Southeast Asia. But there can be little doubt that in the early years of Harold's marriage to Betty, her husband's obligations to both his previous wife and his only child on whom he doted was a cross (albeit a light one) that Betty Hutton had to bear. Yet like most young couples making their way in life, Betty and Harold were too busy and too self-centered to be put off by these frissons.

Harold, in particular, was forever "dreaming dreams and scheming schemes," jotting down long lines of numbers on any piece of paper he could lay his hands on. By holding down their expenses and putting aside what Betty earned, he figured that they could save $3,000 by the end of the first year of their marriage, $5,000 by the end of the second. This money could be used either as a down payment on one of the $10,000 homes being built in West Los Angeles, as Betty at first suggested, or to invest (or "gamble" as she put it) on buying shares in a small refinery on Signal Hill not far from the one where Sam Mosher built his first casinghead distilling plant.

Harold had his way and Betty needed very little persuading. Perhaps she already knew that she and Harold would never have children of their own. Her nesting instincts were not strong. Nor was she one of the *kinder, kuche, und kirche* ("children, kitchen, and church") type of women that middle America still revered in the 1930s. Underneath that demure appearance there beat the heart of her Spennetta and Chuning forebears, who had earned their living as traders and bankers since they first arrived in America. Like Harold, though with less of his power and drive, Betty was a go-getter. She too wanted—and was determined—to win success for them both.

Therein lay the secret of the Huttons' lifelong partnership. Each brought to their marriage very different but complementary qualities. Harold in his thirties was an all-American go-getter, one part gentleman and one part hustler. He was shrewd though occasionally impetuous, tough-minded, and soft hearted—a businessman with a hard head, long vision, and a capacity to stare complex problems in the face and distill out of them the essential points needed for a solution. Harold also loved to make money. Integrity came naturally to him, but there was a touch of piracy, too. Harold was an entrepreneur, a born fighter and promoter, though rarely did he wear his aggressiveness on his sleeve. Rather, he learned the technique that was to stand him in good stead throughout his business career: be slow to speak but quick to pounce when the time comes to clinch a deal.

Harold in his early life could display a rough, tough edge. When he was tipsy, he could occasionally turn sarcastic, though never for long. Harold was self-sufficient, yet he also needed attention. His self-esteem in no small measure depended on the approval of others, especially that of his wife, a characteristic that was to become stronger as Harold got older. But as a young man, his most attractive feature was his appetite for life. Harold combined this with a boyish charm that he knew exactly how to use to his own advantage. Later in his life his personality became much warmer, almost cuddly. James Farley, one of his friends at Chapman College, described him as a "great big cuddly teddy bear." Bears, however, can be surly. So could Harold if he drank too much.

Betty Hutton brought to the marriage a complementary array of qualities. Where Harold was warm and noisy, she was quiet and collected. Even in her midtwenties, during the first years of their marriage when Harold had yet to establish himself in his own eyes or anyone else's, Betty exuded a coolness and peace of mind that neatly balanced her husband's harder-edged enthusiasm. Betty Spennetta had been regarded as a bit of a tomboy during her school days. She was far more a leader than a follower on the baseball mound and hockey field. Yet as a secretary and bookkeeper she was obedient, meticulous, and dutiful; as a young wife she was reserved in public, with a poise and touch of class that Harold greatly admired. Rarely, if ever, did Betty appear insecure. Her attributes were the product of a long line of ancestors who for close to a century had enjoyed a broad margin of security, of comfort, even opulence, in their homes and family habits. Her character was also an extension of the well-to-do orderliness and harmony of her upbringing by an ever-caring mother and an affectionate, if distant, father, who were pillars of the community in the prim city of Orange.

Whatever the reason, Betty, "the cool, calm lady" as one of her friends described her, and Harold, "one of the last of the American swashbucklers" as one of his associates called him, seemed to make an ideal match. Among the up-and-coming oilies they would meet in the late 1930s at the Petroleum Club

A young wife with a touch of class

in Los Angeles, they were one of the most popular pairs. Harold was always ready to buy a round of drinks and play stone, scissors, and paper at a call over lunch. Betty joined in the fun when they made up foursomes at football games, jazz sessions at the Beverly Cavern, and sneak previews in Hollywood.

By the late 1930s, the depression in America was ending. The British and French, sensing that war in Europe was inevitable, stepped up their forward contracts for oil, grease, and lubricants needed for tanks and warships. The oil glut in California eased, then disappeared. Harold about this time switched from St. Helens to Richfield Oil Company. He took a job as senior chemist overseeing laboratory and field tests on specialized lubricants and high-octane propellants that could be tailored for use in airplane engines.

It was 1938, the year when Hitler seized the Sudeten-German border regions of Czechoslovakia. Neville Chamberlain, the British prime minister, signed the Munich Pact that, condemned as it was as "appeasement," garnered for Britain the time needed to re-arm and stock up on oil.

As oil prices rose, Harold in faraway California began to earn good money. It was enough for him and Betty to keep up and step up their savings and indulge their love for fast cars.

Early that fall, they took time out for a delayed honeymoon, driving across the border to Hermosillo for the week-long celebrations of Mexico's independence. Along the way they shot hundreds of photographs and sent postcards to their relatives. In one of these Betty described the trip as "a humdinger of a journey on extremely dusty and very bumpy roads." Returning home via Yuma, Arizona, they moved into a bigger apartment at 1136 South Westmoreland, a two-story stucco building in a development three blocks south of Wilshire Boulevard, where Los Angeles in the late 1930s was reaching out west from the downtown area. A line of thin, scraggly palm trees had been planted along the street, but as yet these were far too small to offer character or shade. The Huttons' apartment was on the second floor, a small, two-bedroom flat with metal windows, fly shades, no air conditioning, and no garage. Looking out, their only view on the opposite side of Westmoreland was an equally humdrum apartment block ornamented with fake, Hollywood-style minarets, built in mock-Gothic manner. Not faraway was one of Los Angeles's landmarks, the now-demolished Ambassador Hotel, where Harold in his down-and-out days had worked as a parking attendant and where later Robert Kennedy was assassinated.

The following year, as the European powers slid down the slope toward war, their orders for U.S. armaments and oil products escalated. The depression was over. Refinery profits rose. The Huttons took a chance and invested their savings in a refining business of their own, a badly run down little "still," as Harold called it, not far from Signal Hill.

Two other young Californian businessmen, George Rawlings and Channing C. Johnson, had joined with James J. Eymann, whose company, Solvents Refining Company, had taken over this plant at 5900 Firestone Boulevard in Downey near Long Beach. Rawlings, who had owned the refinery, sold it to Solvents for $10,000 in cash and the assumption of his liabilities, valued at $3,250, plus a bank debt of $1,000. Channing Johnson chipped in a $4,000 chattel mortgage and $6,000 in shares in Solvents. An outside investor, E. P. Tsant, bought a further $1,000 worth of the new company's stock at $10 per share. Harold and Betty Hutton meanwhile had set up a corporation, Refining Associates, Inc., in Nevada, where no state tax was levied. Refinate, as the company was to be known, leased the Solvents plant with an option to buy.

In 1939, Harold moved into the Solvents offices in Downey as manager of the refinery. Betty became the bookkeeper, leading her brother, Paul, to venture the opinion that "Harold was the one taking risks and Betty provided the keel." The first order they landed was for grease to lubricate the axles of the Southern Pacific Railroad's locomotives and freight cars. Harold also went looking for business with the Russian vessels that called in at Long Beach for cheap bunker oil and lubricants. This Russian trade gave Harold his first taste of the international shipping business. It opened up the Pacific dimension of the global oil business that over the next decades was to become the keystone of his company's future and the foundation of the Huttons' fortune.

OIL FOR THE WHEELS OF WAR

World War II turned the Huttons' risky investment in Downey into a substantial and profitable business. Refining Associates, Inc., small as it was, rose on the tide of the U.S. economy's prodigious wartime expansion.

The Japanese attack on Pearl Harbor on December 7, 1941—"a day that will live in infamy," as President Franklin Roosevelt (FDR) described it—not only shocked the American nation, but also galvanized a still-recession-scarred United States into history's most titanic economic turnaround. It was the perfidy of Imperial Japan, whose ambassador in Washington was still trading the honeyed words of peace while Admiral Tojo's carriers were launching their surprise assault on the U.S. fleet in Pearl Harbor, that infuriated the American public, but it was the response of American industry—under FDR's dynamic leadership—that provided the decisive response to Japanese aggression.

Week after week in the spring of 1942, the headlines told of U.S. and British defeats: "Six U.S. Battleships Sunk," "Japanese Capture Bataan and 36,000 of our troops," "Corregidor Surrenders," "Two British Battle Cruisers Sunk as Japs Invade Malaya." Yet as Allied forces reeled in the face of the Japanese capture of the Philippines, Hong Kong, and Singapore, followed by air and sea landings in Java, thrusts into Burma, and air attacks on Australia, the United States for the first time ordered its entire economy onto a war footing. A draconian War Powers Act, rushed through Congress with little dissent, gave Roosevelt authority to place virtually the whole of America's steel, engineering, vehicle assembly, and aviation industries under the control of an all-powerful national War Production Board (WPB). The U.S. oil industry for all practical purposes was nationalized. The chairman of the WPB summoned the industry's leaders to Washington to give them the government's instructions. These specified that the U.S. Navy alone would require 26 million barrels of diesel oil each year for the foreseeable future; that the Army Air Corps would need hundreds of thousands of blockbuster bombs using toluene, a petroleum derivative; and that hundreds of new air bases, to be built on remote Pacific Islands, would require mountains of asphalt for paving landing strips. With Japan in control of the world's supply of natural rubber, the U.S. oil industry would also be required to manufacture huge quantities of synthetic rubber, of which the basic ingredients was butadiene, another product of oil refineries. Factories and railroads henceforth would be working around the clock, requiring oceans of lubricating oil to keep them running.

Harold, aged thirty-seven when the United States entered the war, was too old to be drafted. By virtue of his occupation as a key oil producer, he was ordered to stay on the job and placed under the jurisdiction of the southern California office of the War Production Board.

A torrent of orders followed for more of everything the Huttons' little refinery at Firestone Boulevard could produce. WPB officials inspected Harold's facilities. He was ordered to double, then redouble output of heavy lube oils for the Navy and Air Corps, axle grease for railroads and the tens of thousands of trucks and tanks needed for an army whose numbers expanded from less than 1 million to 12 million men in less than three years.

Within two weeks of the U.S. declaration of war, Californians had their first taste of the enemy's fury. On December 21, 1941, a Union oil tanker, the *Montebello*, heading for Vancouver from its loading port at Avila, was torpedoed and sunk. As the crew took to the lifeboats, a Japanese submarine surfaced and fired on the tanker with machine guns—but miraculously, not a single one of the *Montebello*'s men was wounded.

Two months later, on February 23, 1942, Harold and Betty were listening to FDR's evening radio fireside chat. His topic was the state of the country's west coast defenses. As Roosevelt's mellifluous voice began, "My friends," the Huttons' telephone rang. There had been an explosion in the Ellwood area just north of Santa Barbara, California. Offshore, said an excited neighbor, was a "giant submarine, longer than a football field!" Local radio reports confirmed that the Japanese navy was lobbing high explosive shells ashore, apparently aiming at two 80,000-gallon gasoline tanks belonging to Richfield Oil Company. But the submarine's gunners were bad shots. Even at point-blank range with the ocean as smooth as glass, no serious damage was done.

Nor was Harold impressed by Japanese navigation. U.S. radio monitors at Point Arguello heard the Japanese skipper boasting via short wave to Tokyo that he had left Santa Barbara "in flames." This submarine, the I/17, was skippered by Captain Kozo Nishino, who in peacetime had often brought Japanese naval tankers to Ellwood to take on cargos of American crude oil. He and his submarine were subsequently sunk with no survivors off Australia during an engagement with allied corvettes and bombers in 1943.

Gasoline rationing was introduced in America in late 1942. It was the first time since their marriage that Betty did not take Harold to share the Spennetta family's turkey in Orange. Instead, they went to Harold's parents' home to say goodbye to his thirty-three-year-old brother Don, who was leaving to join the army. A letter to Betty written by her mother, Edna, the following week captures the spirit of the times:

> Mama and I went up to Los Angeles Friday. I have never seen anything like it. Everybody had the same idea we did; get in one last day before gas rationing started. We drove around for forty minutes before we could find a parking lot. I am very busy now as I have charge of all the work done by my Assistance League. Have to keep thirty women busy. We make surgical dressings as the need for them keeps becoming more desperate as we become more involved in the war. Don't know how we are going to manage about gas. Have a hard time getting meat, butter, eggs but anything to win the war quickly.

The Huttons played their part in the national war effort by working fourteen hours a day to expand their refinery's output. Harold's contracts with the military multiplied as supply officers from all three services pressed for ever more deliveries of specialized lubricants and aviation fuel. One of them told him that the armed forces of the United States and Britain together were now consuming fourteen times as much aviation fuel each day as the entire amount of gasoline shipped by the United States to Europe in World War I!

Betty entertained visiting soldiers en route to the Pacific battlefields. On her twentieth-ninth birthday (February 20, 1942), two young artillery lieutenants spent the weekend in the Huttons' apartment before leaving the next day for Guam.

Up to now the United States had concentrated its efforts on the European front, joining the British in carrying the air war to Germany and helping the Soviet Union beat back the *Wehrmacht*'s onslaught against Moscow. British and United States forces by late 1942 had smashed the German Afrika Korps in North Africa and were poised the following year to launch their invasion of Italy. Now, in 1943, America began to fight back in earnest in the Pacific. U.S. forces under General Douglas MacArthur took the offensive in the New Guinea area. The U.S. Marines secured Guadalcanal in the southern Solomon islands. The U.S. fleet under Admiral Bull Halsey turned back Japanese attacks on Australia. U.S. air power regained control of the western Pacific. And California boomed.

As American war production for the first time drew level with and soon surpassed that of Japan and Germany combined, Henry Kaiser built the first steel plant west of the Mississippi in the California desert at Fontana. Hundreds of new freight aircraft staged through the new U.S. Marine air base at El Toro in Orange County. With tens, then hundreds of thousands of U.S. troops moving into newly built West Coast bases en route to the Pacific battlefields, the ever-observant Edna Spennetta wrote this in March 1942:

We have a lot of soldiers stationed around here. We serve coffee, cake, sandwiches etc., every afternoon and evening. These fellows are all very young boys. Our canteen and recreation room help keep them off the street at a bad time for them to be roaming around on the loose, from 5 P.M. until eleven or after. They talk about their mothers, their homes, sweethearts etc.

The war years transformed California from a mainly agricultural economy best known to the rest of America for the gold rush, the oil boom, and Hollywood into one of Roosevelt's "arsenals of democracy." Los Angeles's economy boomed with the growth of defense installations and the manufacture of weapons and warplanes. As in Michigan, where an influx of black workers from the southern states led to riots in Detroit's huge new tank-building plants, so in Los Angeles there was an abrupt change, turning the city into a dense, smoggy, racially mixed kaleidoscope. The year 1943 began with the "Zoot suit riots." Soldiers stationed near downtown beat up dozens of newly arrived young Mexicans while the police looked on.

Harold Hutton's business rose with the tide of wartime expansion. Oil was the key to California's wartime transformation. His refinery's revenues quadrupled in less than three years. Shipping lube oil and grease to the U.S. armed services and, as the war wore on, direct to U.S. bases in the Pacific and beleaguered allies like the Chinese and Russians, Harold came into contact with a wide network of U.S. procurement and transport officers. He made a point of getting to know them personally, meeting for lunch in Los Angeles, drinking, and telling tall stories at the bar of the Jonathan Club. Harold was an avid jazz fan. Often, he would meet his associates in bars like the Beverly Cavern, where Louis Armstrong and other jazz greats performed. Sometimes, he would take his army and navy pals to meet Betty, play cards, and listen to jazz records at home. From time to time, these sessions would become noisy and rowdy. When Harold in his thirties and early forties had taken in too much of his favorite Scotch whiskey, arm wrestling and playful fisticuffs with his buddies were not uncommon. But he never allowed any kind of brawling at home. Betty would never have permitted it.

The Huttons' contacts with the U.S. military and Armed Services Petroleum Purchasing Agency purchasers paid off handsomely for Refining Associates. Harold added to his expert knowledge of every aspect of refinery operations a savoir faire about liaising with the armed services that was to stand him in good stead as subsequently he reached out into the Philippines, China, and Thailand. He knew who and when to call, how to tailor his bids to ensure that Refining Associates got the best deal at the best price. Harold, in short, matured during the war years from an up-and-coming young fellow on the fringe of the refinery business into a still small but key supplier of heavy lube oil and grease and the high-performance fuels needed for fighter aircraft.

Working as a team, Harold and Betty each brought their own special talents to the business. Harold had flair and drive, Betty had a cool head for numbers and an ability to help turn her husband's brain waves into business plans that worked. One idea that did was a contract to supply lighter fluid for the millions of cigarette lighters in use in a nation where smoking became a national habit during the war. West Disinfecting, a New York family company, was one of the principal suppliers of these lighters. Two of its directors, the Marcuse brothers, had offered to invest in Refining Associates if the Huttons would give them a discount and guarantee supply of the fluid. For Harold, this was good business. The volumes were small, the prices good, and as Betty kept pointing out, they needed the money.

In March 1942, at a meeting of the Solvent Board at 5959 South Alameda Street, Los Angeles, the Huttons had taken over from their partners the lease on the Downey refinery. In 1944, with West Disinfecting's order in their pockets, they now exercised their options to turn this lease into an outright purchase, becoming for the first time owners of the business as well as heavy borrowers from Security First National Bank. It was time to form their own company. Betty did the homework, researching the pros and cons of incorporating in California or as their accountant suggested, in Nevada, where taxes were very much lower.

In spring 1945, as U.S. forces gathered for the assault on Okinawa and U.S. B-29s started round-the-clock bombing of the Japanese mainland, Harold took the train to Carson City with James and John Marcuse. They met an attorney, H. E. Higginson, who restructured their partnership into a Nevada corporation that henceforth would carry on the Huttons' business with lesser income tax liabilities than its directors faced as individuals. Harold was allotted 2,500 shares of common stock, valued at $20,000 to reflect the assets he and Betty had brought to the company, mainly plant facilities and orders receivable. The Marcuse family, acting on behalf of West Disinfecting, bought 250 preference shares at a par value of $100 each, guaranteeing regular dividends. Harold was then named president and a director of Refining Associates Inc., with E. W. Hutton (no relation) as vice president and J. A. Armstrong as secretary-treasurer. To comply with Nevada state law, two local men, G. V. Lamb and A. M. Peters, were named directors of Refining's Carson City office, but the Company's main office remained in Long Beach on Firestone Boulevard.

The gigantic U.S. war effort by this time was building up to its 1945 climax. On the European front, the British and Americans had landed in Sicily, then Salerno, and fought their way up the peninsula to force the surrender of Italy. To support the D Day (June 6, 1944) Allied landings in Normandy, history's most colossal amphibious invasion with 2,000 ships and close to 5,000 airplanes, millions of men and hundreds of millions of tons of supplies of all kinds were flowing across the Atlantic. To ensure that the Soviet Union had the equipment it needed to launch the Red Army's great tank offensives that finally drove back the Germans from the Ukraine and Poland, millions more tons of armaments were being shipped into Russia via Iran and the Arctic convoys that cost the British and U.S. navies heavy losses in escort vessels.

Oil was the crucial ingredient in all of these efforts. Soon on the Pacific front alone, the U.S. oil industry was straining to keep more than 3,200 warships and 6,000 aircraft supplied with the fuel they needed to first smash the Japanese navy, then to leapfrog the U.S. Army and marines from the Philippines to Okinawa as the Americans carried the war closer to the Japanese mainland. Refining Associates was a small but crucial player in this titanic effort. The distillation plant at Downey doubled and trebled its output. Harold hired a fleet of tanker trucks like the ones he himself had driven in the mid-1930s. These trucks carried Refinate's refined products to military bases all over the western states.

By early 1945, Refinate was making a profit. The minutes of its May 31 board meeting included the following:

> The corporation is drawing to the close of its first fiscal year. According to the bookkeeping department, the corporation shows a net profit of approximately $1,200 at this time.

The board resolved to pay a dividend at the rate of 6 percent per annum for the first quarter of 1945 on the preferred stock, giving the Marcuse brothers $1.50 per share.

Soon afterwards, on April 12, four months after his inauguration to an unprecedented fourth term as President, Franklin D. Roosevelt died. For most Americans, including the Huttons, it was a blow more shattering than the one their children experienced eighteen years later when President Kennedy was killed. Harold had disagreed with many of FDR's policies. Like most of his Orange County contemporaries he was no lover of the New Deal's big government and high tax policies. Wartime Washington's red tape, intrusive bureaucracy, and "dictatorial methods," as he once described them, were anathemas to him, as government interference of any kind was to be all of Harold's life. But FDR, the wartime leader, was an authentic American hero for the Huttons and all their acquaintances. They mourned with the rest of the nation as the stricken president's body was laid to rest at his Hyde Park estate in New York. They also resolved, as vice president Harry Truman took over as chief executive, that the best tribute to the fallen leader was for America and its allies to go all out and win the war.

Four weeks later, Nazi Germany surrendered. Hitler was dead. The European war was over. It was time for the United States to turn all its power and energy onto the Pacific front. Hundreds of ships and thousands of aircraft redeployed from the Atlantic to the U.S. West Coast bases as U.S. troops stormed ashore in the Philippines, vindicating General Douglas MacArthur's 1941 pledge, "I shall return." The Allies prepared for what promised to be an eighteen-month or longer campaign against the Japanese home islands.

In the first six months of 1945, Refining Associates turned out more oil and grease than it had in the three previous years. Harold Hutton also took on two new assignments that were to enhance his own and his company's standing in the oil industry. With the defeat of Hitler's Germany, the U.S. Air Force had captured some of the Luftwaffe's Fokke Wulf 180 fighter planes. These together with Britain's Fairey Lightnings were the first to be powered by jet engines and caused huge excitement in Washington. The word went out for the United States to develop its own jet engines.

When the Jet Propulsion Lab was established at Caltech in Pasadena, California, Harold Hutton was one of the first oilmen to be recruited. He worked on the specifications and development of JP5, the first American jet fuel. U.S. forces meanwhile had captured and spirited out of Germany the team of rocket scientists responsible for building the V-1 and V-2 missiles Adolf Hitler had launched against England in the later stages of the war. Under Wernher von Braun, its leader, this team was now put to work on a crash program to develop missiles for the U.S. Army. Harold Hutton took part in this project, too. A note prepared by Betty for Chapman College, when her husband joined its board of trustees, reads:

> We made the first fuel for the U.S. rockets being built at the Jet Propulsion Laboratory. We were the only ones making JP5, a lighter fuel for these engines.

By midsummer of 1945, the Japanese had been defeated and driven back from virtually all of their wartime conquests. Most of their ships had been sunk. The British were on the offensive in Burma, the Chinese were close to recapturing Chungking in the southwest province of Szechwan. The Americans, having won overwhelming air and naval supremacy, had Tokyo and every other big city in Japan at their mercy. Day after day in July 1945, U.S. firebombs rained down on the Japanese capital whose wooden buildings went up in smoke

Hutton's fluid helps fuel early U.S. missile launch

by the tens of thousands. Then on a boiling hot day, August 6, 1945, Harold and Betty Hutton were in their Long Beach office when a secretary burst in and said, "Mr. Hutton, turn on the radio. We've dropped a new kind of bomb on Japan they say could end the war."

The Huttons listened as the news came in of the world's first atomic blast, annihilating Hiroshima, killing 80,000 and wounding more than 100,000 Japanese. Like most Americans, Harold and Betty rejoiced. The staff at Refining joined them in a toast to the U.S. Air Force crew of the *Enola Gay,* which dropped the first nuclear bomb. Four days later, after a second atomic blast killed and injured 140,000 more Japanese in Nagasaki, President Truman announced Japan's surrender. The war was over. It was America's greatest victory ever. Harold gave all his employees the day off. He and Betty drove to Orange to join the Spennetta family in celebrating peace and the U.S. triumph. They took part in one of the tens of thousands of street parties that blossomed across the country, bringing brass bands, dancers, excited school kids, and a parade of flags and banners into the city streets. Harold handed out cigars. He danced with Betty to a recording of Glen Miller's band playing "In the Mood" and "Little Brown Jug." They raised their glasses to the U.S. Navy, to the marines, the army, and the air force, until Harold got tipsy and even Betty lost her reserve.

A week later, as thousands of cheering veterans returning from the Pacific still thronged the downtown streets, Betty moved the Refining Associates office to the Roosevelt building at 727 West 17th Street in Los Angeles. It seemed like a good decision. The company was doing well and needed more room for its staff. Revenues were up, profits were up, the future seemed bright with hope. Betty hugged her husband. He had bet on the oil industry and won. It was the same all over America. Refining Associates, like most U.S. companies, had done well out of the war.

The Hutton team after World War II

A Postwar Family of Two

When the war ended, Refining Associates' sales to the armed services rapidly declined. Whereas for close to four years the company had been able to sell everything it could produce to the government at guaranteed prices, now the Huttons, like all other defense contractors, had to hustle to find fresh markets. As citizens and proud patriots, Betty and Harold were elated by America's great victory; as business people they were nervous. Peace brought fresh anxieties as well as new opportunities.

Harold worried that as demobilization gathered momentum and the world's biggest and most expensive war machine wound down—the U.S. armed forces' strength fell from more than 12 million to less than 1.5 million in eighteen months—this would lead to large-scale unemployment. Harold never forgot how difficult it had been for him to find work in the '30s.

Betty rejoiced in the re-appearance in the stores of a wider range of better food and clothes. She nevertheless took seriously the U.S. Treasury's warnings, which she read out loud to Harold from the business pages of the *Los Angeles Times,* that an explosion of demand for the new homes, cars, and consumer goods that had been denied to the American people by rationing and shortages could unleash runaway inflation. This inflation would be made worse by the release of the massive sums accumulated in tens of millions of families' wartime savings accounts.

Betty's concerns were justified. Harold's proved groundless. He was right in predicting that the Armed Services Petroleum Purchasing Agency would chop its orders for Refining's products. He was correct, too, in thinking that millions of defense workers, laid off with little notice when the atomic bombing of Japan brought the war to a sooner-than-expected close, would join the returning veterans in a scramble for postwar jobs. But peace brought no recession. Instead, there was a postwar boom. Within a year, the U.S. economy achieved its second industrial miracle in less than a decade. Having switched almost overnight from the stagnation of the '30s to mobilization and flat-out war production, all but abolishing unemployment and raising the size of the U.S. work force from 46 million in 1940 to 53 million in 1945 (not counting another 15 million in uniform), America changed gears a second time. In place of the wartime command economy directed mainly from Washington, there was a consumer-led free-for-all.

The Huttons had a ringside seat as California's wartime expansion roared on with scarcely a pause. With the end of rationing, a tidal wave of demand for gasoline, lubricants, and axle grease hit the gas stations. Millions of returning veterans, many of whom had first tasted the joys of the Pacific Coast's sunshine and beaches during the war, moved their families out of the colder eastern states and the Middle West to the proliferating housing estates of greater Los Angeles. From coast to coast manufacturers tried to meet an insatiable demand for cars, household furnishings, radios, and later, television sets. "New look" (i.e., long-skirted) women's clothes replaced the slacks and overalls millions of women had worn to work during the war.

Harold was therefore mistaken. There was no unemployment. Hundreds of thousands of returning GIs went back to school with help from funds provided by the GI Bill. Millions of women were glad to give up their jobs to return home and start the families that had been delayed by war. Betty Hutton's concern about inflation turned out to be nearer the mark. With demand exceeding supply, prices rocketed up. By 1948, the cost of living had risen by more than a third while wages and salaries had risen by only about 15 percent. Yet the spirit of the times was one of optimism and steeply rising expectations. More children, the celebrated baby boomers, were born to returning vets and their wives during the 1945–55 decade than in the whole of the previous genera-tion. America's population leapt from 120 million to 170 million! The construction industry took off, helped by advances in building techniques pioneered only ten miles east of the Huttons' refinery in the new bedroom community of Lakewood, where 16,000 homes were built and sold in less than three years.

The Huttons' first home of their own was in Villa Park, the site of a happy youth for Betty and the place where Harold had been welcomed into her family. So great were the demands of their business that Villa Serena, as Harold romantically named their Villa Park home, took longer to build in 1947–48 than J. D. and Edna's home had in 1915. Not until 1949 did the Huttons move into the house and have landscaping plans drawn up for flower gardens and broad lawns at the front, a wide ceramic tile patio encircling the rear porch, and lower down, a rose garden and fruit orchard screened by brick walls and tall trees.

The Huttons' home in the late 1940s looked out across what still was the uncluttered coastal plain of Orange County, a thirty-mile-wide expanse of citrus groves and dusty country roads. Beyond Newport Beach was the sharp outline of Catalina Island, behind which the setting sun threw up salmon-pink evening panoramas. Sometimes, as the sun disappeared below the horizon, Harold would say to Betty, "It's morning in China and Japan."

Life in Villa Park in the late '40s still was mainly rural. It was a place where, like most housewives, Betty expected to cook her husband's meals, iron his shirts, and hang out her own laundry. But the Huttons did not start a family. A couple of years earlier, Betty had not been feeling well. After consulting a doctor she learned that she had a tumor that necessitated a hysterectomy. She and Harold were never to have children of their own.

Surrounded as she was by classmates and relatives getting pregnant, delivering and bringing up their children, it is hard to imagine that Betty did not occasionally experience moments of quiet desperation about her own situation. In her high school annual, when asked what she would be in thirty years' time, she had written, "A moma." Vivacious, good looking, and high-spirited, a "golden girl," as her father called her, who was deeply in love with her husband,

Betty had overcome her tuberculosis before getting married and seemed a natural to join the ranks of postwar America's young mothers. She could not have been unaffected when she held Harold's daughter's first baby in her arms.

How Harold felt is not known. But as he made a point of paying regular visits to his only daughter, Barbara, to whom he was devoted, Betty could not have failed to notice the spontaneous pride and affection that her husband so obviously felt and displayed in the presence of his only child. Yet no one who knew Betty can recall her ever saying that she wished that she and Harold could have had a family of their own. Their childlessness seems not to have cast a shadow between them.

Betty's maternal instincts no doubt were sublimated in her love and care for her extended family. Starting with her parents and grandparents and extending over the years to her nieces, she showered her affection on them, never forgetting their birthdays and special occasions at school, which Betty always attended when she could. Her love came as naturally and warmly as that which her brother and sister felt for Betty. But early on, she made up her mind that motherhood was not the vocation she was destined to embark on. Instead, she gave her heart and all the affection of which she was capable to Harold, as over the years he did to her. Harold put it succinctly, "We have our own family of two."

The bonding of Harold and Betty grew closer during the postwar years in their work at Refining Associates. Physically, their love life at all times seems to have been fulfilling; socially, they complemented one another. Harold was a natural gentleman, but he could also be brash and boisterous. Betty if anything became more reserved, quieter, more refined. These indeed were the qualities that Harold most admired in his wife. They helped cement a marriage that, lacking children, found fulfillment in the work they did together and joy in the life of travel, adventure, excitement, and business success the Huttons were to achieve as a team.

Most days, as they built up their business during the war and in the late 1940s, they drove together to their small office on Firestone Boulevard, where

Betty had her desk placed beside and at a right angle to Harold's. For several years, they shared the same in-basket, Betty conscientiously reading virtually every document that dropped into it, Harold simply glancing at the headings and asking Betty to deal with the contents. During the early days when the company had only one telephone, they would take turns using it. Sometimes Harold had long chats with his pals in the oil field while Betty, who kept her calls short, tapped her fingers and pursed her lips impatiently.

Throughout the 1950s the company needed to count its pennies carefully. Refining Associates had emerged from the war as a substantial little business but one that was deeply in debt to Security First National Bank. Harold and Betty were also beholden to West Disinfecting, whose orders for cigarette lighter fluid and initial investment of $10,000 entitled its New York directors to the first of any dividends the Huttons might have available for distribution.

West Disinfecting had close connections to the Truman administration in Washington. Its president was a significant contributor to the Democratic party. Harold and Betty by contrast were stalwart Republicans who, like J. D. Spennetta and his conservative friends, had backed Governor Tom Dewey's 1948 campaign to unseat Harry Truman. But for the Huttons, then as always, politics made no difference when it came to doing business. Harold was impressed, not displeased, when he found out that West Disinfecting enjoyed direct access to the White House. President Truman's appointment schedule for Tuesday, April 8, 1952, the day on which he decided not to run for re-election, reads:

12 noon:	Ellsworth Bunker, newly appointed American ambassador to Italy
12:15:	Mr. Alfred Kirsch, President and Treasurer of West Disinfecting
12:30:	Secretary of Defense
1:00:	Lunch at the Supreme Court[5]

5. David McCulloch, *Truman*, (New York: Simon & Shuster, 1992) pp. 895–6.

West Disinfecting's directors rarely attended Refining's board meetings. James E. and John E. Marcuse found the long journeys from New York to Long Beach tiring and unrewarding since the Huttons paid no board fees and Harold's method of conducting discussions, to put it mildly, was casual. Rarely was there any written agenda. Harold would just clear the papers off a small table in his office overlooking the distillation plant, seldom bother to read or sign the minutes of the last meeting, then launch into any items that were troubling him or on which Betty or the company's lawyer had told him that a board resolution was required.

Refining's business in this early stage of its growth more often than not was conducted in the canteen. Harold, as he grew older, became a better organized chairman. He learned to stay silent until everyone else who wanted to speak had done so. Only then would he weigh in with some deprecatory one-line comment like "Charlie, you have the mentality of a grocery man—stay away from the oil business," or "Any deal I cannot figure out on a cocktail napkin is too complicated for me, and I do not want it!"

The minutes of Refining's meetings were equally terse or unclear until Betty in June 1948 became the company secretary. Nearly always until then, it was she who had made notes on Harold's decisions and followed through on the action needed to implement them. With her bookkeeping experience, she kept a sharp eye on the company's accounts, wrote and deposited the checks, filled out the tax returns, and paid the employees' wages. It still took Harold three years to persuade his wife to take her place on Refining's board. Betty had no taste for "shooting the breeze," as Harold was wont to describe any kind of formal meeting.

All her life, until Harold's death left her with no choice but to take over the chair of the company, she preferred to stay in the background, quietly influencing events, not noisily pronouncing her own view or insisting on getting her own way. Betty's only reason for accepting election to the board on August 16, 1948, was to help overcome an emergency. Following a row with Ed

Hutton (no relation), the company secretary, Harold told him to resign or be fired. Betty took his place as secretary and director, formally offering for the first time at the board table what up to now she had provided to Harold in private— wise counsel, shrewd business sense, and an ability to say no to many of his more ambitious schemes.

Her influence was fortunate for Refining since Harold, at this point in his career, had little feel or taste for managing a public company. A wildcatter by nature, he had learned on the job how to run an oil refinery, how to mix and blend crude oil, how to open up new markets for his products. Corporate finance was another matter. Bankers and lawyers and tax men were not his natural partners. Boardrooms never became his chosen place for doing business. He got better at it as the years went by, but conducting meetings with a formal agenda, as required by the regulations that govern corporate bodies, was an obligation that all his life sat uneasily on Harold Hutton's shoulders. By instinct, he was more an operator than a sophisticated executive who preferred to keep his own counsel, to talk one-on-one, to make deals that could be written down on the back of an envelope and sealed over a drink with a handshake.

"Through all the years, in all our dealings with the Huttons, we never had written contracts," said the chairman of a large company in the Philippines, who bought and sold oil for the Huttons. "Nor did we ever need one. Betty was a lady. Harold was a man of his word."

PART V   GOING GLOBAL

Harold Hutton's global vision: oil from the jungles of Asia

THE MANCHURIAN MAFIA

By 1948, when one of Harold Hutton's heroes, Dwight David Eisenhower, took his oath as the thirty-fourth president of the United States, Refining Associates, small as it was, had started to focus its efforts on what Ike advised all Americans to do—"to get involved and prosper overseas."

It was a time when Congress and the media were engaged in a passionate debate about U.S. foreign policy. The reason was self-evident: America, without intending it, had become the number one power in the world. In four years of war, the United States not only had defeated its foes, Nazi Germany and Imperial Japan, but had completed the job started in the 1920s of catching up and leaving far behind its allies and partners economically. World War II saw the United States double the size of its output while Europe's and Japan's were decimated. Only the British Empire, the United States' closest partner, and the USSR, whose armies now held sway in eastern Europe, any longer could hold a candle to the United States—and both countries had been exhausted by a conflict that pulverized large sections of their economies.

The balance of power in the world had been transformed. Militarily, the United States was invincible; for the time being, it was also invulnerable. Only America had nuclear weapons. Only the United States, if its leaders had been so minded, had the ability to project U.S. power into virtually any corner of the earth except the Soviet Union and China while the U.S. heartland remained immune. Economically, too, the United States was paramount. More than 50 percent of all the world's manufactures in 1945 were pouring out of U.S. factories. The dollar was strong. America alone had food and capital to spare.

Harold Hutton, like most of his friends in the California oil industry, only dimly perceived and only gradually came to recognize the scale and global significance of this historic shift. When Congress started to debate the need for the United States to supply food, capital, and know-how to help its former enemies as well as its wartime allies pick themselves up from the ruins, he and Betty engaged in frequent, often heated, debates with family members and business associates over the virtues of the Marshall Plan and foreign aid. The Huttons, instinctively it seems, were more internationally minded than most of their relatives and acquaintances. The Spennettas were "America-Firsters," though Betty's mother in some of the letters she wrote in late 1946 confessed to a good deal more sympathy with the Marshall Plan's help for Europe than her husband, J. D., ever voiced. J. D. and most of his colleagues in the Orange County business community thought it was time for the Americans to "come home and mind the store" as they put it. The United States, as they saw it, had been forced for the second time in their lifetime to go out and settle the rest of the world's problems; now the United States should concentrate on solving the problems in its own backyard.

Harold and Betty took a different view. Both had seen Refining Associates spring into life before the war with sales of bunkering oil to foreign vessels, mainly Russian, trading up and down the West Coast. Their wartime shipments of lube oil had gone to U.S. forces and their allies in Europe, the Middle East, and Africa, as well as throughout the Pacific. Psychologically, the Huttons had put behind them the notion that America's interests ended at its shoreline. At a time when Richard Nixon, newly elected to the U.S. House of Representatives, complained privately that the majority of his constituents in Orange County were "proud to be called isolationists,"[6] Harold and Betty were starting to peer at wider overseas horizons for their own and their company's future.

---

6. Richard Nixon, in a letter to Sir Eldon Griffiths.

One reason for their broader view was a contract Harold had made with one of the defeated Japanese. George Tottori was appointed soon after the war ended to represent in California the Fuji Kosan Company, a sizable Japanese importer of heavy oil for asphalt plants. Striving to rebuild its bomb-shattered cities, Japan had a desperate shortage of oil of all kinds to fuel its power plants, lubricate its industrial machinery, and asphalt its highways; but at the time, the major oil companies paid little attention to the needs of a defeated enemy whose currency, at 350 yen to the dollar, commanded little confidence. All imports into Japan were also subject to government licensing and required special permits from the Japanese treasury, whose officials were reluctant to use its scarce supply of dollars to pay for imported oil. Somehow, Fuji Kosan had managed to persuade the bureaucrats that used oil, which was vastly cheaper, should not be subject to these import and currency restrictions. Tottori asked Harold Hutton if he could supply Fuji Kosan with crankcase drainings removed from American cars and trucks when their oil was changed.

Refining Associates already had developed a market for used oil. A small laboratory at the back of Harold's office in Downey blended and recycled various kinds of crankcase drainings to acceptable standards and sold the resulting product at cut-rate prices to the tens of thousands of California vehicle users who in the immediate postwar years couldn't get or couldn't afford top-quality engine oil for their cars. To export his used oil was a challenge that Harold seized eagerly. Provided Refining Associates' crankcase drainings met Fuji Kosan's minimum requirements, allowing them to be blended with better quality oil and rerefined in Japan, Tottori said his company would pay "cash on the barrelhead." All Harold had to do was to increase his collection of used oil and deliver it raw to Long Beach. Tottori would then pay for the full amount of each shipment with a cashier's check drawn on a U.S. bank.

Harold shook hands on the deal. Working out of their small office on Firestone Boulevard, he and Betty phoned scores of local garages all over southern California. Most were owned by freelancers who so far had resisted the major oil companies' drive to take over America's gas stations as franchises. Harold had known a lot of these independent garage owners since working in his youth as a delivery driver for Richfield and as a St. Helens oil salesman. Most were glad to sell their drainings at the very low prices he offered rather than have to pay for their spent oil to be removed. The Huttons simultaneously signed up large numbers of off-duty tanker drivers prepared to earn extra money by working outside regular hours. Many of these drivers, too, were former colleagues and friends of Harold's.

Within weeks, Refining Associates was delivering to Fuji Kosan's agents in Long Beach freshly barreled "tailored oil," ready for loading onto Osaka-bound tankers. Harold checked random samples in his lab to make sure that they complied with Tottori's specifications. The Japanese accepted Harold's quality certificates without demur. Harold accepted Tottori's checks without waiting for them to go through the time-consuming procedure of being presented to a New York bank; transmitted, sometimes by mail, to Tokyo; cleared by Japanese exchange control; and finally authenticated for payment back in Los Angeles. The memories of war still were fresh on both sides of the Pacific, but George Tottori and Harold trusted one another. Over the years that followed, they built up a large and mutually profitable business that soon extended from crankcase drainings to trade in all kinds of heavy oil needed for road building.

The Huttons, Tottoris, and Fuji Kosan's owners became close personal friends. Betty arranged for the daughters of the Japanese families to work with her in Orange County. Several of them enrolled at Chapman College, now Chapman University, of which Harold and later Betty, were trustees. In return, the Huttons on their subsequent visits to Tokyo were treated royally by the Fuji Kosan board and later became honored guests at the weddings of the girls they now called "our Japanese goddaughters."

Along with his Japanese connections, Harold was developing another and more exciting dimension of his Pacific dream. He made contact with the "White Russians." Actually Manchurian Jews, these remarkable people, with their business acumen and indefatigable flexibility, already had introduced to West Coast America the same kind of talent for foreign trade that the east European Jews earlier had brought to the East Coast. The Manchurians' great contribution to American life remains to be fully documented, but Harold Hutton was quick to spot and harness the brilliance of one of them, Morris Bach, who in the late 1930s was a ship chandler for the Moore McCormick Shipping Line. The two men had met in a Long Beach bar. Harold was intrigued by Bach's stories of Russian minerals, furs, and lumber being exchanged in the 1930s for Chinese and American consumer goods.

Simultaneously, an American friend whom he had also met in a bar had focused Harold's attention on China. A pilot for the Flying Tiger Lines, this man was one of the old China hands who during the war had flown supplies across the mountains between Burma and China under the command of General Clair Chennault. The Tigers had only recently established their first coast-to-coast U.S. freight airline. Their president was a burly Texan, Bob Prescott, who Harold from time to time would meet in restaurants they both frequented in downtown Los Angeles. Prescott was later to become one of the Huttons' neighbors and golfing companions at the Eldorado Country Club in Indian Wells, but in 1948, he and his pilots were struggling to get the Flying Tiger airline off the ground. His fleet of cast-off U.S. Air Force C-54s needed aviation fuel on easy credit.

Harold was one of the few who from time to time helped the Flying Tigers to take off in America. Through Bob Prescott, he was to meet General Chennault on one of his visits to California. Through Chennault on the military side and his "Manchurian mafia" contacts on the civilian side, Harold also came to know a great deal about the intricate relationships between the United States and China during the difficult days when the Truman administration was striving to reconcile the Nationalist government under Generalissimo Chiang Kai-shek with the Communist rebels under Mao Tse Tung. It was a time when U.S. Air Force squadrons, taking over from the volunteer groups who first had trained and fought with the Nationalist air force, were stationed in half a dozen bases in central China. They set up Chinese American Coordinated Wings (CACWs), supplied in part by the Board of Supplies, Executive Yuan (BOSEY), the Nationalist government's supply agency.

BOSEY was in charge of importing U.S. oil for all the Nationalists' armed forces. Harold Hutton, encouraged by Bob Prescott and Morris Bach, began researching the possibilities of selling surplus oil from U.S. military stockpiles to China.

He already had experience selling the secondhand crankcase drainings to Japan. Now Harold set his sights on finding and unloading war-surplus oil in far larger quantities to China. Through Morris Bach, he made contact with another former U.S. serviceman, F. H. (Bud) Lindus, who had an import and export business in Shanghai. Lindus was well known to the oil service firms supporting the U.S. Air Force in Manchuria where the Chinese Nationalists were struggling, with increasing lack of success, to halt the southward march of Mao's Communists, armed and fueled by the Soviet Union. Lindus also knew the Manchurians in Shanghai and Tientsin. When Harold Hutton phoned him over a faint, crackling line from Long Beach, Lindus confirmed that there was a huge market not only in China but also in Russia for any kind of fuel that would generate heat and light.

Harold's questions were strictly technical. Who exactly would import this oil and what kind of permits were needed? Who would pay for it, in what currencies, and at what exchange rate? How much commission would he have to pay to Lindus or to "White Russians" or Chinese middlemen? What taxes would be imposed on Refining Associates in the receiving countries on top of those he paid to the United States? Lindus, too, had some questions, but he asked them first of his U.S. military and White Russian contacts. What kind of man was Hutton? Could Refining Associates procure and deliver used oil in large quantities at a price BOSEY would be prepared to pay and U.S. aid officials would accept, while still leaving room for a cut for his Chinese contacts and himself?

The Manchurian network produced the answers Bud Lindus needed. Having worked with Harold before Pearl Harbor, procuring bunker oil for Russian vessels trading into Long Beach, their California agent said Hutton was a "straight shooter." If Harold said he could deliver, the oil would arrive on time meeting the required specifications and at a price to match anyone else's in the business. Nor would he worry too much about red tape and paperwork. Harold Hutton could be relied on to do the job with few questions asked.

Bud Lindus agreed to join Refining Associates as Harold's first export director at a salary of $400 a month. This was significantly higher than Harold's, which was $300, or Betty's, which was $3.50 per hour. At his first board meeting in Long Beach, Lindus, according to the minutes, proposed that he and Harold "proceed to New York for the purpose of developing business with the Chinese Board of Suppliers, BOSEY, and Socony Vacuum." Impressed, Harold promised Lindus a sizable bonus. The minutes, as written by Betty, were more cautious: "Additional executive compensation shall be fixed as a bonus, when and if earnings of the Corporation justify the payment of such a bonus."

Shortly after they had confirmed in New York that both BOSEY and the Russian trade agency AMTORG were in the market for heavy oil and that bank financing could be made available to cover its export, Harold and Bud Lindus flew to Honolulu. California's oil companies, including Refining Associates, during the war had shipped hundreds of thousands of barrels of heavy oil and grease to Pearl Harbor and other U.S. naval and air force bases throughout the Pacific. Huge quantities had been stockpiled in readiness for the invasion the United States had expected to launch against the Japanese home islands until the atomic bomb cut short the war. Now, three years after the Japanese surrender, the navy had decommissioned hundreds of its ships and had no further use for this oil. Orders had gone out from Washington to sell it but not to the U.S. home market. To prevent undercutting of domestic prices, the National Association of Manufacturers lobbied Congress to forbid the armed forces to bring back their surpluses to the mainland.

On their visit to Hawaii and Guam, Harold and Lindus identified large quantities of this oil, piled up in stocks up to 100 feet tall. Among them were thousands of barrels of grease that Refining Associates itself had supplied to the navy. Harold's bid to purchase this grease at prices as low as 20 percent of those he and the other U.S. oil companies had been paid for delivering it was quickly accepted by the navy. Betty Hutton recorded the next steps. "We didn't repack it. We just restencilled the drums and sent them off to China and the USSR."

It wasn't quite that easy. Finding the necessary space in ships trading into China as the civil war between the Nationalists and the advancing Communists threatened to engulf Tsingtao and Shanghai harbors required shipping contacts that the Huttons themselves did not have. Nor did Refining Associates have the Chinese connections to ensure that its oil would be unloaded and delivered to the customers who had ordered and would pay for it. Harold turned for help to his White Russian friends. He met in San Francisco with the head of a company named Mark Ross Imports and a self-styled White Russian Jew from Manchuria, Charles Clurman, who was to play an important role in the Huttons' future business in the Pacific.

Charlie Clurman's life encapsulates much of the recent history of the White Russian Jews. Known as "Manchurians" because they emigrated to Manchuria from the Ukraine and European Russia to escape the Tsarist pogroms of the late nineteenth and early twentieth centuries, these most resilient of people were the descendants of merchants, artisans, and professional people who moved east to take advantage of the opportunities offered by the Chinese Eastern extension of the Trans-Siberian railway (CER). To help with construction of this 1,800-mile spur, the Chinese emperors in the 1890s donated a strip of land five miles wide on either side of the tracks. European Jews were encouraged to settle in this frontier region, which at the time resembled Buffalo Bill's contemporary Wyoming. Along the railroad, the Russian government waived the anti-Semitic restrictions that applied in the rest of Russia. In return, the Jewish settlers were expected to develop the natural resources, timber, fishing, and minerals and build up trade between China and Russia.

Between 1890 and 1900, many thousands of Russian Jews moved east into this remote region, congregating in a new city founded on the banks of the Amur river by a Russian general named Harbin, who named the city after himself. Thousands more Jewish soldiers serving in the Tsarist forces settled there after the Russian-Japanese war of 1904–5. The war ended with the Tsarist navy's ignominious defeat in the battle of Tsushima Straits, the beginning of Japan's naval power.

Harbin became a haven for Jews escaping from Russia during the Tsarist and Soviet regimes. In the 1920s, it boasted the largest stock exchange in Asia and a Jewish cultural center with synagogues, card clubs, a Yiddish library, a theater, and a boys choir with a celebrated cantor, Shim Zlatkin, who performed at gala balls as elegant as those of New York and London.

Harbin's boom was too good to last. In 1930, China forced the Russians to give up control of the CER railway. Soon afterwards, Manchuria was invaded and annexed by Japan. Renamed Manchu-Kuo, it fell under control of the dreaded Kempetai, the Japanese secret police. Despite protests from the League of Nations, the secret police unleashed a systematic takeover of Harbin Jewish businesses and banks, though never with the atrocities the Nazis perpetrated against the Jews in Europe. Thousands of Manchuria's Jews, including Charlie Clurman, once again had to move on. Many fled to Tientsin, Shanghai, and Hong Kong, where in the late 1930s they were to be seen peddling their wares, running small manufacturing plants, and handling foreign exchange in the French, British, and U.S. concessions.

Clurman was a prototype of these wandering Manchurian Jews. His father, who arrived in Harbin at the turn of the twentieth century, trained race horses for its Chinese generals and warlords. Charles worked as a cowboy, lumberman, and mule skinner until 1935 when Japanese anti-Semitism intensified and he was packed off to Tientsin in north China to attend a British missionary school. He left Manchuria in the nick of time. A month later, his father was arrested, imprisoned, and tortured to death by the Kempetai.

Clurman then worked for his passage with a group of his Manchurian classmates on a freighter to San Francisco. There he Anglicized his name and teamed up with the son of the former Jewish president of the Harbin stock exchange, who at the time was working as a houseboy for an earlier arrival from Manchuria, a professor at Berkeley University who helped invent the first computer. Mark Ross, the Huttons' future associate, was that houseboy. Ross and Charlie Clurman built up a small business peddling fruit and vegetables from a stall near the San Francisco docks on Market Street. According to Clurman, they earned their first $100 by selling the first Christmas trees in the United States to be sprayed with silver enamel.

Harold Hutton got to know Mark Ross and his firm shortly before Pearl Harbor as a result of an introduction by Morris Bach, the ship chandler from Moore McCormick, and his brother Albie Bach. The Bachs always needed—and Harold could nearly always supply—low-cost bunker oil blended to the exact specifications required for the old-fashioned engines of the Russian and Chinese freighters they serviced. It is unlikely that Harold met Ross's partner, Charles Clurman, until after the Second World War. Immediately following Pearl Harbor, Charles, who since the death of his father had declared a personal war on the Japanese empire, volunteered for the U.S. Army. At first, he was rejected as a noncitizen, but when the War Powers Act was passed, he and Mark Ross were given draft cards that enabled them, once in uniform, to acquire U.S. nationality. Charles's draft number was a high one, Mark's number was low, which meant that he would be required to join the army earlier. So the two partners swapped their draft cards, allowing Charles to go straight into uniform. Within weeks, he shipped out to join Merrill's Marauders, a group of American volunteers attached to the British army in northern Burma.

Merrill's Marauders turned out to be one of the most glamorized units to serve in World War II. They linked up with the Chinese in the tangled mountains over which the Flying Tigers later flew supplies to Chiang Kai-shek's beleaguered forces. Charles Clurman possessed exactly the right qualifications to serve with them. Like many of the Indian units in the British 14th Army that defeated the Japanese in Burma, Merrill's Marauders used mules to transport their field guns. Charlie was a mule skinner, who all his life had worked with horses and mules.

Clurman's war service included stints in Guam and New Guinea, but he ended up in Manila, where he and Harold Hutton were to become business associates. The capital of the Philippines was little more than a shell- and bomb-battered ruin when he arrived in 1945 as a sergeant in the 32nd Division. Heavy fighting was still going on in the northern part of Luzon but Clurman, a hardened veteran, made sure he landed a job as a quartermaster, handling supplies for army and navy PXs (post exchanges). Soon he was fluent in Filipino Spanish and learned quickly how to handle the gangs of Manila black marketeers who pilfered U.S. stocks in search of everything from Spam and cigarettes to nylons for their girlfriends. By the time he returned to San Francisco and his prewar job with Mark Ross, Clurman was a man who knew his way around Manila and much else besides.

Shortly afterwards, through Morris Bach, now the third man in the Mark Ross company, Clurman met Harold Hutton. The two men had many similarities. Both stood five feet nine inches tall and weighed close to 200 pounds. Both men, too, were hustlers who enjoyed taking risks. Clurman in his résumé described himself as "adept at working outside the United States in underdeveloped difficult environments with unstable political and economic conditions." It was a description that fit Harold Hutton like a glove, as did Clurman's further comment under the "special qualifications" heading— "resourceful and adaptable, works well with all types of people."

With Morris Bach in the lead, Mark Ross's company now teamed up with Refining Associates to move all the surplus oil Harold could obtain from the U.S. Navy into the Chinese and Manchurian markets the White Russians had at their disposal. "It was a perfect match for the Russian trade," Clurman wrote.

"Morris was fluent in Russian and Harold was an accomplished petroleum chemist, expert in blending various types of products and grades to meet Russian specifications."[7]

Trading surplus navy oil into Russia and Nationalist China was the Huttons' first international success. Harold declared a 1967–68 dividend of $.68 per share to be paid to the company's preferred stockholders and $.50 per share on the common stock, of which the Huttons were the biggest owners. Bud Lindus was paid $2,500; Harold was paid $2,500, and the following March he would also receive a bonus of $4,125.

Refining Associates was now launched into the Pacific trade where Harold, ever since he first set foot on the shore of Huntington Beach, had always dreamed and intended to work. A generation before most American businessmen were to turn their attention to the Orient, he clearly foresaw the coming resurgence of Pacific Asia as the late twentieth century's greatest new source of growth and markets. The Pacific Rim was to be the Huttons' new frontier.

---

7. Charles Clurman, letter to Sir Eldon Griffiths, November 1996.

CANDLE WAX AND KAMCHATKA CRAB

The Huttons' China venture lasted less than a year. By spring 1948, U.S. efforts to save the Kuomintang (KMT) government had failed. In Manchuria, Chiang Kai-shek's armies were outfought and outmaneuvered by Mao Tse Tung's peasant infantrymen, who marched or trotted into battle carrying only a fraction of the heavy gear the United States had supplied to the Nationalists. The whole of north China was lost to the Communists during the winter of 1947–48. The following spring, a Communist army of 1 million men assembled along the northern banks of the Yangtse River. As they approached Shanghai, preceded by rumors of mass arrests and executions, panic erupted among KMT officials and the international merchant community. Papers were burned; bank vaults emptied; railroad stations, docks, and airports were besieged by frightened families fighting to get out before the greatest trading city in the Far East was occupied by the Communists. In April, Mao's army crossed the Yangtze. The Nationalists fled or surrendered, Chiang Kai-shek and what remained of his troops, his party, and their families took refuge in Taiwan. The Chinese civil war was over. The Communists had won!

The consequences for Refining were serious but far from lethal. U.S. trade with China evaporated in a matter of days. Charles Clurman, now acting as Harold's point of contact with Mark Ross's company, arrived in his office in San Francisco to find a message from Hong Kong saying, "Line to Shanghai dead. Business with China finished." Clurman, who had seen many abrupt changes in his life, immediately got on the phone to try to locate other Asian purchasers for Mark Ross's clients. Clurman was well placed to help. A year after his return from the U.S. Army, he had been contacted by another senior member of the White Russian mafia, Jakob Shriro.

Shriro headed one of the largest trading companies in northeast Asia. The Shriro group bought and sold diamonds, lumber, and every kind of vehicle and consumer product that could be traded between Asia and Europe and the Pacific Coast of North America. Jakob Shriro escaped from Shanghai on the USS *Grisholm,* the last vessel to clear the port before the Communists arrived. The *Grisholm*'s arrival in San Francisco intensified the debate between Republicans and Democrats in Washington over the topic of the hour, "Who lost China?"— as if China were America's to lose!

Shriro, a prewar multimillionaire, arrived in America with nothing but the clothes he was wearing and two shabby crates labeled "Personal Effects." In fact, these crates contained his family's collection of Chinese paintings and porcelains, including a number of priceless Ming vases. Clurman and Bach managed to have them cleared through U.S. Customs in San Francisco without Shriro having to pay a penny. Shriro did not forget this. As he rebuilt his trading empire, borrowing $1 million on his signature from a British bank with which he had done business in Shanghai, he needed to set up a new branch in Manila. Shriro offered the job to Charlie Clurman. Shriro's terms were tough: a $100,000 credit line and $10,000 in equity capital, a one-way ticket to Manila, and a pledge that Clurman could manage the business as he pleased. Clurman posted Shriro's motto on the wall of his new office in the Philippines: "Any fool can do it with money." Over the next ten years, he turned Shriro's Manila company into one of the most profitable of its twenty-eight worldwide branches and a major shareholder in two of the Philippines's biggest companies.

Harold Hutton was among the first to benefit from Charles Clurman's reappearance in Manila. One of Shriro's best-selling lines was candles for the tens of thousands of Catholic churches and Chinese shrines all across south Asia that had been deprived during the war of these aids to devotion. Refining Associates provided the heavy oil from which Shriro made wax for millions of candles. Shriro also traded in fish, as did the Mark Ross group. With their shared Manchurian background, Clurman and the Bach brothers were convinced that the lakes and offshore waters of eastern Russia could produce vast quantities of freshwater salmon and crab that could be sold in most big cities in America. Simultaneously, Bud Lindus, still looking for new outlets for Refining Associates' oil after the shutdown of the China market, urged Harold Hutton to look into the possibilities of trading oil and grease to Russia in exchange for one of its most sought-after delicacies, Kamchatka crab.

Lindus and Harold already had discussed this in general terms with AMTORG, the Russian state trading agency. On November 6, 1947, Harold and Betty attended a diplomatic reception at the Soviet Consulate in San Francisco when Consul General Constantine Efremov proclaimed the virtues of the "Great October Socialist Revolution" on its thirtieth anniversary and urged more trade between the wartime allies.

Lindus proposed that Harold and he should get together with Morris Bach, who represented the Sun Corporation, which procured canned fish for United States and Canadian markets, and take things further by paying a visit to the heads of AMTORG in Moscow. This was a bold and, at the time, foolhardy suggestion. Joseph Stalin was on the point of slamming down the Iron Curtain across Europe. The Cold War was about to begin. The Soviet Union would soon be the mortal enemy. Moscow would become as much off limits as Shanghai had become for Americans.

The Huttons could hardly have been unaware of this situation. Only a few months before Lindus suggested their visit to Moscow, the Soviet dictator had denounced the Marshall Plan as a "capitalist plot." Stalin ordered the Red Army to match the United States in thermonuclear weapons, predicting that the next decade would bring the triumph of Marxist-Leninism over decadent capitalism. Soviet troops in a blaze of headlines returned to Czechoslovakia to assist in the Communist takeover in May 1948. President Truman, determined to resist Soviet expansion, responded by giving the go-ahead for the United States to re-arm. Winston Churchill, visiting Fulton, Missouri, with Truman, pronounced his fateful warning that "a new dark age," symbolized by the Iron Curtain, was about to descend on Europe. And in Washington, yet another "red scare" exploded. Senator McCarthy and his anti-American committee unmercifully savaged "fellow travelers" in the State Department while in the Huttons' backyard, California's home-grown red-baiters harassed supposed Communists in Hollywood and the educational establishment in Orange County.

It was against this ominous background, proclaimed in banner headlines on every front page and debated on radio and television across America, that Bud Lindus, home from China, got Harold's agreement to plan a sales trip to Moscow. Trade between East and West was grinding to a halt—but did the (would-be) merchant adventurers of Refining Associates know or care about this? The evidence is that they did know—and did not let it bother them. Harold, age forty-four, and Lindus, thirty-six, were convinced that they could look after themselves in Russia. "Politics is politics," said Bud, more than likely raising his glass. "Business is business," said Harold.

Convincing Betty proved to be more difficult. When she first heard of the proposed Russian visit, in the teeth of the confrontation flaring up between the United States and the USSR, she told Harold that this sounded like a "very dangerous fishing expedition." When he rejected this notion, Betty's response was that she would be going, too. Harold at first said no, but Betty overruled him and set about making the arrangements.

It took several weeks of phoning, writing, and telexing to obtain Russian visas. The Russian consulate in San Francisco asked for advice from the Soviet embassy in Washington. The embassy asked for advice from the foreign office in Moscow. The U.S. State Department advised against the trip. Bank of America issued travelers checks but could not offer any estimate or even guess at the exchange rate the Huttons would receive. Hotel reservations had to be made through the Soviet travel agency, Intourist, but none could be confirmed until the party had permission from Moscow.

Despite the gathering war clouds, Betty succeeded in getting the necessary papers for Harold, herself, and Bud Lindus with Morris Bach joining them

As the United States came close to war during 1948 Berlin Airlift, the Huttons
nonchalantly went on fishing expedition to Soviet Union

as translator. The intrepid—or foolhardy—party was ready to leave by mid-July 1948.

Looking back, it is hard to exaggerate the contrast between the Huttons' jaunt in search of Kamchatka crab and the diplomatic and military crisis that was occurring in Europe. Berlin was under siege. The United States and its allies were focusing on the possibility of war with a belligerent USSR toward whose capital Harold and Betty were heading.

A good measure of the disconnection between the Huttons' cheerful nonchalance and the menacing diplomatic and military clashes around them can be seen in these contrasting extracts from Betty Hutton's account of their journey and similar extracts from the official biography of the man at the center of the biggest international crisis since World War II, Harry Truman:[8]

> *July 9 [Refining Associates board minutes]*—It was resolved that three directors (H. Hutton, F. Lindus, and B. Hutton) and Mr. Morris Bach go to Moscow to negotiate for the purchase of the total 1948 pack of crab meat from the USSR, same to be sold to Sun Ltd.

> *July 14 [Truman biography]*—The Russians clamped a blockade on all rail, highway and water traffic in and out of Berlin. The situation was extremely dangerous. Two and a half million people faced starvation. Stocks of food would last no more than a month . . . [Later] the President ordered a full scale airlift. He sent B-29s to Germany, the giant planes known to the world as the kind that dropped atomic bombs.

> *July 16 [Betty Hutton's diary]*—Flew from Copenhagen to Stockholm and Helsinki. We have spent 30 hours in the air, plus ground time for refueling. Our Aeroflot aircraft to Moscow is furnished like a Victorian sitting room with plush seats, antimacassars, and heavy Victorian wood. No seat belts and no announcements!

---

8. McCulloch, *Truman.*

July 19 [Truman biography]—Meeting with the Secretaries of State and Defense, the President said, "We stay in Berlin—come what may."

July 24 [Betty Hutton's diary]—Came the great day and we left for New York and thence to Reykjavik in Iceland. We tried to sleep, Harold successfully after consuming a lot of scotch, me unsuccessfully, because of the noise of the engines. Our ground speed is 215 MPH. We should pass 170 miles south of Greenland at 0300GMT. The sun will rise at 0500GMT.

July 26 [Truman biography]—A special session of Congress opened. General Clay, the U.S. commander in Berlin returned to Washington, says the Russians would try to stop any attempt by an armed convoy to break through along the road to Berlin. Did the Russians want war, Truman asked? Clay did not think so. No one could be sure.

Arriving at the Moscow airport, while back home their family and friends wondered if World War III was about to break out, the Huttons and their luggage were searched. They were then taken by an Intourist bus to the National Hotel only three blocks from Red Square. On each floor of the hotel, babushka-wearing ladies in black garments passed out the keys for the rooms. None of the rooms had plugs in the bathtubs and all of them were bugged. There were telephones but no telephone directories. When Harold tried to call, he was told that the hotel operators dealt only with incoming messages. Betty exchanged $100 worth of travelers checks and $30 in currency for rubles. The clerk said that they were the first American business people to visit Moscow that year.

That night Morris Bach's Russian contacts came to the National Hotel to drink the Huttons' vodka and discuss a business relationship. "They wanted to develop a little reverse trade," as Betty described it. At first, the Russians suggested a deal to sell vodka in America, but Harold declined on the grounds that Americans in the 1950s drank beer and whiskey; instead he asked for

Russian king crab from Kamchatka. The Russians said they'd come back the next day.

The Huttons' visit to Moscow coincided with one of the most warlike demonstrations the Soviet authorities ever staged in their capital city. Moscow was plastered with posters of Lenin and Stalin and, on July 25, the whole of the Politburo attended an "air festival" at Tushimo airport where more than 500,000 spectators watched wave after wave of Lavochkin fighters and bombers as they saluted the great leader Stalin. Neither Harold nor Betty was a political sophisticate, but they hardly could have missed the significance of this display of military might. This is how the English language *Moscow News,* delivered to their room on Tuesday, July 27, described the day's proceedings:

> The airdrome was turned into a riot of color by a multitude of flags. The field was swept by stormy waves of applause as thousands of voices joined to cheer heartily their beloved leader.

There followed an account of the flying displays that Harold cut out and brought home in his briefcase:

> The first group of planes flew in perfect formation describing the words Glory to Stalin. Another stormy ovation arose and swept the field. There followed the workhorses of the Red Air Force, Yakovlev, Antonov, and Sukhoi transport planes, then fighters, zooming and banking in dizzy convolutions as breathless with excitement the spectators cheered. It was in planes like these that Soviet flyers captured superiority in the air in battles with the German fascist invaders.

This, then, was the Huttons' firsthand introduction to the Communist system. Harold was decidedly uneasy. He put an X across a *Moscow News* article that falsely claimed that

> USSR production of butter in the first half of 1948 rose to 2/3 above the prewar level while in the United States . . . butter output last year was 28 percent less than in 1940!

As the son of a former Minnesota farm salesman whose Hutton cream dispenser was an expression of the superabundance of dairy products of all kinds in America, Harold knew that was nonsense. The same newspaper went on to congratulate the Ministry of Meat and Dairy on

> ensuring high quality butter in Russia . . . by means of its obligatory state standards; American quality standards by contrast establish only the percentage of fat and moisture, giving proprietors every opportunity for adulteration.

Harold's comments on these claims are not recorded, but if he or Betty had any doubts about the mischief of party control of the media or of the Communist grip on the Russian economy, the contents of several other newspapers they brought back to California surely must have disposed of them. One told of

> notable progress . . . fundamental democratic reforms . . . great strides in agriculture . . . substantial progress in public health and education.

Another reported that

> the generous, unselfish aid of the Soviet Union has relieved Albania from the need to apply for shackling aid from foreign monopoly capital [i.e., the Marshall Plan].

Before leaving Moscow, Harold and Morris Bach signed a deal with AMTORG. Refining Associates would ship oil and grease of the same kind it had been selling to Japan and Nationalist China to the Soviet Union; in return, the Huttons would take Kamchatka king crab from Russia in part payment. Eventually, several shipments of Hutton oil were duly moved out of Honolulu to Vladivostok on Russian ships. Some of the king crab too was shipped from Vladivostok to the Sun Company in the Philippines. But as Betty wrote in a note she later prepared for Chapman University. :

American-USSR relations soon deteriorated. We left 96,000 cases of crab meat in storage in Vladivostok. The Russians let us out of our contract without a murmur. Our affairs with them were always cordial. We had them on 30-day credit and never had a problem over specifications or payments.

While in Moscow, the Huttons called on the U.S. Embassy. They wanted to change their schedule so as to return home via Prague. On their behalf, the ambassador wrote a letter on July 29 to the Czech Embassy saying,

The Embassy of United States of America has the honor to request that visas for transit through Czechoslovakia be issued to the following American businessmen who are traveling in a private capacity[!] Francis H. Lindus, Passport #15496, Morris Bach, Passport #9981, Harold F. Hutton, Passport #115776, Mrs. Harold F. Hutton, Passport #245315.

The Czechs refused. The situation in Berlin made this "inadvisable," they said. By this time, United States and British planes were landing in West Berlin to break the Soviet blockade as often as every four minutes. Allied officials worried about the increased activity of Russian Yak fighters in the air corridors, while back in Washington, President Truman wrote a personal letter to Churchill:

We are in the midst of grave and trying times . . . I hope we can solve [this] without the "sweat and tears" Nazism and Fascism cost.

Were Harold and Betty aware of this? It is intriguing to speculate about the degree to which the Huttons took account of these and the other great events that were to swirl around them during their career. Their business had grown up in large measure on the back of America's participation in World War II. It was soon to be transformed, sometimes for better, sometimes for worse, by political convulsions in Asia, from Korea to Indonesia and Vietnam. Here in Moscow, for the first time, they had a ringside seat as a world crisis of historic proportions unfolded around them. Yet, as was to happen time and time again in Harold's subsequent career, neither he nor Betty showed any sign of being alarmed by, let alone of succumbing to, the pressures of external events that they could not control.

On their way home from Russia, Harold and Betty stayed for two nights at the Palace Hotel in Copenhagen, reveling in the comforts of one of its best suites, number 101, for which they paid 33 kroner per night, less than $10 in those days. On their bill, which Betty saved, there was an interesting note: "The hotel servants, apart from the boots, being salaried, are not allowed to accept gratuities." Harold took no notice of this. Out came his roll of $20 bills. All his life he was a big tipper. On this first expedition to Europe, he started a practice that was to become second nature wherever he traveled—handing out generous tips to everyone in sight at hotels.

Then it was back to Los Angeles via Paris, Betty's first exposure to France, where they spent only one short night. Their return flight refueled at Shannon, Ireland, where Betty filled out a "declaration of origin and health" and meticulously kept a copy, while Harold waited impatiently to get in line for an "Irish coffee," a specialty of Shannon airport containing a heavy slug of whiskey and an inch of clotted cream.

Arriving back in Los Angeles, August 7, 1948, the Huttons found the U.S. media still ringing the alarm bells over a possible war in Europe. Betty wondered aloud whether their oil-for-crab deal was "worth all the costs and risks of such a long flight." Their trip had made the Huttons minor celebrities. The *Los Angeles Times,* under a headline "They Know So Little" that could be read in more than one way, quoted Harold as saying about Moscow, "Everyone's jittery—except the Russians. We were not shadowed or cross-examined or guarded in Moscow." Bud Lindus added, "I don't think Russia can afford a war."

The Huttons were to be caught up in the explosion of anti-Communist emotions that erupted across America as the United States and its allies collided with the Soviet Union not only over Berlin but over Greece, where a U.S. military aid group was dispatched to Athens in late 1949 to help defeat a Communist insurrection. Simultaneously, pictures of Chairman Mao and his Communist lieutenants taking over the former Chinese Empire's Forbidden City in Peking, which they renamed Beijing, enflamed the national debate in Washington. Senator McCarthy and his Un-American Activities Committee hogged the air-waves on Capitol Hill. Trading with any part of the Sino-Soviet bloc was denounced by most conservatives as tantamount to supplying the devil.

In Orange County, some, perhaps a majority, of their friends and business associates were openly critical of the Huttons' appearing in Moscow at a time when Berlin was under siege and China had been lost to the Communists. "Doing business with the Russians was pretty much frowned upon in Orange County," said a former member of Betty's "gang" at Orange Union High School. "Harold was rather defensive about it," said another. But by no means all the Huttons' associates were critical of their Russian venture. G. Abbot Smith, a prominent Orange doctor, said, "You don't have to be a Communist to do business with them." Harold, he added, "had an inside track. He shouldn't have been blamed for trying to do trade with the Russians." Betty's observations characteristically were more prosaic:

> Prices in Moscow are high. Ten eggs cost the equivalent of $4 American. Transportation is excellent, subway, buses, taxis. Some of our business appointments were as late as 1 A.M. Soldiers are to be seen doing common labor, also Russian women.

War in Korea Saves the Huttons' Bacon

After their trip to Moscow, the Huttons needed to turn to problems within their own business. There were personnel clashes at the refinery. Harold had fired a superintendent who drank more than was good for him. Two days after landing in Los Angeles, the Huttons' accountant, C. J. Duggan, presented financial statements that showed disappointing prospects for the next financial year. The chairman was spending too much. The 1948 annual meeting on August 16 led to sharp words between Harold and some of his stockholders. The board minutes as recorded by Betty read as follows:

> The Chairman stated that the Financial Statements do not represent a true picture since some $48,000 had been spent for sales and traveling expenses upon which almost no return had been received, but this expenditure was considered an investment and that he expected dividends for this in the coming year.

West Disinfecting's nominees, James and John Marcuse, did not attend this meeting, Harold having been appointed as their proxy. But the Marcuses later took exception to his having pushed through, at a previous meeting that they had also not attended, a resolution for the company to purchase 458 shares of Refining's common stock, valued at $15,000. This purchase was to be covered by a $10,000 check for cash and a note for $5,000 at 4 percent per annum to be paid in installments of $250 per month. It is not clear from the minutes whether any discussion took place before this resolution was passed. Nor is it recorded to whom the $15,000 was to be paid. The inference is that it went to Harold, since he was the only person to whom common stock shares were issued—a total of 25,000 shares issued without par value for which he subscribed assets valued at $20,000.

Did Harold at that June 1948 board meeting oblige the company to buy those 458 shares of common stock, allowing him to take out cash, because he and Betty needed the money? Alternatively, or additionally, was this the most tax-efficient way of the Huttons' receiving some capital benefit from a company they had created but which so far had paid very little compensation to its founders for their risks and hard work? Harold had paid the equivalent of $8 a share as his initial subscription to Refining's start-up capital. Cashing in 458 of these shares for $15,000 would give him a handsome but by no means an exorbitant return. It was an amount far less than he would have received if his initial stake had been invested over the same period in good quality stocks on the New York Stock Exchange and far more than he would have received from U.S. savings bonds.

The Huttons' benefit turned out to be a good deal less than Harold may have calculated. Subsequent board minutes, recording the decisions of a meeting that took place two months later, state that West Disinfecting objected to the company's buyback of the chairman's shares, but not because the proceeds represented a sweetheart deal for the Huttons. The unforeseen result of the company buying back those 458 shares would be to augment Disinfecting's beneficial interest in the outstanding stock to a level where the Marcuses effectively acquired a controlling interest. Harold and Betty would lose virtually all their own company, but West Disinfecting would become liable for Refining Associates' debts.

The Marcuse brothers had no interest and no desire to see that happen. Disinfecting had more important things to do than take over responsibility for a small California refinery on the other side of the country from New York, whose operations could well collapse without Harold as overall manager and Betty as secretary/bookkeeper. Nor did Disinfecting have any wish to take on Refining's liabilities to its work force and customers, let alone its debt to Security Pacific Bank. Harold almost certainly cashed in those 458 shares to help pay for the new house he and Betty were building in Villa Park, but after several heated phone calls with the Marcuses, there seems to have been an agreement whereby he and Bud Lindus would buy back 209 of them at a cost of $3,438.72 paid by Harold and $3,406.00 from Bud. This had the effect of returning a narrow majority of the common stock and of voting shares of Refining to the Huttons and Vice President Lindus.

In November of that year, the Marcuse brothers resigned, offering as their reason "the great distance between New York and Los Angeles." West Disinfecting stayed on as a preferred shareholder receiving its 6 percent dividends and enjoying its 15 percent discount on purchases of lighter fluid and kitchen cleaners until March 1957, when the discount was cut to $7\frac{1}{2}$ percent. When the Marcuses, who had subsequently acquired 875 shares of Refining's common stock, sold their remaining shares in Refining, their discounts were discontinued. Harold Hutton by that time had moved on from lighter fluid. He had his eye on bigger deals in the Pacific.

The late '40s and early '50s were difficult years for the Huttons. They had a steady and rising income from oil sales to Japan, where Fuji Kosan was expanding rapidly as one of the largest producers of asphalt. To help increase his sales in Japan, Harold rented a suite in the Imperial Hotel in Tokyo, where on the tenth floor, Refining Associates opened an office alongside the four-room apartment the Huttons were to use over the next twenty years for the accommodation and entertainment of their Japanese clients. With the dollar selling for up to 400 yen, Harold, like most Americans in Japan in the early '50s, could afford to live like a prince. And he did.

Through one of his contacts in the U.S. occupation forces, he imported a Cadillac and hired a chauffeur whom he nicknamed Poncho after the Mexican thief of that name because of this driver's tendency to use the allowances Harold gave him for meals and out-of-town lodging to line his own pocket or, more likely, to keep his family during the days when most Japanese were short of good food and clothing. Harold also became a regular visitor to one of Tokyo's top nightclubs, the Copacabana, owned by a lady named Madame Cherry who always made a fuss over him when he went out for a good time. Among the singers he met there was Frank Sinatra.

Back home, however, the Huttons were having a hard time. Sales to the U.S. military were falling as the Truman administration and its Republican critics in Congress competed with one another to cut defense spending in the hope of balancing the budget. Under strong pressure from the Audit Committee of the Senate, the Armed Services Petroleum Agency bombarded the oil industry with questions about alleged overcharging, forcing small companies like Refining Associates as well as the major companies who were the main targets of the pressure to double and redouble the staff time and money they had to spend on unproductive paperwork. Betty, feeling the strain, caught a bad case of the flu in January of 1949 and didn't attend the next two board meetings. To assist her, Irene Anderson, a blond Norwegian-American who was to become an indispensable aide, was hired to help with the bookkeeping.

By the summer of 1949, Refining was in difficulties. Harold was still spending too much on his by now extremely heavy overseas travel schedule and on entertaining his customers when they visited California. His Japanese contacts in particular enjoyed going with him to Las Vegas for long weekends of partying and gambling. On one occasion, Harold spent $25,000 to cover his losses and theirs at the poker tables. To make sure that his check to the casino didn't bounce, he had to hurry home to arrange an extra loan from his bank.

To underwrite this spending on business expansion, Harold extended the mortgage he and Betty had taken out on the new home they were building in Villa Park. Betty was not amused. At Refining's annual meeting on August 15, she recorded another set of "poor results" for fiscal 1949. She and Irene Anderson were the only persons present apart from Harold and Vice President Bud Lindus, and much of the discussion centered on the two men's big spending habits. Betty put her foot down. "Sales and travel development expenses were cut by 50 percent," read the next set of board minutes.

The following January, after one row too many with Harold, Bud Lindus quit as vice president and director. Harold agreed to acquire his shares for $3,406. But Refining's troubles worsened. Nothing reveals this more clearly than their decision to move the company's office out of downtown Los Angeles. Board minutes tersely described the scope and urgency of the problems:

> *June 15, 1950*—"Chairman reported the distressed conditions of the corporation which he states was caused by general decline of business and also cancellation by the Armed Services Petroleum Purchasing agency of two contracts." Resolution: "That the Los Angeles office be closed and moved to the refinery location at 5900 Firestone in Southgate, that the Corporation discount its lease at Parr Terminal in Richmond, California, and suspense [sic] with the services of Harry Thompson" (one of the managers).

> *August 15*—Annual Meeting at Southgate Office. "Financial statements not available. Chairman stated that preliminary work on them indicated a considerable loss which was attributed to a great extent to cancellation by the Armed Services Petroleum Agency of various contracts."

For Betty, the most painful decision when she closed Refining's office in Los Angeles was to lay off Irene Anderson. The two women had become close friends. "They just didn't have enough money coming in to pay me," said Irene. Nor could she afford to undertake the additional daily journey to and from the refinery in Long Beach to which Betty had returned the Huttons' office. "The only car I had was a 1936 Chevrolet in which I had driven to California from New York. It couldn't be relied on in the heavy traffic that was building up along the road between my apartment and Long Beach." Out of the blue, Harold dropped in on Irene at her home. All his life he hated dismissing any of his employees. When Irene told him about her car, his response was, "You can have mine. I'll ride with Bets." It took Betty two days to talk her impulsively generous husband out of that idea.

To help keep the company solvent, Harold pegged his 1950–51 salary at $11,600, a good deal lower than the pay most middle-rank executives earned in the early '50s. But his confidence in the future remained. The board minutes limiting his pay went on, "Should conditions warrant, the president's salary may be increased up to $24,000 per year with an appropriate increase for other employees according to length of service."

By cutting the payroll and borrowing $9,000 from Betty's father, J. D. Spennetta, the Huttons saved their company. Once again, they benefited from events in the overseas world—the outbreak of the Korean War.

On June 26, 1950, while Harold and Betty were driving to work in Downey, a bulletin on their car radio conveyed an ominous message. Communist forces from North Korea had rolled across the thinly defended thirty-eighth parallel dividing the peninsula along the line where U.S. and Soviet forces had met at the end of World War II. A new war had broken out in Asia. Within days, North Korean tanks had rolled into the South Korean capital of Seoul. The South Korean army, supported by little more than a skeleton force of Americans, was in headlong retreat. It looked as if the Communists, who only two years earlier had won control of China, were on the brink of another great victory in Asia. Harold Hutton, like most of his California contemporaries, sat glued to the radio that evening, waiting to hear what—if anything—the United States could do to prevent this.

President Truman bit the bullet. Within hours of South Korea's plea for help, he sought and won the support of the U.N. Security Council to repulse North Korean aggression. With British, Australian, New Zealand, and later, Turkish and South African support, Truman mobilized a huge U.N. operation to rescue South Korea. California once again was the jumping-off point for war in the Pacific. As Harold and Betty watched, a U.S. Marine expeditionary force shipped out of Camp Pendleton under escort of a huge naval task force led out of San Diego by the aircraft carrier *Valley Forge*. They arrived in the port city of Pusan just in time to prevent the vastly better-equipped northern tank forces from driving the demoralized South Koreans into the sea.

There followed a trans-Pacific air and sea lift of World War II proportions. Close to a million American troops shipped out to Okinawa and Japan as well as to South Korea. The U.S. Air Force undertook a huge airlift to U.S. bases throughout the Pacific. The Flying Tiger Line was engaged to help fly men and equipment to Japan. The U.S. Navy came back into the market for heavy lubricants.

Refining's order book once again expanded on the back of its military business. Further growth came when Harold won an unexpected and substantial contract from an Indian government company, Victor Oil Company of Calcutta, for "considerable quantities of our products." By the summer of 1951, Refining was making a comeback. To boost production and finance overseas sales, Harold borrowed large sums of cash, some of it at 9 percent, from one of his friends, Allen O. March, and more in the form of a new credit line up to $500,000 from the Bank of America. With sharply rising sales, the company was profitable again, though its problems with the federal government were not over. With their business expanding rapidly, the Huttons had to appoint a corporate attorney, Marie Gowdy, "to transact and otherwise represent Refining Associates in all matters, things, and business with the U.S. Collector of Customs." That August, the board was told, "due to extensive audit by the Collector of Internal Revenue, no financial statements (were) available." Yet with Betty recovered from a second bout of the flu that had laid her low the previous winter, the administrative as well as the commercial side of the business was improving. The company's housekeeping improved, its accounts were returned to good order, and its office under Betty's direction modernized and simplified its procedures.

During a visit to the Spennettas' beach house on Balboa Island one bright September evening in 1951, Betty and Harold walked on the beach. A huge brass-red sun was sinking below the horizon as the Pacific surf foamed end-lessly up and down the beach. According to Edna Spennetta, Harold spent some time gazing at the ocean. His words to Betty are not recorded, but she several times recalled to one of her friends that he said something that evening to the effect that since they had married and set up their company, they had "cast a lot of bread" on the waters. Soon, Harold added, gripping Betty's arm, "the other side of the Pacific's going to rise up from the ashes. When it does, we'll rise up with them, mark my words."

A SECONDHAND REFINERY NEAR CHIANG MAI

The Korean War, like the Second World War, did far more than strengthen the market for oil products of all kinds. It refocused West Coast America's attention, and soon the rest of the world's, on the vast region of Pacific Asia where over their lifetime the Huttons were to see—and reap the benefit from—some of the greatest economic changes human history has ever recorded.

When in 1945 Harold and Betty celebrated the U.S. victory over Imperial Japan, much of east Asia was in ruins. China's great cities had been bombarded and ransacked during a decade of Japanese occupation. Seoul and Jakarta were devoid of a single high-rise building. Hong Kong and Singapore were little more than colonial slums. Tokyo and Osaka, second in destruction only to Nagasaki and Hiroshima with their radioactive rubble, were burned-out hulks from fire bombing. Poverty was endemic for the people of east Asia in those days. From the outer islands of Indonesia, still in the 1950s a rebellious province of the Dutch empire, to the northern isles of Japan, newly seized by the Soviet Union, hunger stalked the land. Illiteracy and disease to most east Asians seemed to be the natural order of things.

Outside Japan, life expectancy in Asia in the early 1950s was rarely higher than forty-five for men and forty-eight for women. Civil conflicts that were to kill and maim ten times more Asians than died in the struggle between the United States and Japan still lay ahead—between Communists and Nationalists in China, North and South Koreans, Dutch and Indonesians, French and Vietnamese, Americans and North Vietnamese. Yet as the old European empires retreated, new Asian nations were emerging to take their place. From Tokyo to Kuala Lumpur, from Seoul to Manila and Bali, they were borne along on a tide of economic growth, stimulated first by America in the late '40s and '50s, by Japan in the '60s and '70s, and then by the "little tigers," Taiwan, Hong Kong, and Singapore. Not far behind were east Asia's coming superpowers: China, for sure; India, perhaps; Indonesia, then as now, a blood-stained question mark.

It was this global transformation that provided the leitmotif of the second half of Harold Hutton's life. By early 1952, the United States and its allies had 500,000 men and thousands of vehicles and aircraft deployed in Korea. Further south, the French had an army of 240,000 men backed by armored vehicles and airplanes fighting their last colonial war in Vietnam. The British, who had fought and won a prolonged struggle to defend Malaya against Communist guerrillas, maintained a powerful fleet and air force in Singapore. Oil was the fuel on which all these forces depended. And Harold Hutton agreed with Henry Luce, the editor-in-chief of *Time,* the magazine Harold and Betty read every week, that the American Century, as he called it, would be "the Century of Oil."

The Huttons by the early 1950s already were selling considerable quantities of oil to Asia. In the fall of 1952, on one of his visits to Honolulu to check into Refining's shipments of oil to Japan, Harold flew on to Manila. Striding into the Shriro building, he called on the White Russian, Charles Clurman, with whom the Huttons had first done business when selling used oil to China. Harold went straight to the point. "Charlie, you've become a legend in the Philippines. Get me a contract with De La Rama."

Clurman was the right man to ask. De La Rama Steamship Line was the Philippines' only big national carrier; Shriro company served as its ship chandlers. Most of De La Rama's ships had been sunk or captured by the Japanese during the war, but under the reparations agreement the United States imposed on Tokyo, three Japanese liners, surrendered to the Americans in 1945, had been made over for De La Rama as compensation. These three vessels were now carrying passengers and freight between ports in the Philippines and countries in the South Pacific, and at every port they called, Shriro agents supplied them with bunker oil.

Harold Hutton was not without experience of the bunker trade. Before the war, Refining Associates had supplied modest quantities to the Moore McCormick Company whose agent, Morris Bach, had helped him get some of the bunkering business with Russian and Chinese freighters trading up and down the West Coast.

Clurman told De La Rama that Harold had a reputation for being a straight shooter and a brilliant chemist who could deliver oil of exactly the type required for their former Japanese ships. A deal was made whereby Refining became one of the Philippine line's suppliers at half a dozen of the lesser-known ports in the Philippines archipelago where the major oil companies had no facilities. De La Rama was also a member of the Westbound Pacific Conference, the trade association of the bigger shipping lines operating between Southeast Asia, Australia, the Philippines, and Hawaii. Two other members were the British Blue Funnel and the Swedish East Asia lines, each with three other large ships. Harold's bid to provide bunker oil for these vessels came in at a lower figure than that of his competitors. With Shriro's help, Refining Associates won a year-to-year contract to supply small portions of the oil needed by all nine ships of the conference.

Working with Shriro's group and the new friends he made at De La Rama, Harold Hutton developed a taste for trade across the Pacific in many other products besides oil. His early experiences as a purveyor of grease and crankcase drainings to China and Japan and his exposure to trade in the Philippines had sharpened his native business talents. Harold's horizons now expanded from those of a small-scale refiner to those of an international purveyor of the goods and services needed by the expanding economies of Pacific Asia. He was quick to recognize their needs for know-how and equipment to open up their natural resources. He saw, too, the high margins of profit that could be earned by anyone who knew where and how to procure the goods and services, machinery, and technology Asian companies needed and the shipping space required to transport them. Harold, in short, saw his chance and took it. Over the next twenty years, the Huttons were to become not only used-oil suppliers but also traders in every kind of construction and oil field equipment into Thailand, Singapore, Hong Kong, and most of all, Indonesia.

Harold's first love remained blending and refining oil. On his return to southern California from a later 1954 trip to Japan, luck or fate intervened to remind him of this. An envelope postmarked Bangkok was waiting on his desk. Under the letterhead Oriental Import & Export Company, a Thai businessman, Kriang Jiarakul, wanted to know if Refining Associates was interested in supplying lubricants to Thailand. Kriang, the son of a Thai-Chinese merchant whose trading company had served as an agent for Japanese products in the 1930s and during the war, was looking for a U.S. connection. With Japan still on its knees, America was the only source of the engineering and consumer products Oriental had been set up to sell in south Asia. Kriang wrote his letter after an American lawyer practicing in Bangkok drew his attention to a business magazine that contained a list of U.S. companies seeking agents in Thailand. One of them was Refining Associates.

The timing was propitious. The United States in 1954 was building up Thailand as the centerpiece of SEATO, the Southeast Asian Treaty Organization designed by Secretary of State John Foster Dulles to halt what Washington saw as the onward march of Communism into Indochina and Malaya. President Eisenhower, one of Harold Hutton's few political heroes, only recently had warned that Vietnam, Laos, and Cambodia, followed by Malaya and Singapore, would one after another "fall like dominos" unless the Western allies joined forces to help defeat them.

The United States at the time already was openly assisting the Chinese Nationalists in Taiwan to stave off threatened attacks on the offshore islands of Quemoy and Matsu. U.S. military advisors were helping President Magsaysay of the Philippines in his struggle against Communist guerrillas in Luzon. In September 1954, while the Huttons coincidentally were paying a visit to Manila, Secretary Dulles convened a conference that would set up what he regarded as the Asian counterpart of NATO to resist any further Sino-Soviet aggression in

Pacific Asia. Meeting in the Philippines' capital, the representatives of Australia, France, New Zealand, Pakistan, the Philippines, Thailand, the United Kingdom, and the United States signed a "collective defense treaty" permitting the eight member nations to assist one another in "preventing and countering subversive activities" (i.e., Communist penetration) and in "promoting economic and social progress" in the region. A separate protocol provided for military aid to Vietnam, Cambodia, and Laos.

It was shortly before Harold Hutton received Kriang Jiarakul's letter that this new alliance established SEATO's headquarters in Bangkok. A Thai general was its first secretary general. U.S. aircraft commenced flying reconnaissance flights over Indochina from Thai bases. It was the start of the process that within a decade was to lead to America's involvement in the Vietnam conflict.

Such was the background of Harold Hutton's first business venture into Thailand. Harold was no politician and certainly no diplomat. It is doubtful if he knew anything more about SEATO than he had read in the newspapers during his long flight from Los Angeles. But like most Americans of his generation who had watched the fall of China to the Communists, followed by North Korea's attack on South Korea, Harold applauded the creation of SEATO. He thought it was "necessary and appropriate." He also recognized that the U.S. decision to build up Thailand as a barrier to Communist expansion could open up a sizable military market for Refining Associates' products and perhaps also increase his sales into the local Thai market.

Harold responded positively to Kriang Jiarakul's enquiry. Following his next trip to Manila, Harold arranged to spend a week in Bangkok. Like most Americans, he and Betty knew next to nothing about "the little kingdom," as Harold called Thailand, save what they had gleaned from the movie *Anna and the King of Siam*. Flying into Bangkok, he read a brief provided by the U.S. Oil and Gas Trade Association. It told how King Phumiphol had succeeded to the throne after the 1946 murder of his older brother, Rana, and how the Thai army had removed the postwar civilian government. It went on to report that a strong man, Field Marshall Pribul Sanggram, who was prime minister during the war years when Thailand sided with Japan, had again seized the reins of power.

The central valley of Thailand, according to the article, was "the rice bowl of Asia," and the long peninsula reaching down toward Malaya boasted large reserves of tin, iron ore, and manganese with the possibility of offshore natural gas. Finally, the article said—Harold underlined this with his red ballpoint pen—Thailand's economic potential was held back by a shortage of fuel oil.

Arriving in Bangkok, Harold moved into a suite at the Oriental Hotel, newly refurbished and promoting itself as Asia's finest hostelry, where Somerset Maugham and Joseph Conrad had written their famous novels. The Oriental, situated on the broad Chao Phraya River next door to the French embassy, was to become one of Harold and Betty Hutton's most frequent stopping-off points in Southeast Asia. For many years, they rented one of its luxurious apartments and several adjacent rooms to serve as their company's office.

Harold met Kriang Jiarakul over tea and cakes in the Author's Lounge at the foot of an elegant staircase leading up to the bedroom where James Michener at that time was writing his novel *Taipan*. Speaking passable but by no means perfect English, Kriang described how his father had built up the Oriental Import & Export Company in the 1930s, when Thailand progressively became more dependent on the rising power of Japan. During the Second World War, the company had acted as the Bangkok agent for Mitsubishi Trading Co. Kriang openly admitted that his family had collaborated with the Japanese. Given the still-painful memories of the Japanese war, this admission might well have created a barrier between the two men. But Harold Hutton, ever since he sold his used oil to Fuji Kosan, had traded regularly with the Japanese. He quickly decided that Kriang Jiarakul, whom he was to rename Edwin Chia, was a man with whom he could do business. The Thailander agreed to set up a distribution network for Refining's lube oil in Bangkok. Harold undertook to establish a line of credit for Oriental Import & Export Company and, once he had obtained firm orders, to start shipping his products to Bangkok.

Two or three meetings later, sitting alongside the broad brown river that laps against the Oriental's outside bar, Harold raised a very different question. How would Edwin Chia feel about joining with Refining Associates in bidding to build a refinery for the Thai National Oil Co.? This project, which Harold had learned about from his contacts with the U.S. military, required the construction of a small refining plant in the remote northwest section of Thailand, sixty miles north of Chiang Mai, not far from the Burma border. The attractions for Refining were twofold. First, with U.S. forces now active in Thailand, locally produced refinery products that could meet the supply officers' specifications could find a ready market. Second, the growing inflow of U.S. and other Western aid funds made it likely that economic activity in Thailand as a whole would be stimulated, increasing demand for oil. An alliance between Refining Associates and the Thai National Oil Co. could be a potentially lucrative partnership.

Edwin Chia was enthusiastic. He had a family connection to Thai General Narongsaleerattavibak, who commanded the northwest region where the refinery was to be located and undertook to make further enquiries. Harold agreed on his next trip to Bangkok to pay a visit to the proposed site for a refinery at Fang, a small town on the Nore River.

On this occasion, Betty Hutton joined her husband for the long flight across the Pacific to Tokyo, and thence via Hong Kong and Bangkok to Chiang Mai. With Edwin Chia, they bumped their way over red mud roads through the forests to Fang. Harold brought a 16 mm movie camera to take hour after hour of pictures, but most of the time it rained. From their hotel near the royal palace, Phu Phing Ratchanivet, the Huttons looked across a mile-wide river at a mountainside rich in teak, with its lower slopes covered in tea plantations. It was Betty's first exposure to the Asian jungle, and she wrote home to her mother that she "loved the incredible density and silence of the green, damp forest." Harold was intrigued and challenged.

Along with officials of the Thai National Oil Co. and an escort of heavily armed soldiers, Harold led a small team of Refining Associates engineers to inspect the site for the refinery. They needed to know who would clear the forest, build the roads, and truck in steel and cement to lay the foundations. The Thais said they would guarantee the supply of crude oil to the new refinery if Refining Associates would bring in technicians to design and supervise erection of the towers and boilers. Harold and Edwin Chia met with General Narongsaleerattavibak. He was a man in a hurry. The refinery was needed urgently, he said, to supply fuel and lubricants for his armored vehicles' operations against Communist rebels.

By the time they returned to Bangkok, Harold and Edwin had agreed to form a joint company to bid for the refinery project. Both men knew the risks. This remote semiwilderness area was still the center of insurrectionary activities stemming from unrest and drug running among the tribes along the Burma-Thai border. It was not the kind of place where U.S. banks or major oil companies were ready to risk investment. But Harold relished the challenge. Working out of an office at the Oriental Hotel, he and Edwin Chia sketched out the main lines for a joint bid. Harold located a disused refinery in Bakersfield, California, that could be disassembled and shipped out to Thailand. Betty worked the telephones, instructing their California staff to get started on figuring out prices for the large quantities of other U.S. equipment and materials that would be needed and to hire structural engineers and other specialists to assist the Thais in completing the job on time.

*****

It took months, then years, to complete the negotiations. Then, one day in early 1957, the telephone rang in the Huttons' office in Long Beach. Edwin Chia, calling from Bangkok, told Harold that they had won the Fang Refinery contract. It was the Huttons' first big construction job, their first success on the mainland of Asia!

Within six weeks Harold and his team moved onto the site, joining forces with the Thai oil company's civil engineers. Work proceeded throughout 1957 and the first half of 1958. The disused Bakersfield refinery was broken down and sent by truck and rail to Long Beach and then shipped to Bangkok. More than 600 riverboat shipments were needed to move it up the Chao Phraya and Ping Rivers to the nearest point to Fang.

Conditions were far from easy. Rain, floods, flies, and a frequent shortage of essential parts made for delays at every stage of the work. The Thai army alone provided protection against tribal warfare along the nearby border with Burma and frequent—and bewildering—changes of government in Bangkok. But Fang's first refinery was completed on time. A senior member of the Army Chief of Staff, General Pachern Nimitbur, formally opened it in 1958 with Harold, Betty, and the entire Chia family on hand for the ceremony. Soon afterward Harold moved his Bangkok office from the Oriental Hotel to a new building owned by Edwin Chia on Sripraya Road. The company was by now buying and selling a wide range of products other than oil, including pharmaceuticals. The Huttons and Chias became close friends, frequently entertaining officials in the Thai government and military establishment, whose goodwill was indispensable for anyone, especially a non-Thailander, wanting to do business in Bangkok.

As Thailand's economy grew in the '50s, Harold hoped to win further contracts with the Thai National Oil Co. He and Betty labored long and hard on complex new tender documents. But by now they faced strong competition from local firms allied with the big international oil companies, among them Shell and Caltex. The Thai authorities, too, demanded ever higher commissions (i.e., bribes) to steer contracts into foreign companies' hands. This way of doing business was a foretaste of the "crony capitalism" that a generation later was to puncture Southeast Asia's economic miracles and plunge Thailand and its neighbors from boom to bust in the late 1990s.

Harold Hutton refused to pay "slush money." It was a time when the U.S. Congress, fired up by scandals arising from U.S. defense companies bribing foreign customers in Europe and the Middle East, was crafting legislation to punish any American who engaged in such corrupt practices; but the Huttons required no laws to keep them honest. Despite the prevailing culture of the countries where they did business, neither Harold nor Betty ever spent a penny on under-the-table bribes.

Refining Associates retained its office and continued to sell its products in Bangkok until the mid-1960s. Edwin Chia went on to become a founder of the Bangkok stock market and eventually its president. He and his wife built a number of the high-rise buildings that transformed the center of Bangkok into a mini-Manhattan. The Huttons' personal relationship with the Chia family prospered. Betty Hutton introduced their daughter Ann (her Thai name was Tasnee Jiarakul) to Chapman College in Orange, where she received her master's degree in business administration before returning to Thailand. Ann Chia became a top executive at 3M.

But having made their mark and no small fortune in Thailand, Harold and Betty Hutton concluded in the mid-1960s that Refining should look elsewhere. They had neither the desire nor the funds to get involved in the political manipulations that increasingly seemed to determine who prospered in the Thai oil business. Nor did they need to do so. New and bigger opportunities beckoned in Indonesia.

PART VI   PIONEERING IN INDONESIA

Indonesian soldier greets Harold at oil compound in north Sumatra

TO SUMATRA—
HUNGRY FOR ADVENTURE

Harold Hutton went to Indonesia for the first time on a suffocatingly hot day in the late summer of 1956. His journey, which he described as "a preliminary reconnaissance," was prompted by conversations he had with the chairman of Edgington Oil, a neighboring company in Downey, California, and a visit to the Indonesian Embassy in Washington. It took place against the background of an international oil crisis blowing up in the Middle East.

On July 27, Gamal Abdel Nasser, president of Egypt, nationalized the Suez Canal Company, which had built and, for close to a century, managed the "lifeline of the British Empire" linking the Mediterranean to the Indian Ocean. Through the Suez Canal flowed 90 percent of Europe's and a rising proportion of America's oil. Anthony Eden, the polished but irascible diplomat who succeeded Churchill as Britain's Conservative prime minister, likened Nasser's action to Hitler's pre–World War II seizure of the Sudetenland from Czechoslovakia. Eden and his French counterpart, Premier Guy Mollet, were determined not to repeat the "appeasement" policies of Munich that started the countdown to World War II. Most Americans who thought about this agreed with Eden. So at first did President Eisenhower. With the Soviets encouraging Nasser, Secretary of State Dulles flew to London where he and Eden concocted a Suez Canal Users Association (SCUA) that would establish an international regime to keep the canal open to the ships of all nations, including those of Israel, which Nasser had said he would exclude. SCUA, backed by Australia, New Zealand, the United States, Britain, and France would insist on compensation for the assets confiscated from the Suez Canal Company.

Every international oil company without exception backed this plan. So did Harold Hutton in conversations with colleagues in Long Beach. If Egypt got away with its seizure of an international waterway, violating the treaties that protected free passage, what would there be to prevent Panama from doing the same? Or Turkey in the case of the Bosphorus? Nationalization without compensation was equally abhorrent to American businessmen as well as to the U.S. government. If Nasser could thumb his nose at the most basic principles of private ownership and due process of law, would not other dictators be tempted to seize foreign investors' property, including the assets of U.S. companies in South America and Cuba?

As the Suez crisis deepened, the price of oil on world markets started to climb sharply. Even the prospect of the canal being closed, forcing two thirds of the world's tanker fleet to detour 6,000 miles around the southern tip of Africa, adding three to four weeks to the average voyage between the Gulf and Europe, had produced near panic on the stock markets. There were fears of a massive fall in deliveries of Middle East oil to western Europe's power stations, bringing factory closures and widespread unemployment in the winter of 1956–57. Anthony Eden underlined the gravity of the situation by quoting an ominous phrase used by one of his predecessors a few days before World War I: "The lights are going out all over Europe."

Harold Hutton was only one of thousands of U.S. oilmen who reacted to the Suez Canal crisis by casting around for new sources of oil. He sensed that the sharp rise in Middle East oil prices spelled opportunity for entrepreneurs like himself, unburdened by the political and economic baggage of the big international oil companies. With his friends at the Jonathan Club in downtown Los Angeles, where oilmen gathered to have lunch and talk business, Harold discussed the prospective reduction in deliveries of Kuwait and Saudi crude and the corresponding rise in prices. Japan would be especially hard hit, its treasury being desperately short of hard currency to pay more for imports of oil. One of Harold's Japanese contacts mentioned Indonesia as a potential source of "non–Middle East" supplies, as it had been for Japan during the 1942–45 period of Japanese occupation during the war.

By coincidence President Eisenhower had invited the president of Indonesia, Bung Sukarno, to visit Washington earlier that year. Following the 1955 conference of nonaligned nations in Bandoeng, when China and India joined with Indonesia in condemning "western imperialism" and blaming America for the Cold War, the U.S. was anxious to wean Indonesia away from the Soviet bloc into whose clutches Secretary of State Dulles feared President Sukarno was leading it. Sukarno, with his black pitji hat, sunglasses, and silver-headed swagger stick, at first made quite an impression in the U.S. capital. He opened his speech at a glittering White House dinner with the words "I am just a little brown man and I wonder what I am doing here." He delivered an address to a joint session of Congress that led one of its more gullible legislators to remark that this was "the best speech ever made by a visiting statesman with the possible exception of Winston Churchill."

The love affair quickly faded. Within a year the United States was engaged in covert operations to overthrow Sukarno, whose own version of his talks at the State Department included this description of his conversation with Dulles: "I tried to explain that we had no desire to echo the Soviet Union nor to strictly follow the path that America had laid for us. Mr. Dulles's reply was that America's policy was global. Neutralism is immoral. You must be on one side or the other." Sukarno then went to see President Eisenhower in the Oval Office. Their conversation, described by the Indonesian as an "immediate nonmeeting of minds," included these translated exchanges, which Harold, who read them in a well-thumbed biography of Sukarno he kept in his study, enjoyed quoting to his friends:[9]

> *Ike:* I hear you like movies, President Sukarno. Tell me, how often do you see them?
>
> *Sukarno:* Three times a week in the palace.
>
> *Ike:* What kind of film is your favorite, President Sukarno?

---

9. Cindy Adams, ed., *Sukarno, An Autobiography.* (Hong Kong: Gunung Agung, 1966), 75–277.

Sukarno: Adventure stories, history, and biographies.

Ike: Is that so? Well, I like only Westerns. And I bet you'll never guess who my favorite star is?

Sukarno: No. Who?

Ike: Randolph Scott.

The Huttons often quoted this story, especially in later years when they became neighbors of Randolph Scott's when they all lived in the desert.

From Washington, Sukarno flew to Los Angeles, where he shocked Dulles but greatly amused Harold by making a public pass at Jayne Mansfield and visiting a lingerie store where he lined up a group of shop girls to help him decide what size of "bust holders" he needed to buy for his wife. The Huttons kept newspaper clippings reporting Sukarno's comments. Of California life, he said, "I find only one fault, Americans are too full of fear—afraid of B.O., afraid of bad breath, haunted by fear of dandruff." Harold especially enjoyed—and quoted to his colleagues—another of Sukarno's jokes about politicians: "American candidates shake hands with the mothers and kiss the babies. The Sukarno way is to shake hands with the babies and kiss the mothers."

The Indonesian president's visit nonetheless had a serious side. In meetings with California businessmen, Sukarno urged them to help open up his island country's rich resources of lumber, minerals, and oil. There were not many takers. Neither the oil companies nor the banks were impressed by the claims of a faraway country still technically at war with the Dutch, whose economy was in near chaos and whose legal system was in tatters. Harold Hutton, however, was intrigued. His early forays into Pacific Asia had gone well. Selling war surplus oil out of the Philippines to the Chinese Nationalists had netted useful profits. His business in Japan was prospering. The refinery venture in Thailand seemed likely to pay off handsomely. One evening Harold said to Betty, "Why don't we take a look at Indonesia?" He ticked off his thinking on the fingers of his left hand:

One, the world needs more oil.

Two, oil prices are rising.

Three, there's oil in north Sumatra that the Big Boys can't touch.

Four, the Japanese need it.

Five, we've got connections in Japan.

Betty urged her husband to check carefully whether the Japanese would risk buying Indonesian oil. Like Harold, she knew very little about the vast Indonesian archipelago except what she had read in *Time* magazine and the Los Angeles newspaper reports on Sukarno's visit. Betty was especially cautious because she realized that following Egypt's seizure of the Suez Canal and Iran's previous grab for the Anglo-Iranian Oil Company's assets in the Gulf, the United States and its allies had pledged to take legal action against international trafficking in the fruits of these, in Western eyes, unacceptable acts of expropriation without compensation. Wasn't Indonesia doing exactly the same to the Anglo-Dutch oil company Shell as Egypt and Iran had done to Anglo-Iranian (now B.P.)? she asked. And would the Japanese, still heavily dependent on American goodwill, risk buying Indonesian oil in the face of worldwide disapproval and a possible breach of international law? Betty's concerns were well founded. Lawsuits from the big oil companies, their bankers, and Wall Street seemed inevitable if Refining got involved in trading oil from Indonesia, to which Shell Oil Company might have a prior claim.

Harold shared his wife's reservations with his friends at the Jonathan Club. Like him, they paid little attention to international politics. One man whom Harold consulted seemed to think that Indonesia was an extension of Indo-China. "A bunch of savages," said another who ranked as an expert because he had served in the U.S. Navy in the South Pacific. J. D. Spennetta's advice was to "pass." Only one of his drinking friends, a big burly oil driller named Ross McClintock who was working for Fluor Corporation, echoed Harold's own views. "What's there to lose? Go down there and take a look."

On his next visit to Bangkok, Harold met a group of Japanese businessmen introduced to him by his Thai partner, Edwin Chia. They talked, somewhat wistfully Harold thought, about the natural complementarity between Japan's rising demand for non-Arab oil and the possibilities of increasing output in Indonesia. But would an importer be legally permitted to bring into Japan oil from fields that had been seized from their previous owners without compensation? To Harold's questions on that subject, the Japanese offered no response except enigmatic smiles.

Back in Long Beach, Harold talked over the possibilities of getting oil out of Indonesia with one of his neighbors, Ralph Edgington, whose refinery on Artesia Boulevard was just around the corner from Harold's office. Edgington Oil was a much larger company than Refining. Its main interest was in heavy crude for asphalt. Ralph Edgington was a cautious man as well as being a stickler for details, but as an entrepreneur, he shared Harold's hunch that there was big money to be made in Indonesian oil. Edgington also disliked the major companies, which Harold, when he had a couple of shots of scotch inside him, was wont to describe as "SOBs" and "rascals." He liked the thought of what he called "cocking a snoot" at the likes of Caltex, Stanvac, and Shell who monopolized all but a fraction of the supply of heavy crude in east Asia.

With the help of a lobbyist named John Wright who claimed to have "connections" in Jakarta, Edgington made contact with the Indonesian Embassy in Washington. On June 26, 1956, he and Harold met Wright and the commercial counselor, Achmad Pousem, at the Indonesian Embassy. Counselor Pousem said he was looking to identify American independents to assist the Indonesian national oil company his government was struggling to establish. Such independent companies must have, he said, "sufficient resources, and must be strong enough to withstand pressure" from Shell and the other Seven Sisters.

During the course of their meetings with Counselor Pousem at the embassy in Washington, Ralph Edgington and Harold Hutton listened to views of George

Jellison, a former employee of Caltex whose operations in south-central Sumatra at the time were the biggest source of Indonesia's exports and foreign exchange. Jellison and Wright pointed to north Sumatra, where the prewar fields lay in ruins and Shell had made no move to re-occupy or redevelop them. It might be possible, they said, to make a deal whereby a consortium of American independents would help Indonesia restore production in the Langkat area, taking out crude oil in return for equipment, know-how, and marketing. The Americans would be paid in crude oil.

This was only one of hundreds of similar proposals for tapping fresh sources of oil that were making the rounds in Washington and other Western capitals in the context of the Suez crisis. But both Edgington and Harold were impressed. On June 29, Wright sent a telex to Edgington's office in Long Beach saying that the Indonesian government was asking for a quote on 20,000 tons of asphalt and urging Edgington to stress in his negotiations his willingness to help with the building of schools and the training of Indonesian oil workers.

While in Washington, the two Californians attended a garden party with the Indonesian ambassador, Moekart Notwiddidja, and a visiting politician from Jakarta, Sudjo TritJitrokusom. Edgington told Sudjo that he was ready to send a team of technicians and geologists to north Sumatra. Harold said that on his next visit to Thailand he would go on to Jakarta to join them. Sudjo's only questions were the same ones that Pousem, the economic counselor, had asked. Did Edgington and Refining Associates have deep enough pockets to finance the restoration of production in the north Sumatra fields? Did they dare face up to hostility from Western governments and legal action by Shell? Ambassador Moekart added that they would need to work under the control of the Indonesian army, which he knew (but the Americans did not) was about to take over responsibility for his country's indigenous oil industry.

Ralph Edgington's response came in a letter to the commercial attache after Harold and he had returned to Long Beach:

> I want to confirm the interest of this company in assisting your government in opening, developing, and selling petroleum from the north Sumatra oil field . . . We are an independent and therefore smaller oil company in the world's petroleum business, but we have our own production refineries, marine terminals, and even drum manufacturing plant . . . We are presently contemplating the construction of a refinery in the vicinity of Manila, Philippines. The crude oil might fit into such an operation or, it might develop, it could be preferable to erect a refinery at Sumatra.

Edgington proposed a fifteen-year deal whereby his company would "assume the obligations of producing and developing this oil field" and "training Indonesian citizens for the purpose of . . . operating it." Edgington Oil at this stage seemed fully committed to this venture, and Harold Hutton agreed to work with the company. The rough outlines of a partnership between Edgington and Refining Associates were drawn up. Ralph Edgington told the Indonesians that one of his executives, George Pennebaker, together with Harold Hutton would visit Indonesia "within the next ten days for a preliminary survey of the possibilities."

There was, however, a difference between Edgington's approach and Harold's. The first indications could be seen in two key sentences of Edgington's letter:

> We realize that there may be international claims and complications that might have to be settled or adjudicated . . . There are innumerable phases of such an agreement that must be discussed, considered and mutually worked out.

Edgington's caution was understandable. In a painfully similar preview of its descent into chaos in 1998, Indonesia in the mid-'50s was sliding into a state of near–civil war. Many of its outer islands were in open revolt. Guerrillas stalked the jungles surrounding the derelict oil fields of north Sumatra. Communist-led trade unions dominated the government-owned industries. President Sukarno was quoted as saying of his country's condition, "Political parties grow like weeds . . . We face disaster. Endless conflicts. Hair raising confusion."

For a man of Ralph Edgington's age and conservative disposition, the prospect of investing time, money, and his company's reputation in such faraway bedlam seemed less inviting back in Long Beach than it had at the Indonesian ambassador's garden party. The State Department's advice was that Shell Oil almost certainly would sue to win possession of oil brought out from north Sumatra. Nor did the Indonesians do much to reassure Edgington. He had asked for a clear-cut commitment. "Before going into details, it is of course necessary to know that your government is interested in this project." Weeks, then months, went by without a response from Jakarta.

Harold Hutton, meanwhile, flew to Indonesia on that suffocatingly hot day in August. It was his second visit, the first having taken place in the course of a selling mission on behalf of Refining Associates in the spring of 1956. The international news lent urgency to his midsummer journey. The Middle East crisis was deepening. As Harold arrived in Jakarta, British and French task forces were steaming across the Mediterranean with orders to forcefully re-open the Suez Canal if Nasser did not yield. Israel and Egypt mobilized. Arab mobs in Iraq and Jordan threatened to burn Western embassies. The U.S. government, worried that the Arabs might cut the pipelines from Baghdad to the Mediterranean, ordered 300,000 tons of oil from its strategic petroleum reserves to be made ready for shipment to Britain, with another 200,000 tons to be added if circumstances warranted.

Harold could not have enjoyed his exposure to Jakarta that August. His hotel, the Soviet-built Indonesian, in later years was upgraded to the best international standards, but in 1956 the air conditioning system worked only fitfully in temperatures of 100 degrees. The elevators kept breaking down. The food, said Harold in a letter to Betty, was "just awful."

Following the advice he had been given in Washington, Harold called a series of numbers in the Ministry of Oil and National Planning, including one in the personal office of the Minister, Dr. Djuanda. He got no answers there. Instead, Harold was informed that he should see a lawyer named Nirwonojudo, who until recently had run the central Java oil fields for the government. Nirwonojudo indicated that he was the only person with whom Americans needed to deal in connection with north Sumatra. He claimed to have a lot of influence in this remote and violent region and clearly knew all the ins and outs of the politics of Indonesian oil.

A few years earlier, while some of his U.S.-oriented colleagues in Jakarta were trying to come to terms with the international oil companies including Shell, Nirwonojudo had set up his own organization, PTM, to take control of the Sumatran fields at Rantau and Pangkalan Brandan. His idea, supported by the aggressive Communist trade union, Perbum, was to sell north Sumatran oil directly to Singapore, thereby excluding the central government of Indonesia. Though this project failed and brought temporary disgrace to Nirwonojudo, this facile lawyer went on to become managing director and president of one of the three main divisions of the national oil industry, charged with developing the Javanese fields.

Lawyer Nirwonojudo did not impress Harold Hutton. Their different assessments of "Nirwo's" importance also helped widen the gap that was opening between Edgington's approach and Harold's. In October 1956, Tam Edgington, brother of the chairman, had flown out to Jakarta. He fell ill and was confined to a hospital bed, but in a series of letters written in longhand, Tam complained that Harold Hutton had "upset" Nirwonojudo and this was damaging their prospects of winning the Sumatran deal. One letter said:

> Nirwo has the full authority of the central government to carry out
> the oil business in north Sumatra . . . but until now, it seems that
> Hutton neglects him. I am afraid that Hutton will spoil the business.

Another, written in longhand, went on to say that Harold, on behalf of Ralph Edgington:

> has not got the oil and the money moving . . . I do not understand
> this, after all, Nirwonojudo is the man now. So will you please have
> Mr. Hutton send me all papers.

Exactly when, why, and how Harold and the Edgingtons parted company is unclear. Harold's freewheeling approach evidently made Ralph Edgington nervous. He was older and far wealthier than Harold and at the time was almost certainly better informed about the change of front that in early 1957 had overtaken U.S. policy toward Indonesia. Thus Edgington knew, though Harold may not have known (or cared), that Washington now regarded Sukarno as little more than a tool of the Soviets and that dissident elements in Sumatra, with tacit U.S. encouragement, were threatening to break away from the Sukarno regime in Jakarta. Edgington's attitude was that if north Sumatra's oil business could be won away from Shell without undue risk, he was willing to invest, but Edgington was under no pressure and had no need to cast his family bread—and/or reputation—onto the waters of Sukarno's faraway archipelago.

Harold's situation was different. He was a younger man in a hurry. Aggressive and self-confident, he was temperamentally less inclined to meekly follow Washington's warnings. Harold was neither rich nor poor, but he possessed in abundance the wildcatter's determination to strike it rich or go broke. He was also attracted by the prospect of becoming a trader, supplying the Indonesians with whatever they needed to build up their own industry in return for payment in oil. Harold, too, was hungry for adventure. Eager for a challenge, he was unafraid or unaware of the scale of the risks he was facing.

Harold Hutton, in short, had a vision of Pacific Asia as the "new frontier" for American enterprise. His business instincts were aroused. He was ready to risk all he and Betty had on the opportunities he smelled in Indonesia.

*****

The break between Edgington Oil and Refining Associates almost certainly came when Harold decided that Nirwonojudo was the wrong horse to back in north Sumatra. In their magisterial history of the Indonesian oil industry, Dr. Anderson G. Bartlett III and his Sedjarah team of American experts had this to say about Nirwonojudo:

> To some he was a visionary—idealist, socialistic, and impractical.
> Others are more harsh; in their view he was simply a political
> opportunist. Although not a Communist, he shared the view of
> many in Indonesia that he should work with the Communists.[10]

Harold's comment was more direct. "Nirwonojudo didn't ring any bells. So we started looking for a more solid approach." He struck solid ground when he lunched with a twenty-five-year-old Belgian-American named Joe Gohier at the home of the Jakarta agent of Isthmian Steamship Lines. Gohier was married to a Javanese lady with family ties to senior figures in the Sukarno government. Since the Dutch withdrawal, he had represented American and British firms in Indonesia and had just imported several shiploads of asphalt to the country. Gohier was impressed by Harold Hutton. Later in life, he would describe him as "my role model . . . Harold became almost a father to me. Betty was like a mother."

In the fall of 1956, Harold asked Joe Gohier to take over his negotiations with the Indonesian oil ministry. "As far as Refining was concerned," Gohier recalled, "I was the only American with a permanent visa permitted to work in Indonesia."

For nearly a year, at his own expense, Gohier worked to advance the Huttons' cause. All Refining's business in Indonesia in 1956–57 was done under Gohier's name. Harold's bank accounts in Jakarta were held in Joe Gohier's name. Making use of his connections with the newly decisive force in north Sumatra, the Indonesian army, Gohier made arrangements for Harold to meet the important people in the infant oil industry. One was Gohier's brother-in-law, Major General Suhardiman, who later was to become vice president of Indonesia's national oil company, Pertamina. Another was Dr. Djuanda, who not long afterwards became prime minister of Indonesia.

---

10.   Anderson G. Bartlett et al., *Pertamina, Indonesian National Oil*, (Djakarta: AmerAsian Ltd., 1972).

By the summer of 1957, an elated Harold sensed a breakthrough. Djuanda cross-examined him about how Indonesia might go about developing its own independent oil industry and marketing its products to Japan. Harold described his work in Thailand, his interests in the Philippines, and his sales of oil to Japan. He made a specially good impression on Ir Anondo, head of the Directate of Mining, who joined in their meeting. "Mr. Hutton spoke no Indonesian but he clearly knew his way around oil wells, refineries, pipelines, and the international marketing of oil," one of those present commented.

Harold on his return to California was optimistic that, as he told Betty, "we've got one foot in the door." But as the weeks and months went by without any firm offers from the Indonesians, the early promise started to evaporate. Back in Jakarta, Harold's calls to the Oil Ministry produced only polite evasions. Suddenly, "when the time was right," as Gohier put it, General Suhardiman phoned. He took Harold to a house in one of the wealthier suburbs of Jakarta. There Harold was to strike what proved to be for the Huttons the equivalent of the oil gusher on Signal Hill that made Harold's boyhood hero, Sam Mosher, a billionaire.

Harold's host that morning was Ibnu Sutowo, the army brigadier general in charge of north Sumatra. Ibnu was to become Indonesia's oil supremo. It was one of those rare personal encounters that changes the lives of both parties. Harold Hutton was to become a catalyst for Ibnu's transformation from medical doctor and army officer into Indonesia's oil king and international trader extraordinaire. Ibnu in turn proved to be the driving force behind Refining Associates' take-off in the Indonesian oil business, the source of both the Huttons' and his own great private wealth.

A gregarious Harold (middle photograph) was a hit with the boss of Sumatra's oil fields, Brigadier General Ibnu (left at top and bottom)

MEETING THE BOSS IN JAKARTA

I bnu Sutowo when Harold first met him was forty-three, the fifth of eleven children, seven boys and four girls, of a former Netherlands East Indies civil servant. Ibnu entered medical school in Surabaya at age sixteen, completing a ten-year course, combining university and medical studies in nine years during which he also mastered German and Dutch and later Japanese and English.

After graduation in May 1940, Dr. Ibnu was assigned to south Sumatra as a public health officer charged with fighting the high incidence of malaria and secondary diseases. He told Harold a story about an Indian patient who had been attacked by a crocodile. Afterward, because Ibnu's orderly had fainted at the sight of so much blood, the patient refused to pay Ibnu's fee. During the Japanese occupation, Ibnu organized a vigilante corps to distribute food and medicine in his district of south Sumatra. As chairman of a revolutionary youth group, he organized nationalist groups against the returning Dutch and in 1947, when the Dutch commander delivered an ultimatum to evacuate Palembang or it would be bombed, took the last train out with his expectant wife, Sally, and their two-year-old daughter.

The new revolutionary government appointed Ibnu military commander for south Sumatra with the rank of major. His friend and colleague, Chief of Staff General Nasution, asked him to come to Jakarta in 1956 to reorganize army logistics and later, when martial law was declared, gave Ibnu the double assignment of deputy operations officer and chief administrator of the nationwide military regime.

Professor Bartlett in his book *Pertamina* relates a story, probably apocryphal, concerning Nasution's selection of the first director for the new national oil company he was empowered to set up in 1957. Three officers were being considered, a lawyer, an engineer, and a physician. After careful consideration,

Nasution concluded that the lawyer would argue too much, the engineer would plan too much, but that Ibnu Sutowo, the doctor, could and would cure this ailing industry.

Ibnu's approach to his assignment in north Sumatra was more martial than medical. With two assistants, Major Harijono, who had worked for a German company and had experience in the purchasing branch of the army, and Major Jeudong, who took charge of the finances, he set up his headquarters in a small sitting room of Jeudong's home. In the early stages, his staff used bicycles to collect the mail and had no official cable address until an important telegram from the United States was returned to its authors "addressee unknown."

Such was the small group of army men who in 1957 were asked to develop the oil resources of north Sumatra—a primary producing field at Rantau in Atjeh province, the oil refining facilities at Pangkalan Brandan, and the port of Pangkalan Susu. Ibnu was quick to admit that neither he nor any of his lieutenants knew anything about oil. "Consequently, I have no other choice but to learn by doing," he told his subordinates. "Our motto will be, 'learn while you work and work while you learn.'"

When Ibnu and Harold Hutton first met, thanks to Joe Gohier, the two men superficially could not have been more different. Harold, blue eyed and fresh faced, had the hands of an oil tanker driver. Ibnu, short, slim, dark, and boy-ish looking, had the slim soft fingers of a surgeon. The Asian spoke quickly, quietly, and precisely. The American had a gravel-voiced drawl and affected the good-old-boy language of the oil patch. Even their dress seemed to jar: Ibnu in trim, olive-green army fatigues, neatly creased, with black, polished shoes; Harold in a casual sports coat, open-necked floral shirt, slacks, and canvas loafers to keep his feet from sweating in the 100-degree temperature.

Yet even if there was little in their very different backgrounds that seemed likely to create an affinity between the Javanese physician-turned-army-commander and the California oil-man-turned-international-entrepreneur, something impor-tant transpired between Ibnu and Hutton that day. They liked one another.

Instinctively, they felt that each could bring to the table what the other wanted and needed; they could do good business together. Trust was yet to grow. For now, it was enough that Ibnu felt a need for the blunt-spoken American's lifetime of experience in the oil industry and Hutton was looking for a break, a chance to throw himself into a new adventure that he recognized as the chance of a lifetime.

The next day they discussed the details. When Ibnu asked him what a barrel of oil was worth, Harold gave him the exact sum as quoted in that morning's financial press. It was the same figure that Ibnu's staff had already placed in front of him. "This was the first time I had ever received a straight-forward, honest answer from any foreign oil man," Ibnu commented later. "All the others talk about posted prices and discounts, concepts that I hardly understood—but here was a man who didn't try to bargain nor pad his answer to me. As a novice in the field, I liked that." Harold, in return, laid aside the formalities that he and the Edgington brothers had exchanged with the Indonesian ambassador in Washington. Instead, he told Ibnu that Refining Associates would help Indonesia set up a viable national oil company in north Sumatra without asking for any of the concessions that Shell and Caltex had insisted upon in the past. All Harold wanted in return was a share of the oil.

As the negotiation developed, Ibnu specified that the key to any business relationship must be that the oil belonged to Indonesia and no one else. Indonesians must also manage and control its production and export. Refining Associates would be the junior partner. Its role would be to provide technical assistance in restoring production, funds to purchase the spare parts, and engineers, geologists, and drillers to re-open the pipelines and port and to explore for fresh sources of oil. Only later, when the oil started flowing, would the U.S. company have a chance to recoup its investment by selling a share of north Sumatra's production to overseas markets.

This was a very different arrangement from any previously accepted by the international oil companies. The Indonesians, despite their lack of capital and know-how, would have operational responsibility as well as clear legal title; the Americans would be contractors, suppliers, and marketers. Everywhere else, the oil majors insisted that in return for their risking their money and labor to develop "Third World" oil and gas fields, they must own or share the product at the wellhead and retain management control. But Harold Hutton did not argue. He accepted Ibnu's terms without demur. His comment on their deal came later in a response to the authors of *Pertamina*:

> In 1957, Indonesia was suspicious of foreigners and big foreign companies. They wanted to try it on their own and I encouraged them. Evidently, I was the first foreign oil man to believe that an all-Indonesian oil company could succeed. I told Ibnu, "All it takes to build an oil company is oil."

At the end of their first and decisive encounter, General Ibnu did something unusual for an Indonesian in those days. Looking Harold Hutton straight in the eyes, he held out his hand and said, "I believe you can help us." Harold jumped out of his chair, grasped the general's hand and said gruffly, "You've got a deal."

Joe Gohier, meanwhile, had worked out the main lines of a contract with Ibnu's staff and the director of mining, Ir Anondo. This document was placed on the table when two days later he and Harold returned to see Ibnu and Major Harijono. "Far too long," said Ibnu rifling through pages. "I am in a hurry. My country needs oil now."

"You are a man after my own heart," said Harold, pushing aside the multipaged draft. He and Ibnu spelled out the main points of their agreement. While they spoke, Gohier and Harijono incorporated them into a very much shorter contract on a typewriter in Ibnu's office. This contract stipulated the following:

> 1. Refining Associates would "provide engineers and oil technicians to rehabilitate the Pangkalan Brandan refinery facilities and tank farm; repair the pipelines from Rantau to Pangkalan Susu; repair or replace the Susu storage tanks; reconnect them to the loading jetty; and get the oil moving as quickly as possible."

2. Refining Associates was to open up "a line of credit covering the supply of all necessary spare parts for the existing installations and any and all new equipment required; purchase this at the best possible prices from U.S. and other suppliers; and ship it into Susu together with trained engineers able to assist in introducing new technologies to the Indonesians."

3. The Indonesian side would "retain ownership and management control up to the point when the oil was loaded onto tankers that Refining Associates was to procure in timely fashion at Susu." Once loaded, however, the Americans were free to market the oil at the best possible price, sharing in all profits earned.

For Harold Hutton, the latter point was the key. Refining Associates would risk virtually everything the Huttons owned—"bet the farm," as he put it—on rehabilitating the wells and pipelines and loading the oil into tankers. Its dividends would come from 35 percent of the markup between the cost of the oil at the point of loading and the price at which he could sell it on the world market. Harold's luck confirmed his judgment. As oil prices rose in the '50s and '60s, Refican's profits soared, mainly from its sales to Japan.

Once the draft contract was typed, Major Harijono wanted to take time out to review it with the Indonesian side's attorneys. General Ibnu would hear nothing of that idea. Glancing through Gohier's typescript, he said, "Let's get started." He and Harold scribbled their signatures at the bottom of what Professor Bartlett described as "probably the shortest oil sales contract on record: single spaced it would be less than two type-written pages."

Within a week, Harold and Joe Gohier were on their way to the oil fields at Rantau and Pangkalan Brandan in one of Ibnu's military planes. They were the first Western oilmen to visit north Sumatra since the Dutch left in 1942. Landing at the regional capital, Medan, they found a situation even worse than Ibnu had described. The whole area was a shambles. Basic services did not work, roads were impassable, and the authority of the central government long since had been usurped by feuding local chieftains, dissident army officers, and trade union bosses. Business conditions could not have been more repellant. Escorted by heavily armed soldiers whose loyalty to Ibnu's local representative, Major Jeudong, could not be taken for granted, the two men made their way north along what remained of a former Dutch colonial highway. Whole sections had disintegrated into little more than a muddy trail. Bridges had been bombed out. Washouts required wide detours through the forest. It took forty-eight hours in an army jeep to cover the thirty-four miles to Pangkalan Susu, the small port on the Siak River from which General Ibnu hoped to export Indonesia's first nationally owned oil. Susu was in ruins. The wrecks of ships bombed by the Allied air forces in World War II littered the waterway leading from its broken down pier to the Malacca Straits and the South China Sea. Most of Susu's oil storage tanks built by Shell were out of action. The pipelines through which oil had flowed south to Susu from the production centers of Rantau and Pangkalan Brandan were overgrown with roots and jungle moss.

Continuing into the next day, the two Americans needed another eighteen hours to travel the eighteen miles from Susu to Langkat where they were met by representatives of several rival organizations, each claiming to have control of the oil fields. One was still reporting to the Jakarta lawyer Nirwonojudo who, it transpired, had recently been sacked as chief assistant to the military commander on charges of "smuggling." Nirwo was closely associated with the aggressive Communist union of oil workers, Persatuan Buroh Minjak (Perbum).

Another much larger group was headed by a heavyset forceful man named Djohan, whose lifelong experience in refinery maintenance made a deep impression on Harold. Djohan's recent life history provided the two visitors with a vivid insight into the turbulent events that had closed down the north Sumatran oil fields. One of the few Indonesians with technical training in Holland, he had been given the military rank of sergeant when Shell was making preparations to resist the Japanese invasion in 1941. Djohan was ordered to destroy the Pangkalan oil installations to prevent their falling into enemy hands. He refused and was arrested by the Dutch for insubordination. Freed in 1942 by the Japanese invaders, Djohan rebuilt the damaged oil works in north Sumatra in less than eight months. His friendship with the wartime Japanese garrison commander at Pangkalan Brandan led the Japanese when they surrendered in 1945 to turn over control of the fields to Djohan and his workers.[11]

Harold, given his close connections with Japan, listened carefully as Djohan explained the tangled story of north Sumatra's oil fields. After the war, the workers had formed themselves into *lasjkar minjak,* groups of oil freedom fighters to resist the return of the Dutch and reconstruct the fields for their own use. The pipelines, refinery, and port, still severely damaged by Allied wartime bombing, were then torched by the *lasjkar minjak* to prevent their falling into the hands of the returning colonialists. During the first Dutch police action against the new Republic (August 13, 1947), Djohan and thirty of his comrades re-occupied the burned-out refinery. A second "police action" by the Dutch in December 1948 led to a further round of destruction of nearly all that remained of Brandan's operating equipment. Eventually, in the early 1950s, Djohan led a number of workers and their families back to Pangkalan Brandan where, as time went on, they repaired what they could and built up a small local trade in kerosene.

Now, as Harold Hutton and Joe Gohier arrived, Djohan was operating as general manager under a charter issued by the governor of north Sumatra. He had a staff of 425 and was working on a modest rehabilitation program involving construction of two small oil stills and planning to build four more. Harold drove and walked around Pangkalan Brandan and the oil facility's compound. He and Joe Gohier noted that Djohan seemed to be popular with

---

11. The Japanese head of personnel, Nagaharu Nakamura, who conducted the formal transfer from the Imperial Japanese Army to Djohan, entered the oil business after the war. He returned to Pangkalan Brandan in 1961 when the Japanese consortium introduced by Harold Hutton to sell Pertamina's production to Japan undertook to assist in the rehabilitation of the oil fields. Nakamura joked that he should have kept what he had, since he seemed to have spent the rest of his life buying it back. Bartlett, *Pertamina,* 68–70.

his men. The operations, such as they were, appeared to be well run. There was no technical reason why the wells, the small refinery, and the port of Susu could not be rehabilitated given the money, materials, and professional expertise Harold was confident of recruiting from California.

The big question in Harold's mind as he returned to Medan was, "Who is in charge?" Over the eight years since independence, the Indonesians had failed to develop any coherent policy on foreign investment in their oil fields. Lacking the capital and technical know-how needed to restore the north Sumatran fields themselves, the new country's squabbling oil bureaucrats had set up three successive parliamentary committees to advise on whether to allow Shell to return to Langkat and, if so, on what conditions. No decisions had been made. Djohan was in possession, but the Nirwonojudo faction and the Perbum Communist union were competing with him for control.

On his return to Jakarta, Harold Hutton put his question to General Ibnu, "Who's the boss?" Ibnu replied, "I am." There was no doubt about this. Before sending Hutton and Gohier to Pangkalan Brandan, the youthful-looking Ibnu had made sure that he had virtually absolute authority, both as army commander and director of a new government company set up to run the north Sumatran oil fields. The Indonesian cabinet, as part of Sukarno's most recent confiscations of all Dutch assets, in October 1956 had announced that its oil properties would not be returned to Shell. Instead, a government corporation would manage the fields under the jurisdiction of the army chief of staff, General Nasution, whose powers as war administrator he deputed to Brigadier General Ibnu Sutowo for the next fifteen years.

In north Sumatra, Ibnu's word was law. He had learned the oil business from the bottom up, but he ruled his oil fields with an iron hand from the top down. Ibnu's personal crusade was to build a national oil industry run by Indonesians for Indonesia. In the process, he became rich and powerful. Harold Hutton prospered with him. The slim, brown, Indonesian doctor and the thickset, ruddy-faced American became partners and lifelong friends.

MAKING OIL FLOW IN THE JUNGLE

Immediately after his initial handshake with Ibnu, Harold Hutton had started work to fulfill his side of the bargain. It was to be a dangerous as well as a complex and exciting undertaking. Four things were required most urgently. First, men, materials, and equipment were needed to help the Indonesians rebuild their north Sumatran oil production facilities, repair the refinery and the port, and re-open the roads and pipelines. This meant quickly building up an operating base in the oil fields with repair, road building, and as soon as possible, oil exploration facilities. Second, Harold would need a lot more money or credit than Refining Associates ever before had commanded to finance the purchase and shipment of these spare parts and new equipment required during the period before the oil started to flow; only then could Refining get paid with a share of the oil. Third, the Huttons must ensure that the oil, once it started to flow, could be sold on the world market. The risk, which potentially could prove fatal, was that Shell Oil Co. would take legal action to recover compensation for the seizure of its Sumatran assets. Fourth, it was necessary to establish back in Long Beach a sophisticated purchasing and ship-chartering agency. This agency was to be Betty Hutton's job. Competent managers had to be hired to handle what over the next thirty months would become a daily flow of 11,000 barrels out of Sumatra and a $5 million-a-month movement of supplies from the United States to Southeast Asia.

Getting his men and equipment into north Sumatra was Harold's first big challenge. He chose as team leader Walt Redman, a well-muscled and experienced chemist who had supervised the construction of the secondhand refinery Harold had shipped from Bakersfield to Thailand. The Indonesian army major chosen by Ibnu to secure north Sumatra against guerilla attack and rehabilitate its oil fields was Johannes M. Pattiasina. He and Harold took an instant liking to one another when they met in Medan. Probably the main reason for this bond was Harold Hutton's personal frankness and gregarious good humor, which contrasted sharply with the more formal manner and patronizing style that Indonesians had come to expect from European and American oilmen working in Asia in the 1950s. Harold had an ability to make people of all races and colors feel comfortable. He never put on airs. Describing his approach, the military attache at the U.S. Embassy, George Benson, who later was to become a senior advisor to Pertamina, said to one of the authors:

> If you had gone to central casting in search of a swashbuckling American oilman of the '50s, they would have brought out Harold Hutton. He was gruff, a little bit paunchy, but he didn't put on airs. He listened very carefully to what the Indonesians had to say. There was never any condescension or sense of color between them, as was the case among many Americans as well as Dutch in Southeast Asia at that time.[12]

For Major Pattiasina ("Patti"), his new American colleague's people skills were a crucial asset. Like Harold, he had been in the oil business since the early '30s, when Patti served an apprenticeship as a Shell Oil technician. During the Japanese occupation, he had been jailed, then released to help rebuild the Pladju refinery in south Sumatra. Patti recalls, "Mr. Hutton and I talked the same language, the oil-man language. I told him, 'if you want to succeed here, you must send someone who understands oil as much as I do.' So he sent Walter Redman to work with me."

Together, Redman and Patti faced up to the task of repairing the blown-up wells and rebuilding the burnt-out refinery with virtually none of the necessary materials, spare parts, or at first, many skilled technicians. Patti's solution, reflecting his earlier reconstruction of a number of small refineries destroyed in

---

12. Personal conversation with Sir Eldon Griffiths.

the Dutch police action of 1947, was to requisition all the scrap dealers' yards in the Medan district. From this heap of secondhand plate, pipe, and machinery, he recovered fifteen box loads of workable piston rods, pipe couplings, and other oil field iron that over the years had been sold as scrap.[13]

Working together, Patti's soldiers and Djohan's teams of *lasjkar minjak* undertook the heavy work of rehabilitating the oil fields. When they needed specialist advice or replacement parts, the Indonesians turned to Redman and the team of Americans he built up at Pangkalan Brandan. "Nearly all the equipment had been destroyed," wrote Patti, "so I had to repair them [sic] all, not only the pipelines but the oil tanks and jetties too, while all the time keeping guard to fend off the rebels."

It was backbreaking work in 100-degree heat with 90 percent humidity surrounded by flies, mosquitos, and water snakes. What was worse for the Americans, many of them young and working for the first time overseas, the local population had greeted them on arrival with a mixture of suspicion plus, in some cases, death threats. Leaders of the Perbum oil workers union portrayed the Americans as lackeys of Shell hired to take back the oil fields Djohan and his people had started to reclaim. At every stage, they encountered physical and bureaucratic obstacles that for months foiled even General Ibnu's attempts to cut through the red tape and subdue his own people's latent hostility to "palefaces."

The Americans, in turn, were appalled by the hideous poverty in which many of the local Indonesians were living. In a land of lush paddy-fields, palm trees laden with coconuts, and rivers filled with fish, they could not understand why so many children were as thin as matchsticks and so few people were over sixty. The reasons were not hard to find. Not only had the war and two subsequent Dutch police actions destroyed north Sumatra's oil industry, Sukarno's vainglorious mismanagement of independent Indonesia had made things ten times

---

13. Bartlett, *Pertamina*, 74.

worse. A country that under the Dutch had exported rice and sugar now had to import both to keep its people from starving. Only 20 percent of its cotton mills were working because of a lack of the cotton that Indonesia once produced in abundance. By every normal economic yardstick, Indonesia in the late 1950s was as bankrupt as it was again to become in the 1990s. And the human cost was painfully visible wherever Refican's oilies looked when they arrived in Pangkalan Brandan.

Slowly, the attitude of the poorly fed and badly housed Indonesian villagers changed. Looking back on his first encounter with "these men who looked like the Dutch but couldn't speak their language or ours," an old man at Pangkalan Brandan recalled the arrival of Walt Redman's crews in 1957:

> At first, the children were frightened by their thumbs-up signs and "Hi y'all" calls. Then they handed out candies and Coca-Colas. It was the first time we had seen this kind of drink. After a while we started to like it and the Americans.[14]

Another explanation of the Americans' success in overcoming the initial hostility of many Sumatrans was offered by one of the most admired of Indonesia's indigenous oil leaders, Julius Tahija, who ended up as president of Caltex.

Quoting a phrase that many of his older countrymen still use, "An American who speaks only English is better than a prejudiced European who speaks Indonesian," Tahija relates his own experience with a Dutch supervisor who was supposed to teach him about oil rigs but never found time to train him:

> I asked to be switched to an American. The difference was dramatic. Teaching me to handle oil rigs seemed to make him happy. The work required great strength. His huge hands turned the valves easily but I could not move them. The American laughed, "I have the muscle and you have the brains," I like the Dutch but I rarely heard them say anything kind about Indonesians' intelligence![15]

---

14. Personal conversation with Sir Eldon Griffiths.
15. Julius Tahija, *Horizon Beyond* (Singapore: Times Books International, 1995).

Tahija could have been describing Harold Hutton and his American oilies in the mid-1950s.

Working as a team, Patti's troops, Djohan's engineers, and Harold Hutton's oilies pressed forward with the task of clearing pipelines and re-opening pumps and valves:

> They welded, patched, clamped, hammered, soldered, fixed it with chewing gum and bailing wire—and put together a workable connection between the wells and storage tanks.[16]

Progress was painfully slow amid the torrential downpours and 100-degree heat, but the pace of recovery increased as supplies arrived from Long Beach. Harold had promised Ibnu that there would be no problems between the Americans and the Indonesians. And there weren't!

✳ ✳ ✳ ✳ ✳

In the wider context of U.S.-Indonesian relations, the spring and summer of 1958 was a time when the perception of most Indonesians with whom Walt Redman and his pioneers had been thrown together was that the United States was their enemy, even though the individual Americans working alongside them were colleagues and friends. The U.S. government or large parts of it had persuaded itself that President Sukarno was leading Indonesia into the Communist fold. Covertly, Washington had decided to arm and finance groups of military and ethnic secessionists in the outer islands against the central government in Java. One of the hot spots of this anti-government activity was Medan, the center of a coup by a flamboyant colonel, Simbolon, who proclaimed "a state of war and siege" in north Sumatra. Further south, in Bukit Tinggi, near the Caltex oil fields, his co-conspirator was Lt. Col. Alimed Hussein, whose exploits against the Dutch had earned him the nickname Tiger of Kuramji.

---

16. Bartlett, *Pertamina*, 149–150.

Hussein had ousted the Javanese governor and now declared himself in charge of central Sumatra.

Which side was the United States on—the rebellious colonels in Sumatra or the central government in Jakarta? Neither Harold nor Walt Redman—nor for that matter the U.S. Embassy in Jakarta—had any firm information. In Washington, Secretary Dulles saw in the colonels' revolt a made-to-measure opportunity to halt what he feared was Indonesia's drift towards Communism, if necessary by detaching the outer islands from Java. In March 1957, while Refining Associates' engineers were assembling in Medan, Dulles had despatched a senior U.S. diplomat, Gordon Mein, deputy director of the Office of South West Pacific Affairs, to assess the possibility of a breakup of Indonesia. Mein's secret report to Dulles listed the arguments in favor of the United States backing the separation of Sumatra. Among them were "the concentration of Communist strength in Java while the islands are anti-Communist"; the "high percentage of Indonesia's foreign exchange revenues arising from Sumatra's rubber, oil, perhaps tin, and other strategic raw materials"; and the fact that "Sumatra dominates the straits of Malacca."

Mein's conclusions, though unpublished until thirty years later, were leaked to most major oil companies within a year of his writing his report. They highlighted the difficult circumstances into which Refining Associates was about to plunge its people. "Sumatra," according to Mein, was "a sea of jungle with at least five distinct, mutually hostile, ethnic and cultural groups linked by a single circuitous road impassable in the rainy season." Referring to Atjeh province, where Harold had undertaken to set up drilling platforms, Mein told Secretary Dulles:

> Atjeh has already been for the past four years in armed rebellion against the central government. It appears unlikely that the fanatically Moslem Atjehnese would make their peace with the staunchly Christian Batiks and submit to any inter-regional Sumatran authority.

Mein's leaked report, to Harold Hutton's relief, recommended against U.S. intervention to separate Sumatra and the other outer islands from Java. But the CIA had different ideas. Unknown to the U.S. ambassador to Indonesia, its operatives had provided money and weapons to the rebel forces of Colonel Simbolon in Medan and Colonel Hussein in Bukit Tinggi. During the weeks and months immediately before Harold Hutton sent Walt Redman to Pangkalan Brandan, the CIA was covertly using U.S. submarines to land mortars and machine guns at small ports held by the rebels in northeast and south Sumatra. The same CIA-sponsored submarines took anti-Communist recruits for training at U.S. bases in Okinawa and Saipan. Heavier arms for the rebel forces were brought in by a freighter and barges from Taiwan.

Throughout the early months of 1958, at almost exactly the same time as Redman and his men started work in Pangkalan Brandan and Rantau, CIA-chartered aircraft—some flying direct from the Philippines and Thailand, others using the British air base in Singapore—delivered substantial quantities of guns and ammunition to the opponents of the Indonesian government for whose fledgling oil industry Refining Associates was working. "We heard rumors, but we knew nothing about this until much later," recalled one of the engineers, who served at Pangkalan Brandan. Fortunately for the Huttons, the colonels' revolt in Sumatra was quickly suppressed. The Indonesian army stayed loyal to its chief of staff, Nasution, a man who was to play a large part in the Huttons' future. Harold's men nonetheless were exposed to grave danger when crowds incited by PKI (Communist) and trade union leaders gathered in Medan to protest the arrival of a U.S. naval task force off Sumatra. The fleet was under orders to "protect American lives and property." Its presence actually placed the Refican team in Medan in far greater and more immediate danger.

Worse was to come. On May 18, 1958, a B-26 bomber conducted a raid against Ambon on the east Indonesian island of Amboina. After sinking an Indonesian naval vessel at its pier, the plane bombed a church and the central market, killing and wounding scores of civilians, before it was brought down and its pilot captured. He was an American, Allen L. Pope, carrying U.S. military identification papers. In his pocket were recently dated orders from his U.S. superiors and a current post exchange card for Clark Air Force Base in the Philippines. Pope's capture made it clear that the CIA, without the knowledge of the U.S. Embassy in Jakarta, was involved in armed support for those who wanted to see Indonesia dismembered.

For Walt Redman and his pioneers in north Sumatra, the Pope incident turned an already tense situation into one fraught with immediate peril. Harold, who made frequent trips to Medan to meet his men and inspect their progress with Major Patti, had to face the possibility that his Sumatran gamble was too dangerous and might have to be abandoned.

Betty Hutton's letters and diaries contain only passing references to these "problems between the U.S. and Indonesia." Harold, who did not want to alarm her about the hazards their men were facing, seems not to have shared his worries about the possible failure of their whole Indonesian venture. But Betty sensed what was happening. On April 26, 1958, she wrote what was in her heart: "I am so worried about Harold."

In the end, Nasution's paratroopers speedily recaptured Medan, restoring full authority to the Indonesian army and the central government in Java. The Huttons and their men breathed a collective sigh of relief. In Jakarta, President Sukarno's position for the time being had been restored. The U.S. ambassador urged Dulles to "give Indonesia another chance," as if it were in Washington's power to determine the vast archipelago's future. By the fall of 1958, the evidence was overwhelming that General Nasution and the Indonesian army, if not Sukarno, had the will and the power not only to tame the regional rebels but to beat back the Communists, too. The U.S. State Department, gravely embarrassed by the Pope incident, ponderously changed course. In place of its piecemeal support for anti-Communist insurrections in the outer islands,

American policy swung back to more diplomatic attempts to wean the Sukarno regime away from the Soviet bloc. Later, when that too failed, the United States ended up backing the Indonesian army, one of whose generals, Suharto, ten years later was to become the strongest—and most pro-Western—ruler Indonesia had ever seen.

* * * * *

Tensions in north Sumatra in the meantime had abated. Harold Hutton's engineers were able to get on with the job. Describing the situation in which they had to work, Major Pattiasina wrote the following to Sir Eldon Griffiths:

> The military situation was still dangerous, we had rebels wandering around in the jungle. I had to fight them to keep them from the oil rigs. We had to start rebuilding from scratch. We had to start with nothing. All we saw were ruins everywhere, completely blank. That's why I am grateful to Mr. Hutton. He helped me to get many things that I needed to do the work.

The distance from Long Beach to Medan in north Sumatra is 7,900 miles: nine time zones plus the twenty-four-hour change involved in crossing the International Date Line. The Huttons found it hard to manage their risk-laden new venture in Indonesia from a faraway office in California. Telephone connections were uncertain and often broke down. Telegrams and mail took days or weeks to arrive. Financial and manpower issues needed on-the-spot personal decisions and total immersion in the political and social culture of a world very different from that of inward-looking California of the 1950s.

Harold had also decided that his men and his company needed better and more reliable support than he so far had been able to provide. He made two important decisions: (1) the company must transfer its operating base to Singapore, and (2) its forward operations in Sumatra would also be better conducted from the safety of a ship at sea, rather than from its vulnerable Langkat office on land.

Singapore was the natural choice for the Huttons' forward base. Its chief advantage was that Singapore was very much nearer to Medan and the northeast Sumatran oil fields than Jakarta. Still a British crown colony in the early 1960s, Singapore also offered, then as now, a business and social environment vastly safer, more efficient, and more comfortable than anything to be found in the chaotic Indonesian capital. Telephone operators spoke English. The air conditioning rarely broke down. Singapore, too, was full of British bankers and traders, Chinese merchants, artisans, and agile-fingered seamstresses whose cheap but good-quality garments already were starting to attract a growing stream of tourists and American servicemen on leave from Korea and Vietnam.

Finding an appropriate place for Refican's headquarters in Singapore was not easy. Harold's daughter, Barbara, and her husband, Tom Chambers, undertook the search. Chambers, formerly general manager of an Oldsmobile dealership in Hollywood, married Barbara in Las Vegas, Nevada, and soon afterwards had been hired by Harold with a goal of setting up an automobile spare parts business in the Pacific islands. This was to be combined with a small oil refinery that Harold had in mind to build in Okinawa. To that end, the Chambers with two young children flew from Los Angeles to Okinawa in July 1959, arriving during a typhoon. Harold flew out a month later, but his plans for a refinery were quickly abandoned. Caltex had an unbreakable monopoly. Nor did it prove to be feasible to establish an auto-parts business. There was not enough demand for spare parts among the U.S. garrisons that Harold and Tom Chambers visited in either Okinawa or Guam.

Harold therefore transferred the Chambers family to Singapore. Tom was to become Refican's on-the-spot liaison between Harold and General Ibnu in Jakarta, using Singapore as his headquarters. And so it was that the Chambers located first a home for themselves and later one for Harold and Betty in Singapore.

The Chambers' home was in the exclusive Holland Park area. Harold first rented the home, then purchased it. Soon afterwards, with Joe Gohier's help, they found what Betty was looking for: a former British army officer's home in the Queen Astrid Park area of Singapore, whose concrete block houses still are known as "black and whites" because of the regulation color scheme bestowed on them by the military authorities. The house was cool and quiet, surrounded by a large garden with shade trees. The Huttons moved in at once, but within a year, as their business expanded, the company needed bigger quarters. Barbara Chambers found just what they needed: 28 Pierce Road, the retirement home of a former sea captain who had built in what was then a jungle-surrounded dell just outside the city center, a large stone-and-clapboard "dream house" complete with servants' quarters and a large swimming pool. The sea captain was prepared to lease but not to sell, even though Harold offered three times the asked-for rent in return for an option to buy at the best market price in six months' time. Not long afterwards, the sea captain died and his executors found the Huttons' offer on the dead man's desk. Two days later, Harold and Betty moved in as freehold owners of one of the most sought-after houses in Singapore in early June 1962.

* * * * *

Betty, meanwhile, had started to search California for a ship. The company needed a vessel big enough to carry its men and all but the heaviest equipment across the Makassar Strait from Singapore but small enough to get into the narrow waterways of the Sumatran coast. Such a ship would also serve as a floating hotel during times when it was unsafe for expatriates to go ashore in the still dangerous political circumstances of north Sumatra. Later on, as Harold developed the offshore drilling rights he had obtained under his contract with Ibnu, the ship could be equipped to do seismic surveys and provide support for his drilling barges.

The Huttons located a former U.S. Navy minesweeper that had been converted by a wealthy Los Angeles businessman, C. S. Jones, into a luxury yacht. Built and launched towards the end of World War II, the *Destination,* as the minesweeper had been renamed, was a 268-ton vessel of all-wood construction

Harold's oilies in newly independent Indonesia: back-breaking work in 100-degree heat

with a relatively shallow (eleven-foot, four-inch) draft that would allow it to steam into most of the larger creeks along the north Sumatra coast. Harold made a flying trip to see the *Destination,* which was berthed in the marina at Mazatlan on the southwest coast of Mexico. He liked what he saw: a sleek but sturdy ocean-going cruiser, powered by twin 8-cylinder General Motor diesels rated at 500 horsepower apiece, whose 126-foot length and 24.5 foot beam provided ample cargo space on the deck and below for all but the bulkiest items. His surveyors valued the vessel at $75,000, subject to its being returned to Long Beach for inspection and overhaul. Three months later, the *Destination* would set off for Southeast Asia and its new role as the Huttons' operations base and support vessel off Sumatra.

To finance the rapidly growing shipments of materials and equipment for the Sumatran oil fields, Refinate, as Refining Associates now was known, needed something more than a Singapore base and a ship. The company must have more cash. The Huttons' fortunes had improved with the worldwide rise of prices for crude oil that followed the Suez crisis. At a June board meeting in 1957, Harold was able to announce an increase in sales from just under $2 million for the year ended June 1956 to some $9.8 million for the year ending June 1957. Betty's minutes reflected the board's decision:

> In recognition of the extra work that the Thai refinery and the new
> Indonesian contract involved, the chairman was awarded a bonus
> of $6,000. This bonus was considered under normal, but necessary
> to conserve cash reserves at the present time.

As secretary, she too got a raise. Her hourly rate was increased to $5.50, "in recognition of her increased responsibilities in handling overseas contracts."

But while 1957 and 1958 continued the improvement in Refinate's revenues, Harold now was spending large sums to support his side of the contract with Ibnu. To meet Walt Redman and Major Patti's ever-increasing calls for more equipment and manpower, the company needed to raise more cash and credit. Harold and Betty met with their bankers.

They were not helpful. Though the port of Los Angeles was expanding rapidly, most of the bankers Harold knew were unfamiliar with overseas business. They were unsympathetic toward his need for ever-larger loans collateralized on forward contracts underwritten by people with foreign-sounding names in far off places. The U.S. Export Import Bank was of little help either. Indonesia's credit rating was zero. Taxation was another problem. The Internal Revenue Service required U.S. companies operating abroad to present their accounts in conformity with American practice, even though, in many cases, foreign countries' methods of preparing and presenting accounts differed so widely that it could cost thousands of hours of work by lawyers, accountants, and translators to conform to U.S. regulations. Nor was Harold enamored by the prospect of paying tax twice, once in Indonesia, which had no tax treaty with the United States and little prospect of negotiating one, and a second time back home where the United States required all its citizens to pay taxes on their overseas operations as if they were being conducted in America.

Harold and Betty sought advice. They were advised to set up a foreign corporation outside IRS jurisdiction. Canada was the obvious choice in 1958. Harold and Betty flew to Toronto, where two Canadian lawyers, Ronald Merriam and Paul Hewitt, completed the formalities for a new company, Refining Associates (Canada) Ltd. Refican, as it became known, henceforth would conduct the Huttons' overseas business under Canadian law, which at the time was far less rigorous than that of the United States with respect to overseas profits. Jimmy Perkins and Ernie Moyer became vice presidents. Betty was named as Refican's corporate secretary.

Thanks to their success in Thailand, the Bank of America extended the Huttons' lines of credit to cover extra monthly purchases up to $250,000 but this was nowhere near sufficient to meet their needs for cash. To keep the Indonesian contract with General Ibnu alive, Joe Gohier arranged and financed the first shipments of material to Medan from his own resources in Singapore.

Back in Long Beach, Harold and Betty hustled up every dollar of extra credit they could find.

Elated by the prospects, excited by the risks, Harold one day proposed that they remortgage the new house they had built in Villa Park to obtain an extra $30,000. Betty was not pleased. Her imagination too had been stirred, but it was only with the greatest reluctance that she agreed to risk her home for the business. It was the biggest personal gamble of her life. One of her family's bankers, an old friend of the Spennettas to whom Harold had turned, commented that it was the only occasion when he saw Betty in tears. Years later, she confided, "I knew very little at the time about Indonesia. But I knew Harold, so I backed *him*."

The Huttons' gamble in Indonesia was eventually to pay off handsomely. For several years, however, the outcome was uncertain. One of their closest associates said later, "When they got started in Indonesia, their total net worth in the world was half a million dollars, including their home. That is all they had and they committed every penny." Tom Chambers, Harold's son-in-law, added a further comment: "They both knew this would make or break them, but Harold talked Betty into it. He was a great salesman."

The Huttons' first oil shipment leaves Sumatra on the Shozui Maru

A LARGE LEGAL SPANNER IN THE WORKS

The rain was tilting down in buckets, as it nearly always does just before or after lunch in Singapore, when Harold Hutton in early April 1958 got a delayed telex message from Walt Redman in Medan. The first oil from the Rantau field had started to flow. Section one of the battered old refinery the Refican men had helped repair at Pangkalan Brandan was ready to go back on stream.

Working sixteen hours a day in double shifts, Patti's troops and Djohan's workers had opened enough of the Aceh and Rantau wells to feed the pipelines that led to the stills. As a bonus, Redman and Patti had also restored the prewar Shell Company golf course at Langkat. Both Patti and Ibnu, who flew into Langkat in his helicopter, were soon to become passionate golf players. Each left a set of clubs at the numerous courses in California, Indonesia, and Japan where the Huttons henceforth would entertain them. But business always came first. Whenever Patti played a round at the restored course at Langkat with the Americans, he recalled:

> I would explain to Walter what materials and tools I needed and he would get onto Harold. Then Harold would send me the latest models, the best equipment available, every single one of them I wanted.

The oil that started to flow from the Rantau field in April 1958 proved to be an exceptional quality—waxy Katapa crude with minimal quantities of sulphur, "so pure that you could run a Volkswagen on it," said one of Harold's oilies. As the number 1 storage tank above the port of Susu started to fill, Harold made arrangements with a Japanese company to charter a small shallow-draft tanker to sail to Sumatra to load his first cargo of Indonesian oil. Despite the political storm clouds and the hostility of Perbum officials in Medan, General Ibnu's dream of a wholly owned Indonesian national oil company producing its own oil seemed to be at the point of being realized. The Huttons could start to contemplate the first returns on their go-for-broke investment.

It was then that Refican's lawyers tossed what Betty described as a "large spanner into the works." Harold, at her urging, had asked a Washington law firm to look over the simple two-page contract he had signed with General Ibnu. The lawyer picked out a critical clause on which the Huttons in effect had bet their fortune and future. He warned that it might not stand up to challenge in U.S. or Japanese courts. The dubious clause read as follows:

> Seller represents that the oil to be produced from the above property and the right of the Seller to deliver the same as free and clear of encumbrances or other obligations, and the Seller hereby guarantees the title to all crude oil delivered thereunder.

As the authors of *Pertamina* reported, the Seller's (i.e., Ibnu's) ability to offer this guarantee rested on the Indonesian government's regulation number 34 of 1956. This asserted its "authority over" the north Sumatra oil fields, but in the lawyers' eyes "authority over" was not the same thing as "ownership." Shell Oil Co., the prewar concessionaire, had located and developed the oil field. Its title to the oil had never been formally assumed by Indonesia or abandoned by Shell. On this basis, shipments of oil produced in Rantau could be subject to seizure by Shell.

For Harold Hutton this was a bombshell. He and Betty had invested all they owned in north Sumatra and were heavily in debt. Their men in the field had worked hard and braved serious hazards for eighteen months on the project. And now, suddenly, the Huttons were faced with advice that their guarantee clause was defective. It followed that no shipping line would carry their oil out of Sumatra without high-priced insurance coverage that Refican could not afford.

As Harold waited to board the next available plane for Indonesia to share the bad news with Ibnu, Joe Gohier phoned from Jakarta. One of Ibnu's aides, Major Harijono, who previously had recommended a Greek company, Sea Oil & Gas, instead of Refining Associates as Pertamina's partner, was urging that the Huttons' contract be canceled and switched to Harijono's friends in Athens. "Harijono, a political animal, gave me an ultimatum of one week to remove the legal obstacles," Gohier recalled in a letter to Sir Eldon Griffiths. Harold told him to "stall." Gohier therefore took Harijono on an all-expenses paid jaunt to Singapore where the two men would await news of the cloud over Refican's title being cleared. Harold meanwhile arrived in Jakarta worried, though he did not show it, that his luck was running out. His home as well as his company was on the line. General Ibnu, however, was unmoved. He appreciated the fact that Harold neither whined nor made excuses, but his only comment was, "You are the ones with experience, you solve the problem. Your share of the oil is yours once you load it into your tankers."

How Refican and the Indonesians solved this problem and avoided Harijono's threatened deadline offers a classic example of legal, diplomatic, and political intrigue of the kind that oil politics thrives on.

Urged on by Joe Gohier, the Indonesian army's judge-advocate general already had worked out a simple if drastic "solution." To this officer, Dr. Basarudin Nasution, the answer lay in the State of War and Siege Law, in effect in Indonesia since March 1958. This gave the army chief of staff the power to promulgate ordinances in lieu of parliamentary law. It was typical of Indonesia that the chief of staff was the judge-advocate's brother, General A.H. Nasution.

Apprised of the risk to Indonesia's first national oil shipment to Japan, General Nasution immediately agreed to use his powers to revoke the Shell concessions. The revocation was drafted, discussed with Prime Minister Djuanda, who initialed his approval, and issued on February 1, 1958. This came as a surprise to both President Sukarno and the Indonesian parliament who, according to Gohier, knew nothing of it until Nasution's order was promulgated.

The effect of this high-handed edict was to cancel the Shell concession and take ownership of the designated oil fields, including north Sumatra. For Ibnu Sutowo, that was the end of the matter, but within a month the repercussions had spread far beyond Indonesia. As recounted in *Pertamina*,[17] the British Embassy in Jakarta claimed compensation on behalf of Shell. The Indonesian Foreign Office did not understand what had happened or why:

> [When] the diplomats called . . . for an explanation at the Foreign Office, [the Advocate General] faced a battery of a dozen lawyers and officials. Basarudin [Nasution] argued successfully that the emergency War and Siege Law prevailed [over Shell's concession contract].

Once explained, the Foreign Office accepted this.

> [But] what could they [tell] the attorneys at the British embassy to establish a justification for taking these Shell properties? [The Army's] answer was that the Dutch had abandoned these areas in 1942 with [their] scorched-earth policy. Thereafter they never reoccupied these areas. [Djohan's] local workers had [also] been in occupation of the fields for the past 15 years.

All that remained to discuss was compensation.

For Harold Hutton there was a larger question. What would be Shell Oil's reaction? The big Anglo-Dutch company decided to test the Huttons' nerve, wrote Professor Bartlett:

> Two of its senior men flew from the Hague to meet them in Los Angeles. Over dinner they asked Harold Hutton if he was serious in his intention to purchase oil from the new Indonesian company. Harold said he was. After dinner the Shell representatives and the Huttons shook hands and went their separate ways.

Meanwhile in Tokyo, a Japanese import company, probably with Shell's support, sought an injunction barring the landing of Refican's oil on grounds

---

17. Bartlett, *Pertamina*, 145.

that its title was defective. The Huttons engaged a Japanese attorney who had won a major case involving the revocation of another international company's oil leases in the Middle East. Copies of the Indonesian constitution and General Nasution's revocation ordinance were translated from Indonesian to English to Japanese and telexed to him from Jakarta. Harold's attorney then moved that the hearing be moved out of Tokyo, away from the gaze of the Japanese government and the embassies of Britain, the Netherlands, and the United States, all of which were concerned about preventing any upstart company from profiting from the Indonesians' confiscation of foreign investment without compensation. The case was tried at a remote port in the province of Kainan where Harold had arranged for his first ship to be unloaded. This proved to be a very smart move. The local magistrates ruled against outside interference with badly needed Japanese imports and, by inference, in favor of Refican.

That was enough for Harold. Without waiting to see if Shell would appeal—they did not—he radioed the captain of the small shallow-draft Japanese tanker, the *Shozui Maru,* that was to load Pertamina and Refican's first shipment of national oil. "Safe to proceed," he said. Harold also telephoned Joe Gohier in Singapore to tell him that he no longer needed to keep plying Major Harijono with liquor and girlfriends. Refican's title had been cleared. No longer was there any risk of Ibnu canceling the Huttons' contract. The legal spanner had been removed.

Betty poses with troops for Harold's camera

PART VII   THEIR ASIAN EMPIRE

HARD SLOGGING IN THE
SWAMPS AND RAINFORESTS

May 24, 1958, the day the Huttons shipped Refining's first small tanker load of oil out of Pangkalan Susu, was an important occasion for Indonesia. This was the first Indonesian oil produced and wholly owned by an Indonesian oil company for the benefit, according to the constitution, of the Indonesian people.

General Ibnu was delighted. Looking back on the first shipment at a ceremony of Jakarta's university, where he received an honorary degree, he used unaccustomedly flowery language:

> This first export of 1,700 tons of crude oil was an historical day for Indonesia. It gave proof that we could develop our country's natural resources ourselves, for the sake of our national development . . . From then on, we were in a position to promote the further growth of our own company. The spirit of development caught fire.

For the Huttons, the occasion was more hazardous than heroic. The day dawned warm and overcast. By 10 A.M. it was humid as a laundry. Lead-colored clouds dripped fat raindrops onto the muddy green surface of the mile-wide creek that separates Pangkalan Susu, then as now little more than a huddle of tin shacks, mud huts, and a leaky storage tank, from the mango swamps and forest that stretch to the horizon on the opposite shore. The channel to the open sea and the nearby Malacca Straits was littered with underwater wrecks. Most had lain there, uncharted, since the bombers of World War II, British, Australian, and American, came swooping in from their aircraft carriers to deprive the Japanese Empire of its Sumatran oil.

Harold and Betty arrived at the jetty in midmorning, together with Joe Gohier and Jimmy Perkins. They were escorted by heavily armed troops and Ibnu's representatives, Major Harijono and Major Pattiasina. Patti recalled:

> There were still plenty of rebels about on the islands. I had therefore placed my soldiers and several gunboats to guard the tanks and the jetty. My men were also on guard along the pipeline all the way from Pangkalan Brandan to the harbor, so it was safe for the first shipment.

Only one of the patched-up pipelines as yet was carrying oil, but the tank overlooking the harbor was full and a hose connected it to the rusty little Japanese tanker tied up at the jetty. A dribble, then a steady stream of crude oil had been flowing into the tanker for several days before the Huttons arrived. Now, at a signal from the ship's engineer, the valves were closed. All three tanks on board the *Shozui Maru* were full.

"Time to go," said Harold, urging Patti to precede him up the gang plank.

"Harold, this is your first shipment and ours but I cannot come with you," Patti told him. "I have to stay here to make sure your next ones are safe. We have to keep up our guard. The pumps must keep on working, day and night. If they stop, the next shipment of Indonesian oil will be delayed."

A watery sun broke through the clouds as the four Americans and Major Harijono climbed aboard. Colonel Pattiasina saluted. Harold clambered up the gang plank with difficulty. Weeks of strain and jet lag were starting to take their toll on a body already feeling the effects of smoking and drinking. Not so for Betty Hutton. Trim and cool in pale blue dungarees, she said hello to the tanker's captain, who bowed low in Japanese fashion. Betty then took a turn around the deck snapping pictures over the rail before going below to inspect the quarters where the Huttons, Gohier, and Perkins were to spend the next three weeks. The *Shozui Maru* cast off, heading for a gap in the mango-covered sand spit through which it needed to pass to reach the open sea and the long slow journey to Japan.

An anxious moment came as the small tankers moved closer to the opposite side of the creek. Major Harijono urged the Americans to take shelter on the starboard side in case the guerrillas, thought to be lurking there, opened fire. Joe Gohier made notes. Jimmy Perkins joked. Harold Hutton smoked. Betty was taking photographs when, suddenly, from the bridge came a shout, "Smoke ahead!"

Through their binoculars, the Huttons could see a thin column of smoke rising over the spit behind which a bigger tanker lay at anchor. For a while, it looked as if this vessel might be on fire. Had it been attacked by rebels? Not until the *Shozui Maru* rounded the offshore spit and came in sight of the bigger ship was it clear what was happening. An Indian crewman had lit a brazier on its deck to cook his evening *chapattis*. The pillar of smoke had risen when the chef had used a hose pipe to douse the still-glowing coals.

The Huttons went ashore from the *Shozui Maru* in Singapore. It took the little tanker twenty-one days to complete its passage to Japan along what in those days was the most hazardous coastline in Asia, through the pirate-infested Malacca Straits, across the stormy South China Sea, then north along the coast of China where Chiang Kai-shek's Nationalist forces on the Quemoy and Matsu islands still were exchanging gunfire with the Communists on the mainland. In years to come, the Huttons were to navigate portions of this route many times in far smaller vessels, prospecting for oil and fish. But for now, as General Ibnu put it, their voyage in the *Shozui Maru* "opened a door and a new chapter" in east Asia's economic history. "It enabled Indonesia's own oil to flow to the rest of the world."

Shipping Indonesia's first national oil cargo to Japan was the beginning of a trade that gave the Huttons greater satisfaction and earned them far more millions than Harold in his most ebullient moments had dreamed of or promised Betty when they met in the desert at Palm Springs.

It was also the start, though only a start, of the redevelopment of the oil fields in north Sumatra and Aceh. Refican now had the task of working with the newly promoted Colonel Patti in Sumatra and Ibnu in Jakarta to rapidly step up the flow of crude oil from the existing Rantau wells and drill onshore and offshore for more. Patti by now had met Betty. They got along very well. Patti once commented, "The Huttons wanted to have steady, regular profits from the oil we produced. That was natural and fair, but they always sent me the best equipment and materials and no questions asked."

Jakarta was a different matter. Harold and Tom Chambers took on the frustrating job of maintaining contacts with the rapidly changing membership of the Sukarno government, and more profitably, maintaining Ibnu Sutowo's trust. Throughout 1959 and 1960, Harold flew in and out of Jakarta, staying at a company apartment in the diplomatic quarters. He became a familiar figure in the clubs and bars that American oilmen frequented.

At the U.S. Embassy, Harold got to know George Benson, a Korean War veteran recently appointed as U.S. military attache. Benson's wife was studying Indonesian. In her class was Ibnu's wife, Sally Sutowo, who was learning to speak English. When they met Harold, the two women took an instant liking to the blue-eyed Californian with his gruff drawl and inexhaustible store of oil-patch stories. Sally Sutowo was to become one of the Huttons' best friends.

To get to Refican's field headquarters in the Langkat compound in Pangkalan Brandan, Harold had to make frequent 2,000-mile round-trip flights from Jakarta and back. Quarrels between Indonesia and Singapore made it impractical for him to make the five times shorter "puddle-jump" across the Makassar Straits direct to Medan from Singapore. But Harold and, before long, Betty never failed to visit their men in the Sumatran jungle where Refican was now starting to drill.

A succession of the company's geologists, engineers, construction men, drillers, and roughnecks had followed Walt Redman to Singapore from the United States. Among them, in addition to Tom Chambers, were James (Jimmy) Perkins, who was to take over as the chief operating officer in California, and another of Harold's vice presidents, Ernest Moyer, a chemist who visited the oil fields two or three times a year while serving as head of purchasing in Long Beach. Joe Gohier's office manager, Franz Herrnsdorf, a Dutch-American, took charge of the Jakarta office.

Conditions in Sumatra were rough. The men flew from Jakarta to Medan on airplanes that were poorly maintained and subject to ground fire from rebels. In times of political crisis—"which means most of the time," Harold warned them—they would often be held up for several days or even weeks at a time. Once in Medan, the Americans could never be sure of finding transport to Susu or the oil fields. "The roads were unbelievably bad," said Willie Chapman, an engineer. "Very narrow with wet clay, no bridges, black ooze, and landslips."

Working with Walt Redman was a small army of Indonesians, Australians, and a score of American oilies. The head of the Sumatran office, until Betty set up Refican's administrative headquarters in Singapore, was the gruff and likeable Arkansan, Jimmy Perkins. Jimmy, like Harold, would figure out the details of what to do and how to do it on the back of paper napkins that he then filed away in his office. Perkins loved working with numbers, which made him closer to Betty than to Harold. He impressed the Indonesians with his capacity to write shorthand. He subsequently became, with Betty, the effective head of the company's worldwide procurement business. He was a man with a quick temper but much respected by his staff.

Ernie Moyer was quieter than either Perkins or Redman. His face still showed the scars of a chemical fire in which he had been badly burned before joining Refican. Moyer, a chemical engineer, was described by one of his contemporaries as "the guy who walks about talking about viscosity." He took charge over the next decade of the technical aspects of Refican's operations in Sumatra.

Joe Gohier, the quick-witted, hardheaded, and charming Belgian-American, became Refican's indispensable link to the Indonesian army and oil company bureaucrats whose language Gohier spoke fluently, whose reactions he could anticipate, whose quixotic demands and desires he instinctively knew how to handle.

Wilson ("Willie") Chapman came to the company in 1960 after a wartime career flying B-26s in North Africa and B-29s out of China on raids over Japan. Willie was hired as "the engineering department." For several years he was the only person in it. On his first trip to north Sumatra, Walter Redman asked, "How long do you plan to stay?"

Willie answered, "Until the job's done."

Walt replied, "That is a change. Once they've seen this place, the first thing most guys ask is how soon they can go home."

Harold gave Chapman the job of drawing the blueprints and helping to supervise construction of a gas plant and carbon black plant near Susu and a small new refinery at Pakning. He spent most of his time in the Long Beach office but like Moyer visited Sumatra several times each year, living in the company's cottages at Brandan and Rantau and construction huts at Pakning. From time to time, he encountered hostile bands of Communists. Colonel Patti provided Willie with an armed escort and drove ahead of him on one such occasion when fighting threatened to break out. Patti's truck was ambushed. Chapman's sailed past unscathed.

Another of Refican's managers, a contemporary of Willie Chapman's, was Bill Merrill, a geophysicist and registered engineer who had worked in oil companies all over the Pacific before he joined Refican. Harold put Merrill in charge of the operations at Susu. His main task was to keep port operations moving. Merrill landed a Refican construction team and its heavy equipment on the mangrove-covered island opposite the jetty from which the *Shozui Maru* had sailed. Clearing forty acres of the jungle where guerrillas previously lurked, the team built a repair yard for the company's boats and warehouses where higher-priced equipment and materials could be held until they were moved upcountry.

Merrill also repaired the sagging jetty at Susu. Lacking structural steel to replace the struts and pilings, he and Pattiasina scavenged hundreds of Dutch-built metal lampposts from local scrap yards.

As oil production increased and Refican made plans to drill more wells and build larger downstream facilities, an urgent task was to rebuild the road between Belawan, the port of Medan, and Pangkalan Brandan and hence to the dock at Susu. Harold made a deal with one of his neighbors in Singapore. Near the front gate of the Huttons' home on Pierce Road was an enormous tree that overhung the entrance to the drive of their next-door neighbor, a contractor named Koh Bock Thye. One morning, a short Chinese man knocked on Harold's door to ask if he could cut down the tree. The two men got involved in an animated conversation about the political situation in Indonesia. Harold asked his Chinese visitor, Koh Bock Thye, if his firm would be interested in building roads in Sumatra. When Koh said he would, Harold made arrangements for him to travel to Medan. "Aren't you going to tell him if he can cut down the tree?" asked one of Harold's secretaries. "Not until he tells me that he'll fix my roads in Sumatra," replied Harold.

Koh Bock Thye was nervous about his first visit to Sumatra. Between Indonesia and Singapore in the early 1960s, there was a state of near war arising from President Sukarno's suspicion that the island's British bases were still being used by the CIA to support secessionists in Sumatra. "No problem," said Harold, "we'll sign you on as a deck hand on one of my boats. That will make you an American when you go ashore."

Met in Belawan by Pattiasina's troops, Koh Bock Thye and Willie Chapman were joined by a Refican site engineer, a tough American named Lein Uttecht, who spoke fluent Indonesian. Uttecht strapped them into his Land Rover and set off into the jungle. "Where is the road?" asked Koh Bock Thye as they plunged into a ravine. "You're on it," replied Uttecht, a man with "muscles of iron, a head like teak and a heart of gold," according to one of his associates.

It took twelve hours to navigate the track from Medan and Susu. Several times the Land Rover got stuck in deep black mud. Uttecht would scramble out and lash a cable around a rubber tree so the vehicle could haul itself clear. Once it slid into a hole big enough to drown a bus. "Be careful or you will bury us," said Koh. "If I bury you, I'll bury you deep" was Uttecht's reply as, covered in slime, he revved up the engine and foot by foot juddered up out of the hole.

Koh Bock Thye eventually agreed to undertake the job of relaying and resurfacing the roads that Colonel Patti's troops were digging out. His geologists located suitable quarries for rock and large deposits of gravel and sand. Harold then started ferrying Koh's plant and machinery into Susu, while teams of barefoot Indonesians unloaded thousands of tons of cement brought in by surplus U.S. Navy landing craft. Refican also built an asphalt plant to provide tar for the road surface, but because of the high clay content of the soil, oil-based materials proved unsuitable. Koh Bock Thye solved the problem by mixing dry cement with the existing soil to form the road's foundations. The Indonesians and Harold's men then poured thick, heavy asphalt on top of the cement mixture and rolled it, mile after mile, to create the first paved road to be built in northern Sumatra since the Dutch left in 1941.

Once the highway and Port Susu were completed, Refican's operations in 1960 moved into high gear. Building a carbon black plant to utilize waste gases from the stills at Pangkalan Brandan was a major job, requiring the import of large quantities of specialized machinery. Environmentalists would soon make it impossible to operate these smoke-belching plants in North America, Western Europe, and Japan, but with the demand for carbon black, a key element in tire manufacturing, rising sharply among the world's car makers, less-developed countries like Indonesia were more concerned with earning foreign exchange than they were with protecting their air quality. Over the next ten years, the Huttons' carbon black plant at Pakning proved to be one of Refican's most profitable investments. Next came the drum-making plant, another successful investment. Its thousands of moving parts, many bought secondhand,

Perhaps the first American woman to visit north Sumatra after World War II

were procured in the United States and shipped to Medan and Susu in surplus U.S. Navy landing craft.

Refican's drillers meanwhile moved onto a dozen sites in the steamy interior. Some were completely inaccessible except by barges along the waterways. Exploring for oil in these circumstances was the kind of work—rough, tough, and dangerous—that earned Harold's roughnecks top dollar wages, free of U.S. income tax. Not all of them could handle the job. Some gave up and went home. Others got drunk every night. But most enjoyed the hard work and camaraderie of the jungles. They also got on well with the Indonesians, as Harold had promised General Ibnu his men would do.

Betty Hutton made her first visit to her husband's Sumatra operations in 1962. In her Christmas letter to her family she wrote:

> From Pangkalan Susu to Rantau by Land Rover for overnight stay and a tour of gasoline and carbon plants, pump maintenance shop, road construction, etc. Next day back to Brandan guest house for a visit to lube plant, oxygen plant, trumble plant and Pertamina's IBM computer division. Most surprised to find them now processing their inventories and payroll.

The next morning the Huttons embarked in a Trojan speedboat to visit Refican's more inaccessible drilling sites in the jungle. The wash of the Trojan disturbed crocodiles basking along the banks of the broad green Lepan River. Flocks of colored birds rose from the bayous, gibbons yammered in the mango trees. Occasionally the boat passed groups of huts and canoes gathered around small stick-like jetties. Harold shot hundreds of photos. Betty wrote to her mother:

> Very early by speed boat to Charcoal Landing. The jungle trip to Sungaidung camp and No. 1 drilling location was a never to be forgotten experience. We traveled along a path, sometimes up, sometimes down hill through swamps of thick black oozing mud, clear over our boot tops. Thick jungle on each side of the path but occasionally a small clearing with a native hut and people living out in the middle of nowhere.

It took a three-hour march along this jungle path before, sweat-drenched, dirty, and thirsty, the Huttons reached a knoll above the trees where in bright sunshine Betty saw Refican's camp and down the trail, a couple of miles further, its Number 1 drilling site. Betty continued her thoughts to her mother:

> Our men are busy rigging up, trying to get all their materials moved
> in and the rig set up before the rains really set in. It is a marvel how
> these drilling locations can be set up in spite of the obstacles.

Back on the river, the Huttons continued upstream past long stretches of fish traps. The Trojan's wake rocked dug out canoes propelled by naked paddlers, sending strange-looking water birds skittering across acre after acre of water lilies. Apart from the roar of the engine, there was an all-encompassing silence. Harold tried to fish with no luck. They were moving too fast. Betty took photographs before they ate lunch and drank cold beer. Her diary notes:

> We reached the drum plant and gas plant. The men were pleased to
> see us but frustrated. Work had stopped on both plants, due to lack
> of steel.

This was one of the innumerable occasions when the presence of Betty Hutton, most likely the first and probably the only American woman to visit the drilling sites in north Sumatra in the early 1960s, worked wonders for the roughnecks' morale. She and Harold spent the afternoon chatting with the men about their homes and families. She noted:

> They all came up with mail and final messages prior to our departure.
> I hated to wave goodbye as we set off down the trail and finally got
> back to the landing where the Trojan was waiting.

Tokyo When the Yen Was Cheap

T he delivery by the Huttons of the tanker *Shozui Maru*'s first cargo of crude oil to Japan enhanced Refican's stature in both Jakarta and Tokyo. General Ibnu now had his first international outlet for nationally owned Indonesian oil. Both sides were starting to deliver what Harold and he had agreed on. As world market prices rose, especially for north Sumatra's light Katapa crude, the profitability of their business sharply increased. The two men's relationship expanded and prospered. Both became multimillionaires. Mutual trust reinforced common interests. From now on, the Huttons were to occupy a special place in Ibnu's thinking. Their families became friends and henceforth each would go out of their way to look after the other.

Harold had also won the confidence of the still small but rapidly growing Japanese oil import industry. Refican was a major supplier to the Fuji Kosan company with which Harold had been doing business since he sold them his first barrels of U.S. war-surplus grease. "The Japanese returned the compliment," said Betty. Harold played golf with chairman Sugimoto Yoshida, whose enthusiasm for the game lasted until he fell dead on one of Tokyo's new courses in 1974. Another Fuji Kosan man, Frank Iwase, became Refican's agent in Tokyo, serving the Huttons loyally until Harold died. One of Fuji Kosan's biggest Japanese customers was the Kobayashi Group, headed by senior industrialist M. A. Kobayashi, who as chairman of the Japanese War Reparations Commission for Indonesia was responsible for assessing compensation for World War II property damage inflicted by Japanese troops.

Reparations to Indonesia were nowhere near as substantial as those paid by Japan for the vastly greater devastation and atrocities its forces had inflicted on China. Many Indonesians, after all, had greeted the Japanese as "liberators" and in many cases had actively collaborated in trying to restore production during the occupation. As reparations commissioner, Kobayashi paid frequent visits to Jakarta. He soon echoed Harold's views about the "complementarity" of the Japanese and Indonesian economies. Japan needed the minerals, lumber, tropical fruits, and oil the vast archipelago could produce. Indonesia, in turn, required the capital, technology, and markets Japan could make available.

In 1957, an old Indonesian hand, Mr. S. Nishijima, joined Kobayashi's commission. Nishijima had represented a major Japanese trading company in Jakarta before the war and spoke the language fluently. During the Japanese occupation of Indonesia, he served as a liaison officer for the Imperial Navy in Jakarta and got to know many of the leaders of the Indonesian freedom movement. Jailed by the victorious allies as a suspected war criminal, Nishijima was back in Indonesia by the mid-1950s as a purchasing officer for a Japanese group that was looking for liquified petroleum gas.

Nishijima met General Ibnu at about the same time as another Japanese group approached Pertamina with an offer to send a team of geologists and engineers to search out new energy sources. As soon as the Japanese realized that they were competing against one another, they re-organized into a single investment consortium, the North Sumatra Oil Development Corporation Co., Ltd. (NOSODECO), with Kobayashi as its chairman.

Ibnu consulted Harold Hutton about NOSODECO. Harold found himself in the middle, since Kobayashi had already invited him to brief the Japanese on Refican's experiences in north Sumatra. Harold responded favorably, if tersely, to Kobayashi's enquiries about Ibnu and the problems of doing business in Sumatra. The Japanese evidently needed all the encouragement he could offer. A report by the Kobayashi survey team had revealed good prospects for oil and gas both on and off the shore of north Sumatra, but Kobayashi was still apprehensive about the political and security risks of a country where only recently Japan had been both occupier and loser.

NOSODECO's advisors also shared the views of both the Japanese foreign office and the U.S. State Department that Indonesia under Sukarno was tilting towards Communism and more than likely would plunge into economic chaos. "Whoever entered this political and financial wonderland would need some exceptional faith in Indonesia's long term future and a great need for Indonesian oil."[18]

To what extent the Japanese were influenced by Harold Hutton's example in risking all he had to overcome these difficulties is hard to judge. It is certain that Ibnu in the course of his efforts to persuade Kobayashi to invest in Sumatra made much of the willingness of an American independent to cast his lot with Indonesia. Harold told Ibnu that the Japanese with whom he had done business negotiated long and hard but stuck to their word once they'd given it, and invariably paid on time. In a comment to a friend he added that the Japanese in Indonesia were like "blind cats in a meat shop, they don't know which way to turn."[19]

He offered Refican's help on Ibnu's visits to Japan. Refican provided a car and chauffeur and a suite at the Imperial Hotel that helped Ibnu maintain an independent stance during the protracted negotiations that followed with Kobayashi. Whatever Ibnu needed in Tokyo during the days before the Indonesian national oil company became a power in its own right, Harold and Betty Hutton made sure that he got.

Harold's advice on negotiating with the Japanese undoubtedly helped Ibnu during the innumerable trips to and from Tokyo the Indonesian was to make in the early 1960s. The association between Japanese capital and Indonesian oil was to become a major factor in east Asian trade and industry. When this association frayed in the 1990s as Japanese companies withdrew large sums of

---

18. Bartlett, *Pertamina*, 155.
19. Grant (Buck) Buchanan, then a Fluor executive in Singapore.

the liquid capital they held in Indonesia and largely ceased to invest more, Indonesia came to collapse. The relationship began in earnest when the Japanese government agreed to provide $53 million in credit for the purchase by the still virtually bankrupt Indonesians of oil-field equipment, materials, and technical assistance. In return, Japan was to get a 40 percent share of the increase in crude oil production above a target figure of 36 million barrels in the fields it was pledged to develop. Ibnu still insisted on the same kind of agreement with NOSODECO as he had pioneered with Refican. "Price is the main source of friction," he told Kobayashi. "So, why not let us divide the production: thus, there will be no need for profit calculations in determining the Indonesian share?"

The Japanese firm took a lot of persuading. Eventually, when Ibnu prevailed over Tokyo and Washington, NOSODECO opened an office in Jakarta and sent a large technical support group to Pangkalan Brandan. Its first managing director was Mr. S. Nishijima, the same ex-naval officer who had advised Kobayashi's reparations commission. He and Harold became good friends and business acquaintances, further enhancing the Huttons' entree into oil circles in Japan.

Refican by now had established its own representative office in Tokyo. Harold rented five rooms on the eleventh floor of the Imperial Hotel, designed by Frank Lloyd Wright on the most sought-after site in the Japanese capital, facing the imperial palace. Robert Dowling, a Californian married to an American lady who specialized in Japanese calligraphy, took charge of the Huttons' expanding business, marketing Refinate's used oil to Fuji Kosan and managing Refican's sales of oil from Sumatra. Japan was soon to become by far the largest market for Indonesian oil. Switching from coal-based to oil-fired power stations, Japanese oil consumption increased by 25 percent per anum during the 1960–64 period. In 1958, the Japanese lagged far behind the Americans and Europeans as oil consumers; by 1969, they were the third largest importer of oil after the United States and Germany and soon would be the biggest importer.

The Huttons found Tokyo to be an exciting city in which to do business as the Japanese shrugged off the traumas of defeat and postwar poverty. The Korean War had greatly increased the presence of American troops and tourists. The U.S. dollar fetched 300 yen. Japan's great steel, engineering, and shipbuilding industries were roaring back to life. No Japanese cars were assembled after the war until 1953, but ten years later the production lines at Toyota and Nissan were among the best in the world. Admiration for Nipponese art and culture was also starting to dilute America's wartime images of Japanese aggression and cruelty. Suddenly U.S. collectors were shopping for Japanese paintings, lacquered screens, wicker ware, and kimonos. U.S. fashion houses also discovered the demure smiles of Japanese models.

Betty and Harold were well placed to share in the resurgence of Japan. Harold had gambled on the sale of oil to the Japanese when their economy was in ruins; he now shared in their reviving prosperity. He and Betty imported a huge Lincoln Town Car. Their Japanese driver, Seiji Arakawa, known as "Poncho" (another person Harold renamed), served as an interpreter and became a valued member of their Tokyo team. Betty Hutton on her frequent visits worked extremely hard in Japan, according to Miki Hirano, whom Betty hired as an executive secretary. She and Harold also played hard, entertaining a never-ending procession of Japanese clients and visiting U.S. businessmen. One of their favorite haunts was the Copacabana nightclub, owned by a lady called Madame Cherry. She always made Harold welcome when he and Betty went out for a good time. Among the singers appearing at the Copacabana nightclub was Frank Sinatra. Harold's choice meal was steak, but in Tokyo he often dined at the Cresson restaurant, whose steamed duck and grapes with rich white sauce was his favorite. Betty would try to limit his intake of heavy foods, generally with little success.

In October 1964, Tokyo was to stage the Olympic games. They were a dazzling success for the defeated enemy. More than anything the games marked a turning point for the Japanese people, the end of the postwar era of hardship and poverty. At last, all the hard work had paid off. In 1960, Prime Minister Ikeda had promised that he would double the national income in ten years; in fact, it took four. As preparations began for the games in the spring of 1964, the Huttons drove out to the Harajuku area, where Kenzo Tange's spectacular Olympic stadium was beginning to take shape. They were impressed by the long, straight roads (in many cases made of asphalt) that had been quickly built to take Olympic traffic from the airport to the stadium. Three raised expressways, the first in Tokyo, and two ring roads were under construction. A new monorail serving the airport, new subway lines, and splendid new high-rise buildings were planned. The first *Shinkasen*, "bullet train," the fastest train in the world, linking Tokyo and Osaka, was scheduled to open in time for the Olympics.

With Refican's business thriving, Betty Hutton became an avid shopper for Japanese antiques. In a letter to her mother in the spring of 1964, from the Imperial Hotel, she wrote:

> I did quite a bit of shopping mostly for Pierce Road, and was lucky to get some pieces of silver which included a beautiful silver chafing dish for only $30.00 and a wonderful old teapot (rather large), a green celadon (Ming vase) incense burner, same finish as tea pot, all with chrysanthemum design.

For their visitors from the United States, Betty and Miki Hirano arranged tours of the Japanese countryside. Taking the train to places like Hokana and Kyoto, they would be met by Poncho in Harold's Lincoln to visit temples and medieval villages in the mountains. J. D. and Edna Spennetta flew out from California to join their daughter on several of these expeditions. They shared her liking for Takumi-screened calendars of which Harold and Betty bought thirty to forty each year to send to their friends and business acquaintances. "Each November," Miki Hirano said, "the Takumi manager would phone up and ask how many calendars were needed that year. In the '60 and '70s they were relatively cheap but as the yen strengthened against the dollar, the cost must have risen very sharply."

Betty still made a habit of purchasing several dozen of the calendars each year for annual Christmas gifts. Many were used to decorate the office she later came to occupy in the city of Orange, California.

In spring 1964, a Japanese company, Maruzen, made an offer to purchase Refican's drilling rights offshore as well as onshore of Sumatra. The Japanese firm was eager to secure its own sources of supply. When the Huttons agreed to sell, complex and often tiresome negotiations ensued. Harold found himself spending less time in Singapore and more around the bargaining tables in Tokyo, where Betty, Miki, and sometimes Poncho frequently had to take over when Harold needed to be elsewhere.

Month after month, during the summer of 1964, the negotiations continued at the Imperial Hotel with Japanese government officials in attendance. The price was quickly agreed on, but every time news broke of some fresh round of instability in Indonesia, the Japanese would request a time extension, which the Huttons were reluctant to grant. Betty gradually took over as chief negotiator. After one particularly grueling negotiating session, she revealed her irritation over Maruzen's tactics in a letter written to Harold on a flight between Tokyo and Singapore:

> We are really mixed up now—didn't get our Maruzen deal arranged satisfactorily until yesterday afternoon and then because of new management, they requested that papers be signed in person next Tuesday. So today, Wednesday, we are on Japan Airlines direct to Singapore and will then return to Tokyo again for completion next week.

Betty's diary continued her story of an American woman's bargaining sessions with some of Tokyo's top lawyers and oilmen:

> Mother and Sally (her niece) sat in with me during the last three weeks of frustrating negotiations. Without them and Poncho I would never have made it. What a wild wild time! Arguing with the Japanese each afternoon and evening, getting the day's happenings

into writing that night for delivery to the Japanese at the opening of business next day and then talking to Long Beach by telephone between 2:00 A.M. and 5:00 A.M. each morning! Finally at the zero hour (actually 15 minutes after) which was midnight on November 30th, the formal agreement was signed. You won't believe it, but on that final evening when it looked as though things might completely fall apart, the Japanese took one and one half hours out to watch a championship boxing match on television!

Eventually Maruzen paid Refican more than $10 million for its drilling rights, plus continuing royalties. Harold and Betty collected the checks only days before the 1964 Olympic games opened. Betty's diary read:

Harold left for Beirut. Sally and I are heading for the beach at Waikiki in Honolulu. As we left, Olympic flags were unfurled and on the very same day, the new, fast bullet train to Osaka, the monorail to the airport, and the freeway system were all operating right on schedule. I can't believe it after struggling through the four-year construction period.

THE HUTTONS GO TO SEA

Harold Hutton had made a big and as it turned out, a strategically wise decision in March 1961 when Refican took to the sea. The colonels' revolt of 1958 and the anti-American outbursts that in 1959–61 had endangered the company's people in the face of U.S. support for the secession of Sumatra from Indonesia were bad enough. The extra hazards and high costs of moving men and materials to and from Sumatra via Jakarta and of supporting their operations in jungle terrain where access by road was impossible were other compelling reasons why a ship would be far better than the unreliable airlines.

Harold's decision made good financial sense in those pre-helicopter airlift days. The cost of supporting Refican's expanding operations in north Sumatra by any other means than a ship would have been many times greater. The converted U.S. Navy minesweeper Harold had purchased and reconditioned in Long Beach would also prove to be a huge operational asset. Built and launched toward the end of World War II, the *Destination*'s relatively shallow (eleven-foot, four-inch) draft allowed it to steam into most of the larger creeks along the north Sumatran coast. It served the Huttons as a ferry and transported urgent supplies from Singapore to Belawan, the port of Medan, as well as to Pangkalan Susu. It was a floating hotel for Refican's technicians and managers in time of need, and later, when Harold turned to offshore drilling, it acted as a support vessel for seismic explorations.

The Huttons took possession of their new flagship in Long Beach in December 1961. Refurbished by its previous owners, it was now more luxury yacht than minesweeper. Harold's grandson, Don Chambers, who saw the *Destination* for the first time as a boy of six, said, "It was beautiful. Very special. No one on the West Coast had anything like it at that time." Forward of the *Destination*'s gangplank, there were three cabins on each side with their own bathrooms to accommodate 12 guests. Aft was a spacious salon and the air-conditioned area where drinks and five-course meals were served from a modernized galley and pantry. A boat deck had been added to make it easier to launch two Trojans with 125-horsepower engines. The main deck had been extended to include an enclosed bar and lounge, where Betty and Harold were to spend much of their time when on board.

From Long Beach the *Destination* sailed to Penang where the vessel was home ported. To own and manage the ship, Harold set up a company, International Geophysical Associates (Panama) S.A. with articles enabling it "to engage generally in oceanographic exploration, conduct research and activities for the exploration, mapping, or survey of oceans or any other bodies of water and underwater formations." Betty invited their staff to join them for

The Destination

an introductory cruise around Long Beach harbor, followed by dinner aboard one of the Maersk Line cargo ships, which Harold used for some of his exports. The next day, December 8, 1961, the *Destination* departed on its first voyage to Southeast Asia, with Captain Hansen on the bridge.

It was to meet the Huttons in the Philippines at Davao City in southern Mindanao. Harold had arranged to use his new ship en route to Southeast Asia to conduct a survey on behalf of an Indonesian company, P. N. Perikani. This was headed by Iman Sutopo, a senior officer in the Indonesian navy and a close relative of General Ibnu. Perikani had formed a venture with a member of the American Van Kamp family to create a joint U.S.-Indonesian fishing business. The American partner, Fisheries Associates, consisted of a group of U.S. investors that included Gilbert C. Van Kamp. Harold was chairman and George Ellington was president and chief executive. Refican subscribed $1,500 in cash in return for two founder shares. The contract stipulated that

> Perikani will fish the entire Indonesian waters and adjacent waters
> . . . Fisheries will supply the most advanced tackle, technicians,
> refrigerated transportation . . . and buy Perikani's marketable fish
> at average world market price.

This venture was not a success. One of the participants later described Ibnu's brother as a "former admiral who needed a job." Nor was the *Destination* properly equipped to conduct a scientific survey of the potential for fish in the waters off West Irian and Borneo when on January 27, 1962, it arrived from Kwajalein Island at the small harbor of Davao City in the Philippines.

The party joining the *Destination* at Davao was a large one. Three days earlier they had assembled under the auspices of Charles Clurman at the Swiss Inn in Manila: Iman Sutopo and his assistant from Jakarta; Dr. W. M. Chapman, director of research with Van Kamp Company; Betty Hutton, who had flown in from Honolulu to enjoy the first cruise of the *Destination*; and Harold, who arrived last after a heavy schedule of business appointments in Bangkok. The Clurmans wined and dined the Huttons at the Casino des Espinol and then took them to watch jai alai games at the Skyroom before they serenaded them onto a small aircraft for Davao. There, as Betty wrote in her diary:

> It was fabulous to find the Insular Hotel, located in the middle of the jungle on the beach with beautiful mahogany panelling and mother of pearl everywhere. If the sun had only come out for a peek, I would still be there as I have never pretended to be much of a sailor and as the time for boarding drew closer, my doubts became greater.

The Huttons boarded the *Destination* to the sound of gunfire. One of the ship's engineers, a man named Brown, had a revolver and began firing it in his quarters. The rest of the crew took refuge behind the engines. Eventually, the third engineer, Antrekin, wrestled the gun away from Brown. Betty wrote:

> After discussing this with the Captain, Harold decided to let Brown remain onboard for the remainder of the trip. In the end, this almost turned out to be our undoing.

Getting the *Destination* to sea proved to be almost as difficult as disarming engineer Brown. Parts for the ship's water evaporator and air conditioners had been shipped from Refining's office in Long Beach, but after cables, telephone calls, and endless trips to the airline office, the Huttons gave up and decided to sail without them. Betty recounted:

> We devised a plan to place sponges in the air conditioner drip trays to keep the water from slopping out and spent considerable time searching for these. I finally located some prayer kneeling pads which we bought for the purpose.

The *Destination* finally departed with its cargo of Fisheries Associates and Perikani executives at 3:30 P.M. on January 13, 1962. Extracts from Betty's diary illustrate the hazards and follies of its first voyage in the South Seas:

> *Wednesday, January 31*—Entering the Celebes Sea, we had the first of the wonderful breakfasts consisting of fresh fruit, sweet rolls, eggs and bacon, or ham. Harold and I took sun baths—all this

about 8:30 A.M. After lunch Edna and I began our series of three-deck canasta. Dr. Chapman started his writing: he was like the Davao rain, he never stopped.

Thursday, February 1—Running along the west coast of the Celebes we were amazed to learn that we do not have proper charts for the fishing waters. A few flying fish came aboard of their own volition; however, this wasn't very impressive when one is out on an eight-day cruise to explore for fish.

That evening we made [our] one and only attempt to operate the air conditioner. After cutting and fitting the prayer mats into each of the tin trays; the refrigerator was turned on. It took exactly 10 minutes for the stateroom trays to overflow and we spent the next few hours mopping up . . . but on a lurch from the ship at least ten gallons of water came pouring through the ceiling, so that was the end of that. The heat was unbearable. In heavy seas, all doors and windows and portholes were secured to keep the water out.

Friday, February 2—Crossed the equator last night . . . ship now rolling considerably, passing through rain squalls as we enter the Java Sea. All hands were getting the knack of holding on with one hand while eating with the other. Iman was sick after dinner.

Saturday and Sunday, February 3 and 4—The sea became rougher and rougher. We were really rolling but life continued in the same routine, sleeping, napping, eating, reading with a bit of canasta and gin rummy.

Monday, February 5—Changed course, entering the South China Sea. About 10:30 P.M. as we were playing canasta, the honk honk of an engine room warning was heard. One engine stopped due to an airlock. The ship was rolling to such a degree that the fuel tanks which had not been completely filled were failing to deliver fuel; however this was not determined until 1:30 A.M. next morning when both engines along with the generator went out.

I was truthfully never in such a deadly silence. It is quite an experience to be in a heavy sea with no engines, no lights. As I was sitting up in my bunk peering out of the window, there came the Captain searching over the side of the ship with a flash light as though trying to spot the bottom. In the distance I could hear the surf breaking. I was convinced that we were about to go on a reef. We drifted and rolled about last night until 4 A.M. when the *Destination* got underway again.

Tuesday, February 6—The sea was so heavy that Edna and I found it hard to get out of our cabin with the water pounding over the deck and every few minutes a swell breaking over the windows. We stuffed towels [under] the door and windows to stop some of the leakage. We finally made it [to] the galley for breakfast and were no sooner seated when the whole works went out again. We rolled through the meal and were then ordered back to our cabin as a protection against the roll which was very heavy. The seas continued heavy making lunch in the galley a necessity. We were comfortably seated and what happens: the whole works went out again . . . The ship came to a halt.

Up to this time the *Destination*'s engineers "had acted very secretive," said Betty. "However this was enough, and Harold blew his stack." It took six hours with the ship rolling from side to side to repair defective valves in both engines. By 11:00 that night, the *Destination* was proceeding northwest on two engines, but Iman was so sick that Betty was afraid he was going to die. She continued recording the experience:

We were all rather uneasy. With dead storage batteries we had no signal devices whatsoever, also the radio phone was not operating properly even on the emergency wavelength.

Tuesday, February 6—Still confined to the galley for dinner. Imagine our surprise on being served soup, roast duckling, and hot pie together with champagne in iced glasses. As rough as it was the bridge game went on. Dr. Chapman rolled over three different times and there went the legs on three more chairs: in fact at the end of the trip only 5 out of 12 chairs still had their legs intact.

Wednesday, February 7—Last night in the middle of the China Sea was by far the roughest. I never closed an eye during the night.

Edna and I were confined to quarters. Our steward then brought a breakfast of fried egg sandwiches in a bucket. Edna took to it all like a duck but I wasn't eating too eagerly by this time.

Due to the sea conditions, Captain Hansen decided to take the *Destination* further north to reduce the hazard of making a 90-degree turn to port. Betty's notes told more of the story:

Once the ship had the weather behind it, heading for Singapore a great calm and a great sense of relief settled over us.

Thursday, February 8—With decks washed off, the stewards cleaned a thick coating of salt from the salon windows. We are all confirmed sailors by now and have given up computing how much less time it would have taken to make the trip by plane. As the wind died down, we stood along the rail watching the ships coming and going along the main route into Singapore. We were planning to get all dressed up for the last evening on board when Harold came breezing along with the announcement that we were out of water. What a let down!

As the *Destination* sailed into Singapore that night, Tom Chambers came alongside in a water taxi. Refican's battered "flagship" anchored off Clifford pier where the Huttons and their guests went ashore in the Trojans.

By noon the next day Betty was luxuriating in a hot bath in her Singapore home on Pierce Road. The last page in her diary speaks volumes:

Many mysteries of the trip were resolved, on learning that 18 bottles of Philippine gin were removed from the quarters of the Chief and the Second Engineer after their departure. We all felt more than thankful to have come through this experience in view of the fact that the Singapore press reported the loss of four small ships in those waters during the time we were passing that way!

A gracious hostess in the Huttons' spacious home in Singapore

AN OLD SEADOG'S HOUSE IN SINGAPORE

Once their business in Indonesia was established with Japan as their principal market, the Huttons found themselves on a never-ending merry-go-round of air and sea voyages. They flew back and forth from Los Angeles to Tokyo and Singapore, to and from Jakarta to Medan and the oil fields, intermittently to New York and Washington, and from time to time across the Atlantic to Europe and to the Middle East. They worked hard, traveled hard, and dined at the best hotels and restaurants with business colleagues who Betty more often than not turned into personal friends.

Wherever she went, Betty wrote letters and postcards to her family. Hundreds of these letters survive, allowing one to select at random a number that reflect the hectic and incredibly varied life the Huttons led as Betty sought to balance her family ties and domestic chores in two different places, Singapore and southern California, with their business responsibilities in the United States, Japan, the Philippines, Thailand, and now Indonesia.

Typically, she wrote to her mother on airline notepaper. In one three-week period in the fall of 1962, her letters included the following excerpts:

> [Quantas] Late as usual. Away from Tokyo yesterday evening (Sat) just before 7 A.M. [sic] Didn't get to Bangkok until 1:30 next morning, by the time we got to bed it was 4 A.M. Tokyo time. Bad electrical storm. Heavy rain off and on all day.

> [Japan Airlines] Arriving tomorrow night in Singapore . . . it has not been definitely decided but we may go to Medan for two days and then to Rangoon on a sales deal for Pertamina, or vice versa. Harold had a badly infected finger but we were finally able to obtain some Terramycin yesterday.

[Cathay Pacific Airways] At least we don't have any quiet dull moments in our life. Monday Harold had decided we would wait in Singapore until Saturday to see George Ellington then take off for Israel and Europe, but we had news yesterday regarding reorganization of Maruzen Oil Co. so here we are off again for Tokyo. I have been almost crazy working this last week . . . Right now we plan to return to Singapore on the weekend and then head for Europe as soon as possible.

Singapore by now had taken the place of Long Beach as the Huttons' main operating base. The chief advantage of Singapore was that it was much closer to the Sumatran oil fields than Jakarta. Its business and social environment was vastly safer, more efficient, and comfortable than anything to be found in the chaotic Indonesian capital. Under the leadership of British-trained autocrats like Lee Kuan Yew, whose family the Huttons befriended before he became chief minister, the island state was on the way to becoming a world class port and communications center that soon would be regarded as a rival to Hong Kong and number one example of the "Asian model" for rapid economic development with only limited political freedom.

The house at 28 Pierce Road turned out to be exactly the place the Huttons needed as a residence plus office, hotel for Refican's executives, and entertainment center for large numbers of visiting Indonesian and Japanese associates. It was a large and, for its time, elegantly appointed house set in nearly six acres of lawns. The garden ran down to a small stream and copses of jungle plants festooned with bright flowers and creepers and alive with croaking frogs and monkeys.

The house was situated well away from the noisy center of Singapore, and visitors to Pierce Road reached it via a winding lane up a hill that is now lined with some of Asia's most expensive homes. The gate, marked by tall stone pillars, opened onto a driveway that curved down past flower beds and a koi pond to a turnaround in front of the three-car garage and apartments for the *amahs,* three Chinese live-in servants who were to become Betty's close friends. Betty was to become very fond of her three *amahs,* so much so that when she sold her home on Pierce Road in Singapore, she made arrangements for them to be financially taken care of by the Hutton Trust until their deaths. (The only remaining *amah* is Madam Chin Ah Siew, who in her nineties received Sir Eldon Griffiths and Tom Parker at her home in Singapore in 1998.)

The house was constructed in a vintage '50s style, a stone-and-glass manor built by the retired sea captain who evidently visualized himself living out his sunset days at the sedate pace described in Somerset Maughan's South Seas novels. The sedate pace certainly ended when the Huttons moved in!

On her first visit, entering the teak front door past another small koi pond to its left, Betty found a huge living area with high ceilings and large plate-glass windows overlooking the swimming pool and garden. The downstairs rooms, though large, looked square and chunky to her, but the large reception rooms were "just right for Harold." She especially liked the grand dining room with adjoining butler's pantry and floor-to-ceiling wine rack. Harold, in an effort to cut down his drinking, once filled this with Coca-Cola bottles.

Upstairs was a semicircular balcony overlooking the lawns and swimming pool. The balcony was lined with ugly iron rails, behind which the sea captain would sit and smoke his cigars at sunset. His bedroom, which Betty identified as the best one for Harold, offered a wide range of hanging closets. Betty had a separate dressing room with eighteen built-in chests of drawers and closets.

Betty replaced all the furniture and redecorated her new home from top to bottom. But she kept what she described as "the greatest treasure of 28 Pierce Road"—*amah* Ah Siew, its indispensable housekeeper. Ah Siew was born in south China, from which in the turbulent 1930s tens of thousands of young girls walked barefoot to the coastal ports to escape the civil war and the rampaging armies that made poverty endemic and plagues of all kinds commonplace. Singapore in Ah Siew's youth was a mecca to which these migrants traveled to find jobs in the homes of its Chinese merchants and British colonial officials. When the Huttons bought the house, Ah Siew stayed on. The small flat she occupied over the Pierce Road garages was her only home. For the Huttons she was a godsend, a fluent English speaker who knew everything they needed to know about their new house, including how and where to shop for food and household necessities and, above all, how to cook both the western and oriental meals that Harold insisted should be available four times a day. With Ah Siew's devoted help, Betty and Barbara Chambers re-equipped 28 Pierce Road as an American-style combination of residence and office. Together they shopped for fresh wallpaper, lacquered Chinese screens, Thai silk cushions, handmade rattan chairs and sofas for the veranda. The previous owner's heavy teak table and twelve chairs they kept for the dining room, which was to serve as Betty's place for writing letters and office memos. Pierce Road's dining table became the center of both the Huttons' business and social activities in Singapore.

Harold's first concern was to set up Refican's office. Crates of duplicate files were shipped in to a rented building in the business and banking section of downtown Singapore. He and Betty had adjoining desks, exactly as they had in their first small office in Downey, California. A telex room provided direct connections to Tokyo and Long Beach.

Before long, 28 Pierce Road became the home to which, more than any other except the one in Villa Park, the Huttons were to become most attached. Betty went out of her way to make it a family place, where a succession of her nieces and other relatives were invited out from Orange County for two- and three-month vacations. Their dining table where four, sometimes five, meals each day were on offer became one of the most hospitable in Southeast Asia.

Harold developed a compulsive taste for Ah Siew's puddings and sweet-meats. He started to put on weight, soon weighing in at 250 pounds and rising. One of his nieces told of a bet she and Harold had made during her visit to Singapore. "Harold and I made a $2 bet about who could lose the most weight in two weeks. I starved myself to win but one night I was really hungry. I went downstairs to eat something. There was Harold in the kitchen having a middle of the night snack. He gained two pounds, and lost [the bet] paying me the $2."

Among the Huttons' near-neighbors in Singapore were Harold's daughter, Barbara, and her husband, Tom Chambers, who joined Refican shortly after his marriage to Barbara. Chambers had started out as Refican's representative in Okinawa and Guam, where Harold at one point believed they might open up a market for used cars parts. He then moved to Jakarta to help open up the Refican office, joined Harold and Betty in Singapore, and eventually became chief executive officer of Refican in Southeast Asia. With his sardonic humor and fund of comic stories, Tom knew how to make Harold laugh!

Both the Chambers were natural athletes—Tom, one of Singapore's top tennis players, and Barbara, its ladies champion golfer in 1962–63. Harold was delighted by his only daughter's prowess as a golfer. As always, he doted on her. He showered her with presents and jewels. Barbara Chambers and Betty put aside the coolness that had separated them during Barbara's teenage years, and the two women became fast friends and shopping companions. Like Betty, the Chambers collected antiques and paintings, filling their basement in Singapore with a treasure trove of Chinese paintings, Javanese silverware, and precious stones. Throughout their time in Singapore, the Huttons and the Chambers were active members of the colony's social set.

* * * * *

The Huttons' hectic travels left them with too little time to spend more than a few weeks at a time in Singapore. "We are always packing and unpacking our bags and leaping on and off airplanes," Betty wrote in 1962. But her letters to her mother and sister, Mary, kept on flowing, interspersing the personal and business items that characterize the life of a professional woman at the height of her career:

> September 19, 1962—Finished shopping for the Medan household items and will get one shipment off to the packer this morning. Shell phoned Wed. morning for a meeting with their head Sales Manager, Refinery man and Tanker man. I about died. I studied for about 4 hours on the thing and realized Wed. evening that the figures we had received from Long Beach were incorrect. Fortunately was

High society in Singapore, the Huttons with Barbara and Tom Chambers

able to talk to Ernie (Moyer) Thur. morning early so we got everything straightened out. The meeting with Shell went fine. I was so relieved that I decided to take the rest of the day off. Did some nice and different things at the S.A.T.A. work shop which has things made by people confined with TB.

October 26, 1962—We are waiting for Walker from California and Redman from Medan. Harold and Tom flew away to Burma. They are coming back this evening—won't know until then if we have to make a return trip but I imagine so. I had quite a bit of business here so had to stay behind. It has been very windy here, quite like Santa Ana—and no rain lately. Is Mama still eating candy? Is she taking the vitamins?

November 4, 1962—Al Kerr arrived Sat. afternoon. We had the whole gang for dinner that evening. The children had a Halloween party. I worked most of Sunday. We gave Tom and Barbara an electric ice cream freezer so Barbara was busy trying to figure out the recipe. It turned out good although too rich!

The Huttons' home and office became a regular stopping point and watering hole for California executives looking for advice and counsel on how to do business in Singapore. Harold's telephone seldom stopped ringing as visiting oil and construction marketing men invited him to help them open doors in all parts of Southeast Asia. At a meeting with the president of one of America's biggest engineering firms and his opposite number from a major U.S. oil company, Harold characteristically sat silently in his chair while a team of accountants and lawyers spent close to an hour wrangling over what kind of offer to make to their prospective Indonesian partner.

"What do you think, Harold?" asked the construction company president.

"Forget all this MBA talk," growled Harold in his best oil patch manner. "Just give me the numbers you need and I'll figure out what it will cost you. All you need to do is tell the guy on the other side of the table how much money he's going to make."

Harold Hutton's directness was to become a legend in the Singapore of the 1960s. So was the Huttons' hospitality. Asians and Americans alike were welcome at their table, in their swimming pool, and on the patio where the best of food and drinks was always at hand. Betty loved entertaining. She and Harold became especially friendly with the family of Chief Minister Lee Kuan Yew. Betty was charmed by Lee's father, a Chinese craftsman who, still active at the age of 93, made exquisite silver jewelry.

Pierce Road was also to become a regular point of call for General Ibnu who, like Harold in his middle life, developed a passion for golf. Ibnu kept a set of golf clubs at every one of the half-dozen houses and offices the Huttons put at his disposal in Orange County, the California desert, Honolulu, Manila, Guam, and Tokyo as well as in Singapore. Later, Ibnu's family was to take over more than half the rooms at Pierce Road as their own, ensuring the general a refuge when in the late '60s he temporarily fell out of favor in Jakarta.

* * * * *

In the summer of 1963, the Huttons were invited to attend a Pacific Indonesia Business Association meeting in Jakarta sponsored by Stanford Research Institute. It offered an eerie preview of events more than thirty years later when Indonesia's currency collapsed in the late 1990s. The association's stated purpose was to calm international concerns about the political instability of Indonesia and the financial recklessness of its government.

With foreign bankers' attendance far greater than expected, every hotel in Jakarta was packed as Betty and Harold moved into Refican's far more comfortable air-conditioned guest house. Betty wrote in her diary:

> It was a revelation to see presidents, chairmen of the boards etc., from many of the largest corporations of Australia, Hong Kong, Japan, Philippines, Singapore, United States west coast. Julius Tahija, president of Caltex, was chairman of the meeting. He and the Indonesians who participated did themselves proud.

The Huttons by now were well established in Jakarta. At the conference they were guests of General Ibnu and his wife, Sally, at an elegant dinner with linen, silver candles, wine, and "a menu far surpassing any such dinner I have ever attended at home," wrote Betty.

Concluding the conference was a side trip to Bali. Harold and Betty flew with Sally Sutowo and her daughter Endang on the Pertamina aircraft, which featured a pretty Indonesian stewardess serving tidbits the whole trip. The Huttons were later to help Ibnu build a golf course and hotel on Bali, but this was their first visit to the island. Betty's letter to her mother relates her impressions:

> Much different than I had imagined, Bali is a primitive island dominated by the volcano Agung which is rarely completely visible because of the cloud halo surrounding it.

Bali already had become the home of many European artists. The wife of one of them, the Belgian painter Le Mayeur de Merpus, invited Betty to their beautiful home in the vicinity of the Huttons' hotel at Sanur beach.

> She has an exhibit of her late husband's paintings. They will revert to the Indonesian government on her death. Our visit terminated at the home of an American painter named Blanco. We had a tour through his home and studio and to a summer palace, a favorite of Dewi Kapa, Sukarno's Japanese wife.

The Huttons had arranged to return from Bali by sea. Betty wrote:

> The good ship *Destination* was waiting in Saragan harbor. We sailed along the southeast coast of Bali through the Badung strait . . . into the Java sea . . . then along the west coast of Borneo into the South China Sea which as usual was more than rough. After five days eating, sleeping, and fishing, Harold is feeling better. We dropped anchor in Singapore returning to civilization once again. This voyage from Bali to Singapore is one of my happiest experiences of life in the South Seas.

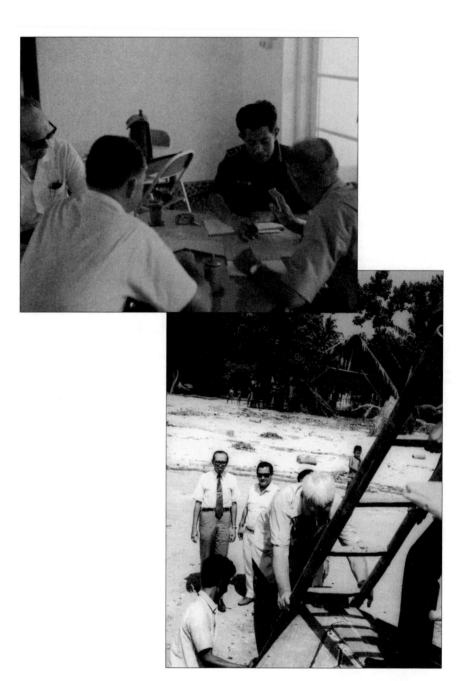

Refican's engineers negotiate oil contract as Harold, climbing ladder, goes looking for more opportunities.

PRODUCTION SHARING UPSETS
THE SEVEN SISTERS

B y the late 1960s, Refican was well on its way to becoming a money machine for the Huttons. Its prime profit maker was its share of the crude oil produced by the Aceh and Rantau wells, which Harold marketed to Japan and West Coast American refiners. The volume of crude oil coming through the pipe lines to Port Susu stabilized at around 11,000 barrels per day by 1964. Of special importance to Harold was the high quality of this Sumatran crude known in the trade as Katapa. Spouting out of the Rantau wells at a temperature of 95 degrees and hardening when it cooled, Katapa commanded premium prices, especially in Japan where oilmen regaled Harold with wartime stories of Katapa oil being poured into wicker baskets where it solidified into wax. The baskets were then floated down the rivers to waiting tankers, which warmed it up into liquid for transport to Japan. "Katapa was our ace in the hole," said Ralph Wathey, the Hutton company's controller. "It's the best crude in the world. You could run a Model T Ford on it."

Refican's crude oil business was driven by a new type of contract pioneered by Harold with General Ibnu. Their production-sharing agreements revolutionized the way in which Indonesia and, later, most producer countries would henceforth do business with the world oil industry. Together, Ibnu as head of one of the smaller national oil companies and Harold as head of a small independent U.S. interloper, had taken on the world's oil giants by producing Indonesia's first national oil out of fields confiscated, without compensation, from one of their number, Shell Oil.

Now Ibnu and Harold made a further arrangement that turned a page of oil history, irreversibly changing an important sector of the international oil game.

No longer would the source country, Indonesia, hand over control of the oil under its soil to foreign companies in return for a share of the profits. Instead, the producer country would own and control its own oil all the way from well to tanker. Its foreign partners henceforth would receive a proportion of the output, not the profits, that the foreign companies had helped to produce.

Production-sharing agreements (PSAs) had their origins in visits made by Ibnu with Harold's help to Saudi Arabia, Iran, Iraq, and Venezuela. As an observer at OPEC meetings in the early '60s, the Indonesian was surprised to learn that none of the governments of these producer nations, heavily dependant as they were on oil for their national income, were masters in their own house. When Ibnu spoke to the Shah of Iran about building a new refinery, the occupant of the Peacock Throne said he'd first have to consult the Anglo Iranian Oil Company, which in 1962 produced nearly all of Iran's oil and 60 percent of its government's revenues.

The problem, as Ibnu saw it, was that the world's oil business was dominated by the Seven Sisters: Esso, Shell, Texaco, Mobil, British Petroleum, Atlantic Richfield, and Caltex. These giants, according to Ibnu, spent more on road maps than Pertamina's total earnings in 1960. Globe-girdling multinationals with far wider interests to consider, notably in the Middle East, the Seven Sisters looked on Ibnu's fierce desire to own and manage the oil Indonesia produced as both unrealistic and politically unpalatable. It was bound to set a precedent that their vastly more important Middle Eastern partners might adopt. The Seven Sisters preferred their own system of "profit sharing" between national governments and foreign oil companies. They were determined to hold onto this arrangement as long as possible, even though the oil companies' share diminished as OPEC's pressure increased, while that of their host governments rose sharply.

Ibnu objected to profit sharing. First, because the majors generally controlled the marketing of oil by selling mainly to their own affiliates. To that extent, they could determine the price on which the profit split with the producer states was determined. "I have hundreds of men who can sound a tank and tell me how many barrels our share of the oil amounts to, but I have very few men who can follow that oil through complicated transactions and tell me how much of it should show up in the company's profits," Ibnu said.

Not so, the oil companies replied. Prices are a function of market forces. Ibnu's retort was that the integrated world oil companies kept their books at their international headquarters, making it impossible for producer countries to discover the full facts about the prices and costs on which their profits were calculated. "Those books may have been correct," he said, "but the governments had no way of checking and this created considerable distrust."

Refican was a pygmy by comparison with the giants of the oil industry. It still offered Ibnu a way out of the "profit sharing" system to which he objected. The crucial issues for Ibnu were ownership at the wellhead and national management control. The Indonesian constitution, like those of most OPEC countries, stipulated that all its natural resources, including oil and gas, "belonged to the people," but Ibnu wanted to go further.

Pertamina must also be able to oversee and, where Ibnu thought it necessary, to undertake the day-to-day management of the process of production. Essentially, what Ibnu wanted was foreign partners who would act as contractors, not co-owners.

The Seven Sisters could not accept this. All over the world they had sunk hundreds of billions worth of their shareholders' money in exploration and development. Much of this money was invested in countries that lacked any local ability to drill wells and pump oil, let alone refine and market it. Nor was there any guarantee that spending vast sums on exploring for oil would lead to finding it. More than a third of all exploratory drilling turned out at the time to be a failure. Political instability in the host countries meanwhile competed with revolutions and arbitrary confiscations to make the oil business exceedingly hazardous. For all these reasons, the Seven Sisters were doubly cautious about sharing the ownership of their hard-won production, as distinct from a percentage of the profits, with the oil states' politicians. As for ceding management control to local companies, whose personnel lacked training, know-how, and experience, this was unthinkable in the late 1950s to the American and the European multinationals that dominated the global oil trade. Management control was critical. Without it, there could be no assurance either that the oil once found would flow or that their companies would earn a sufficient return on capital to retain the confidence of their bankers and shareholders.

Harold Hutton's approach was different. As a seasoned oil man he understood the major's anxieties, but Harold was far more a trader than an investor. True, he had "gambled the farm" on helping the Indonesians bring the north Sumatran oil fields back into production. But ownership of the oil was never an issue for Harold, nor was management control. Harold was an individual. He did not think like a corporation. He was content to rely on the 35 percent share of the production that Ibnu had agreed to allot to him once it was loaded onto tankers. Refican's return would therefore depend first on making sure that Ibnu got his oil. In the process, the Huttons would earn a profit on the supplies of materials and equipment they traded to Sumatra. Thereafter, they would count on Harold's skill and luck in selling their share of Pertamina's oil on the world market. Refican, in short, would share with Indonesia the tangible product, oil, not the notional profits of the business. That was the crucial difference between PSAs and the profit-sharing agreements that up to that time had ruled the world oil industry.

General Ibnu signed the world's first production-sharing agreement with Refican on June 10, 1961. The reaction of the bigger oil companies and oil advisors in Western governments was one of anger and exasperation. Harold was variously described as a "pirate" and "an innocent abroad." One of his California contemporaries condemned Refican for "going native"; another mixed his metaphors by accusing the Huttons simultaneously of "rocking the boat" and "queering the pitch." PSAs, this man said, would "cause chaos in the world oil market."

Neither General Ibnu nor Harold was moved by this outcry. Six months later, Ibnu signed a second PSA with another American independent introduced to him by Gohier and Harold.

Asamera Oil Co. in the early 1950s was a relatively small company with a refinery and a few wells in Canada. Its president, Tom Brook, for years had been attempting to expand his operations into Sumatra, using a succession of local agents, but until he met Harold in 1960, Brook had been unable to put a satisfactory deal together. Refican at the time was drilling south of Rantau. Asamera had greater experience in this type of work, so Harold agreed to join forces and obtain a production-sharing agreement for Asamera in the Geudong Dong area. General Ibnu's support was crucial. With Joe Gohier's help, Harold took Brook to meet him. The result was that Asamera in November 1961 was granted the second PSA to be awarded to a foreign oil firm, the first being Refican's. Ibnu also put Asamera in touch with Mobil Oil, which needed extra drilling capacity in its offshore exploration areas. Brook was able to make a highly profitable arrangement with Mobil that paid off handsomely when natural gas was found in the Brunen field.

The Geudong Dong field covered in Asamera's PSA proved to be highly productive. Its drillers brought in a large number of wells that substantially increased the company's size and profitability. Asamera went on working the fields of north Sumatra and remained a large producer until it was taken over by Gulf of Canada. Refican received a 10 percent interest in Asamera and the right to sell all the crude oil produced in its first exploration area, another highly profitable business. But Tom Brook's relationship with Harold deteriorated. The two men in the summer of 1967 got into a shouting match at Medan airport. They did no more business together, though Refican continued to market large quantities of oil produced by Asamera in north Sumatra until Harold Hutton died.

General Ibnu's third production-sharing agreement was signed in July 1966 with a consortium of American independents who had pooled their interests to form the Independent Indonesia-American Petroleum Company (IIAPCO). Headquartered in Billings, Montana, these latest arrivals on the Indonesian oil scene shared Harold's complete "lack of deference" towards the Seven Sisters, as one of them described it. Instead, they took Harold's advice that PSAs were the right kind of agreement and that Ibnu was the man they must deal with. IIAPCO signed a PSA that specifically allotted management control to the Indonesians and was duly awarded drilling rights offshore of northwest Java. A Japanese independent, JAPEX, was next with the fourth PSA, agreed to on October 20, followed by a fifth signed by Ibnu and Harold for Refican to explore the seas offshore of the southeast coast of the huge island of Borneo, now Kalimantan.

Each of these contracts involved choice exploration areas and was signed with relatively small oil companies unconcerned about the effect of these production-sharing contracts elsewhere in the world. The Seven Sisters were outraged. They brought pressure on the U.S. State Department and the Japanese foreign office to support a new face in the Indonesian government, oil minister Ir Bratanata, in opposition to Ibnu. The countries' diplomats in Jakarta backed Bratanata in attacking PSAs. One of them described Harold Hutton as "a fly in the ointment."

The dispute ended up on the desk of General Suharto, newly installed in 1968 as president of Indonesia. Most of the maneuvering took place behind the scenes. The Seven Sisters wanted the clause in PSAs that gave management control to the Indonesians to be abandoned. Emerging from the Hotel Indonesia, where the heated negotiations were going on, a Shell representative tactlessly remarked that "Indonesians did not possess the skill to implement this clause."

A U.S. company spokesman added, "My company will never sign a contract based on production sharing."

These were rash words. On January 19, 1967, President Suharto took personal charge of the main oil directorate in place of the ministry of mines. When the showdown came, Bratanata lost. So did the Seven Sisters and the Western governments that had backed them. Ibnu and the "fly in the ointment," Harold Hutton, had won the fight for PSAs. As one of the U.S. oilmen ruefully put it, "Ibnu knew both Suharto and the oil industry. He also knew that the only way to gain acceptance of production sharing was to utilize the independents and proceed on an ad hoc basis." Harold Hutton's was the "ad hoc" approach. Refican opened the door and led the way for the independents.

It was only a matter of time before all the major oil companies signed production-sharing agreements. Some fought a long losing battle, among them a large French company whose negotiator, still insisting that the management clause be struck, reacted to Ibnu's refusal by getting up from the table with the threat, "I am leaving to report this impasse to Mon General [DeGaulle]." "Please do so" was the reply of Ibnu's representative. "I shall report to my General also." The Frenchman never returned.[20]

The breakthrough came on May 12, 1967, when Continental Oil, whose vice president, Harold Dubuisson, had opted to negotiate with Dr. Ibnu, as recommended by Harold, rather than with Bratanata, as advised by the U.S. Embassy, became the first of the big U.S. companies to sign a production-sharing agreement. Continental obtained drilling rights in the Barito Basin off Kalimantan. Union Oil then signed its first Indonesian contract in January 1968 with rights to drill offshore and onshore in northwest Sumatra. Once these two big companies had accepted the model that Harold Hutton and Ibnu had pioneered, fourteen others signed on in 1968. Thirty others followed in 1969, among them all of the Seven Sisters!

---

20. Bartlett, *Pertamina*, 298.

Above: The MV Torrey, *one of Refican's oil-drilling barges*
Below: The Narcissus, *a shaky launch for sonar probes*

SURVEYING THE SULU SEA

"I want to lay a sonar probe in here," said Harold Hutton, stabbing the forefinger of his right hand onto a map of the Gulf of Tomini between two of the outflung peninsulas of Sulawesi, better known as the Celebes Island. The map was on the wall of the Shriro company's offices in Manila. Harold, who had marched in without knocking on a hot and sticky afternoon in March 1962, followed up with a question to the large man with close-cropped hair who was sitting behind the desk of Shriro's managing director. "Who owns the drilling concession?" he asked.

Charles Clurman was the right man to ask. Since he and Harold had joined forces to sell surplus navy grease to Nationalist China, Clurman had expanded his activities as head of the Shriro Trading Company in the Philippines into manufacturing, food processing, a foundry, and machine shop. He employed 300 Filipinos at Regal Manufacturing, producing sewing machines, rice hullers, and water pumps. As chairman of California Manufacturing, he hired 800 more at peak times, packing fruit and meat for Ladies Choice and Best Foods. Clurman's response to Harold's question was "What do you mean here? Your finger is covering 200 square miles."

It was not long after Refican's venture in Sumatra started to grow that Harold had turned his attention to offshore drilling. His contract with General Ibnu required the exploration of several blocks of Indonesian sea-space allotted to Refican. To that end, the company had purchased, in addition to the *Destination,* a drilling vessel, the MV *Torrey,* already operating in the Malacca Straits. Now, as a result of the steep rise in oil prices led by the Shah of Iran and the Arab oil sheiks in the early 1960s, the technology of deepwater drilling was advancing rapidly. With the British government opening up wide areas of the

North Sea off the coast of Scotland, sonar and seismic surveillance was becoming more reliable and accurate. U.S. companies had joined B.P. and Shell to build ever bigger and more complex drilling platforms.

Harold Hutton, who as a youngster had watched Sam Mosher and other U.S. wildcatters open up offshore wells in California, followed the progress of the North Sea's drillers with keen interest. Refican was not even remotely in the same league as the majors who led the way, but Harold, who had promised General Ibnu to bring offshore as well as onshore drilling techniques to Pertamina, believed that he could apply some of the lessons learned in the deep water and harsh conditions of northwest Europe to the shallower and warmer waters of the South Seas.

Harold had hired and then bought the MV *Torrey* drilling barge from Westpac Offshore Drilling Company of Long Beach. Its previous operator was a dashing Irish-American named Ross McClintock, one of the more colorful figures in the California oil patch. McClintock, a school friend of Betty's, shared Harold's tastes for fine scotch and high-stakes gambling. In many ways, they were alike. The two men would meet in Refican's Long Beach office to talk business and end up sharing tall stories with Jimmy Perkins in the nearest bar. To entertain their overseas visitors, especially the Japanese, McClintock began flying them to Las Vegas in a private jet, complete with a butler who served drinks on a silver platter and a five-course meal en route.

A story Harold loved telling about him had McClintock occupying the limelight at a black-tie reception in Hollywood, then taking his plane to Las Vegas where he indulged in a bout of heavy drinking. The next morning, the telephone rang in his bedroom. An English voice said, "This is Rolls Royce in Beverly Hills."

"Oh yeah," said McClintock.

"It is our practice," said the voice, "to advise the head of the household when someone in their family has purchased one of our cars so I am phoning to congratulate you on the Corniche model your wife purchased last night."

McClintock by now was thoroughly awake. "I bought no Rolls Royce," he snapped.

"But Mrs. McClintock's name is on the check."

"Cancel the sale."

Only then, according to Harold, did Ross McClintock recall that the big event in which he had starred the previous day had been his own third marriage to film actress Mamie Van Doren. The postscript to the story, as told and no doubt embellished by Harold, came over breakfast:

"Ross, you're crazy," said Harold.

McClintock's reply was, "If you haven't tried it, don't knock it!"

Like Harold, Charles Clurman in Manila was also a friend of McClintock, with whom he later shared a cattle ranch in Nevada. Now Clurman, furrowing his heavy brow in Shriro's office in Manila, concentrated on Harold's proposal to drill for oil near Sulawesi. With his pen, Harold pinpointed a remote area halfway between the Sulu and Turtle Islands. "I have a hunch we could find oil there," he said. Clurman already knew who owned the drilling concession: American Asiatic Oil. He also knew that Asiatic was little more than a shell, one of a score of companies owned by one of Manila's most notorious entrepreneurs, Harry Stonehill. Like Clurman, Stonehill had served in the U.S. Army, ending the war as a sergeant in charge of one of the PX stores in Manila selling fast food and cigarettes.

Stonehill at best resembled Sergeant Bilko of the popular television show of the period. At worst, he was a black marketeer and a smuggler. A great deal of his fortune, it was later discovered, was made by selling cigarettes at cut-rate prices by counterfeiting the excise stamps. Clurman said he could work out a deal whereby Refican could conduct a survey of Stonehill's Turtle Islands concession. He also warned Harold that the Sulu Sea was subject to typhoon force winds that could blow up at any time and that insurance rates were sky high

because of pirate attacks on vessels without naval escorts. Harold was unde-
terred. "Find me a boat," he told Clurman.

The only vessel available in Manila to conduct a seismic probe at that time
was a 60-foot-long launch, the *Narcissus*. This, too, was owned by Stonehill but
equipped for nothing more dangerous than trips around Manila harbor. To fit
the *Narcissus* for deepwater cruising required a major overhaul, extensive
rewiring, and a welding job. Scores of custom-built components had to be flown
in from California, where Betty Hutton at her husband's request was making
arrangements to hire a sonar probe and technicians to man it. During the time
it took to refit the *Narcissus* and install the sonar equipment, Harold passed the
time sunning himself alongside his hotel pool, playing cards, and shooting dice
in the Riviera Club. His high stakes and fat tips—it was nothing for Harold to
hand out $20 bills to bellboys whose weekly wage in those days was barely one
quarter that amount—quickly marked him as a high roller. Clurman warned
that he was setting himself up as a target for one of the criminal gangs that
infested the metroplex area, but Harold's luck held out. The word went out
from the Riviera management, "Lay a finger on Mr. Hutton and we'll break
your legs."

Watching the *Narcissus* being loaded when its refit was complete was Kari
Beck, managing director of Asiatic. Apart from the sonar probe, he told
Clurman, the largest crate that was boarded was full of whiskey. Beck brought
Harry Stonehill to meet Harold and have their photographs taken together.
Years later, when Stonehill was arraigned on charges of smuggling in the
Philippines and tax evasion in the United States, this picture proved to be a
minor embarrassment to the Huttons.

Stonehill eventually was thrown out of the Philippines. At a party one
evening, he reportedly said of the president of the republic, "I have Diosado
Macapagal in my pocket." On another occasion, one of Refican's staffers
recalled an uniformed Filipino general coming into Stonehill's office to collect a
thick roll of bank notes. "Stonehill treated him like dirt," this man said.

Deported from the Philippines, Harry Stonehill made a deal with the U.S. tax authorities whereby he flew to Mexico City, surrendered to a U.S. Marshal, paid a $5 million fine, and was then allowed to return to Beverly Hills.

The *Narcissus* sailed out of Manila Bay on Good Friday, April 13, 1962, heading south in choppy waters past Cavite Naval Base and Corregidor. On board were eight Americans—three geologists, a sonar-probe technician from Fairchild Company, and two electricians, plus Harold Hutton and Tom Chambers, his son-in-law. The boat was a mess, showing the signs of hasty repair and refurbishment that left many of the pumps unworkable. "We will be lucky if this thing holds out," said Harold. Tom Chambers, a nonswimmer, went below to find a life jacket. Nearly all of the sixty jackets he checked were rotten and torn; eventually the mate found a fairly good one, which Chambers tried on. All the straps broke.

At Stonehill's insistence, two heavily armed bodyguards had been assigned to defend the *Narcissus* against attack by pirates. They had four shotguns and two rifles and were to be reinforced en route by two more armed guards with Browning automatic rifles, who came on board at Jolo Susu. The crew were all Filipinos except for a Chinese cook on loan from Manila's top restaurant, the Swiss Inn.

On the first day out, the crew, all ardent Catholics, celebrated Good Friday by praying at a makeshift shrine. "This religious respect is catching," wrote Harold in a letter to Betty. The next day, April 14, was his birthday. His letter to Betty reminded her of their courting days in Palm Springs:

> We are sailing toward the Southern Cross with the Big Dipper and
> the North Star at our stern. This is one of the few places in the
> world in which this is possible.

For Harold's birthday lunch, the cook prepared pigs' knuckles and sauerkraut, his favorite. That afternoon, as the winds increased to fifty miles per hour from the east, the boat started rolling, and several of the Americans experienced their first touch of diarrhea. Tom Chambers swallowed motion sickness pills. When dinner was served, Harold tucked into calf's liver and bacon.

As they sailed into the Sulu Sea, twelve-foot waves threatened to capsize the *Narcissus*. The Captain sought shelter in a tiny cove on the southern tip of the island of Panay. Muscular islanders were waiting in outriggers. The entire village of Anniny gathered on the beach, but when the captain of the *Narcissus*, who could speak the local dialect, told the local chieftain it was Harold's birthday, the villagers took the Americans to an amphitheater with hot springs and a sulphurous water hole. As Harold and Tom Chambers distributed drinks and candy for the kids, the villagers passed out five-foot-long bamboo poles filled with beer made of fermented coconut milk. The party lasted five hours, during which time the Americans consumed the contents of five bamboo trunks. "It was a real Hollywood setting, beautiful beach, coconut trees, cock fights, and everything," said one of the geologists. Harold wrote the following to his wife:

> Maybe not my best birthday party because you were not there, but
> one I will remember a long time.

Taking a roasted pig aboard with them, Harold's survey crew departed Anniny in quiet waters with rolling swells. The cook served the pig for hors d'oeuvres followed by veal chops, potatoes, and ice cream for dessert. The sea was calm as a mirror as they entered the Mindanao Sea and refueled at Damaguete, a picturesque town with sixteenth-century watch towers built by the Spaniards to guard against pirate attacks. Eventually, in a temperature hovering near 100 degrees, the *Narcissus* reached the "Flower Island" coast of Mindanao. During the night, the generator blew out. Harold and Tom Chambers lounged on the quarter deck playing gin rummy.

Harold wrote all this and more to Betty:

> I am starting to tan and go barefoot. So far, I am ahead of Tom in
> gin. He keeps everyone laughing and happy.

With its phonograph blaring out the latest hits from *South Pacific*, the *Narcissus* approached Zamboanga. Harold and his team had steak, eggs, and mangos for lunch before disembarking to a noisy greeting by another flotilla of small canoes manned by boys and girls beseeching them to toss coins into the crystal water. The Americans went swimming in Panusco Bay and then had dinner and an air-conditioned night's sleep in Zamboanga's Bayot Hotel. The local movie house was showing *Girls Town,* a movie with Mamie Van Doren. Of course, Harold retold his story about her Rolls Royce and Ross McClintock.

The *Narcissus*'s last port of call before commencing its sonar probe of the continental shelf north of the Turtle Islands was Jolo Susu, a small harbor on Jolo Island. An unruly squad of officials and military officers came on board and started drinking Harold's whiskey at 9:00 A.M. Ashore, he met the city mayor, surrounded by a posse of gunmen. "All carry guns and make their living smuggling," wrote Tom Chambers in his diary. The next morning Harold was wakened at dawn by an explosion fifty yards from the boat. A local fisherman had thrown a stick of dynamite into the water to kill a school of fish so that his crew could pick up the dead ones. Chambers it seemed was the only one able to detail those events:

> I was the only one without a hangover this morning. Had to repair generators again. Hot and sticky by lunch, hot soup, pork and mangos. Played gin with Harold until dinner.

With fuel tanks replenished and a ton of ammunition for the Browning guns stored below decks, the *Narcissus* rode more easily as it slid through the Sulu Sea en route for Taganak, the main island of the Turtle Island group where the survey was to commence.

High winds produced a heavy swell, the roughest so far on the trip. So with the Sulawesi mainland only eighteen miles south, the captain sailed into a bay in the nearest island. The chief of police of the nearest village presented a supply of turtle eggs supposed to make everybody "very ready." Harold's comment was "Who needs them!"

The next day, the *Narcissus* was on station, ready to make its first survey run in the hope of locating oil. It was then that the weather intervened. Tom Chambers' diary describes what happened in vivid detail:

> *April 22*—What diarrhea! Up and down the ladder 10-12 times to the can. Got started on the run at 5 A.M. but a short in the calculating machine holds us up 2 hours. Had horse cock and eggs for breakfast. I just ate the eggs. Equipment went wrong all day, one thing after the other. We stopped to fix this and that. Hope this contraption will work. At least the fishing was good: the Cook landed a 70 pound Tangingi.

> *April 23*—Typhoon to the north of us. Took off 2 days beard with cold water. Equipment ready to go. Started on runs at 8 A.M. Same old stuff between 3 and 4 knots. Lousy fishing . . . too slow. Just found out we are getting low on fresh water.

> *April 24*—Rained all night, lousy sleeping. Weather is not good for work. Can't get water until midnight as a big ship is taking on water at the nearest port. On edge of a typhoon.

> *April 25*—Started run on northern islands. Geologists, Harold, and I took motor launch and guards ashore to see volcano and survey island. After walking two miles up and down the volcano being eaten up by mosquitos we decided to have lunch and cold beer, and to hell with the other islands. Picked up the geologists at 5 P.M.

Harold Hutton's first South Seas expedition prospecting for offshore oil ended in the waters off Sandakan in northern Borneo. The *Narcissus* then returned to Zamboanga where Harold and Tom Chambers caught a Philippine Airlines plane for Sebu City and Manila where Charlie Clurman offered to let them stay in the bridal suite at the Bayview Hotel. Harold left there at midnight for California, taking with him copies of the geologists' handwritten reports on their preliminary findings from the probe.

The results were inconclusive. The sonar equipment had worked less than perfectly; the readings, though mildly encouraging, were incomplete. Harold told Betty that the cost of this "preliminary reconnaissance" of the South Seas, which she estimated could not have been less than $100,000, should be written off to experience. "There is oil there, I know it," he insisted. "We just have to keep looking."

* * * * *

During the late 1960s, the Huttons commissioned a number of further surveys in the waters around Indonesia. Betty wrote the following tartly in her diary in June 1964:

> We now have quite a navy. To support the *Torrey* meant purchasing two tugs, two personnel boats, and several motorized sampans, as well as support vessels for the *Destination*.

Once, when the *Torrey* was drilling in Sumatran waters, Harold brought the *Destination* alongside to replenish its supplies. Betty, who was also aboard, wrote this:

> We thought we would be enjoying a perfect balmy tropical evening. Instead we ran into a terrific storm with 50 mph winds and the heaviest rain I have ever seen. Lightning flashed all around us, 360 degrees. We ran into one storm right after another for four days and nights in a row.

One by one the lines holding the *Torrey* over the hole where she was drilling came loose, making it difficult to keep the drills rotating. Finally, wrote Betty:

> *Torrey* broke all the lines connecting her to the hole. The *Destination*'s anchor chains also parted. We almost blew right into the Torrey broadside. Next night we were close to blowing ashore on Sembilan Island.

It took two weeks to repair the *Torrey* after this incident. Later the same year, the barge suffered another shock when a successful hole it was drilling at Besitang Number 1 zapped into a gas pocket. The explosion sent a shaft of gas bubbling up through the water and erupted 200 feet into the air. The gas column caught fire as the well blew up. Betty recorded this in her diary:

The fire was extinguished without serious injuries, but we finally
lost the hole because of the gas.

The *Torrey* survived several more fires and blowouts during the years it
was operated by Refican. It also made some promising finds, on one occasion
locating a sizable gas field north of Sumatra. To utilize this, however, meant
building an undersea pipeline from the ocean to Pangkalan Brandan and the
price of gas proved too low to justify this. Harold closed this well without
exploiting it.

Offshore drilling was to remain one of Harold's passions. All in all, his
offshore explorations were successful. Harold covered his costs and earned
useful profits by selling to Japanese companies the seismic data he built up in his
deepwater surveys.

To judge by the videos and hundreds of photographs they took of sweeping,
sandy beaches and fish being hauled aboard their small fleet of vessels, Harold
and Betty also enjoyed some of the best times in their lives in the South Seas.
They swam, fished, and sunbathed and tossed coins into the limpid waters
where youngsters dove into the depths to retrieve them. Betty treated these trips
as her second, third, and fourth honeymoons. Harold pointed out the different
constellations of stars that are to be seen south of the equator, recalling the days
when he took her courting under the night skies of Palm Springs.

PART VIII   CONFRONTATIONS AND CRISIS

Indonesian troops board Refican oil-survey vessel

CRUSH MALAYSIA

E vents in Indonesia took a turn for the worse in the mid-1960s. Oil was flowing in increasing quantities from the north Sumatran wells. Refican was doing well on the basis of what Harold Hutton called his "two-way street." He was both a broker of the heavy crude exported from Pangkalan Susu and a supplier of materials and equipment for Colonel Patti and the other Indonesian operators on the spot in Aceh and Rantau. Harold's own drillers reported good progress and high hopes of finding more oil in the locations he had been allotted for exploration. Construction work was progressing on Refican's drum plant and carbon black plant at Pakning. Harold also had negotiated an arrangement with General Ibnu for Refican to sell direct to the local market the lube oil he was making at the Pakning refinery from the heavier waxy crude produced in some of the Sumatran wells. This deal effectively bypassed the oil ministry whose ownership extended only to crude oil coming out of the ground and exported from Indonesia. The income from this lube oil was to be shared by Harold and Ibnu, rather than being handed over in its entirety to the government. It was for both a financially attractive—and mutually beneficial—sideline.

Into this generally encouraging and profitable scene, political convulsions in Jakarta and yet another rapid deterioration in United States–Indonesian relations injected a series of shocks. In the latter half of 1964, the Huttons once again were caught up in the interplay of international politics and the oil business. Refican suffered vast inconvenience, some loss, and no little danger to its employees on the ground in Sumatra. The source of the problem was Konfrontasi, the cold war declared by President Sukarno on May 23, 1965, against Malaysia. The British in 1963 had proposed to combine their crown colonies of Sarawak and Sabah with Singapore and the new nation of Malaya that they had defended against Communist onslaught in the previous decade. The federation made sense. The majority of its people were of Malay stock. Neither Sarawak nor Sabah was viable on its own. Singapore, cut off from its natural hinterland, badly needed free trade with the rest of the Malay peninsula. Great Britain, too, wanted out. Despite the pleas of many Malays that its forces should remain to defend them, the British government had decided that its Southeast Asian empire imposed too great a strain on the United Kingdom's armed forces and finances.

President Sukarno of Indonesia reacted with fury to the proposals for a Malay federation. Secretly he had hoped that Britain's withdrawal would allow Indonesia to "pluck the former North Borneo colonies like a ripe plum," as the U.S. ambassador, Howard P. Jones, wrote in his memoir, *Indonesia: The Possible Dream.*[21]

Denouncing the new Malaysia as an "imperialist plot," Sukarno in May 1965 imposed an economic blockade on Malaya and Singapore. The following year, after a United Nations mission sent to test the opinions of the people of north Borneo concluded that they vastly preferred to federate with Malaysia than to join a turbulent and chaotic Indonesia, Sukarno gave orders to the Indonesian army to "crush Malaysia."

The upshot of Konfrontasi for the Huttons was two years of grave political uncertainty and restrictions on travel between Indonesia and its neighbors. In the summer of 1964, they already had been caught up in riots that broke out between Chinese and Malayans in Singapore. The rioting started when a Chinese reportedly threw a Coke bottle at a parade of Malayans celebrating Mohammed's birthday. As the parade passed Raffles Hotel, Betty and her niece Sally Struck, who was visiting from Orange County, took photographs from the back of Harold's blue Lincoln.

---

21. Howard P. Jones, *Indonesia: The Possible Dream.* (New York: Harcourt-Brace Jovanovich, 1971), 304.

Betty wrote in her diary:

> Everything seemed normal until that night. Then everything started
> to happen. Harold turned on the radio. All stations were off the air.
> The city was placed under curfew.

Betty's housekeeper, Ah Siew, bustled in to say that there was fighting in the Chinese area. "It started where we were parked in front of Raffles Hotel," said Ah Heng, the chauffeur. "It was terrible."

Harold immediately turned on the outside lights at Pierce Road but the *amahs,* his Chinese servants, would not stand for that. Instead all lights were extinguished and the draperies drawn. Betty wrote:

> The *Amahs'* reasoning seemed to be that no one would be able to
> see us. They were worried sick, remembering similar experiences as
> the Japanese were taking Malaya during the war.

One of Refican's staffers then arrived with a message that the water line connecting Singapore's main supply on the mainland had been blown up. The Huttons filled their bathtubs and plastic containers with water. Betty wrote in a letter to her mother:

> Tension was eased by playing Gin and Dominos until it was
> announced that water rationing would not be necessary and the
> curfew was raised. Early next morning, the fighting exploded
> again, the whole city fell apart.

Within two days the Singapore authorities announced that the city was quiet. Everything was under control. Police arrested as many of the violators as they could lay their hands on. Hundreds were sentenced to jail. Heading for the airport with a heavy military guard, Betty wrote:

> We all heaved a sigh of relief as our plane took off in a heavy
> downpour. So ended those days of anxiety which started with a
> Chinese throwing a Coke bottle. Many were of the opinion that it
> was just one of those outbursts of temper displayed from time to

time between the Malays and Chinese but this was overshadowed
by the feeling that it was done with Communist backing and defi-
nitely connected with the confrontation between Malaya and
Indonesia.

By this time, President Sukarno's policy of Konfrontasi had switched from
strong words to near war. The Soviet Union supported Indonesia's threat to
"crush Malaysia." Already, Sukarno had opened the door for the introduction
into Indonesia of large quantities of Soviet military equipment and the
technicians to handle it.

Sukarno also announced that he would purchase an entire navy costing
hundreds of millions of dollars from the Soviets, including twelve submarines
and an aging cruiser the Red fleet was happy to dispose of. For Indonesia, whose
agriculture had been run down by its ruler's profligacy to a point where rice
production was 10 percent below its people's minimum needs, this was an
expensive *folie de grandeur*.

Worse problems were to follow. Incited by Sukarno's fiery rhetoric against
Malaysia, which he condemned as an "imperialist conspiracy by Britain and the
United States," mobs set fire to a building directly opposite the Hotel Indonesia,
where the Huttons often stayed when visiting Jakarta. This was the British
Embassy, whose ambassador, a canny Scot, responded to threats to kill him by
having his aide parade up and down the veranda of the Embassy residence playing his bagpipes.

The United States backed the new Malaysia. President Kennedy at first tried
to mediate, but ended up joining the British in sending the Malaysians weapons
to defend themselves against Sukarno's attacks. Among these attacks were a
number of comic opera paratroop raids on the Malay peninsula. For the
American community in Jakarta, these were hazardous times. In December
1964, the PKI (the Indonesian Communist Party) with Sukarno's support had
launched an all-out anti-American campaign. The U.S. information center in

downtown Jakarta was sacked by angry crowds, spitting, waving their fists, and shouting "There's an American, let's get him" whenever they spotted one. The rioters tore to pieces the American flag, before sacking this diplomatic building and burning it to the ground.

Refican's staff in Jakarta was cautious but there were times when Harold's offices in Medan and Jakarta had to close for fear of mob violence. Communications between Singapore and Jakarta were blacked out. Supplies from Long Beach continued to arrive in Pangkalan Susu but less frequently and with far greater delays. The Huttons stopped making air trips to Jakarta and limited their visits to north Sumatra to occasional trips to Port Susu on the *Destination*. Describing one of these visits in August 1964, Betty wrote in her matter-of-fact way:

> Due to internal unrest we were not permitted to go ashore except to visit the company guest house which is in close proximity to the landing dock. Most of the first quarter of 1964 was spent flying around in circles trying to keep ahead of the cold war between Indonesia and Malaysia.

During the three years of Sukarno's Konfrontasi, Walt Redman and his roughnecks never complained. There was no sign of panic among his construction workers though the office in Long Beach detected increased orders for bar supplies. Harold made good use of the *Destination* and its Trojans to make sure that these were delivered and that his men could take time out aboard the ship or on weekend furloughs in Singapore.

Ashore, ugly crowds frequently threatened Americans and other expatriates in Sumatra. Their trucks were pelted with stones and jeered at. Once, an army jeep with a heavy machine gun mounted in the rear pulled up outside a club used by the oilmen in Medan. The gun traversed until it pointed at a group of Refican oilies seated on the veranda. For two hours there was a tense standoff until troops marched into the building. One of the Refican men recalled:

They said they were looking for local officials accused of taking bribes. The situation was pretty threatening. It remained very unstable until Colonel Patti got things straightened out and we could get on with the oil business.

By January 1965, when Harold and Betty managed to fly into Jakarta en route to Medan and the oil fields, the Indonesian capital was the scene of another Sukarno tantrum against Malaysia. Indonesia, he announced to a banner-waving crowd of close to a million PKI supporters, would withdraw from the United Nations. American as well as British rubber and oil companies were to be placed under government control. American movies were outlawed. Communist unions then halted the supply of water and electricity to British and American homes, including the house Refican had rented in the diplomatic section of the city. The U.S. ambassador to Indonesia, Howard P. Jones, until then an apologist for Sukarno, wrote in a report to Washington:

Takeover committees threaten American-owned plantations in Sumatra; a communist dominated union instituted a mail boycott against the U.S. Embassy and AID Mission and the Consulate; Indonesian telecom people refuse to handle copy for U.S. newsmen.[22]

Asked by the State Department what he thought was likely to happen in Jakarta over the next months, the ambassador replied that no one could be sure what would happen over the next six days or six hours.

Harold Hutton was marooned in Jakarta for weeks at a time during the worst of the anti-American riots of the summer of 1965. He made a point of dropping in on the U.S. Embassy for briefings. A new ambassador, Marshall Green, had replaced the gentle but disappointed Howard Jones.

Harold was never a regular at diplomatic cocktail parties, but he and George Benson, the U.S. military attache, struck up a warm acquaintance. With their wives, they met at barbecues given by Ibnu and Sally Sutowo where John Wayne

---

22. Jones, *Indonesia.*

movies were shown on an outdoor screen. "Harold listened far more than he talked," said Benson, "but when he did drop a couple of lines in the west Texas drawl he liked to affect, the Indonesians listened. Ibnu was impressed by Harold's line, 'You don't need to know a lot about oil to set up an oil company; all you need is oil.'"

Harold never drank at Ibnu's home, respecting the Moslem tradition. He still made everyone laugh at dinner parties he and Betty attended with groups of worried Americans by reminiscing about the Prohibition era of the 1920s. Harold loved W. C. Fields's crack, "We were caught in a storm off Sumatra and I lost my corkscrew. We were forced to live on nothing but food and water for several days." Betty Hutton, with her memories—and fears—of Harold's occasional binges, could not have enjoyed her husband's drinking jokes as much as their companions did, but at a time when many of these expatriates were openly alarmed at the prospect of anti-American violence getting out of hand, Harold's calm good humor was welcomed by most as a tonic.

CROCODILE HOLE CAUSES A BLOODBATH

T he night of September 30, 1965, was hot and sultry as the Huttons sat out on their balcony overlooking the swimming pool and garden at Pierce Road in Singapore. The moon was pale and full as it rose over the Strait of Malacca separating the Malay peninsula from Sumatra and over the great throbbing metropolis of Jakarta 800 miles further south. It was Jakarta that was in their minds as Betty sipped a whiskey and Harold inhaled the smoke from his Camel cigarette. The BBC had broadcast an "unconfirmed report" of yet another threatened military coup in the capital of Indonesia.

Next morning, the rumors were substantiated. Squads of Communist-infiltrated units of the Indonesian army and air force had secretly made their way into Jakarta, bearing the photographs of seven men they were to kill or capture. The seven were the minister of defense, General Nasution; the army's top field commander, General Rani; four other senior generals and the intelligence chief. But the Gestapu putsch as it was to be labeled, was not directed against President Sukarno. Its target was the high command of the only force guaranteeing law and order and resistance to a Communist takeover in Indonesia—the army.

Six of the generals were seized in their homes, then murdered and mutilated. One of them, Brigadier Sudojo, was a friend of the Huttons who frequently had visited their home in Jakarta. General Nasution alone foiled the assassins by leaping over a wall, breaking his ankle in the fall but escaping to rally loyal troops with the aid of a tough brigadier in charge of a standby force deployed outside Jakarta. This brigadier was Suharto, the "savior" of Indonesia as he was to become known. Eighteen months later, Suharto succeeded the quixotic

Sukarno as Indonesia's second president. He was unchallenged for the next thirty-eight years, the architect in the '60s and '70s of Indonesia's massive shift from neo-socialism to crony capitalism. In the '80s and early '90s Suharto was courted by successive U.S. presidents and depicted in Washington first as an ally and partner and later as a tyrant and bumbler when the "miracle economies" of Asia stumbled into the financial crises of the late 1990s, ending his rule ignominiously in June 1998.

Suharto came into office as Sukarno left, in a welter of rioting and bloodshed. Immediately following the Gestapu putsch of September 30, 1965, a long period of military skirmishing and civil unrest lacerated Jakarta. The rebels, it was revealed, were members of Communist-supported groups in the army and air force, among them several senior commanders and by inference, General Nasution believed, the commander-in-chief himself, President Sukarno!

Public horror and the army's determination to destroy the Communist party exploded three days later when the bodies of the murdered generals were found in a pit known as Crocodile Hole. Their exhumation caused massive public protest in a Moslem nation that reserved the greatest horror for mutilations of the human body. Grisly photographs showed eyes gouged out, limbs chopped off, and bodies torn apart in an effort to force the six captured officers into false confessions.

The Huttons were still in Singapore as news trickled out about the Gestapu putsch and the discovery of their friend, Brigadier Sudojo, and the other five victims' bodies. Was this the start of the civil war in Indonesia that many observers had predicted and that Harold had hoped and prayed would never happen? Betty's diaries offer no clue about the depth of their concern for Walt Redman and his crew in Sumatra and Franz Herrnsdorf in Jakarta. She noted only that Sudojo's mutilated corpse was one of those exhumed from Crocodile Hole and wrote simply, "I am so sorry and distressed for Mrs. Sudojo." She also noted that the widow's first husband had also been killed by the Communists when he fought against an uprising in east Java in 1948.

The Huttons' dismay over the massacre of the generals, which seemed to threaten their entire business and future, escalated as the BBC reported further violence in Jakarta. Alerted by Nasution, General Suharto's Siliwangi division had moved into central Jakarta where the putschists had seized the radio station and assembled two battalions of dissident troops in Merdeka Square. There followed a tense fifteen-hour standoff that threatened open conflict between rival elements of the military. Suharto's superior numbers and heavier weapons ensured that he came out on top. His troops disarmed the rebels without violence. Fears remained that the air force would order the bombing of the city because several of its commanders had supported the coup. The next day, Sukarno's paratroopers recaptured Halim Air Force Base and that threat, too, was eliminated, but finding President Sukarno at Halim added to the army's belief that, secretly, he had encouraged the plotters attempt to eliminate his own chiefs of staff.

Whether Sukarno had actually connived against the Indonesian army's commanders has never been finally determined. But within a year, the "Father of the Nation" who, by any measure, had been the inspiration of his country's independence movement, had been discredited. Placed under house arrest, Sukarno saw his powers one by one stripped away and handed over to the new strong man, Suharto.

Then came retribution. Within days of the Crocodile Hole murders, the Indonesian army launched an all-out offensive to root out all those who had backed the Gestapu movement. The main target was the Communist Party (PKI), the only force that might have challenged the army's supremacy. All told, there were estimated to be 15 million members of the various organizations that made up the PKI: 8 million in the peasants' organization (BTI), 3 million in the trade unions (SOBSI), plus 4 million more in the youth and womens' organizations. Tens of thousands of these Communists were armed with weapons shipped in from the Soviet Union and China. A few, not many, were Chinese, members of the minority community that then, as now, dominated much of Indonesia's trade and commerce.

On all of these people there now fell the vengeance that the Indonesian army exacted against anyone and everyone who might be connected with the Communists. Suharto's troops led the way. Their orders were only to disarm the Communist Party, but the soldiers were much less merciful. In an orgy of popular revenge, Moslem youth groups also took to the streets to settle their scores with the Marxists in every corner of the archipelago. During the killing that went on for close to a year, hundreds of thousands of actual and alleged Indonesian Communists were slaughtered. Many were ethnic Chinese, merchants, craftsmen, and street hawkers whose conspicuous success as traders had aroused the jealousy and hatred of the less-wealthy Indonesian majority.

At first, the Huttons knew little about this bloodbath. While the killing went on, the Indonesian army blacked out the media and silenced Jakarta radio. But day by day, as the horror stories trickled out of Indonesia, Betty and Harold realized that they were in the presence of one of postwar Asia's greatest holocausts.

Many of the press reports concentrated on Bali. There, as the army stood by, black-habited Hindus working in teams systematically went through village after village checking off names against Communist Party lists. The subsequent executions, which ran into the tens of thousands, were nearly always by sword or knife. Men and women marked for death were run through with spears, then decapitated. Some Balinese villages carried out communal executions as hundreds of alleged Communists were gathered together in the central square and clubbed or knifed to death. Among them were hundreds of completely apolitical Chinese and Javanese merchants whose only crime had been to prosper or raise rents while most Balinese Hindus went hungry.

The Huttons' chief concern was focused on north Sumatra where, in the area surrounding their oil facilities at Pangkalan Brandan, many of the agricultural workers were controlled by Communist trade unions. There, the army commander was Brigadier Kemal Idris, who heard the news of the Crocodile Hole massacre at his base southeast of Medan. Idris didn't wait for orders. Occupying Medan, where Refican's engineers were holed up in a large apartment, the brigadier and his troops pointed their rifles at every official in sight. "Are you for or against Suharto?" they shouted. "Support for Suharto," said an American observer, "suddenly was one hundred percent!"

There is no evidence that Colonel Pattiasina's troops were involved in the massacres of trade union members in the rubber plantations near Medan. Their task was to guard the oil wells and keep open the refineries. More likely, Patti's men, like Djohan's, had no choice but to stand by while Idris's troops, according to one of his closest associates, killed "not less than 20 percent of the rubber workers in the Medan area."

Meanwhile in Jakarta, General Suharto looked the other way as army-inspired mobs smashed and looted PKI's headquarters. None of this sacking and burning was particularly novel in the turbulent political life of Jakarta in the 1960s. What was new was that it was the Communists, instead of the Americans and the British, who were now on the receiving end. Yet to the Huttons' amazement, just two weeks after the Gestapu affair, when for the first time in decades the Communists were on the run, the U.S. Embassy ordered officials' wives and children to be evacuated. John Hughes, *The Christian Science Monitor's* Pulitzer-prize winning correspondent, noted in his book:

> It was a decision that to many outsiders seemed incomprehensible. Many U.S. officials privately spoke out militantly against it. After all, the Embassy for months had been the target for Communist mobs at a time when it seemed to be in the ascendancy. With courage and fortitude, the Americans and their dependents had sat out that crisis in Jakarta. Now with the Communists on the run and the Indonesian army in apparent full control, the U.S. had decided to pull its dependents out. The new President, Suharto, who regarded himself as a friend of the United States, was astonished by what looked like an American vote of no confidence in their best friends, the Indonesian army![23]

23. John Hughes, *Indonesian Upheaval* (New York: Van Rees Press, 1967), 142.

Exactly how many Indonesians, Communist or otherwise, were killed and wounded during the months of October, November, and December 1965 has never been exactly determined. The *New York Times* estimated 400,000 but conceded that the total could be far higher. The *London Economist* set the figure for Java at about 800,000, plus 100,000 in Bali, almost as many in Sumatra, and several thousand in the outlying islands. Indonesia's 1965 blood-bath, concentrating as it did in many areas on the ethnic Chinese, ranks with the slaughter of the Jews in Nazi Europe and the killing fields of Pol Pot's Cambodia as one of history's most terrible massacres. The death toll far exceeded that of the killings in Bosnia or Rwanda in the 1990s. Yet because of the censorship and radio blackout imposed by the army, neither the United States nor most other nations at the time made anything more than offhand, even perfunctory, protests about the holocaust in Indonesia. On the contrary, as the shootings and mass executions tapered off, many Americans, including Secretary of State Dulles, were more inclined to regard one of the century's greatest acts of military-supported genocide as little more than a regrettable but understandable act of self-defense against a Communist conspiracy.

Harold Hutton's view was that the emergence of President Suharto in place of the discredited Sukarno almost certainly avoided a civil war that could—and probably would—have brought about even more deaths and suffering. Indonesia, he feared, would have suffered the same fate as Korea, Vietnam, and Cambodia if the army had not moved decisively to prevent the vast archipelago's being torn apart. As for the discredited Sukarno, he was not mistreated. Instead, the ousted president was placed under palace arrest at his home near Bogor and formally removed from office the following year, 1966. Sukarno's survival, to live and die in luxury, offers a comforting harbinger of the likely fate of his successor, President Suharto, when thirty-two years later, he too was forced out of office in 1998.

One of Suharto's first acts was to turn his back on the Soviet Union and sever Indonesia's relations with Communist China. As president, Suharto held out the hand of friendship to the United States. When the United States returned its diplomats' families to the embassy in Jakarta, relations between Washington and the new military regime improved. Five U.S.-trained economists were placed in key positions in the new government. Their orders were to dismantle Sukarno's socialist monopolies, beat back trade-union control of the economy, and provide incentives for the peasants to sell their rice and cotton at free market prices. Over time, the prescription worked. By the late 1960s, Indonesia once again was able to feed itself. Exports increased. Foreign investment moved in as year by year the standard of living of most Indonesians visibly improved. True to his anti-Communist rhetoric, Suharto cut Jakarta's trade links with China and Russia while opening up his huge country to western investment. Oil was to become by far its biggest asset and earner of foreign-exchange income.

The Huttons were among the main gainers from this change. Their entire Indonesian gamble once again had come perilously close to disaster, but at the last minute had been rescued from the risk of all-out civil war. In Sumatra, Walt Redman and his men could safely travel outside the refinery compound at Langkat. Colonel, soon to be Brigadier, Patti could get on with the job of developing the Aceh and Rantau fields and maximizing the flow of crude oil out of Pangkalan Susu. Most important for the Huttons, Brigadier, now Major General Ibnu had been confirmed by his friend and commander-in-chief, Suharto, as the undisputed chief of the Indonesian oil industry. For Harold and Betty that confirmation was critical. Without Ibnu they would have been doomed.

Harold and Betty in their prime

THE TEAM AT THE TOP

Throughout their lives together, Harold and Betty Hutton worked as a team. Those who knew them best described their relationship as symbiotic—each nourished and grew out of the other. In Asia, Harold concentrated on what he was best at—getting oil out of north Sumatra and marketing it in Japan. Betty took charge of their companies' "engine room"—finance and shipping. Three "pistons" in this engine room powered the Huttons' business and profit. One moved and marketed crude oil. Another procured and shipped the materials, equipment, and manpower Refican and Pertamina needed for their operations in Sumatra. The third provided support for speculative ventures of the kind that Harold relished undertaking and Betty as often dreaded—in exotic places like Lebanon, Guam, Dahomey, and the Philippines.

The Huttons' shipping activities were Betty's special responsibility. It was a major challenge for a woman in the still male-dominated 1960s, especially in an industry where a female voice on the telephone was assumed to be a secretary's, never that of a senior executive. The number of Refican-commissioned tankers at sea at any one time was often as high as fourteen. Betty took charge of hiring these big vessels, winning the respect of brokers from Singapore and Hong Kong to London. She took pleasure in working out the costs, capacities, turnaround times, and loading schedules of all Refican vessels.

At one point these ships were leaving the tanker terminal Harold helped Pertamina build off Pangkalan Susu at the rate of one every eight days. Not all the oil the Huttons moved was Sumatran. Another of their profitable contracts was for a monthly shipment of Venezuelan crude to Osaka, Japan. Others involved the shipment of Esso crude from the Middle East to markets throughout the Pacific. Refican's marketing department from time to time was tempted to switch supplies to U.S. brokers who offered higher prices, especially for top quality crude, while the tankers were still at sea en route from Sumatra. Harold refused to do this, insisting that Fuji Kosan, his first big Japanese customer, never should be shortchanged or disappointed. Betty, too, made a point of keeping Fuji's purchasing agent, Frank Iwase, happy. As the Japanese market for asphalt and other oil-based products soared in the '50s and '60s, she would negotiate additional supplies and tanker tonnage from the gulf and Saudi Arabia to meet Fuji Kosan's needs. Iwase and the Huttons became fast friends.

In late 1962, the Refican board authorized Ernie Moyer to make arrangement for regular shipment of its oil in a Texas-based tanker, the *Fernhill*, operating out of New Orleans. In 1965, the company set up a shipping subsidiary, International Associates, Liberia. Pertamina acquired six shares, Refican four. General Ibnu joined Harold and Betty on the board as a director. International Associates held its first meeting in rooms 2055-57 at the Indonesian Hotel on July 27, 1965. Not long afterwards, Harold said to Betty, "Let's buy some tankers. I know where I can get three."

It was not a good idea. Owning and managing ships is a very different business from chartering them. Prices for big tankers soared in the early '60s, but it wasn't long before they started to fall as the big Korean shipyards, Hyundai and Daewoo, started to challenge the Japanese in mass-producing ever-bigger oil and bulk carriers. Betty put her foot down. "We don't need to buy ships and we can't afford these," she told Jimmy Perkins. Harold discarded his plan to buy a fleet of tankers.

It was a decision that came just in time. Refican narrowly avoided the 1973–74 crash in tanker values that bankrupted dozens of shipyards and brokers and in the process, cost Pertamina—and Ibnu Sutowo—dearly.

The second piston pumping profits into Refican's coffers by the late '60s was its oil field supply business. Harold told his wife, "Whatever Ibnu wants, make sure that Ibnu gets!" Johannes Pattiasina, who had been promoted to brigadier general, said of the Huttons at that time, "Without their help, our oil industry wouldn't be so successful as it is today. Every time I needed equipment or materials, they just sent the best and the most modern, and no questions asked." Harold sometimes went overboard, sanctioning shipments that Betty knew Pertamina didn't have the oil to pay for. "Don't do what Mr. Hutton says; do what he really wants," Jimmy Perkins told the staff as he ignored those kinds of orders. Betty strongly approved.

From its Long Beach purchasing office, Refican's supply line now reached to Tokyo and Osaka, Manila, Hong Kong, Bangkok and Singapore, Jakarta and Pangkalan Susu. Betty supervised every detail. Her task was to dovetail the steadily increasing oil business in Indonesia with Refining's other U.S. and international activities, all of which expanded rapidly in the 1960s. Her main challenge was to run a multimillion dollar purchasing agency capable of procuring and shipping whatever was needed to the Sumatran oil fields while staying within the limits of Refican's still erratic cash flow. It also fell to Betty and her Long Beach staff to locate, interview, and hire engineers, geologists, and drillers with the skills and aptitude for working in tough and dangerous conditions.

Refican soon had more than a dozen construction and drilling sites in the Sumatran jungle, a house and two apartments in Jakarta, houses, offices, and workshops in Medan and Susu, and condominiums for its workers in Pangkalan Brandan. Betty made the arrangements for each of the properties to be furnished with American-style bathrooms and for doctors and nurses to be available at all the work sites in case of medical emergencies. Recreational facilities were also needed to keep the men in Sumatra from becoming homesick and bored. Betty shipped over billiard tables, movies, and slot machines.

Indonesia being a Moslem country, it was one of Refican's rules that heavy drinking and indiscretions with Sumatran women would lead to instant dismissal. Enforcing this was not easy, but on several occasions when Bill Merrill and Walt Redman had to discipline their hard-driving crews, it was Betty more often than Harold who stood solidly behind the company's line managers.

At Susu, Merrill fired one of his roughnecks for drinking and womanizing; the employee hit back by threatening to sue. Merrill sent him home and told him to go to see Betty. At a time when very few women occupied top posts in U.S. businesses and virtually none in the predominantly masculine oil industry, the roughneck could not imagine that a woman would fire him. Back in Long Beach, he confidently expected that a sob story from a husky male, topped off with a plea for forgiveness, would be enough to reprieve him. Betty listened carefully, then confirmed the man's dismissal. He was more surprised by this than he was by Merrill's action. "Betty was never a soft touch," said Merrill afterwards. "On personnel matters, she was tougher than Harold. The guys respected her for it."

Refining's purchasing operation in Long Beach was managed in the early 1960s from a small office on Artesia Boulevard. In its purchasing, shipping, engineering, geology, and accounting departments, there were twenty-five employees by 1962 and thirty by 1967. All but a handful were women. It was rare, indeed, in those days to phone an oil service supply company and find the voices at the other end of the line to be feminine, especially in the technical departments. But Betty Hutton had confidence in her "girls."

Among them were some impressive women. Ruth Muggli, daughter of a Shell Oil executive, who had worked in the Signal Hill oil patch for most of her professional life, would answer the telephone with "Good morning, this is Miss Muggli" in a voice that rose and fell by two octaves from beginning to end.

Connie Martin, an auburn-haired Californian, went to Hong Kong to help open the company's new offices in the Hilton Hotel. Later, she was to nursemaid the sons and daughters of some of Asia's top business families when they visited California as the Huttons' guests.

Jerry Baker moved to California from Manhattan, complaining that her office in Long Beach was "certainly not a suite on Fifth Avenue." But not for long. Betty put her to work as a secretary to the executive staff. Jerry said:

> It took me some time to relate to nebulous entities like offshore drilling, production sharing contracts, support vessels, carbon black, LPG, seismic surveys and names like Kobayashi, Kriang Jiarakul, Pattiasina, Ibnu Sutowo, Pangkalan Susu. My knowledge of Asian geography, geology, paleontology, deadweight tons, tanker draughts, metric drilling tools, driller, roughneck and riggers responsibilities, air routes, inoculations and visas qualified me at best as a Trivial Pursuit champion.

By the mid-1960s, Betty and her crew were handling ships' cargos worth tens of millions of dollars a month, including $5 million a month of exports to Indonesia. "We purchased everything from nails to heavy construction equipment," recalled Sylvia Law, who joined Refining in 1961 and stayed on to become Betty's personal secretary, friend, and confidante. Betty had a knack of delegating to her staff as much responsibility as each could handle. According to Jerry Baker:

> She felt that if she could do it, then so could the rest of us. In my mind, this was a vote of confidence. She always inspired us to do more. Nothing seemed like too big a task.

* * * * *

The Huttons' Artesia office, rented from a garden equipment company, consisted of six square rooms set around a small glass atrium, with asphalt tile floors, metal desks, and a reception area that lacked windows or carpets. A small petroleum chemistry lab in the rear—"often smelling awful," said a new recruit—tested the reclaimed drain oil the Huttons processed in their small refinery. Incoming telegrams bringing messages from Tokyo, Manila, Hong Kong, and Singapore as well as from Walt Redman in Indonesia were received each morning from Western Union via the house telex machine, retyped by the receptionist, and distributed to the relevant departments.

The Huttons shared a corner suite, their desks side by side. Harold preferred to leave the day-to-day operations and bookkeeping to Betty and her staff. As chief executive, he was often overseas or lunching at the Petroleum Club and playing golf with visiting customers. When he did appear, Sylvia Law recalls that Harold would go straight to the coffee pot at the end of the hall. "He would eat one donut, then put another on his plate and go into his office, so that Betty thought he had just one." Jerry Baker reminisced this way:

> There was a strong physical resemblance between Harold and Ernest Hemingway, especially when his hair was cut in a certain way, and the resemblance, I suspect, went further, including their adventuresome spirits, their restlessness and strong appetites.

Yet popular as he was among the staff, Refinate's California office was Betty's domain far more than Harold's. Betty blossomed as a manager. The company's three top executives were men—Jimmy Perkins, who returned to Long Beach as president of the Huttons' original—and still very active—U.S. company, Refining Associates; Ernie Moyer, the company chemist, who paid frequent visits to Sumatra; and Sammy Struck, husband of Betty's sister, Mary, who had special responsibility for looking after its overseas customers, especially the Japanese.

"Mrs. Hutton," as Betty invariably was addressed by her staff, insisted that her women staff members at all times must look ladylike. She herself wore smart suits with pastel-colored blouses, spoke softly and seemed almost to tiptoe around the office. Her talent was to make each person she was with feel special. "She seemed genuinely interested in each one of us and in what we had to say," said Jerry Baker. Betty Hutton could also be tough. "Businessmen would come to her office and be awed," wrote Sylvia Law.

Once when Jimmy Perkins yelled at the front office staff because his mail wasn't ready, Betty went into his office and closed the door. Two minutes later, Vice President Perkins apologized for his "ungentlemanly conduct." On another occasion when the Huttons were abroad, a bright young temporary employee persuaded Vice President Ernie Moyer that the atrium in the center of the office should be redecorated. Moyer agreed, with the result that a collection of plastic trees, rubber plants, statues, and a fountain were installed in the atrium. The lobby furniture was re-upholstered in turquoise vinyl. "Hideous," wrote Jerry Baker.

On Betty's return, she inspected the new arrangements in silence and immediately went behind closed doors with Moyer. Her voice, rarely raised, could be heard saying something about this "garden of delights." The next day, the display in the atrium was dismantled, the plastic trees offered to employees to take home if they wished. The room in the atrium was refurnished to make space for more members of the staff but not, Betty commanded, for the bright young temporary employee; her help no longer was required.

By 1967, the Huttons' business had greatly outgrown its premises on Artesia Boulevard. Betty decided to move to more spacious surroundings in the city of Orange. For most of the employees, this move involved a longer drive to work. A memo signed by all of the staff questioned whether there would be an increase in salary or mileage allowance to compensate. "No raises," said Betty. "Those who do not want to make the move are welcome to look for a job elsewhere." Everyone moved!

Betty's new office in Orange consisted of a large ground-floor emporium with a patio garden and a beautiful tiled entrance. It was located at 436 Glassell Street not far from Chapman University. There and at her home in Villa Park, she entertained a steady procession of Chinese, Indonesian, Japanese, and Thai visitors as well as Harold's associates in the California oil industry. As Refican became more widely known, her guests included golfing friends like General Ibnu, the actor Randolph Scott, and actress Mamie Van Doren, the former wife of Harold's friend, Ross McClintock.

Sometimes Betty took on the role of troubleshooter, sending Sammy, her brother-in-law, to appease impatient customers, notably the Japanese. More often, she acted as the group's chief financial officer, working with Ralph Wathey, the controller, who joined her in 1967.

"Mrs. Hutton was on top of everything," said Ralph Wathey. "Harold had the ideas but Betty kept the business going. Everyone who worked for them knew this."

* * * * *

The third—and more erratic piston—that helped and sometimes hindered the Huttons' business in the late '60s was Harold's penchant for "deals." He nearly always kept $1 million in cash in half a dozen separate bank accounts to enable him, as he put it, "to get up and go when I need to." Some of his off-the-cuff speculations did very well. He bought condominiums in Honolulu, a large house in Guam, homes for his top executives, and above all, the freehold of the Pierce Road estate in the heart of Singapore, which appreciated in value close to 100 times between its purchase in 1961 and its sale in 1976.

There were other occasions when Harold's appetite for adventure got the better of his business judgment, such as the Fisheries Associates venture referred to in "The Huttons Go to Sea." The idea was to fish Indonesian waters for a 60,000-ton catch of marketable fish each year. Fisheries Associates commissioned a number of expeditions to trawl the South Pacific using a Japanese technique whereby a flotilla of small boats paid out fifteen- to thirty-mile-long lines with hooks every few feet. The Indonesians, however, insisted that only half of each crew should be Japanese; the rest must be Indonesian. Persistent squabbles between them led to operations being discontinued. Harold thereupon assumed at a board meeting held June 12, 1964, at 840 Van Kamp Street in Long Beach, "full responsibility for management of the operations."

But Harold's troubles with Fisheries Associates were far from over. The American directors resigned. Six months later, George Ellington quit the company, which gradually became a joint venture between Refican and an Indonesian company named Refican/Perikani. The fishermen's unions frustrated

Perikani's attempts to land the fish in either the Philippines or Indonesia and Harold's fishing venture was a flop. The company disappeared without a trace in the late 1960s.

Another of Harold's bright ideas that went wrong was a proposal for Refican to build a refinery in Africa. He spent a lot of his time on this deal, which was put forward in 1965 by Mario and Aturdi Araktingi, a pair of Lebanese entrepreneurs. They wanted his help to put up a refinery at Port Nova in the former French colony and now independent republic of Dahomey (since renamed Benin) in west Africa. The Araktingis proposed that Harold should negotiate a partnership with the Dahomey government with themselves as agents. Dahomey was to provide the necessary planning consents, a site, and construction labor. Refican would take on the job of commissioning the refinery and arranging to bring in crude oil, initially from Nigeria and later from newly discovered fields in Gabon at the mouth of the Congo. Harold knew nothing of Dahomey, except a story he remembered about its legendary women archers who, like the Greek Amazons, cut off their right breasts to improve their aim. He nonetheless agreed to pursue the Araktingis' proposal in New York and Geneva, where he discussed the possibilities of obtaining the necessary financing without result. He and Betty still agreed to meet the Lebanese in Beirut.

Beirut in 1965 was one of the world's most sophisticated cities. Before it was destroyed during the Israeli invasion of Lebanon, it combined the elegance of its former French rulers with the Arab traditions of Syria and a climate and snow-covered mountains like those of California. Lebanon in those days was the Middle East's most sought-after center of money, beaches, shopping, and business deals. When Harold and Betty arrived there jet-lagged from New York, they were driven to the Phoenicia Hotel overlooking a harbor filled with many more yachts than there were at that time in Newport Beach, California. "No rooms left," said the clerk at the reception desk. Betty then changed her travelers checks, and Harold put the equivalent of $100 on the desk. The clerk immediately found them a room. "We will only charge you the Aramco rate," he said, referring to the deal negotiated by the U.S. oil company whose executives used the Phoenicia while on leave from the Saudi desert. "That will save you the money you have just given me."

Mario Araktingi arrived the next day for lunch. He and Harold discussed details of the proposed refinery for Dahomey. They spent the rest of the afternoon going through the drafts for a possible contract. Aturdi Araktingi then joined them for cocktails and dinner. By the time they went to bed, the Huttons thought they had a deal.

The following morning they drove to Tabarkja where Harold especially enjoyed the succulent Lebanese hors d'oeuvres. That evening, they had reservations at a restaurant in the world's oldest recorded city, Byblos, perched on a promontory overlooking the Mediterranean. Harold sat in the hulk of a former sailing ship amid a mass of fish nets and paper lanterns while a barman served licorice drinks. When the Araktingis arrived for dinner, he sniffed the evening air. A huge barbecue was cooking prime ribs in the Le Panache restaurant. Discussion of the Dahomey deal continued over large plates of beef and a grand St. Emilion red wine. And then it was off to the casino where Harold dropped more than $6,000. "We finally got to bed at 3:30 A.M." wrote Betty. "Everyone was dead tired."

The Dahomey deal quickly went sour. Neither the Araktingis nor the Dahomey government had either money or credit. Yet Beirut still worked its magic. Mario had a friend who knew a man who knew an advisor to one of the Persian Gulf oil sheiks. The ruler of Sharjah, said the Lebanese, was eager to link up with an American independent oil man just like Harold. Sharjah needed help to drill for oil in its offshore waters.

On the face of it, the story made sense. Sharjah at the time was feuding with Iran about the status of two small islands in the Persian Gulf. To press his claim, the ruler wanted to start drilling on his side of the median line. If Harold was interested, the Araktingis could set up a meeting.

"Where and when?" asked Harold. The Araktingis said that the sheik just happened to be in Beirut, vacationing with his brothers.

Harold and Betty met the ruler of Sharjah at a restaurant near the Pigeon Rock grotto, one of Beirut's most attractive beaches. They were frisked by the sheik's bodyguard, a huge fierce man in flowing robes, a dagger at his waist and a high-powered rifle in his hand. Only then were the Huttons ushered into the presence of two slight, dark-faced men wearing well-cut European white suits, seated cross-legged at a table filled with another array of hors d'oeuvres. Betty counted as Harold and the Ruler of Sharjah tucked into "this assortment of liver, lamb, cheeses, pistachio nuts the size of almonds, barbecued chicken, and finally small pancakes with a sweet whipped-cream filling and turkish coffee."

The sheik then turned to business, speaking a mix of Oxford and Texas English. Sharjah, he said, had plenty of oil in its offshore waters. All he lacked was the means to prospect and develop it. All Harold had to do was to put enough money on the table, and the drilling concession would be his.

"How do I know that there is any oil there?" asked Harold.

The sheik said, "You can take my word for it."

The magic of Beirut by now was wearing off. Harold's response was that he would bring in an oil barge with all the necessary equipment "to determine if there is oil we can get out at competitive prices. But nothing down just as an advance. We can share the oil and the profit afterwards if there is any." That remark proved to be the deal breaker. Without a large upfront payment, the Sheik of Sharjah was not prepared to open his waters to U.S. drillers.

A year later, an American and two European oil companies agreed to the deal that Harold, just in time, had rejected, but not with the ruler he met. A coup in Sharjah removed the sheik with whom the Huttons had lunched from any further influence on his country's affairs. As for the Araktingi refinery in Dahomey, that, too, came to nothing. The Huttons' journey to Beirut had been a wild goose chase. But in this case, they were lucky. Dahomey over the next decade swallowed up huge quantities of drilling effort and investment, with little result.

PART IX   HAROLD'S FOURTH QUARTER

Hosting General Ibnu at the Eisenhower house in Palm Springs

LIVING IT UP IN THE DESERT

One afternoon in the early summer of 1969, Ralph Wathey peeked around the door of Harold Hutton's office on Glassell Street in Orange and said, "I thought you'd like to know. You've made a million dollars today."

Wathey, financial controller of Refinate, had just sold another tranche of the stock Harold had obtained in one of the independent oil venture partnerships he had acquired in Indonesia. It was one of the many profitable spinoffs from his relationship with General Ibnu.

Harold was now approaching his sixty-fifth birthday. He celebrated April 2, 1969, at a lavish party thrown by Betty at their Villa Park home. Harold had plenty of reasons to be content with his life. By any material measure, he was rich. He was the head of two large and prosperous international companies—Refican, operating in nearly all parts of Asia, and Refining Associates, the Huttons' original U.S. company, still pumping out handsome profits in North America. Harold and Betty owned virtually all the stock in these and a dozen other companies, some less than successful (like Fisheries Associates), others returning a handsome yield on originally very small investments (like their California real estate investment companies). Harold had also made substantial capital gains from the sale of his drilling rights off the coast of Sumatra and Kalimantan to the Japanese and of his shares in partnerships with other U.S. independent oil companies whose stock he had purchased or received in return for advice or help.

Asamera Oil was a case in point. Tom Brook, its chairman, had allotted 55,000 shares of the stock in its Indonesian subsidiary to Harold when with

Refican's help he negotiated the 1961 production-sharing agreement that opened up a section of northwest Sumatra. Asamera made a big strike. Over the months that followed, its stock price scored a series of sharp rises on the New York market. Harold cashed in his shares in tranches of 5,000, 20,000, 15,000 and 15,000, on one occasion earning the $1 million profit in one day that attracted Ralph Wathey's attention.

Most of the Huttons' assets in 1970 were tied up in oil rights, property, and accounts receivable. The cash flow from their businesses at its peak was running at the rate of scores of millions each year. Neither Harold nor Betty ever took a large salary out of their companies. They did not need to. But if they had chosen to receive competitive executive salaries in each of the various countries where they worked, they would simultaneously have been multimillionaires in Singapore, Japan, and Thailand as well as in the United States and Canada.

There is no evidence whatsoever that they evaded paying taxes. Both were too scrupulous, as well as too cautious, to do that. Refican's nonresident status nonetheless reduced its tax liabilities in America, and by living and working overseas, the Huttons minimized their exposure to U.S. capital gains taxation.

The Huttons undoubtedly lived well. Personally, they were modest, unpretentious, and unspoiled by their good fortune; they nonetheless had acquired the habit of expecting and getting the best that money could buy. Betty dressed simply and stylishly, but her rings and other jewelry were priceless. Wherever they traveled, Harold bought her pearls, diamonds, rubies, emeralds, sapphires, and whole displays of gold and silver trinkets whenever they caught his eye. Betty collected and became something of an expert in oriental art, much of which is now housed at the Hutton Foundation in Santa Barbara.

Harold was naturally generous, "fast on the draw with his wallet," as one of his friends remarked. Recalling his days as an impoverished car park attendant, he took pleasure in handing out large tips to every carhop, porter, cleaner, or bartender he saw at the hotels and restaurants he patronized. Ever ready in his later years with $100 bills, he would pay whatever gratuity was needed, or more, to get hotel rooms, airline tickets, choice tables in the best restaurants, or front-row tickets to the theater. When his grandson, Don Chambers, muttered something about this being "ostentatious," Harold responded that he liked giving away money. "Makes me feel good and them feel good. It's my way of spreading the wealth."

Another of Harold's pleasures was to wear well-tailored clothes. As a schoolboy, cadet, and salesman, he'd made a point of dressing well. Now he wore stylish suits and Hermes ties, tasseled Gucci loafers, and gold collar stays in his shirts. "I remember a call from his jeweller, saying they had received his Petek Philippe," recalled one of his secretaries. "I knew Rolex was good, but this turned out to be the thinnest watch I have ever seen."

Big expensive cars were another appurtenance that Harold liked to indulge in. Ever since he bought his first Stutz Bearcat while struggling to make ends meet at Howard Hughes's studio in Hollywood, he'd longed for the day when he would drive the world's finest automobiles. He had his large blue Lincoln in Japan and another in Singapore, where Harold's car was often seen with his driver, parked outside Raffles Hotel. In Tokyo, Poncho the Thief, as Harold still affectionately called his Japanese chauffeur, was on call twenty-four hours a day, just as Harold himself had been when he drove for Abe Lyman in Los Angeles in the 1930s. In Jakarta and Hong Kong, he hired stretch limousines with hotel drivers whom he tipped with $50 bills.

In California, he drove a snappy gray Ferrari, which was destroyed one October evening in 1968 when he drove it into a tree. The next day Harold bought a replacement, another gray Ferrari costing $17,000, at a time when a middle-range import could be purchased for less than $5,000.

By the early 1970s, the Huttons had cut down on the incessant traveling they, in particular Harold, had engaged in over the 1950s and 1960s. They now were able to spend more time in Orange County and at their new home in the California desert, not far from the gas station where he and Betty met years earlier.

There, Betty and her mother one morning were sunning themselves alongside the swimming pool. Their sunbath was rudely interrupted when a golf ball flew between the palm trees that separate the fairway from the yard and plopped down into the pool. Two men in a golf cart drove up. One, the striker of the ball, was Gerry Ford, former president of the United States; the other, driving the cart, was comedian Bob Hope. The Huttons knew both men slightly, but this was Betty's first social encounter. She found Ford "extremely nice." Bob Hope, who was in a hurry, "sat in the golf cart yelling at him to move on but President Ford stayed and talked and ended up posing for a photograph."

Ford's interest in the Huttons and their desert home arose from its previous owner, his predecessor Dwight David Eisenhower, the thirty-fourth president of the United States. The house on Amethyst Drive was where Ike in his later years lived and played a couple of rounds of golf every week. Mamie, his wife, had her friends over to play bridge in the evenings.

Harold and Betty had started looking for a place in the California desert after they sold out most of their drilling rights in Indonesia to the Japanese. They wanted to go back to the sunshine and starlit skies where thirty years earlier they'd met and courted. Betty, recalling her youth in Palm Springs, was keen to find a winter home with guaranteed sunshine. Harold, now sixty-six, had resolved, a trifle unconvincingly, that he wanted to enjoy his remaining years playing golf and cards with his friends. Eldorado Country Club, a former grapefruit orchard tucked into a series of rocky coves of the Santa Clara mountains, was then and still is today one of California's most exclusive resorts. The concept of an amateur golfer and the professional at the nearby Thunderbird Club, Eldorado had been built by Robert McCulloch, founder of the McCulloch chain saw company, as one of the world's finest golf courses.

Among Eldorado's first members were Bob Hope, Bing Crosby (the first club champion), Desi Arnaz, Greer Garson, Rosalind Russell, Dean Martin, Jimmy Stewart, and Randolph Scott. The club's first few years proved to be difficult. Not every one wanted to buy one of McCulloch's $10,000 plots in a patch of desert whose summer temperatures reach 110 degrees Fahrenheit. The club's luck changed in 1959 when, as Harold Hutton had noted on one of his weekends in the desert, two golfing "firsts" put Eldorado on the world map. One was the 1959 Ryder Cup match between the United States and the British Isles. This made global headlines when the entire British team and members of the press were nearly killed as their plane, en route from Los Angeles, was caught in a violent storm. The next day, Lord Brabazon of Tara, president of the British professional golfers association, opened the door of his cottage to find a thick blanket of mist covering the fairway. "How thoughtful," said his lordship, delighting the media and Harold. The Ryder Cup match put Eldorado on the map.

The club's second coup was President Eisenhower. Introduced to the club by Freeman Gosden of *Amos and Andy* fame, the General, as he was known, frequently arrived in the presidential helicopter, alighting in his golf shoes to avoid any delay in getting onto the links. Ike and Mamie occupied the home at Amethyst Drive as guests of Bob McCulloch. When the U.S. Secret Service feared that an attack on their lives might be imminent, the entire mountain overlooking Eldorado, now known as Mount Eisenhower, was illuminated in a spectacular night time display recorded coast to coast on television.

Later, when Ike left the White House, he was made an honorary member of Eldorado and spent most winters at the Amethyst house. Among his visitors, lending Eldorado still more—by now unwanted—publicity, were his successors John F. Kennedy, Lyndon Johnson and Richard Nixon, West German Chancellor Konrad Adenauer, President Mateos of Mexico, and the Reverend Billy Graham, who partnered Ike on the golf course. Once when Graham missed a two-foot putt at the fourteenth hole, Eisenhower inquired why the reverend's "heavenly sponsor's" vocation wasn't more helpful in his putting. Graham's reply is not recorded, but the story was one that Harold Hutton often related to his guests.

Ike left Eldorado for the last time in April 1969 because of the heart disease that was to end his life. His house was put up for bids, though McCulloch characteristically insisted that he would not accept any profit on the sale of his hero's home. That Christmas, Harold and Betty were visiting the club. Both were life-long Republicans, like the Spennettas, and had contributed to Eisenhower's election campaign. Betty inspected the house with her usual thoroughness. The living room with its high ceilings, round table for bridge, and chaise lounge under a picture window overlooking the swimming pool reminded her of Pierce Road in Singapore. The kitchen, painted bright yellow, suited her very well. One wall of Ike's study was paneled in pine with shelves for his books and photographs of foreign leaders. Alongside the general's chair were two black-handled chests that had seen service with him in both Europe and the White House.

As soon as Betty said "Yes, let's have it," Harold took out his checkbook and wrote a check for the down payment. The Huttons purchased the Eisenhower house for $225,000. They were going back to the desert where their lifelong romance had begun.

Their Eldorado home became a refuge and oasis for Betty. She loved its lofty ceilings and space to display items from her collection of oriental art shipped back from the Far East. Harold enjoyed getting into the overheated pool and paddling back and forth with his slow, ponderous crawl. Most winters, the Huttons invited General Ibnu and other friends from Indonesia, Japan, and the Philippines to join them for the Bob Hope Classic golf tournament. Harold arranged for Ibnu to play golf with his California oil friends. His son-in-law, Tom Chambers, who bought a winter home in Rancho Mirage, often joined them to make up a foursome.

It took some time for the old-timers at Eldorado to accept the presence of these dark-skinned visitors from Asia. It was one thing for them to play on the links and something entirely different to see them in the club's locker rooms and dining hall. Once, when a young guest of the Huttons, newly arrived from Jakarta, ventured into the locker room, one of the staff ordered him to leave. "Caddies are not allowed!" he roared. It took a great deal of time and tact on Tom Chambers' part to erase that obnoxious slur.

Harold, when he was informed, recalled an incident on one of Indonesia's golf courses. An American oilman, visiting Jakarta to win a valuable contract, had been kept waiting by the oil minister for several days. Taking time out from business on the golf course, he felt even more exasperated to find a group of Indonesians arguing and gesticulating as his all-white foursome waited to make their approach shots to the eighteenth green.

"Out of the way," shouted the oilman.

"Who is that guy?" demanded one of the Indonesians.

"I'm the president of the company," said the American, naming his famous firm.

"Well I'm the minister of oil," replied the little Indonesian.

The next day, according to Harold, the oilman's local agent arrived at the minister's office to offer his boss's apologies. He was handed a piece of paper ordering the company's president to be deported immediately!

Harold at the peak of his power

RETREATING FROM THE FAR EAST

Because they had spent most of their time in the Far East and most weekends while home at Indian Wells, the Huttons' wealth rarely attracted the attention that big money nearly always commands in Orange County, California. Behind the scenes, however, they contributed to a wide range of local and national charities as well as to the Republican Party during Richard Nixon's campaign against John F. Kennedy and more significantly, when President Ford and later Ronald Reagan ran against Jimmy Carter. Harold only rarely attended its meetings, but he was a substantial donor to the Lincoln Club of Orange County whose conservative views—and whose funds—carried a good deal of weight at the state and local level. He and Betty developed a cordial relationship with Ronald Reagan when he was governor of California and with Gerald Ford and his wife, Betty, whom they met in Indian Wells.

The Huttons were equally generous to educational causes, especially in Indonesia. Their interest was stimulated by the requirement in Refican's contract that it must help build schools for the children of Pertamina's workers at Pangkalan Brandan and, later, at the refinery built by the Huttons in Pakning. Two primary schools and one large secondary school were constructed in north Sumatra with materials supplied by Walt Redman and funds from Refican. On many of their visits, Harold and Betty would drop by to join the children and their teachers over lunch or in the classrooms. Harold shot dozens of movies. Others, taken by Betty and showing her husband gambolling with those Sumatran school children, raise the question of whether, and to what extent, she regretted that she and Harold had none of their own.

A chance encounter in Singapore with a group of visiting Orange County ranchers, meanwhile, had rekindled the Huttons' interest in Chapman College.

The Sunkist Co., seeking to promote sales of its oranges, had organized a party of its growers to visit Japan and Southeast Asia. Seated in the bar of the Raffles Hotel in Singapore, the group saw a large American shouldering his way up to the counter. "Where are all those Californian orange growers?" Harold Hutton called out. Ed Pankey, one of the growers, got to his feet and held out his hand. Harold, grasping it, immediately told the bartender—"a good friend of his," observed Pankey—to fill the glasses of the entire delegation. "He was a barrel of a man, maybe 275 pounds, with a tremendously loud voice," said Pankey. "You just couldn't help liking him. A sort of instant empathy developed between us."

Before the drinks party ended, Harold Hutton had the six Americans offering toasts in the Malay phrase, *yam seng* ("here's to you"). He took them home to dinner and on learning that their next stop was Penang in Malaya, invited them aboard the *Destination,* which was tied up in Penang harbor. "His hosting us on his boat at a gourmet dinner with his skipper, Captain Groundwater, was one of the highlights of our tour," said Pankey, who that day made up his mind that the Huttons were natural targets for the next fund-raising drive by Chapman College.

Pankey was a member of the president's council of what in the '50s was a small liberal arts college. Most of its buildings occupied the former campus of Betty Hutton's beloved Orange Union High School. Chapman was only a stone's throw from the Huttons' offices on Glassell Street in Orange and both Betty and Harold knew it well. In 1970, taking advantage of the good fellowship they had developed in Singapore, Ed Pankey invited Harold to become a contributor to the college's funds. A year later, Harold became a Chapman trustee. As far as can be discovered, he never made any contributions to his own schools, St. Johns Military Academy and Carleton College, but over the years the Huttons, especially Betty, became major benefactors to Chapman. Its gymnasium was named in Harold's memory, The Harold Hutton Sports Center.

Alas for Harold, his health in the 1970s did not keep pace with his wealth. All his life he had smoked unfiltered Camel cigarettes, and his gravelly voice was the result. He had also put on weight, so much that a visitor who sat with him by the swimming pool at Pierce Road in Singapore, noted in her diary that "the rolls of fat on his back were so thick that you could lose a quarter in them." (This was an exaggeration. Harold had a deep scar on his back as a result of a surgical procedure to remove a painful boil.) Harold's increasing propensity to eat more as he aged almost certainly reflected a somewhat surprising recurrence of the anxieties he had suffered as a young man. For all intents and purposes, he was at the peak of his career in the early '70s. Yet as often can happen when a successful man appears to have everything he wants, Harold started to exhibit signs of vulnerability whenever even a small detail went wrong with his companies or his contacts.

The first tell-tale signs of his late midlife crisis already had appeared in letters Harold wrote to Betty whenever they were separated. Flying to Hong Kong to meet General Ibnu and the directors of a company named Tunis Inc., in December 1966, Harold on arrival found that no one from Ibnu's entourage had come to the airport to meet him.

In his letter to Betty that night he complained bitterly about this unaccustomed slight. He went on to explain that after checking into his hotel and turning in early, he got a midnight call from one of the Tunis men saying that they would meet with him the next morning at 11:30 A.M. However, when he returned to his room after breakfast, another voice called at 11:00 A.M. to say that Ibnu and the Tunis directors were waiting for him in the Mandarin Suite, making it seem as though Harold were late.

Harold's exasperation, related in detail in his next letter, suggests that the chairman of Refican was overstrained and overanxious. Another of his letters described a tense meeting with Ibnu at which Harold tried to persuade him to keep up Pertamina's oil shipment to California so that he and Betty could meet their contracts. He wrote:

> Ibnu has been convinced that he didn't have any oil for us. This, I
> soon convinced him, was not true and we should go my way.

Yet if Harold's powers of persuasion prevailed on this occasion, his apprehensions remained. The meeting with Ibnu abruptly ended as a beautiful Chinese girl entered the general's suite. Hurrying back to his room, Harold wrote again to his wife:

> I have a feeling that our days are limited on sales of crude, etc., in
> Indonesia. Everyone seems to have gotten to Ibnu and are taking
> everything away from us as fast as they can find out how it works.

It is possible that Harold was undergoing nothing more than a transitory moment of despondency in the face of the rapidly widening disparity between Pertamina, now a huge and powerful force in the Asian oil industry, and Harold's own very much smaller company. Refican's net worth had risen from the paltry $50,000 with which Harold and Betty founded it on the strength of Harold's first handshake with Ibnu, to not less than $100 million in 1970. Pertamina's valuation over the same period had shot up from $215 million to nearly $5 billion, raising Ibnu's company to twelfth among the world's top oil producers. General Ibnu was now one of the emperors of world oil, feted by heads of government, global bankers, and business leaders. As he gained in corporate weight and even more in personal stature among the movers and shakers of big oil, Ibnu needed Harold less, while Harold needed Ibnu more.

International events also conspired to highlight the disparity between them. Following the Yom Kippur War, when Israel in October 1973 beat back a surprise attack by the Arabs and invaded Egypt, the OPEC oil states retaliated against the United States and its allies for their failure, in Arab eyes, to rein in the victorious Jews. OPEC unlimbered its "oil weapon." The Arabs cut back oil production in Saudi Arabia, Kuwait, and Iraq, forcing up prices by 200 percent, then 300 percent, and severely limiting, for the second time in a decade, deliveries of the vital fuel on which Americans, Europeans, and Japanese depended to run their industries and drive their cars. Pump prices doubled in America. The United States came close to re-imposing wartime rationing.

For the Huttons' business, this would have been positive news if they had been able to keep their supply of Indonesian crude flowing. The opposite happened. General Ibnu was happy to supply all the heavy crude Refican needed for its lube plant in Pakning, whose output went almost entirely to the local Sumatran market (with Ibnu and the Huttons sharing the profits); but with the world's oil markets running out of crude and every major oil company scouring the world for supplies to make up for the shortfall in Middle East production, Ibnu had more important buyers than Refican. Spurred on by Pertamina's huge earnings and overseas loans, he launched three jumbo projects—a huge 100,000-barrel-a-day refinery on Batam Island south of Singapore, another of the same size in central Java, and an enormous storage-tank farm for the Japanese on the island of Lombok. Only one of these enormous investments, the refinery in Java, paid off, but their sheer magnitude, coupled with the willingness of western banks to finance them on the strength of Pertamina's huge earnings, served only to emphasize the size of the gap between Refican and the diversified multinational conglomerate that General Ibnu now commanded.

Jakarta in the early '70s saw an explosion of the flamboyant and, as it turned out, recklessly extravagant spending that Indonesia's early oil boom precipitated and its fat cat beneficiaries thrived on. Pertamina led the way, splashing out on ambitious new offices and luxurious apartments for the company's executives and their friends. Hot money poured into Jakarta. Japanese and American banks competed to press large loans into the hands of joint venture companies and partnerships with "connections" to the ruling party and President Suharto's family. Typical of the oil boom's projects was a $400 million showplace island, run by Ibnu's son Pontjo, with hotels, factories, office buildings, and a casino.

A quarter-century later an even greater and more extravagant property boom fueled by even more reckless investment by overseas banks was to bring

Indonesia to its knees when confidence in the rupiah collasped in the 1998 currency crisis. The 1960s extravaganza offered an almost exact preview of this. General Ibnu built the world's first floating fertilizer plant at an estimated cost of $150 million, a twenty-eight-story Pertamina tower, a mosque for the University of Indonesia, a television station at Medan, and a circuit of hotels and country clubs. (Harold Hutton supplied the architects and a plane load of best-quality seed for two new golf courses in Java and Bali.)

Over all of Pertamina's grand schemes General Ibnu presided with what his critics condemned as "autocratic splendor." His management style was like Donald Trump's: Ibnu personally initiated every major project, approved every overseas loan and purchase order. His private investments ranged from an aluminum plant to a textile factory and a private club for Jakarta businessmen. But Ibnu was a patriot and visionary as well as business genius. To critics who complained that his wealth and lifestyle matched that of President Suharto, he retorted:

> People think it unseemly for us to work in air conditioned offices, drive big cars and live in good houses while there are citizens who still lack food and clothing. But if we are to build a modern nation we must discard this notion of poverty being normal or inevitable. In the oil business we are dealing with some of the largest and richest companies in the world. To negotiate as equals and obtain the best terms for Indonesia, we must maintain some level of affluence that will make our role credible. Men who wear threadbare clothing and ride in old cars or betjaks cannot negotiate satisfactorily with men who earn $50,000 a year and fly by company jet aircraft.

As 1974 receded over the horizon, it became clear to Pertamina's creditors that Ibnu had overreached himself. To take over control of Indonesia's oil exports, he had invested in forward leases on a fleet of the giant supertankers the Japanese and Koreans were building to carry the world's fuel supplies. At one point, wrote the *Wall Street Journal,* Ibnu had outstanding contracts with a single Geneva-based shipping tycoon named Bruce Rappaport exceeding

$1.2 billion. Later, he claimed in an affidavit that Pertamina had been "outsmarted by Rappaport's deviousness."

Ibnu's enthusiasm for these supertankers mirrored Harold Hutton's of the late 1960s, but in Refican's case, Betty had vetoed the idea and the Huttons dropped their plans to lease and buy tankers of their own. General Ibnu was not as cautious as the Huttons. The market in these big vessels collapsed in the face of the recession of the early 1970s. Pertamina's multibillion dollar leases for a score of supertankers came due as the bottom fell out of the market. Ibnu's company was stuck with ruinous forward commitments it neither could fulfill nor finance.

The first glimmerings of Pertamina's difficulties appeared in the fall of 1974 when Ibnu had to tell President Suharto that his national oil company no longer could deliver the huge stream of revenue and taxes on which Indonesia depended. Instead, Pertamina's revenues were mortgaged to meet the costs of its overseas debts. Foreign banks released the details of the company's over-borrowing. The western media, in an uncannily accurate preview of Indonesia's financial collapse of twenty years later, revealed a web of corruption and sleaze permeating every level of the Indonesian government and the oil company. Yet while the U.S. press condemned this, the administration in Washington preferred at the time to look the other way. "Sukarno is anti-Communist, so he is our guy" was the theme at the White House and Pentagon, echoing twenty years in advance the same misjudgments that official Washington was to maintain right up to the point when "our guy," the impregnable Suharto, was pushed out of office by the student rebellion of 1998.

It was only a matter of time before General Ibnu paid the price for his overinvestments. To Harold Hutton's deep regret, the man who had built up Pertamina from the ashes and created a great national oil industry out of the rusting oil fields abandoned by the Dutch, wrecked by the Japanese, and bombarded by the Allies, was caught up in the financial crisis that arose from the collapse of the tanker market.

Ibnu survived Indonesia's mid-1970s crisis. By dint of his unrivaled achievements and the force of Ibnu's remarkable character, the government and its foreign creditors recognized that the father of Indonesia's greatest asset, its national oil industry, could not be discarded. By the late 1970s, Pertamina had written off close to a billion dollars in losses and bad loans and undergone a top-to-bottom restructuring. The vast company was on its way to recovery. Financially and operationally, Ibnu was back in business.

But Harold's business in Indonesia was nearly done. While Ibnu was its executive head, Pertamina kept just enough of its crude oil flowing to Refican to pay for the Huttons' profitable supply business that shipped valves, cranes, steam shovels, and rebar to its oil fields in north Sumatra. Harold, however, long since had seen the writing on the wall. His premonitions dated back to letters he wrote to Betty as early as 1967, one of which described how they might cut back operations in Asia and even reduce their work force in Long Beach:

> Ibnu told me that Pertamina has made a deal with Caltex for finished lube oil. I think they are going to buy this from now on, instead of ours.

General Ibnu and the Huttons remained close friends. Ibnu and his family took over half of the Pierce Road home in Singapore and sent their son to play golf with the Huttons at the Eldorado Country Club and their daughter to enroll at Chapman College. But by early 1974, Refican was winding down its operations in Indonesia. As pioneers in Sumatra, the Huttons had opened up north Sumatra and lasted a long and profitable time. Both now hoped to retire, to enjoy the fruits of their labor back home in California.

* * * * *

There was another factor that hastened Refican's pullout from Indonesia. As his business there tapered off, Harold had become disillusioned by the rapacity of the black markets that exploded in the international oil trade of the early 1970s. Some of his executives urged him to sell Refican's products to brokers in South Vietnam, but Harold refused. It is unlikely that this reflected any opposition on his part to the increased involvement of the United States in the Vietnam War. Harold, like most of his Orange County friends and business associates, backed the U.S. military and the extension of the air war into Cambodia and Laos. But Harold was repelled by the bribery and corruption that spread like a fungus across both the U.S. and Vietnamese procurement agencies engaged in purchasing supplies for the government of South Vietnam.

This distaste for bribery was nothing new for Harold. More than anything else, the Huttons' unwillingness to engage in it was the reason why Refican had stopped chasing further opportunities in Thailand after he built his first refinery at Fang. Harold was no prude. All his adult life he'd been a shrewd businessman well versed in the ins and outs of the oil business and no stranger to its darker recesses. But Harold drew the line at bribery. Refican would have no part in it. Nor was Harold prepared, as the oil crisis of the 1970s spawned a new breed of swindlers, to follow the "daisy chains" of contacts that were on offer to anyone looking for hard-to-get crude in the aftermath of OPEC's decisions to cut production in 1973.

A typical daisy chain would usually start with a phone call from a self-described oil broker claiming to have contacts in Egypt, Iran, or Qatar. The "contact" could bring in an oil prince, usually in one of the gulf states, who allegedly could provide 300,000 barrels of crude—that was the usual number—for a price below the market guaranteed for up to five years.

Such a case, well known to Harold, occurred when a southern California oil trader received a call from a mysterious Canadian who claimed that he could obtain a huge quantity of Indonesian crude. The oil trader was told to proceed to Toronto and meet with the principals. There, he was introduced to a Pakistani who claimed to be married to the sister of a Saudi prince who was also on the board of Petromin, the Saudi national oil company. What happened next was related some years later by a well-known Los Angeles oil consultant, James M. McDonald, on whose judgment and integrity Harold had always relied:

> The Pakistani had an incredible story. Indonesia was short of money as General Ibnu had tried to develop steel mills, cement plants, automobile plants, etc., all under the banner of Pertamina. The Indonesian debt had risen to a level which was dangerously high. Saudi Arabia would therefore loan Indonesia four billion dollars and then get paid back in Indonesian crude. At $20 per barrel this would come to 200 million barrels. Repayment at 300,000 barrels per day would stretch out for some two years more or less depending on interest payments.

Time was of the essence if this scheme was to work. A team of four people was flying from London to New York that very day. The team consisted of a high official of Pertamina, a financial officer of Petromin, an interpreter, and an attorney. They were supposed to be carrying a contract signed by General Ibnu and certified as legitimate by the Indonesian Embassy in Washington, D.C. A meeting was to be set up in New York the next evening.

McDonald's story continued:

> The Los Angeles trader acted very quickly and got two people from Amerada Hess Oil Company to meet him in New York the following morning. Hess was looking for a firm supply of low sulfur Indonesian crude for its Virgin Island refinery (rated at over 700,000 barrels per day). Hess asked that two bankers for Chase Manhattan Bank also attend. These bankers specialized in Indonesian monetary affairs. The Los Angeles trader met the team in New York at 10:00 P.M. The high Pertamina official turned out to be the former police chief of Jakarta under the ousted president Sukarno. He was now out of favor with the new regime of President Suharto, and persona non grata in Indonesia. The Saudi financial man was actually a Chinese-American from the Bay area. The interpreter was a friend of his. The attorney was a promoter from God knows where. The contract was a telex from Jakarta signed by General Bambang Suomantri (close). It was later learned

that this man had been executed for making offers like this (not verified but an oft repeated story).

The conclusion of this strange tale was that the Los Angeles trader, realizing that he had been conned, canceled the proposed meeting and returned humiliated to California. But as McDonald related it—and as Harold Hutton would have concurred—this kind of chicanery was commonplace in the oil trade of the mid-1970s:

> No one will ever know how many thousands, if not millions of dollars were spent chasing these very elusive pots of crude oil at the ends of countless rainbows. Very often the money spent was in travel, entertainment, phone calls, telexes, and the like—not to mention the time. One man traveled for two years on the back of a wealthy heiress who seemed gullible enough to believe him. He got to her for at least $50,000 per year while chasing fictitious crude oil contracts.[24]

Harold Hutton had learned his own lesson the hard way. He recalled his own 1969 visit to Lebanon to negotiate a refinery in Dahomey and meet the Sultan of Sharjah. Never again would Refican go chasing the daisy chains in search of a swindler's crude!

---

24. James M. McDonald, "Psst, Wanna Buy Some Crude?" *Pacific Oil World.*

INTIMATIONS OF MORTALITY

"Now I know I've finally made it," said Harold Hutton when he agreed with Ross McClintock in 1971 to join forces with Charles Clurman in investing in a 20,000-acre cattle ranch in Nevada. "I've joined the Manchurian mafia."

Harold's investment in the Nevada cattle business was part of his plan to ease himself out of the excitements of east Asia to a last and less exacting chapter of his life back home in America. Betty was strongly in favor of the idea. With her husband's health far from robust, she was determined that they should enjoy more leisure and fewer worries together. She also knew that Harold's never-failing self-assurance had been shaken by a number of personal blows that hit him hard in the late 1960s.

His mother, Carrie Hutton, died in 1967. She and Harold in his adult life had seldom been close. He was far more grief-stricken by the death of the closest companion of his youth, his brother, Don, of whom Harold had always been fond. He and Betty attended Don's funeral service on January 23, 1968, at Fairhaven Memorial Park in Santa Ana. Five of their colleagues from Refining Associates joined Don Struck, Betty's sister's husband, as pallbearers. Harold chose a childlike memorial hymn, hauntingly reminiscent of the songs he used to warble as a teenager in Albert Lea:

> God hath not promised sun without rain,
>
> Joy without sorrow, peace without pain.
>
> But God hath promised strength for the day, rest for the labor,
> Undying love . . .

After his brother's internment, Harold seemed to many of those present to look and feel that he, too, might not have long left to live. Did he, perhaps for the first time, feel those "intimations of mortality" that from time to time afflict even the most robust of men when younger relatives predecease them?

By the fall of 1973, Harold's health was visibly deteriorating and with it his optimism. In his youth, Harold had always worked out in the gym and kept fit as an amateur boxer, though all his life he suffered from heavy colds made worse by his addiction to smoking. As Harold drew closer to his seventieth birthday, he had put on a great deal of weight. He still was a heavy smoker, breathing with difficulty and unable, as General Ibnu discovered when they played golf together at Indian Wells, to get in and out of his golf cart without "puffing like a steam engine." His taste for rich desserts grew more compulsive, leading one of Betty's friends to make the observation, "If Harold doesn't stop eating, he'll kill himself." Betty's pained reply revealed her concern for her husband, "I'd rather he died overeating than overdrinking."

Betty's anxiety was justified. Harold was struggling, as Don Hutton and his brother-in-law, Sammy Struck, had also struggled, with a revival of his taste for alcohol. Several of the letters he wrote to Betty in the early '70s, especially those from airliners flying the Pacific without her, revealed his handwriting to be much more sprawling, his composition erratic, his sentiments muddled and maudlin. One of these epistles, written on Betty's birthday, borrowed eloquently if inaccurately from the Scottish poet Robert Burns, but the sentiment was undercut by Harold's prefatory remark that "I was cold sober when I started, but not so good now."

Coaxed and cajoled by his wife, Harold would go for long periods without touching a drop of alcohol, but when his resolution flagged and he sipped even a small glass of champagne, he would suffer agonies. His liver and stomach linings protested, and he could hardly sleep at all during the nights. Yet it wasn't until 1974 that Harold gave up drinking altogether. His doctor gave him an ultimatum: "If you don't stop drinking you will die." Harold stopped, but he ate even more.

About this time, a subtle change also seemed to be occurring in by far the most important emotional element of Harold Hutton's life—his relationship with Betty. Theirs was both a business partnership and lifelong love affair. Harold had always been and still was the dominant partner in the business. It was he who took the risks and made the decisions; Betty provided the backup and follow-through that translated Harold's strategic judgments into reality while she injected a note of caution or even a veto into some of his more impulsive ideas.

The 1970s saw the couple's respective roles subtly reversing themselves. Harold was still the boss, but there was less, much less, for him to do. His executives handled virtually all Refican's business in Asia. With Tom Chambers in Singapore, Franz Herrnsdorf in Jakarta, Roland Kuppinger in Hong Kong, Robert Dowling in Japan, and Jimmy Perkins and Ralph Wathey in Orange, the company's activities required little, if any, day-to-day intervention by Harold.

Betty, meanwhile, had taken charge of virtually all of their companies' financial activities. "It was Betty, not Harold, to whom one went for decisions," said one of their business associates in 1972. Harold still occupied the chair, but Betty was now running the day-to-day operations of their business.

The Huttons' personal relationship also seems to have altered in the 1970s. Harold began spending more time at their Villa Park home. He became attached to the cats that Betty kept in their homes. Before, Harold had tolerated his wife's pets. Now he started to dote on a Siamese he named Cassius, for Cassius Clay, the heavyweight boxer who was to rename himself Mohammed Ali. Most evenings Harold's first action when he returned home was to stand Cassius on the dryer and brush his fur until it gleamed. "Cassius," he would say, "can knock the socks off any other cat on the block."

Weekends, when driving to their Eldorado Club home in the desert, Cassius would travel alongside Harold in his Ferrari while Betty brought down the provisions in her Cadillac. According to Sylvia Law, Harold got very upset when his cat one day chased a roadrunner and fell into the swimming pool, emerging looking like a drowned rat.

Harold, as he got older, clearly needed Betty more. Harold never lacked self-confidence. Yet his self-esteem, unimpaired in his thrusting youth and middle age, became more dependent as he aged on the approval of others. To look good in his own eyes, Harold, like most men, needed recognition of his achievements and worth by his peers. As his operational role in Refican's activities diminished, Harold could count less and less on the deference of colleagues and partners in the oil business. And as his weight increased and his breath grew shorter, Harold could not compensate by excelling in other fields such as golf. He had also lived overseas too long—and too often had been a thorn in the sides of large U.S. companies—to be invited to join local boards as a nonexecutive director. Harold was a leader and a loner, well liked but not gregarious. Outside his family and business acquaintances, he had few close personal friends. He was a private man. It followed that, as he grew older, Harold needed and longed for the support and approval of his lifetime partner, his wife. Betty, in short, had become his "one sure guide and staff to comfort me." Hers was the only shoulder on which he could cry a little—though it is doubtful if he ever did.

Harold's deep love for his wife continued to pour out from the letters he wrote whenever they were separated. A moving note he wrote to her from a Japan Airlines plane in 1970 contained this revealing passage:

> Many things have been running through my mind, mostly that I want to soon end all this rat race and enjoy some sort of life with you—I really don't want to be rich and don't need it. Neither do I want to be broke, and have to worry about that.

Yet when they were together, there rarely was an instance when Harold and Betty ever embraced in public. Harold was never a man who enjoyed hugs. Perhaps that is why after his death Betty was to remarry another man, Chester Williams, who had none of Harold's blunt strengths but who put his arms around her, kissed her on the cheek, helped her into her coat, and showered her with all the tactile courtesies Harold rarely displayed.

Betty never faltered in the care and attention she devoted to her beloved husband. She looked after his clothes, packed his luggage, renewed his credit cards, checked his calendar, and entertained with meticulous care Harold's long list of business acquaintances. Yet they had none of that bonding of shared parenthood that keeps older couples close. Harold spoiled Betty's nieces, just as she took time and trouble to get closer to his daughter, Barbara, and his four grandchildren. They still lacked the emotional cement that might have come from children of their own.

Betty, too, by the mid-1970s was her own woman. All her life she had been more self-contained than Harold. Now she was also more self-fulfilled, more determined to live her own life. Her love for Harold was unabated and she would do her duty by him, but she also needed—and wanted—some space she could call her own.

It was a combination of all these factors—Harold's presentiment that before long he might become a fifth wheel on the wagon of his business, the lack of other challenges into which he could throw his still-abundant mental energy, and above all, his desire to please Betty—that led Harold in 1974 to make plans to buy a huge yacht and undertake a "six star" voyage around the world. It was if he were looking for a second *Destination*. He wanted and he needed one more great adventure.

As Harold pored over the details of some of the world's finest yachts, any of which would have cost him well over a million dollars, Betty's reactions were mixed. Some of the best times of their lives they had spent together on cruises in the islands of the South Pacific, but Betty was not a great sailor. The oceans had less appeal to her than they did to Harold. But if his heart was set on an ocean-going yacht and one final round-the-world voyage, Harold should have it was Betty's attitude.

Arrangements for the Huttons to purchase a 120-foot yacht were going forward when suddenly came "the sound of trumpet," as Harold described it. The trumpeter, fittingly enough, was the White Russian who had helped launch the Huttons on their career in the Pacific, Charles Clurman.

Last photo taken of Harold

HAROLD'S LAST HURRAH

All his life, Harold Hutton had a soft spot for Charlie Clurman. He therefore listened carefully when one day in September 1974 Clurman made a call that set the adrenalin coursing through the sharp brain in Harold's overweight body. International events, it seemed, once again had created an opportunity that the Huttons might like to grasp.

Long since retired from the Shriro group in the Philippines, Clurman phoned from Reno with news of a curious proposition from the Soviet consulate-general in San Francisco. The context was the first faint easing of tensions between the United States and the Soviet Union. Detente, as this was called, followed President Nixon's 1973 SALT I agreement with Leonid Brezhnev to reduce the number of nuclear missiles the two superpowers were pointing at one another. The Huttons were well aware of this treaty. SALT I was signed at the Casa Pacifica, the "Western White House," where Nixon and Henry Kissinger entertained their Soviet guests in the gardens of a home not ten miles from Betty's future beach house at San Juan Capistrano.

On the night of this historic Summit meeting, Pat Nixon, it later transpired, had walked in her sleep while the Soviet leader was staying at Casa Pacifica. To the consternation of the U.S. Secret Service, the somnambulating first lady was headed off and returned to her bedroom by one of Brezhnev's security men. Earlier that day, Secretary Kissinger and Soviet Ambassador Anatoly Dobrynin, who had flown in and still felt jet-lagged, took the opportunity to saunter down to the beach where, instead of pursuing the diplomatic dialogue they had opened up in the Nixon's dining room, both men fell asleep on the sand and sustained painful sunburns. Such were the stories, confirmed later by Ambassador Dobrynin, that made the rounds among the Huttons and their Orange County friends following the Salt I signing. Soon afterwards, it was announced that the USSR would have the same "most favored nation" trade arrangements with the United States as all other countries enjoyed. One of the trade-offs, it was assumed, was that U.S. oil firms would be admitted to Russia to explore for oil.

Charles Clurman's phone call brought a curious twist to these diplomatic moves. Only a month before, on August 9, 1974, Richard Nixon had been forced to resign by the Watergate scandal. Would his successor, Gerald Ford, continue his discredited predecessor's foreign policy of detente with the Soviet Union? Harold thought he would. "Business is business," he told Betty, recalling their 1948 foray into Russia at the start of the Berlin Airlift that came close to catapulting Europe into a third world war.

Clurman's call seemed to confirm Harold Hutton's hunch that trade with Russia could now proceed. The senior commercial officer of the Soviet consulate in San Francisco had told Clurman of Moscow's desire to develop U.S.-Russian joint ventures in the Soviet far east. This followed President Ford's assurance, given to the Russian ambassador in late August, that his administration was "just as committed to detente" as Nixon's.

The Soviet commercial attache in San Francisco was Vladimir Kronin. According to Clurman, he said, "We understand you know Mr. Harold Hutton. We have checked on his credentials and know that he is a man of independent mind and that he does offshore drilling for oil. We also know that Mr. Hutton has a lot of money in his Hong Kong bank account. Please tell him that we would like Refican to help us drill for oil off the Pacific coast of Russia."

Relayed by Clurman, this strange message was as much of a tonic as a surprise to Harold Hutton. It reminded him of Morris Bach's proposal twenty years earlier to exchange oil for Kamchatka crab. His first instinct was to have nothing to do with the idea. He told Clurman to forget it. But Harold's business instincts by now were fully aroused. Could this be a case of history repeating itself?

Kamchatka was the barren peninsula from whose shores his Russian partners had expected to harvest the crab that he and Betty had purchased in exchange for U.S. surplus oil. Now, twenty years later, the Russians were offering him a chance to drill for oil in the same area. Further conversations with the consulate produced details of exactly where the Russians wanted the Americans to help them drill—off the shore of Sakhalin, the island north of Japan that the Red Army had recovered in 1945 when it entered World War II six days before the Japanese surrender.

Clurman's family had some knowledge of the waters around Sakhalin, having fished there on vacations in the 1930s. The island, whose southern half imperial Japan had seized and renamed Karafuto following its defeat of Russia in 1905, was cold, stormy, and desolate, not unlike those parts of Scotland that bordered the North Sea oil province. Harold's geologists confirmed that portions of the continental shelf between Sakhalin and Kamchatka have petrological characteristics consistent with the presence of oil-bearing beds. Japanese oil prospectors had also offered to explore the area but were rebuffed by the Russians, with whom Japan was engaged in a furious quarrel over four small islands between Sakhalin and the northern-most Japanese province of Hokkaido.

When Harold spoke directly with Vladimir Kronin, the Russian envoy continued to press his invitation. "You will be our guest in Russia," he said. "We will meet you in Hong Kong, then take you to Vladivostock, all expenses paid. We can promise you a very interesting trip."

Whether Harold ever mentioned the Russians' exotic invitation to Betty is not known. For the past two years, he had been promising her to "wind things up (so we can) stop doing things we no longer need to do. I just hope I haven't waited too long—we both need and are entitled to a few years." But the prospect of just one more adventure, one last search for oil, had re-awakened Harold's wildcatter instincts. Suddenly, it seemed, his late midlife crisis was over. He would seize this opportunity on Sakhalin. He would show Betty and the world that there was life in the old boy at seventy.

Harold's preparations for his last adventure took place in conditions of great secrecy. By late 1974, the East-West political barometer had turned from fair to stormy. Detente with the Soviet Union was the word of the hour in Gerald Ford's White House, but the U.S. Congress, like many of Harold's friends, had very different ideas. Conservatives had never liked the SALT I treaty, believing that it would "freeze in" the USSR's numerical advantage in long-range missiles. Liberals like Senator Henry Jackson seized on the Soviets' imposition of an exit tax on Jews to thwart the administration's efforts to improve U.S.-Soviet trade relations. Restrictions were imposed on U.S. credits for exports to the USSR. The President of the AFL-CIO, George Meany, told Congress, "Detente is U.S. weakness . . . Detente means intensification of ideological warfare . . . Detente means ultimate Soviet superiority." According to a *Washington Post* editorial, "a significant number of Americans believe that it is neither desirable, possible nor safe to improve relations with the Soviet Union."

Harold Hutton, as always, was unimpressed by the political tergiversations in Washington. He sensed a new opportunity comparable with the ones that had taken him first to the Pacific islands and the sale of war surplus oil to China and later to Thailand and Sumatra. Refican would shift its operations from southeast to northeast Asia, this time as part of a consortium to which, in one last big effort, Harold would provide strategic direction and seed money. He mooted the possibilities of drilling for oil off Sakhalin with half a dozen of his business friends, among them Ross McClintock of Fluor whose drilling expertise would be crucial. When they agreed to a "fishing expedition" with Vladimir Kronin, Harold sent instructions to his staff in Singapore to have a large sum of cash available, in case he needed it for a new venture. At the time they erroneously thought this venture would be in China.

Charles Clurman and his Russian-born wife, Miriam, meanwhile made arrangements for the Russians to meet Harold and his friends. They met in a private room at the San Francisco airport, those present including Consul Kronin, Harold, Ross McClintock, and, according to Miriam Clurman who made the arrangements, three or four other oilmen who flew in by private jet. Charles Clurman himself was absent in the Philippines. His brother-in-law, Alex Grant, acted as Harold's interpreter.

The result of this meeting was an agreement that Harold would take the lead in making arrangements for a contract to be drawn up between the Americans and a team of Russian specialists at a meeting the following week in Hong Kong. A visit to Sakhalin was envisaged for the summer of 1975, as soon as the weather improved.

Six days later, Harold advanced the date of the next visit he was due to make to Refican's offices in Asia. He told Betty nothing about his latest adventure, hoping to surprise and impress her.

Leaving Los Angeles with a bad head cold, he arrived in Japan, lacking the hat or topcoat that Betty, if she had known of his plans, ordinarily would have been sure to pack for him. He was soaked in a sudden heavy downpour at the Haneda airport while waiting to climb into his car. Overnight in Tokyo, his cold turned to influenza. Without waiting for medical treatment, Harold caught a plane the next day to Hong Kong.

Barbara Chambers, who flew up from Singapore to meet him, was surprised that her father was not at the Hong Kong airport when she arrived. Instead, he was in bed in the Thai Suite in the Hilton Hotel. "A doctor was there and a nurse but he had not spoken to anyone," said Barbara. "He was unconscious. I thought he wasn't breathing." The hotel's Chinese doctor ordered Harold to be taken to the nearest hospital. At a time when Hong Kong was teeming with refugees from China, all its wards were overcrowded and none of the porters spoke English. Harold, barely conscious, was placed on a trolley and wheeled into a corridor to await his turn to be examined. What happened next is unclear, but it appears that he lapsed into total unconsciousness and in the press of business, was ignored.

Barbara's account continues:

> I sat in the waiting room all night. I fell asleep on the bench and they covered me with a blanket. When they let me see Daddy, he was still on a trolley in the corridor. He opened his eyes and got angry. "Get me out of here," he said. I demanded a nurse and got one. With help from the U.S. Consul General we found a place in a private ward in Canassa Catholic Hospital. It was a very bad bumpy trip to get there in the ambulance. Daddy had severe pains in his back. On arrival he was very weak.

By the time Harold Hutton was installed in Canassa Hospital, Barbara had sent urgent messages to Betty in Orange and alerted Refican's executives. Roland Kuppinger, the Hong Kong manager, picked up Tom Chambers and Joe Gohier, who had flown in from Jakarta.

They were too late. Staphylococcal pneumonia filled Harold's lungs. A massive coronary thrombosis ended his life at 3:30 P.M. on February 24, 1975. Harold was not eight weeks short of age seventy-one.

*****

Taken by surprise, Betty, still in Orange, was devastated. Harold and she had spent the best part of their lives together in east Asia; now they were parted, forever, on different sides of the vast ocean in and on whose waters they both had found fortune and happiness. Betty made arrangements to fly to Hong Kong, but Tom Chambers dissuaded her. It was far better, he advised her, to wait until Harold could be flown home in a matter of days. There was nothing that his widow could do for him in Hong Kong.

Harold's homecoming proved difficult. Under Hong Kong law, a post-mortem examination had to be done before a dead body could be removed from the Crown colony's jurisdiction. Due to a shortage of coroners, this examination was delayed for three days. The corpse had then to be embalmed before Pan American Airlines would accept it for the flight to California. The embalmers did not do a good job. Harold's ordinarily crisp gray hair was plastered down on his skull. Tenderly, his only daughter washed her father's hair, then boarded the plane with the casket.

Except for the grief-stricken Betty, waiting at Los Angeles airport, every senior member of the Refican Company was on the Pan Am aircraft as Harold Hutton left Hong Kong for the last time on March 1, 1975. "If it had gone down, that would have been the end of the company, as well as Daddy," Barbara observed.

Part X Life after Harold

SAYING FAREWELL

Betty Hutton looked pale and strained as, clad in a black suit and mauve blouse, she waited at Los Angeles airport for the Pan American Clipper flight to arrive from Hong Kong. It was midmorning on March 1, 1975. The California sky was gray and overcast as the big-bellied Stratocruiser with her husband's casket on board taxied to a halt, allowing its weary passengers to stream into the terminal. Among the first to disembark were Harold's daughter, Barbara Chambers, and her husband, Tom, an executive of Refican in Southeast Asia. Betty embraced her stepdaughter. The two women had not always been soul mates but now they were united in grief.

One by one, Tom Chambers and the other members of the Refican team, among them Joe Gohier and Roland Kuppinger from Hong Kong, Franz Herrnsdorf from Jakarta, and Frank Iwase from Toyko, squeezed Betty's hand, kissed her on the cheek, or clasped her in their arms. There was no doubting the depth of their sadness. Each felt he had lost a friend as well as a generous boss. There was no question either about the sincerity of their concern for the woman who over the years had given every one of them unstinting support in the field.

Harold had provided Refican with its leadership, business sense, and inspiration, but it was his widow who, especially in recent years, had provided the indispensable back-up its executives needed in the jungles of Sumatra or in the offices where they worked in Jakarta, Hong Kong, Tokyo, and Singapore. Hers was the name that more often than not appeared on authorizations for new equipment. Hers was the signature on their year-end bonus checks, the shoulder on which their wives and families could lean in times of adversity.

Now it would fall to Betty as the sole heir and executor to decide what would happen next, not only to Refican and its people but to the California end of the business: Refining Associates. It was therefore only natural that behind their expressions of sympathy and grief, each of the thirteen top Refican managers who had accompanied Harold Hutton's casket on its final journey across the Pacific harbored inward anxieties. How would the change of command from bluff and bold Harold to cautious Mrs. Hutton impact their jobs and prospects? How would a woman on her own in a still male-dominated industry handle a complex international oil business whose special relationship with its largest supplier, Pertamina, had developed problems and most likely would not survive Harold Hutton's decease? On whose advice would Betty rely? Refican's overseas business had been the powerhouse of the entire Hutton empire with Refining Associates serving principally as its supply arm and marketing department. Would the office workers in southern California now take over from the field men in Asia?

All those worries, however, were for tomorrow. Now, the time had come to say goodbye to Harold. As his widow watched, the casket was trundled from the freight bay, inspected by customs officials, and passed into the safekeeping of the undertakers Betty had hired from Fairhaven Memorial Park in Santa Ana. The funeral took place two days later at the same Waverley Church where seven years earlier Harold had arranged the obsequies for his beloved brother, Don Hutton. Betty assuaged her grief by busying herself with the details. Ever since that first tearful telephone call, when Barbara called from Hong Kong to give her the news of Harold's death, she characteristically had thrown herself into a flurry of activity, drawing up announcements to the media and notices to staff and customers, preparing the list of invitations and the order of the service for the funeral, making arrangements for the reception that would take place afterwards at the Huttons' now eerily empty home in Villa Park.

Waverley Church was overflowing with mourners on the morning of March 3. Many figures from the world oil industry attended, Japanese and

Thai as well as Indonesian and American. Among them was Tom Brook, chairman of Asamera Oil Corporation. He and Harold had not met since they quarreled in the far-off Sumatran city of Medan. Brook flew in specially to offer his last respects. Betty, supported by her sister, Mary, took her place alongside Barbara and Tom Chambers in the front row of the church. Outwardly, she appeared calm and composed. She displayed no overt signs of the emotions that were stirring within her as the organist played Wagner's great funeral march and the choir sang Harold's favorite hymn, "Rock of Ages." Harold's daughter, Barbara, had been given the choice of the lesson that should be used. The tears coursed down her cheeks as Tom Chambers read the words from the Twenty-Third Psalm. "The Lord is my shepherd, I shall not want." But it was the eulogy that stayed longest in most of the mourner's memories. Ross McClintock, Harold's old friend, had been a buccaneer like Harold was. His tribute was filled with wry stories and oilmen's anecdotes. McClintock was a strong man, but he came close to tears as he recalled his friend's most endearing qualities: "courage . . . vision . . . enterprise . . . love for his fellow man."

Bearing the coffin to the hearse that would take Harold to his grave, Sammy Struck, Harold's brother-in-law, was joined by Brad Hovey, Ralph Wathey, Jimmy Perkins, Harold Nelson, and Ross Staton, one of Refican's senior engineers. As they proceeded through the crowd of well-wishers standing outside, where loudspeakers had been set up to enable them to hear the service, bright sunshine broke through the cloud layer. The sky was the same color as Harold's piercing blue eyes as he was laid to rest in a newly opened section of Fairhaven Memorial Park. Betty had purchased this plot and five others alongside it shortly after she got word of Harold's death. She wanted to be sure that she and her family would lie beside him when their time came.

That evening several hundred relatives, friends, and well-wishers attended the reception Betty offered at the place that Harold had called his Villa Serena when the couple thirty years earlier had established their first home in Orange

County. When they were gone, Betty chose to be alone. Waving aside her family's offers to stay with her overnight, she masked her feelings of grief and uncertainty and retired alone. Her only companion was Cassius, Harold's favorite cat.

So began the most difficult period of Betty Hutton's life. At 63, she faced the end of an era. The larger-than-life partner with whom she had built her life, her business, her career was gone. She now had to decide where, how, and with whom to make the best use of her talents and the large fortune she and Harold had earned. Betty was still healthy and strong. She could reasonably expect to survive Harold by twenty years. But she needed time to think, to reflect. The man who since her twenties had taken care of nearly all the big decisions that had shaped her life no longer would be there to rely on. Betty had lost more than a partner. Harold had been her champion, protector, and guide.

Her immediate response was to "carry on as usual." She drove each morning to her Orange office intent on continuing the business she and her husband had built up together. Harold's will, unchanged since he first drew it up in August 1968, made Betty his sole executrix. She was the only inheritor of the half a dozen homes in which they had lived and "all articles of personal, domestic, or household use, jewelry, furniture, books, pictures, plates, household effects and all automobiles, which at the time of my death shall be in, about, or used in connection with my homes." The rest of Harold's assets, held as community property during their marriage, already had been placed in a trust of which Betty, as the surviving trustor, was given "absolute testamentary general power of appointment, exercisable in all events and at any time after the death of the first deceased." The only other beneficiaries were Harold's only daughter, Barbara Hutton Chambers, to whom, under the terms of a separate trust, a sum running into several million dollars was made available in her lifetime and on her death was to be paid in equal shares to Barbara's four children.

Harold's will left Betty an extremely rich woman. It also left her with responsibility for a complex and far-reaching international business, parts of which already were starting to unravel. Betty in many ways was well-prepared to take over from Harold. While her husband had been their companies' captain and navigator, Betty very often had served as its helmsman, purser, and supply officer. From the start, she'd been its chief bookkeeper. There was little Betty did not know about the contracts, finances, customers, and the wide range of political contacts that constituted the working capital of their joint enterprise.

Yet in other ways Betty Hutton was ill-prepared to take over from Harold. She and her husband had been a team, each with separate strengths and weaknesses. Harold had a flair for business. Making deals was second nature to him. With his uncanny ability to "read" people, he could afford to operate on a "handshake for a contract" basis. Harold had learned the hard way how to judge the character and reliability of customers, partners, investors, and employees alike but not so Betty Hutton. If Harold's strength had lain in his ability to "see the big picture" and gamble on it, Betty's lay in organization and details. Harold's forte was that he maximized the talents of those who worked for and with him while minimizing the effects of their weaknesses. Betty almost never judged people; with Harold she rarely needed to. Her instinct was to expect the best, to instill loyalty in her staff by never questioning their motives or doubting their integrity. Betty was a shrewd and experienced businesswoman. But as she took over the leadership of the Huttons' conglomerate, she did not at first respond well to the confrontations that are hard to avoid when strategic decisions must be made. At times she turned away from issues she found painful; on occasion she avoided choices that involved parting with people she had relied on but who failed to repay her trust. Betty Hutton had much to learn over the coming decade, nearly always through trial-and-error and sometimes at great expense.

Essentially, she faced three main options as she sought to craft a new future. One was to follow the advice she for years had been pressing on Harold—to retire and enjoy the riches they had built up together. This would mean selling— or "selling out" as she put it—both Refican and Refining Associates, and this

Betty just could not do. Her pioneer blood forbade it. Her business instincts told her that liquidating the Hutton empire in the midst of the 1970s recession would mean the disposal of its assets at far less than their market value. It would also leave its employees in the lurch.

A second option was to build on the foundations that she and Harold had laid, to stay in the international oil business despite General Ibnu's problems in Indonesia and Pertamina's increasing reluctance to use Refican as a major outlet for its crude. Refican, however, would need either to grow much larger so as to take on its bigger competitors or to identify new niche markets. Betty was far from convinced that either she personally or her management team was equipped, without Harold's leadership, to undertake the job of re-orienting the whole of their business in the highly competitive world of the oil production and supply market of the 1970s.

A third option was to change course, to strike out in fresh directions. The U.S. economy had changed beyond recognition since Betty and Harold had first moved out from California to seek their fortune in Asia. New technology was transforming the business environment. The Cold War had generated massive new investments in aircraft and missiles. Since the Soviets in 1957 launched their first *Sputnik,* the United States had accepted—and was on the way to winning—the competition to explore outer space. From America's great universities poured a series of new discoveries in electronics, lasers, and exotic materials that before long would create vast new industries, churning out ever-more sophisticated computer, telecommunications, and artificial intelligence products. For anyone with capital and vision, this new era seemed to offer gilt-edged opportunities. And California was well-placed to take advantage of them. Wherever Betty looked, campuses such as Stanford and UCLA, both of which she had close family connections with, were turning out graduates in science and business administration (including Bill Gates and Steve Jobs) whose new ventures offered no less exciting—and because they were in America, more secure—prospects for investors than those the Huttons had pursued in Southeast Asia.

It took Betty Hutton six months to determine the direction and strategy her businesses should follow. Rejecting the first option of retirement, she tried at first to stay in the oil industry while at the same time casting around for other technological possibilities. As a rich widow reputed to have substantial cash to invest, she was besieged by inventors and merchant adventurers offering "opportunities too good to miss." For a long time, she reacted to events and other people's self-interested suggestions, rather than taking a grip on her own destiny.

But Betty had to make changes. Within days of Harold's funeral, William Cruikshank, attorney and board member of Refican since 1967, had to resign as president pro tem of the corporation so as to begin the disposition of Harold's estate. In his place, Betty appointed Ralph Wathey, a well-liked and trusted member of the Refinate family, with instructions to explore the possibility of repositioning the oil company in North America.

Together, Betty and Wathey considered the purchase of refineries from Gulf Oil and Douglas Oil. Neither proved to be feasible. There were too many government regulations in America. Uncertainty over Refican's future role in Indonesia likewise led Betty to conclude that the costs and risks of seeking to expand in the South Pacific's exploration and production fields were too great for her to contemplate.

Ralph Wathey, meanwhile had sent a memo to the U.S.-based staff asking for their ideas on what Refining Associates might do besides support Refican and sell oil to Fuji Kosan in Japan. In early June, he told them that the California oil brokerage and supply company no longer could do business as it had done in the past. Scouring the world for hard-to-get crude in the face of the shortages generated by the international oil crisis that followed the Yom Kippur War was an unpromising prospect. Without Harold, there was little prospect of Pertamina's continuing to supply Refican with Indonesian crude oil at a preferential rate when other larger corporations were prepared to pay top dollar to meet their customers' demands.

Reluctantly, Betty accepted that neither Refining Associates nor Refican any longer had the management or resources to compete in the cutthroat oil world of the late 1970s. The trans-Pacific business that she and Harold had spent the best years of their lives developing would have to be closed down. Ralph Wathey and two new Board members, Brad Hovey and Willie Chapman, appointed by Betty soon after Harold's death, began the complex legal process required to sell, liquidate, or write-off more than a score of separate companies that had made up the Hutton group. The dismantling process was to continue for nearly two years. For Betty, it was one of the most troubling periods of her life. She characterized 1976 as the "year of the layoffs."

By early summer, the office staff in Orange had been halved. By fall, the only ones who remained were Ralph Wathey, who directed the dissolution of the company, Brad Hovey, Willie Chapman, and Betty's secretary and confidante, Sylvia Law. Two outstanding contracts made it impossible to close down the Singapore operation immediately. Not until the spring of 1977 did the last tankers with Refican oil leave Indonesia. Then the Norwegian tanker *Dagfred* left Pangkalan Susu for Tacoma, Washington, followed perhaps appropriately by the Japanese-owned *Riyu Toku Maru,* which delivered the last load of Hutton oil to Los Angeles on March 8, 1977. It was just short of nineteen years since the *Shozui Maru,* one tenth its size, had left Pangkalan Susu with the first miniload of 1,700 tons of crude that laid the foundations of both Pertamina and the Huttons' success in the Pacific oil business.

On October 20, Betty left for three weeks to oversee the disposition of the Pierce Road house and office where she had lived and worked since 1962. During this return visit to Singapore, she dismantled Refican's files and shipped back to her Orange County office tens of thousands of documents that might be pertinent to the company's dissolution. Even more distressing than closing the office was stripping bare the Pierce Road home she and Harold had loved so well. Most of the pictures and Betty's priceless collection of Asian porcelain, antiques, and jewelry were carefully itemized and packaged for shipment to

California. One by one, she listed, packed, and shipped home all the books in Harold's extensive library, among them Arnold Toynbee's great *Study of History*, Winston S. Churchill's six-volume *The Second World War*, technical and travel books about China, Indonesia, and Russia, and paperback thrillers by the score (Harold just loved James Bond!). The rest of their furnishings, together with the house and grounds, were sold to a Chinese contractor, Tan Sri Khoo Teck Puat, in January 1977. The price, less than $5 million, was far below the property's international value. Like Tom Chambers, who sold the house in Singapore that Harold had bought for him and Barbara in 1963, Betty was caught by a Singapore law stipulating that all foreign-owned property must be sold only to Singaporeans. Twenty years later, when 28 Pierce Road was again to change hands, this time for development purposes, its selling price was close to $60 million.

It was while Betty was away in Singapore that news leaked out that what was left of Refining Associates' office in Orange would close. Betty, in fact, had made up her mind that closure was inevitable before taking off for the Far East, but she could not bring herself to share this decision with the staff. Two days after she left, the remaining staff received a letter from Roland Kuppinger in Hong Kong telling them that their office was to close. Operations were to cease by the end of November. Speaking by telephone from Singapore, Betty on November 3 gave Ralph Wathey authority to liquidate. By the time she returned home from Singapore, termination notices had been sent to all Refining Associates employees and vendors.

By November 15, it was clear that Refican, too, would be shut down. Corporate Vice President Willie Chapman left on November 29, 1976. His farewell was particularly painful for Betty. Over the past fifteen years, Chapman had become a trusted friend as well as a key player in the development of the company. At his farewell luncheon at the Villa Fontana, one of her favorite restaurants, Betty was visibly moved. Two weeks later, the scene was to be repeated at the Santa Ana Country Club as Betty said her farewells to her assistant, Sylvia Law. "When I got back to the office to finish up some final details, we were both weeping," said Sylvia. She volunteered to return should Betty ever need her. Prophetically, Betty said, "You can count on it."

A formal vote of the Board of Directors to dissolve and liquidate Refining Associates and Refican was recorded in a letter dated December 8, 1976. The Glassell Street office building was for sale. On December 15, Bekins trucks moved in to carry the files to storage in Santa Ana. Enough desks were dropped off to furnish a far smaller office in Tustin for Betty's future operations. Only Ralph Wathey, Brad Hovey, and Betty's sister, Mary, remained until Sylvia Law, returning from a retirement visit to her family in Scotland and Ireland, phoned Betty to say hello. Sylvia was promptly rehired to set up Betty's new office. Ralph Wathey retired in October 1977.

With the empire the Huttons had built now reduced to only Betty and three employees, her thoughts once again turned to the possibility of retirement. Why not put aside the stresses and strains of business and enjoy the freedom she had earned and could afford? Betty had ample income from the trust that she and Harold had established, with enough left over to fund the charitable foundation they both had always contemplated. Why risk her fortune and the security it offered by starting a new career? Family issues, too, demanded Betty's attention. As trustee of J. D. Spennetta's trust, she was responsible for managing her mother's assets. Four nieces, her sister's daughters, were also starting families of their own. During the years she lived in east Asia, there had been only limited opportunities for Betty to entertain these young ladies, when, thanks to Harold's generosity, they had spent long vacations at Pierce Road. Now, she could take all the time she needed to get to know them better and take part in her extended family's activities.

In short, Betty Hutton had every reason to retire except one: her character. She saw herself a businesswoman. She wanted to make things happen. Like her mother, she needed to be busy; like her father, she found in work the source of her greatest satisfaction. Above all, her life with Harold had whetted

Betty's appetite for enterprise and adventure. She felt fit enough, even young enough, to start a second career, and she would do it in the place she knew best, Orange County.

Betty launches a second career

The "Widow Hutton" Re-invents Herself

Growing up in Villa Park in the 1920s, Betty Hutton had seen the county best known for its principal crop, Valencia oranges, change slowly over the years while she and Harold were courting, and more drastically during World War II when the Huttons were building up their business in Long Beach. Since then the pace and cost of progress had accelerated. Wide tracts of the citrus ranches that had covered most of Orange County when the Huttons moved their base of operations to east Asia had disappeared under roofs and concrete by the time of Harold's death. In one ten-year period, 1954–1963, more than 75 percent of Orange County's farmland had been converted from agriculture to housing, offices, shopping malls, public buildings, and highways.

As Betty sought to redirect her companies' development and rebuild her own life without Harold, she was impressed by the avalanche of change. As a citrus rancher's daughter, she regretted the disappearance of the scented blossoms and golden fruit, the empty beaches, and the unspoiled foothills of her youth. Well over half of Orange County's open space had been planted with citrus orchards when she and Harold took up residence in Singapore; now only 65,000 acres of land was under cultivation, and less than 13 percent of this planted with fruit trees.

Betty nonetheless recognized that there was no stopping progress. As the descendant of pioneers who had watched a once-empty continent open up to the demands of its immigrants, she knew that the trend was irreversible. The post-war pressure for homes to accommodate returning veterans had been succeeded in the '60s and '70s by the movement of industry and offices out of Los Angeles into Orange County. Since the Santa Ana Freeway had penetrated Orange County and a prescient Walt Disney had opened America's first theme park in Anaheim, the developers had been building a greater number of homes every year than the 49,000 residences Orange County counted when the Japanese attacked Pearl Harbor. Manufacturing had become Orange County's biggest industry. Aircraft and electronics were employing well over half the work force.

What this meant for Betty personally could be seen in the evening, when she liked to sit out on her patio, looking west toward the setting sun. From the home she and Harold had built among the orange orchards above Villa Park, their view in the early '50s extended across the plain of the Santa Ana River to Newport Harbor and on clear evenings across the thirty-mile channel to Catalina Island. Now Betty found it hard to identify all the tall buildings and clusters of factories, offices, and science parks that by the late 1970s had sprouted up around the new estates in Tustin and Irvine, interrupting her view of Newport Harbor and the ocean.

She made a point of driving around the county with her sister, Mary. They visited old family friends, many of whom had made large fortunes by selling to the developers the ranches the Spennettas had collected oranges from and delivered fertilizers to in the golden '20s. Betty saw for herself how the beachfronts and canyons she had haunted as a schoolgirl had been transformed, not always for the better, by the arrival of more than a million new families. Betty was an avid listener as well as a keen observer. It did not take her long to recognize the opportunities, if not the pitfalls, that Orange County's hothouse growth offered to anyone with liquid capital and credit. The business instincts she had inherited from generations of Spennettas and Chunings stimulated her desire to get involved. Latecomer she might be, but Betty made up her mind to forget retirement. Instead, she launched into a second career in the world of property development and enterprise that was unfolding all around her.

How, where, and with whom to do this was soon the biggest question preoccupying Betty. Throughout her adult life, she had worked in the oil business and overseas trade. She knew how to read a balance sheet, how to buy and sell heavy equipment, and how to be a diligent manager. She inspired intense loyalty among her staff at home and abroad. But Betty was no Harold. She was fascinated by the new technologies that in little more than a decade had added 1.1 million square feet of gleaming new offices and science parks in Anaheim, Irvine, Tustin, and Santa Ana. But it was one thing to recognize the opportunities created by this property boom and quite another for a woman in her sixties, who for the past quarter century had lived and worked overseas to take advantage of them. She would not be able to acquire overnight the knowledge and, more important, the instincts to make a late start in the fiercely competitive business of Orange County in the late 1970s.

Betty did the right thing. She sought advice. Much of it turned out badly and led to Betty's coming perilously close to losing a large part of the Huttons' fortune as well as her sense of security. Nor could Betty herself escape all the blame for the near-disasters that were to befall her business. An intensely private woman who had gladly left the strategic decisions to her husband while she looked after the details, she was about to relaunch herself into the most rapidly evolving sector of the fastest expanding region of the United States. Before long Betty also contracted a second marriage with a former economics teacher from Louisiana, Chester A. Williams. Their union brought sorrows as well as joys and encouraged Betty to indulge the passion for world travel that she and Chester shared.

Betty never fully reconciled these often incompatible objectives—a new and challenging second career in U.S. business and a life of leisure and travel with her second husband. The essence of her problem was what many women in their youth and middle years have to resolve—making hard choices between work and family. Betty, being childless, had never had to confront such dilemmas. Her career and her marriage to Harold were not separate: they were one. Their marriage thrived on their business. Their company was their family. Now in her sixties, Betty for the first time had to choose between a large and complex business requiring a great deal of her time and attention and the space and leisure she needed to enjoy the wealth she and Harold had earned. Betty was also to acquire a second family when she married Chester. She had to decide how much of her time and love to devote to her new husband's needs, especially as his health deteriorated, when this commitment distracted her from the leadership responsibilities she owed to Hutton Associates. Before time, events, and luck resolved these dilemmas for her, Betty learned some costly lessons. Despite her outward serenity, peace of mind escaped her until, finally, she sought help from within her own family, from a younger man, Tom Parker.

* * * * *

Betty's first solo business effort in 1976 was a bank. Like her father, who crowned his success in the citrus and haulage industries by becoming a director of the First National Bank of Olive, she had a fascination for the management of money. Following her father's advice, she had opened a charter account with Security Pacific Bank, which until its merger with the Bank of America was southern California's largest indigenous bank. Now, as the executor of both her husband's and her father's estates, Betty was far from satisfied with her bankers' handling of her own and her mother's portfolio. If only she had a bank of her own, Betty was convinced, she could probably earn more.

It was not to be. On the recommendation of her lawyer, Bill Cruikshank, she pursued the possibility of opening a bank in one of the remotest places on earth, one of the four Bank Islands at the north end of the New Hebrides chain in the South Pacific. Fifteen hundred miles northeast of Brisbane, the New Hebrides consist of forty mountainous islets, many of them volcanic, comprising a total land area of 5,700 square miles. The archipelago had briefly been occupied by the Japanese navy in World War II, but Allied forces were unopposed when in 1944 they recovered the New Hebrides group and returned it to Australia. The total population at the end of World War II was less than 40,000, many still primitive Melanesians. Neither Cruikshank nor Betty knew very much more than that about the New Hebrides when they set out to found a bank in the

Striking out in new directions

Bank Islands. Not even on their most adventurous South Seas expeditions had the Huttons ever come close to visiting this far off corner of the Pacific. But lawyer Cruikshank had heard that the impecunious administrators of the New Hebrides were on the lookout for American investors willing to open a bank that would accept offshore deposits. Taxes would be waived. The bank would handle tax exiles' accounts. Betty was intrigued. The poetic sounding names of the Bank Islands—Gaua, Vanua, Lava, Monta, and Valua—reminded her of the South Seas tales of Somerset Maugham. Nor would she ever forget those happy days when she and Harold had sailed the southern seas on the *Destination*. Fewer things gave her more pleasure than to listen to *South Pacific,* whose tunes she and Harold had listened to day after day while aboard their converted minesweeper.

Bill Cruikshank asked two old Refican hands, Joe Gohier and Roland Kuppinger, who still were on the payroll of Refican, to research the possibilities. On May 28, 1976, he formally incorporated a company named the Bank Islands Bank Ltd., New Hebrides. It lasted for barely five months. Gohier and Kuppinger reported that the proposed venture was a pipe dream. Despite its supposed tax advantages, the New Hebrides produced little but coconut oil and sandalwood. The Bank Islands had neither an airport nor hotel facilities to attract tourists. Nor at the time was there any realistic prospect of U.S. or Japanese investors choosing the islands of the South Pacific with their almost total lack of modern telecommunications as tax havens in preference to far better-situated places like Bermuda or the Cayman Islands. The venture was formally terminated on June 23, 1977, saving Betty from a potential disaster.

By now, however, fresh ventures nearer to home were higher on her agenda. Betty was unhappy with the returns on the trust funds left to her by Harold, which had been held in liquid bank accounts pending final disposition of inheritance tax liabilities. Cruikshank urged her instead to consider investing in a series of joint venture partnerships. These, he said, could yield a return more commensurate with the potential her wealth could expect to command. Among these "opportunities" were a large number that were pitched by Orange County hustlers attracted, like wasps to a honeypot, by the prospects of "assisting" a rich widow returned from abroad. Nearly all of them Betty rejected, but she still needed help to sort the wheat from the chaff. Searching for a manager as well as a lawyer, Betty soon identified a new consultant.

Davis Chamberlin, called "Dave" by many people, was a youthful graduate of Pepperdine who had recently been appointed Chief Executive of Chapman College, now Chapman University. Chapman had a special place in Betty Hutton's heart. It occupied the campus and many of the fine buildings of the former Orange Union High School, where in her teens she had blossomed as scholar, athlete, and leader of the self-styled "gang" of girls who ever since had kept in close touch. Harold had served as a Chapman trustee for the last four years of his life. Betty took his place on the college board on July 28, 1975.

Davis Chamberlin, a deceptively mild-looking man, was an extremely good talker. An aide to one of Orange County's most successful property developers, he had been appointed to Chapman as an interim chief executive, charged to tackle a serious financial crisis that led many to wonder if the college would survive. Betty Hutton was to help rescue Chapman. Her generous support gave her a new and satisfying role, fulfilling her commitment to youth and her zeal for education as well as binding her more closely to her old school and the local community.

Betty, however, was to receive over the first years of her new relationship with Chapman more help from its interim president than she had bargained for. Within a year of becoming a trustee, she found herself discussing her own as well as the college's financial problems with Davis Chamberlin. His verbal dexterity during heated Chapman board meetings had impressed her. So, too, did his enthusiasm for joint venture partnerships as a means by which she might leverage her high liquidity, strong cash, and credit assets into greater returns.

That summer, Betty made her first move as an independent Orange County entrepreneur. From exploitation of the jungles of Southeast Asia, she turned to exploration of the corporate jungle of urban southern California. She set up her own company, Hutton Associates, chartered on August 3, 1977. Its principal assets arose from the trusts established by Harold and Betty, including funds designed to provide for her brother and sister and their heirs. Corporate offices were established at 17581 Irvine Boulevard in Tustin, a building the Hutton Trust would purchase by the end of 1977. As CEO of Hutton Associates, Betty appointed Davis Chamberlin, who by now had been replaced at Chapman. Bill Cruikshank, Betty's lawyer, agreed to serve as vice president. With Brad Hovey and her sister, Mary, continuing as directors and senior staff, Betty herself assumed the duties of secretary to the board and chief financial officer. These were the same positions she had occupied for over thirty years at Refining Associates and Refican.

Davis Chamberlin at first seemed to be an ideal leader. At Chapman he had cultivated a wide range of contacts with the business leaders shaping Orange County's future, an advantage not diminished by the fact that his wife was secretary to the Orange County Board of Supervisors. Betty's knowledge of her new CEO was limited. Chamberlin was neither a trained executive nor a financial manager. Under orders from a strong-minded boss like George Argyros, now chairman of Chapman's Board of Trustees, he could be, and often was, effective on a narrow front, e.g., in cutting payrolls. But as Betty was to discover, Chamberlin was more a self-promoter than a chief executive. He lacked experience and talent to launch a large multifaceted company into the highly competitive environment of a county whose economy, according to the *Los Angeles Times'* carefully researched commemoration of Orange County's 100th anniversary, had become "distinctly high-tech, white collar and successful— so successful that it was creating problems."

Chamberlin's opening gambit as president of Hutton was to engage as his assistant a tall, rangy ex-football player, Bill Zogg, who had worked with him at Chapman. Together with lawyer Cruikshank, they organized the first of what would become a series of "investment retreats," opportunities to brainstorm about future business possibilities. This retreat took place at Betty's desert home in Indian Wells. Its stated purpose was "to provide direction and establish a plan for her future investments." Chamberlin and Zogg brought in specialists from various target areas such as energy, real estate, agriculture, financial services, and education.

Betty threw herself into reading and learning all she could about the exciting new prospects they offered. Two days of concentrated talk and socializing opened her eyes to the latest changes in the business climate and the accelerating pace of scientific innovation. Afterwards, she confided to members of her family that her grasp of both the jargon and the technicalities was limited. Another telling comment was Betty's observation that when she and Harold had been in the oil business, she knew the industry and how to respond to it; now she had to depend on others, to put herself into the hands of the advisors she had gathered around her.

Deep down, as she later was to admit, Betty felt far from comfortable about this situation. Unlike Harold, she had little experience evaluating the technical competence of the people she had now to rely on. Betty always shied away from probing her advisors' own motives. One of her more endearing qualities was that she rarely judged other people or questioned their intentions. During the years that immediately followed the loss of a husband who performed these necessary tasks for them both, Betty's inexperience in picking the most suitable subordinates and utilizing those around her for her own advantage was to prove a shortcoming that cost Hutton Associates dearly.

Before long, the trio of Chamberlin, Zogg, and Cruikshank had stepped up the pace of Hutton's acquisitions. The company invested in a broad range of partnerships, owning railroad tank cars, public storage facilities, a pig ranch, and a jewelry design and sales business, to name but a few. Betty was moving down paths with which she and her executive team were only vaguely familiar. One of the more speculative investments was in Y.Y. Inc., a yogurt chain of which Bill Cruikshank's wife, Rita, was president. Financially, Y.Y. turned out to be a disaster.

By far the biggest investment was undertaken when Chamberlin introduced Betty to a representative from Logical Business Machines, a computer
technology firm based in Sunnyvale, California. Logical sought Hutton's
backing to develop computers to program languages for European customers.
The idea possessed great promise. Personal computing was emerging from its
infancy, but even the best-known manufacturers of computing machinery at the
time had still to establish uniform programming languages. It was an age when
computer technology was paving the way for the rise of new industrial empires
like Microsoft and Apple. Why should Logical and Hutton not follow in the
footsteps of Bill Gates and Steve Jobs?

Betty was impressed and intrigued. Logical offered her a chance to invest in
a technology that was certain to be part of the future. The company clearly
offered global marketing potential; its products could also have applications for
education. With Chamberlin's strong recommendation, Hutton Associates
purchased a majority of Logical's stock. There was only one drawback. Leading-
edge computer technology was alien turf to Betty and her team. The industry,
too, was proliferating at the speed of the latest gigabyte. To stay on top of it
required highly sophisticated and scientifically knowledgeable management.
This was not Chamberlin's forte. He and Hutton Associates had made a
substantial investment in a business about which Betty and her advisors knew
much less than they needed to know. They suffered the consequences for
many years to come.

For now, however, the watchwords of the Hutton company under
Chamberlin and Zogg's leadership were "expand" and "diversify." At a time
when most major U.S. corporations were reaching into unrelated fields, like
sporting goods stores and discount drug chains, it seemed natural for Betty, too,
to invest in an ever-wider range of partnerships and joint ventures. The Hutton
Trust invested in high-grade bonds, notes, and industrial diamonds. Hutton
Associates bought part of a cattle ranch in Nevada and a condominium development near Reno and offered real estate loans. Research began on the purchase
of Newport Beach radio station KOCM.

Another venture was California Business Financial (CBF), the idea of another of Betty's new advisors. Richard Agnello, a friend of Zogg's was a former Bank of America employee. He designed CBF to take advantage of one of Orange County's most lucrative businesses, personal property loans. The potential for profit was high. Agnello seemed competent and experienced. But the project was another disaster. Within two years, Hutton Associates was stuck with a large number of CBF's nonperforming loans. In 1979, the venture was closed down. Agnello was forced to resign.

Dave Chamberlin, meanwhile, encouraged Betty to persevere in her search for a bank. With her support, he explored the possibilities of a new investment bank in the City of Industry, southeast of Los Angeles. Hutton Associates was to invest only a small share in this enterprise. Further research revealed that the project was flawed. It ended the same way as the short-lived adventure in the Bank Islands. Betty quickly withdrew, narrowly avoiding involvement in a questionable venture that was threatened with legal proceedings by state regulators.

Within three years of her husband's death, it was clear that Harold Hutton's widow at age sixty-five had begun re-inventing herself. She had closed down Harold's businesses, set up a new company of her own, assembled her own team of advisors, and followed her new CEO into arenas where neither she nor Harold had ever trodden. If 1976 was Betty's "year of lay-offs," 1978 was her year of takeoffs. But dangers lay ahead. By her overreliance on advisors whose heady visions she shared but whose performance she found hard to measure, Betty had allowed her new company to proliferate rather than focus. Her interests had spread too far too fast. Of the Betty L. Hutton Trust's capital, a larger share than was prudent was being invested in ventures that neither her managers nor Betty was well-equipped to handle if the boom of the late '70s turned down. When it did, Betty Hutton was vulnerable. Too many of the takeoffs she had authorized before long would be faced with crash landings.

Betty and Mabel Ho revisit her former Amahs in Singapore, 1978.

BACK TO OLD HAUNTS—
ON TO A NEW MARRIAGE

All her life, Betty Hutton enjoyed and needed sunshine. From her earliest childhood, she had reveled in the hot California sun of Riverside and Orange Counties. As a teenager, she was sent by her parents to enjoy the clear air and bright sunshine of the California desert at Palm Springs; throughout her years in Pacific Asia, Betty took every opportunity to sunbathe on the after deck of the yacht *Destination*, alongside the swimming pools of the fine hotels she and Harold frequented in Bangkok and Jakarta, or on the patios of her homes in Singapore and Orange County. Winter was the time when Betty sought the sun at the home she and Harold had bought in Indian Wells in 1969. There, around the overheated swimming pool and spacious rooms of 46-300 Amethyst Drive, she and Harold would entertain their family and friends at Thanksgiving and Christmas and almost always at the California desert's premier social event of the year, the early February Bob Hope Classic golf tournament.

Betty continued the tradition following Harold's death. She gave the biggest and best parties of her own and her company's calendar over the weekend before the crowds arrived, and this grand golf tournament teed off with its Classic Ball. Almost always, there was bright sunshine. Her houseguests and business associates, for whom Betty reserved and paid for the best accommodations in nearby hotels, drove or flew in over the encircling mountains that keep the Palm Springs oasis warm during the coldest winters elsewhere.

Betty was the consummate hostess. Her guests would play golf with the Eldorado Country Club's pros or sun themselves during the day before meeting

Betty at her home for cocktails in the high-ceilinged living room of the Eisenhower house, followed by dinner at her favorite restaurants. Conversation was animated; Betty might recount anecdotes from Refining days or speculate on what the walls of her home might have heard during the years of the former president's residence. Often for those staying at the house, the evening meal would be followed by nightcaps at the round table by the bar where old friends relaxed before retiring.

The year 1978 was different. Shortly before the Bob Hope Classic, Betty had received an invitation from Pan American Airways, in those days still the leading U.S. international airline. Pan Am took advantage of the partial rap-prochement with China that followed President Nixon's historic visit to Beijing to re-open its old route from Los Angeles to Shanghai. The airline invited "Mr. and Mrs. Hutton" to join 150 other specially selected passengers on the inaugural flight. Insensitive as it was to Harold's decease, the invitation acknowledged that the Huttons during Refican's halcyon days had been among the airline's most frequent first-class flyers, earning what Pan Am described as Q Class (privileged) status.

Betty was pleased to be asked but unsure about whether to accept. Not only was there was no Mr. Hutton, she also felt emotionally unready to risk the journey's reviving the grief as well as the warm memories of her life in the Orient with Harold. Betty consulted her friends at the Bob Hope Classic Ball dinner. Unanimously, they urged her to go. Davis Chamberlin, as CEO of Hutton Associates, agreed to meet her with his wife in Hong Kong where Chamberlin had various ideas for possible Hutton investments. With such encouragement, Betty accepted. As escorts, she invited Brad Hovey and his wife Ferris to join her. Brad was a natural choice because he attended high school in Tientsin where, coincidentally, he was a classmate of the Huttons' old Manila ally, Charles Clurman. Hovey spoke more than passable Chinese and knew prewar Shanghai well.

The Pan Am trip was memorable. Betty reminisced about the scores of flights she had made with Harold back and forth across the Pacific without ever once touching down in mainland China. Shanghai, too, had a special attraction. It was there that Bud Lindus and the Manchurian mafia in the postwar years had helped broker Refining Associates' first sales of surplus navy oil to Nationalist China. The Pan Am flight returned via Tokyo, where Betty disembarked to undertake her own private pilgrimage. With the Hoveys as companions, she spent thirty-six hours in Japan visiting old friends and business associates at Fuji Kosan and making arrangements for one of her Tokyo "goddaughters" to enroll at Chapman College.

From there, she flew to Hong Kong to link up with the Chamberlins and fly on to Singapore. The Pierce Road house had long since been sold, but Koh Bock Thye, the Huttons' former next door neighbor who built Harold's first road through the jungles in Sumatra, welcomed Betty like a long lost big sister.

The next day, she wept when Hovey drove her and a friend, Mabel Ho, to visit the three Chinese *amahs* who for twenty years had served the Huttons' Singapore household, ending up as virtual members of the family. With Ah Siew, her former housekeeper, Betty went shopping for more antiques to add to her collection of Chinese porcelain. She took the Hoveys and Chamberlins for drinks at Harold's favorite bar at the Raffles Hotel.

These side trips to Hong Kong and Singapore were visits Betty felt she had to make. Her thoughts she kept to herself, but as Hovey recalled, "They probably were deeper than tears."

Business then took precedence. From Singapore, the Hutton group flew over the South China Sea to the Philippines, where Charles Clurman had on offer a number of interesting deals. Looking out from the aircraft window, Betty could hardly have failed to recall the frequent voyages she and Harold had made across these treacherous waters in the *Destination*.

Sadly, this ship, too, had been sold. An Indonesian company had used Refican's former yacht for many years as an inter-island passenger carrier, but lacking regular maintenance, the *Destination* was soon too old and rundown to be kept in service. Left to rot in the harbor, the pride of the Huttons' fleet eventually sank and was abandoned in some far off Sumatran inlet.

Arriving in Manila on April 5, 1978, Betty and her party were met at the international airport as if they were traveling royalty. Charlie Clurman, still active as a trader extraordinaire, rolled out the red carpet, garlanding Betty with flowers and whisking her off to the airport's VIP lounge, where the entire party was plied with drinks and rice cakes.

Clurman had arranged an executive suite at the five-star Peninsula Hotel. The next day, he took the party to Ibaan where his Monterey farms agrobusiness maintained an intensive pig ranch. Betty's advisors already had taken up 33 percent of the shares in one of the breeding units. This unit produced large numbers of six-week-old piglets as a source of the tiny valves required for human heart transplant operations in American hospitals. Because U.S. law forbade the slaughter of pigs at so young an age, ventricular valves of the necessary small size could not be produced in America, but Chamberlin was convinced that large profits could be made—and thousands of heart patients saved—by importing the valves from the Philippines, where restrictions of that kind were unknown.

Betty gingerly inspected several of the pigpens on Clurman's farms. After posing for a photograph, she seemed relieved when Clurman drove her party to a waiting private aircraft for a flight to Isabella Cauayan, a city in northern Luzon Island where they stayed in a sumptuously furnished seventeenth-century hacienda. Clurman brought Betty together with a group of well-to-do Spaniards with whom he was negotiating a complex trade arrangement. Betty bought and wore a dashing Spanish costume with a sombrero and leather tassels, but if the Spaniards had hoped to include her in their deal, their efforts proved to be in vain.

Back in California, Brad Hovey noted that they had flown 12,000 miles, stopping in seven different cities over a period of twelve days between March 30 and April 10. For Betty, it was like old times. Old friendships had been renewed. New contacts had been made. Hutton Associates appeared to have a potentially lucrative contract for heart valves in its pocket. The trans-Pacific flights had also proved to be a bittersweet experience, recalling the most productive and vivid years of Betty's life. Every inch of the way Harold was in her mind and in her heart. In the words of the great song from the musical *South Pacific,* which was making a comeback on Broadway at that time, Betty was "gonna wash that man right out of my hair," but she could not. With all his faults, and they were many, Harold had been the light of Betty's life, the champion and protector on whom, like no other, she could always rely.

Her 1978 journey nonetheless helped Betty to ease herself out from Harold's shadow, to put the past behind her, and to look more confidently to the future. Never would she know a love and a partnership like the one she and Harold had shared, but by retracing their steps in so many of the places where they had worked and prospered together, Betty had come to accept that this chapter of her life was closed. Another was about to begin.

* * * * *

How and when Betty's thoughts turned to the question of remarriage is a question that her friends still speculate about. At sixty-five, she was eminently eligible. She was affectionate, good looking, and affluent, invariably well-dressed and coiffured, a fine hostess and charming companion. The tuberculosis that had flared up in her late teens had cleared up completely. Aside from an old knee injury incurred on the hockey field that was to trouble her as she grew older, she looked the picture of health.

But did she want to remarry? Family and friends alike had tried and failed to penetrate the gossamer veil of privacy with which Betty had surrounded herself after Harold died, but all her life she had made a habit of keeping her thoughts to herself. It wasn't that Betty was an introvert. In her youth she had been a tomboy, an aggressive hockey and ball player. Throughout her business life, she was a vivacious hostess who reached out to those around her. Yet it was only with her family, especially her mother, who remained active and gregarious well into her nineties, that Betty would let her hair down, if not her guard. She was an intensely private person with a core of protective self-sufficiency. Seldom, if ever, did she brood; never did she seem to feel sorry for herself. Betty disliked, though she never would announce it, the tendency of other people to broadcast their troubles. "This made her much loved and admired," said one of her closest friends. "Her style was to stay quiet and listen."

Harold Hutton during their courtship had identified—and fallen in love with—Betty's quiet reserve. In one of his letters, he likened her to the *Mona Lisa*. So it was, as the months and years went by after Betty's widowhood, that her only response to hints that she should remarry was silence and an enigmatic smile. Then came the first clear sign that she might be ready for a second romance. It was close to a year since Betty had paid her first return visit to Asia. The 1978 midwinter social season in Indian Wells was at its peak. Betty, as usual, had invited a large number of her family and friends to the desert for the Bob Hope Classic. As the week was winding down, she had arranged dinner at a posh local restaurant for fourteen of her houseguests.

That afternoon, after Sylvia Law, her secretary, had meticulously arranged the seating plans, Betty returned home late and announced that she would not be joining the group for dinner. She had made other arrangements. "I was dumbfounded," Sylvia recounts. "I had never known her to drop out of her own party like this." Sure enough, as the guests started arriving, Betty was nowhere to be seen. "She was in her room titivating," said Sylvia. "She asked me to fasten her pearls; she looked just lovely. She told me she had a dinner date with a gentleman friend."

Betty's date was a Texas oilman introduced to her by a neighbor and friend, the chairman of Fluor Corporation, Dave Tappan. The Texan had impressed her enough that Betty was willing to forego her carefully arranged dinner with old friends to spend the evening with him. Looking in on her guests who already had arrived at her home, she briskly apologized for not dining with them. Because the desert air was chilly and she did not have a fur coat with her, she asked to borrow one of the other ladies' minks. Just then, the doorbell rang. Betty went to the door and departed, borrowed mink in hand, without introducing her date to her guests.

That evening over dinner, her guests, all close friends, buzzed with speculation. Later, after returning for the nightcap ritual, Sylvia Law recalls:

> We waited and waited, until well after midnight. Finally, Betty came in through the back door. She was floating on air. We all gave a big cheer and told her to sit down and tell us all about it. She would have none of it. Instead, she let the borrowed mink drop, trailed it on the carpet while heading for the bedroom hallway, and gave a lovely smile. Her only words were "Goodnight, all."

The next morning Betty was gone before the household was up. When she returned, she said she had been out for an early morning walk with her new friend. Later, there was talk of her jogging along the perimeter track that circles around the golf club, accompanied by a good-looking man. Nothing came of this friendship with the anonymous oilman. More than a decade later, Dave Tappan speculated that Betty and her Texas friend recognized the problems inherent in a long-distance romance. But Betty clearly had emerged from the emotional "purdah" into which she had withdrawn following Harold's death. She was healthy, wealthy, and alone—but not for long.

At the time, she was exploring the idea of a school for international business education. To be named the Hutton Institute, it would promote the training of young Americans in overseas trade. "My prime interest is international business," she told an interviewer. "Orange County should be focused on overseas trade." The Hutton Institute proved to be twenty years before its time. After much travel and discussion with business schools and trade organizations in the

United States and Japan, Betty recognized its impracticality in the late 1970s. Through this project, however, she met the man who was to become her second husband, Chester Arthur Williams.

It was Bill Cruikshank, her lawyer, who brought Chester to Betty's office on July 31, 1978. Whether or not Cruikshank was playing matchmaker is a moot question. Like Betty's other friends, he and his wife, Rita, were concerned for her happiness, and in Chester, with whom the Cruikshanks had long had a business relationship, they saw a "natural fit." Chester Williams was a fine-looking fellow. At sixty-five, he had thick white hair, an erect carriage, and trim physique. He, too, was single and available, having lost his wife of forty years to complications of liver cancer. Born in Kansas City, Williams had moved to California in the late 1930s after teaching economics at Louisiana State University. Much of his working life had been spent in insurance and financial planning, but his two sons characterized their father as having an educator's mind, much more than a businessman's.

Only Betty could have said exactly what attracted her to Chester. At first, she may have seen in the courtly Kansan many of the sterling qualities that had endeared her to Harold in his prime. Chester, too, dressed meticulously, favoring a tie and French cuffs. Convivial and gregarious, he brought her the same sense of animation as she and Harold had shared in their youth. Betty may also have been looking for the same husband-partner relationship she had enjoyed with Harold, a relationship important to a woman whose business was her only child. Perhaps she needed a shoulder to lean on, a man around the house. What is certain is that Betty and Chester in the late 1970s looked stunning together. Their similarities were far more than cosmetic. Chester enjoyed reading and conversation and, like Betty, he planned his social life meticulously. Having worked in the insurance industry, he claimed to understand how money was made and lost and how to take risks. Chester, too, loved to travel, something Betty enjoyed but preferred not to do alone.

What seems to have clinched the matter was that Chester was naturally affectionate. He was instinctively more demonstrative, more attentive to a woman's sensibilities than Harold in his later years. Chester opened Betty's car door for her. He held her hand, put his arm around her waist, and kissed her on the cheek. Soon he was calling her by pet names, like "Doll" and "Baby Doll," which Betty seemed to enjoy. Chester, too, was generous in the small things that a sixty-five-year-old widow appreciated. In addition to bringing her flowers on conventional occasions, like her birthday and Valentine's Day, he would often stop at his florist's and surprise Betty with special bouquets.

There were other differences between Chester the courtier and Harold the big, bold wildcatter. Harold had been larger than life. Physically and emotionally, Chester was less robust. While he enjoyed meeting people, he was hardly an outspoken extrovert, able like Harold to command the attention of any room he walked into. Chester would never have marched into the bar in the Raffles Hotel in Singapore and bought drinks all round for a group of transient visitors. Nor was Chester at home in the rough-and-tumble world of risk taking. Lacking the innate business skills that Harold possessed in abundance, Chester was "Mr. Nice Guy" and Betty loved him for that.

By November 1978, she and Chester were traveling to Tokyo together to explore the feasibility of the Hutton Institute. Chester, in a letter to his family from the Imperial Hotel, announced that he was in love. He had met the woman he wanted to marry, and he wanted to introduce her to them. Betty, characteristically, made no mention of her feelings in letters and phone calls to her family but on their return, she joined Chester in paying visits to his two sons, Russ and Doug, and his married daughter, Sue. Both young men, one in the painting business, the other a minister, were surprised but happy for their father. Sue at first had misgivings because Betty was to take the place of her deceased mother in Chester's affections. But Sue was quickly won over. She would soon see in Betty the traits that had led her father to fall in love: quiet elegance, personal serenity, a quick intelligence, and above all, a regard for others.

By Christmas, the engagement was common knowledge. Not all of Betty's friends were as elated as she was. A few jealous souls pointed out that Chester's wealth was far more modest than that of his new fiancée, but the truth was that both of them presumed from the outset that Chester would die first, so inheritance never was an issue. Instead, as he told a friend and former business colleague, George Browning, whom he later was to bring into the Hutton Company, Chester had fallen in love. "I am attracted," he told Browning, "to a wonderful lady with a fascinating background who has the same name as the 1940s movie star."

Betty Hutton and Chester Williams were married on May 9, 1979. Before then, they had become business partners. The previous February, Betty had formed a new company that Chester would run. It was named, at his suggestion, Bettlee Investment Company, an assimilation of Betty's first and middle names. The company was set up to buy problem trust deeds at a discount, then collect the outstanding balances. Chester was supremely confident. It was his style to use superlatives, telling Betty that X was the "greatest," Y was "the best ever," and Z was "absolutely the finest manager I have ever met."

A close look at the Bettlee Investment Company provides a snapshot of Betty's business outlook as well as her relationship with Chester at this point in her life. The concept appeared profitable. Betty accepted it without investigating the risks for herself. When Bettlee was established, Chester was close to Betty; they were to marry in four months time. Only later did they both learn that investing in discounted trust deeds is an exceedingly risky business. Collection proved to be difficult. Lawyers' fees escalated as writs and liens proliferated. Betty, by holding back and staying quiet, proved her devotion to Chester, but Bettlee proved to be a failure. After three years, the company had the same fate as Y.Y. Inc.—it was sold at a substantial loss.

That, however, was not until long after she and Chester had sealed their partnership by marriage. Their wedding was an informal family affair. One hundred fifty relatives and friends attended the service at the Santa Anita Church

Wedding photo of Betty and second husband, Chester Williams

in Arcadia, California. Betty looked gorgeous in a mid-length blue dress, three strands of pearls, and high heels. Chester wore a dark pinstriped suit with a gray cravat, diamond pin, and a large white carnation in his buttonhole. Betty's sister, Mary, also in blue, served as matron of honor. Officiating at the ceremony was the Reverend Russell Williams, Chester's older son. His second son, Doug, who later became one of Betty's favorites, was his father's best man.

The couple flew off the same day to begin their honeymoon with two nights at the Fontainebleau Hotel in Miami before boarding the *Sun Viking* for a two-week cruise in the Caribbean. Betty seemed radiantly happy. Once again, she had a handsome husband, a man to share her business interests, a sensitive and caring companion with whom she could travel and enjoy seeing the wide world. As they sailed out of Miami harbor, the new Mrs. Hutton Williams wrote in her diary, "Our hopes are high."

Four Years of Six-Star Travel

Not long after Betty Hutton became Mrs. Hutton Williams, Cassius, the Siamese cat that Harold in his later years had cared for and spoiled like a child, ran away from the Villa Park house where the newlyweds were to make their home. Betty dismissed this as nothing more than a coincidence, but in later years, some of her friends recounted the incident as if it were a foretaste of the bad luck that was to come. During her honeymoon with Chester, Betty became sick and returned home with an infection that with antibiotics soon cleared up.

Chester also developed a high fever that he and Betty thought to be a comparable infection. Instead, following extensive examinations, Chester learned that he was suffering from advanced prostate cancer. This was a demoralizing blow for the newlyweds. Chester's previous wife had died from cancer only two years earlier, and his mother had died from cancer as well. Now his own cancer, with its potential side effects for him and his new bride, threatened the happiness he and Betty so recently had discovered.

Surgery to remove the cancerous prostate occurred July 16. Chester then faced months of uncomfortable radiation treatments interrupted in mid-September for hernia repair. Not long afterwards, Chester returned to his doctor complaining of pain in the right groin area. This discomfort, apparently the result of nerve damage from a metal mesh inserted to strengthen the tissue, would plague him for the rest of his life.

As Chester's health deteriorated over the next decade, Betty increasingly had to play the part of nurse as well as travel and business partner with her second husband. Her devotion to Chester was selfless. Betty put her husband first, even if that meant shortchanging her business.

She and Chester still shared an eventful period of working together at Hutton Associates, though Betty gradually discovered that hers must be the dominant voice if her fortune was not to fall victim to unwise investments. Her company was in the midst of severe growing pains at the time of its owner's remarriage. Betty had to deal with frequent and painful staff changes. Gradually, it dawned on her that Hutton Associates was in the wrong hands. But that problem was put aside till the future so Betty could enjoy with Chester the taste for leisurely foreign travel she had acquired but never sufficiently fulfilled with Harold.

During the late 1970s and 1980s, the names of Mr. and Mrs. Chester Williams were to appear on the first-class passenger lists of nearly all the world's finest cruise ships. There the couple would sink into the luxury of six-star cabins and immaculate personal service. They loved dressing up for formal dinners, sitting at the captain's table, dancing in the ship's ballrooms, and visiting world-class cabarets. Betty's never-failing support kept Chester going. They had made up their minds to get the best out of life while they could.

The log of the world tours and cruises Betty and Chester undertook in the early 1980s reads like an extract from a Baedeker guidebook:

> *June 1980.* Mr. and Mrs. Williams left for a five-week tour of Europe. Chester, the ultimate tour guide, had spent weeks preparing their itinerary, researching sites to visit, picking out restaurants for special meals, buying tickets for spectacular entertainments. The couple toured castles in Spain, shopped in Paris for alligator shoes, gloried in the baroque attractions of Vienna. One magic evening, after attending the Oberammergau Festival, they were dining at a castle restaurant above Salzburg when a dramatic storm passed by. Betty felt romance in the air. A postcard to her mother spoke of "the beauty of the lightning as it illuminated the ancient German city at our feet." The last time Betty had seen lightning of such power and radiance was in the South Pacific.

September 1980. With Chester suffering from asthma and Betty from a constriction of her fingers for which she had just had surgery, the Williams' remedy was a three-week cruise on the Dutch liner, *Veendam.* Sailing out of San Francisco to Hawaii, Guam, Fiji, and Tahiti, Betty was in her element. The sun, sea, and islands brought back memories of the *Destination.* One of her letters to her office staff told of her pleasure at "the sense of settling while we are traveling."

Spring 1981. Over the Memorial Day weekend, Betty threw a party in the High Sierras. According to her diary, "The Spennetta clan gathered at Yosemite . . . The younger members camped out, but the rest of us stayed at the beautiful old Ahwahnee Hotel." Soon afterwards, Chester suffered a relapse. Symptoms of a recurrence of his prostate cancer obliged him to undergo a week of further tests at the Mayo Clinic. The results were encouraging: no evidence of the cancer spreading. He and Betty therefore set off for a seven-week trip around the world. Everywhere they went, to London, Rome, Istanbul, New Delhi, Singapore, and Honolulu they stayed at the best hotels, dined at the best of restaurants. They watched plays, visited museums, and art galleries—and returned home totally exhausted.

August 1981. Less than seven weeks later, Chester planned a cooler, shorter cruise to Alaska. He and Betty sailed to Vancouver, British Columbia, and north through the green waters of the Inland Passage to a string of small logging and fishing ports like Ketchikan and Juneau. En route they played bridge and danced. Betty told Sylvia Law that the cruising brought her "peace of mind in a cabin large enough to hang our things in."

November 1981. Betty and Chester flew to Spain and drove to Lisbon. They spent a connoisseur's week touring the castles and vineyards of Portugal. One of the highlights was sampling white port wine served with "digestive biscuits" before lunch in the cellars at Oporto.

June 1982. Flying to Honolulu, the Williamses boarded the *Oceanic Independence* for a seven-day cruise of the Hawaiian Islands including Maui and Kauai. From there they took a side trip to Anchorage, Alaska, to visit with friends before returning home for the Fourth of July weekend. Betty and Chester celebrated Independence Day, "in a big way," as Betty wrote in her diary. All the members of the Williams and Spennetta families congregated at their Capistrano Beach house.

July 1982. Three weeks later the couple were off again to Europe. They arrived in Paris in time to watch the Bastille Day national celebration from their room at the Ritz. They toured the Normandy Invasion beaches, which Betty characterized in a postcard as "very sobering and inspiring." They spent two days in a hotel at the foot of the great monastery at Mont-Saint-Michel.

The next stop was Oslo, where Betty and Chester were guests of the Norwegian distributor for the Hutton company, Logical Business Machines. Then, in Amsterdam, they boarded the *Royal Viking Star* for yet another fourteen-day cruise calling first at Copenhagen and then sailing into the Baltic, where their ship called at Stockholm, Helsinki, and Leningrad, soon to be returned to its pre-Communist name, St. Petersburg.

August 1982. Drained by these midsummer journeyings, Chester within a week of his return to California checked into the Eisenhower Medical Center for a further series of tests. He was still well enough by month's end to travel again, this time to New York, where he and Betty took a suite at the Waldorf Astoria. And then they were off again, flying to Lisbon for a fourteen-day Mediterranean cruise on the *Golden Odyssey* to Malaga, Mallorca, Monte Carlo, and Crete, before disembarking in a baking hot Athens where, exhausted, they visited the Acropolis. Finally, from Greece they flew back to Venice, where Chester insisted on taking Betty out to tour the canals in a gondola before they climbed into the new Orient Express and tried, with little success, to sleep in its narrow bunks en route across the Alps via Switzerland and France to London.

It had been not only a summer but close to four years of luxurious and compulsive travel. Had Betty and Chester enjoyed it? They'd certainly seen the world, occupying the best suites in the best hotels and cruise ships, visiting Europe and Asia's most famous monuments, driving, shopping, and shooting a fortune's worth of photographs in the old world's most celebrated capitals and the most fabled islands of the Pacific. But was this what Betty really wanted? For her husband, who before he married her had traveled far less than Betty, these odysseys offered a never-to-be-repeated opportunity to travel in a style more lavish than anything he previously could have contemplated. Perhaps, too, as his health deteriorated, Chester felt an urge—which Betty was eager to gratify—to gaze on the glories and partake of the luxuries of the exotic lands outside America before his personal curtain came down.

For Betty, too, "going places" had always been part of her life. For a while in the early '80s it seems to have become a passion as well as a hobby. Friends said that she never ceased to look forward to the next vacation. Yet it is not easy to read through Chester's and Betty's diaries over the first five years of their marriage without pondering about the real purpose of their incessant traveling.

Betty undoubtedly went on cruises in large measure because she cared for Chester and wanted to give him a good time as long as he lived. Was she also motivated by a subconscious desire to avoid the confrontations she sensed were about to surface at Hutton Associates? Betty was entitled to enjoy the fruits of the success she and her first husband had earned. "Seeing the world" was part of the promise that Harold had made to her when not long before he died he sought to purchase a yacht on which they would sail around the globe. Yet it is hard to avoid the feeling that Betty, whether she realized it or not, during her cruises was ignoring problems that by the mid-1980s would shake Hutton Associates to the core.

It was time to stay home and pick up the threads of her business while Chester still was a player.

Hutton Centre and The Hutton Group after sale of Hutton Centre and move to new offices
From left to right: Sylvia H. Law, Sally A. Durham (niece), Jessica L. Wilson (niece), Betty,
Thomas C. Parker, Arlene R. Craig, Mary S. Struck (sister), Thomas A. Pooler

TRIALS AND TRIBULATIONS

The summer of 1979 was one of the hottest Orange County's weather watchers had recorded for many years. Day after day in July the temperatures soared into the high nineties, several times passing the 100-degree mark in inland cities like Tustin, where Hutton Associates had its offices. Betty Hutton Williams, just back from a vacation in Europe with her new husband, Chester, invited her senior executives, led by attorney and Board Director Bill Cruikshank, President Davis Chamberlin and Vice President Bill Zogg to conduct their second Investment Review Session—for which she and Chester had been pressing—at the spacious waterfront home Betty had recently completed at Capistrano Beach.

Built with funds from the sale of her Singapore mansion, this handsome duplex house stored and displayed many of the oriental art and furniture pieces the Huttons had collected in Asia. Betty enjoyed her beach house. There, cooled by the breeze that every morning brought light mist in from the Pacific and most evenings blew the clouds offshore, creating spectacular sunsets, she met the company's top managers and advisors for the second of Chamberlin's "retreats." Those present included Chester, now a member of the board, Charles Martin, one of Chamberlin's consultants, and Christopher J. Felix, a shy young man who became one of the brightest stars in the Hutton firmament.

Felix had been hired and elected as a director to run the bank that Bill Cruikshank and Chamberlin had expected to form with other American investors in the City of Industry. When Betty disassociated herself from this ill-starred venture, Felix moved over to take charge of Hutton Associates' property portfolio.

On the second day of the review session, the Hutton board had one-on-one meetings with the company's joint venture partners. By now these included a dozen real estate investments in Riverside, Los Angeles, and Orange Counties as well as in Reno, Nevada. Four involved partnerships with a young couple, Bob Warmington and his wife, Lori, whose company was becoming known as one of the most adventurous, conspicuous, and profitable developers in Orange County. Betty was charmed by the Warmingtons. They were to play a significant role in her own and her business futures.

The 1979 review session went on to note with approval that large sums of Hutton capital were now flowing into Logical Business Machines, the computer company in Sunnyvale, California. Davis Chamberlin gave a rosy report on the prospects for Logical to invade the exploding market for program language software. Somewhat ironically, it was noted that the Hutton company was the owner of a leading-edge computer business yet still did its own book-keeping by means of a manual single-entry system. Betty's sister, Mary Struck, admitted that this system (which she and Betty preferred) made it hard to keep up with the variety and complexity of the scores of diverse projects that Cruikshank, Chamberlin, and Zogg were pursuing. To support Mary and eventually take over from Betty as secretary and chief financial officer, it was decided to hire a professional accountant. Arlene Craig, the accountant chosen, started working four ten-hour days per week introducing an accounting system for the company's by now kaleidoscopic accounts. Arlene was to become the Hutton company's widely admired chief executive officer and, later, to succeed Betty and, before her, Harold as a trustee of Chapman University.

As the 1979 review session broke up, Betty and Chester dined and wined their fellow directors, managers, and consultants as well as their wives. When they all had left, Betty felt uneasy. She had carefully studied the accounts relating to each of their investments and partnerships. There were no unexplained discrepancies. Yet overall, she sensed a lack of strategic direction and coherence. Chester confirmed her anxieties. Hutton Associates, he told her, was getting into too many different and unconnected ventures. He suggested and Betty agreed that they should seek advice from one of his former colleagues, financial planner George Browning, president of Asset Management in Rolling Hills, California. According to Browning:

> Chester called me and said he'd married a "wonderful woman, Betty Hutton, not the actress," and described her fascinating background. His concern was that their guys (Cruikshank, Chamberlin and Zogg) had gotten her into an eclectic array of investments that could get her into trouble. She needed someone to give her advice on a strategy.

Compounding Betty's concerns were her other financial responsibilities as the executive of two personal trusts. One, set up in Harold's will, required its funds to be invested to benefit both Betty herself and Harold's daughter, Barbara Chambers, and her heirs. The other trust, established by J. D. Spennetta, was designed to generate income for Betty's mother, Edna, and on her death, J. D. and Edna's children, Paul, Mary, and Betty, and their heirs. Supervising these trust funds as well as her company while she and Chester were undertaking so much overseas travel was a problem that had Betty worried. The scale and complexity of Hutton Associates' investments seemed also to be getting out of hand. Betty was feeling swamped. She accepted Chester's suggestion that George Browning be invited to take a fresh look at her investments as an independent consultant.

This was a fateful decision. Browning, a graduate of the University of Southern California's prestigious business school, was a forceful and ambitious fellow. Tall, good looking, and athletic, he saw an opportunity to launch himself as well as Betty into the "big time" in California. Browning went to work to review her entire portfolio of investments, including the real estate partnerships. He asked searching questions about her advisors and what they knew about the businesses they were involved in. Browning's analysis revealed that neither Betty nor her executive directors were skilled in the products or services of many of the partnerships that Hutton was financing. "I came back to her with a simple list of recommendations," he said. "Don't invest in things you don't understand. Get someone who does understand the investments you're already in. You need leadership and a strategic plan that meets your goals—preservation of the estate, income, and long term growth."

Browning's advice made sense, but it took some time for Betty to act upon it. In the meantime, another of the decisions she and Chester had made went wrong. Richard (Dick) Shaw was a friend of Chester's son, Doug. He came to Betty as a certified public accountant (CPA) and attorney. His name was added as a trustee of the Betty L. Hutton Trust. With his flashy Rolls Royce, Shaw brought with him all of the trappings of success. Initially, Betty was impressed. Soon, however, it became clear that Shaw was not all he seemed. Shaw was neither a CPA nor an attorney. The Rolls Royce was leased. Shaw lasted only a few months at Hutton Associates, but as one company official noted, "It was a scary two months!"

During this time, major changes were underway in the company's top management. In July, Arlene Craig became the company's full-time accountant. Betty, though she hated to do this, terminated the services of her longtime friend and attorney, William Cruikshank. Two months after marrying Chester, she amended the Betty L. Hutton Trust to include her new husband and George Browning as trustees.

By the fall of 1979, Browning's influence was becoming more apparent. Chamberlin and Zogg, by contrast, appeared to be out of their depth. Under their management, Hutton's investments had diversified so broadly that there seemed little if any overall theme. Betty, as Browning had advised, felt the need for more focus and fresh leadership.

It was in the last weeks of 1979 that Betty Hutton approached Browning to take over the management of both the Hutton trusts and her company. She asked him to provide the "strategic focus" he had recommended earlier in the year. Browning came aboard as director shortly before the elaborate Christmas party Betty threw that year for all her staff and their spouses at her Villa Park home. By the end of 1979, Browning was taking charge. He was not "a detail man," he said, so he called in Chris Felix to scrutinize the cash flow of each of the company's investments with a view to cultivating the profitable ventures and disposing of those that were marginal. Browning also intensified his efforts to remove Chamberlin and Zogg who, he felt, were giving Betty poor advice; he characterized their management style as "long lunches at expensive restaurants."

While all this reorganization was going on, Betty and Chester left for a three-week vacation in Europe. During their absence, Chamberlin and William Zogg resigned as directors and officers of the corporation. The new directors were Browning, Felix, Chester, and, of course, Betty.

The Browning-Felix strategy that now emerged at Hutton Associates focused on two main targets: computers and real estate. The company's other interests, from medical devices to yogurt bars, were given less emphasis or sold off when buyers could be found. Felix, with his background in banking and commercial real estate, concentrated on property investments. Browning who, like Chamberlin, fancied his chances in the personal computer business, saw Logical Business Machines as the company's future flagship.

Logical in 1980 clearly had immense potential. Worldwide, the computer industry was expanding. Logical had joined with Byte Industries Inc., in which Betty had also invested, to open America's first chain of retail software stores. Its technicians were jockeying to develop computer languages to compete for the massive market opening up in the early 1980s (ultimately captured by Microsoft). Browning sensed huge opportunities, and he was not alone. Among those on the board of directors of Logical Business Machines was Ray Norda, who later distinguished himself with his own Novell Corporation.

Browning recommended that Betty extend her commitment to Logical. Almost every week, some new breakthrough seemed imminent. Hutton Associates already had spent $3 million on the language project without return.

To abandon this investment could be very costly. Relying on Browning's judgment in a field of which she herself had little knowledge, Betty agreed to further large cash injections. Her confidence was boosted by Browning's decision to personally take over the active management of Logical investments while continuing as group president of Hutton Associates.

Soon, George Browning was to spend two or three days each week in Logical's office in Northern California. Gradually—and willingly—he would be sucked into the vortex of leading-edge electronics technology and the intricate—and costly—financial engineering that was needed to feed its research and development appetites. As a result, his other responsibilities as Hutton's chief executive had to take second place.

Chris Felix, meanwhile, as he took over Hutton's property interests, focused first on a major investment in undeveloped residential land in Reno, Nevada. This land had been purchased under the direction of Harry Thompson, a former employee of Refining Associates. Other residential developments were underway in Orange and Riverside Counties in partnership with the Robert Osborne Company and the Sand Dollar Development Company. Many of these Hutton partnerships included their own executives. It was not unusual to provide senior staff with incentives in this way: shares were allotted to them in recognition of their work and enthusiasm. Betty was not entirely comfortable with this arrangement because hers was the underlying responsibility in the event these investments went wrong.

Among her biggest partnerships were those with the Warmingtons. These involved commercial as well as residential development in Riverside and Orange Counties. By far the largest, Warmington Plaza, planned seven large office towers on a forty-six-acre tract in Santa Ana adjacent to the Costa Mesa Freeway and within minutes of Orange County's airport.

Bob and Lori Warmington joined Betty and Chester in 1981 on their five-week trip to Germany, Austria, and Switzerland. Despite an age difference of nearly three decades between the two couples, the Warmingtons and the

Williamses found much to share. Chester and Lori kept the conversations animated. Warmington described their trip as "one of those great vacations." He and Betty, in fact, had been partners at arms'-length since 1976. Among Hutton Associates' early investments were two commercial and two small residential partnerships with Warmington.

Whether Bob and Lori Warmington took advantage of the closer relationship they formed with Betty and Chester during their shared vacation is a matter for speculation. What is certain is that Bob Warmington persuaded the Hutton group to plunge more deeply into his most ambitious venture, Warmington Plaza. At first glance, the project looked like a good idea. Not far from what would become the West Coast's most ambitious shopping mall, South Coast Plaza, and the magnificent Orange County Performing Arts Center, Warmington had purchased the forty-six acres at a rock-bottom price of $7.6 million that seemed to guarantee rapid appreciation. Betty agreed to join forces with Warmington as the developer on the basis of a short talk, a quick look at the site, and a handshake. Confident of the project's success, she plunged in, just as Harold used to.

The projections for Warmington Plaza depended heavily on two assumptions. First, Orange County's boom had to continue. Second, its new office towers also had to attract the leading professional and financial firms that were pouring into the area where the 405 and the 55 Freeways intersected. Construction on the first tower of Warmington Plaza commenced in the fall of 1980. Within a year, it was ready for leasing. Work on the second tower began shortly afterwards, and plans for a third were in hand.

The venture did not prosper. By mid-1982, recession had replaced boom. Rents were falling fast. Barely a quarter of the offices in the first tower block were occupied. Despite all the publicity, Warmington Plaza was also judged by many real estate agents to be on the wrong side of the tracks, i.e., north of the 405 Freeway, which separates it from the airport and the classier buildings in Irvine and Newport Beach.

With the recession of the early 1980s biting into his portfolio's values, Bob Warmington was soon overextended. Several of the other Warmington-Hutton partnerships were also in trouble. Concern over Warmington's ability to see his now controversial business plaza to completion began to grow. Betty saw the warning signals flashing: adverse publicity, mortgage interest rates reaching double digits, occupancy rates falling woefully short of expectations. Before long, Warmington's cash flow turned sharply negative. He was unable to meet capital calls. Warmington Plaza was in jeopardy.

Hutton Associates now faced a make-or-break choice. Betty was too deeply committed to the plaza to cut her losses and walk away. Despite a monthly loss of several hundred thousand dollars, she could not afford to let the project fail or falter. By year's end, Felix and Browning had convinced Betty that they must buy out Warmington's share not only of the plaza but of all his partnerships with Hutton. More than likely, given the recession, they could be purchased at a figure well below their original cost or future market value.

This was a tough choice for Betty. She had little experience on which to base it. And where was she to find the money? She could not, as a trustee, responsibly commit any more of her family trust funds to so risky a venture. The banks, overloaded with nonperforming real estate loans were unenthusiastic. The plaza seemed unlikely to be able to compete with more prestigious and better-located office blocks closer to Orange County's rapidly expanding airport. Hutton Associates, too, faced problems of its own. Conditions at Logical Business Machines continued to deteriorate. George Browning, still actively running the company, was spending at least half of each week in Northern California. Arlene Craig, Hutton Associates' best accountant, was also having to devote two days a week to Logical, drafting a report on the responsibilities of each person in management. Logical still held out the promise of dramatic returns just ahead, but the drain on the group's resources was putting other Hutton ventures at risk. Discontent mounted in the corporate offices, pitting Browning against Felix as the latter's real estate revenues began to fund Logical's outlays.

Betty could sense the tension. Browning, her tall, handsome president in whom Chester had great confidence, was committed to the computer project. Felix, smaller, quieter, and less verbal, warned against the group's deteriorating cash flow. Betty hesitated to choose between the two chief actors and the two main sectors of her business—property versus technology. She did agree to pledge enough of the Hutton assets to buy out the Warmington partnerships. By February 1983, the company had added to its property portfolio six new real estate developments, formerly pioneered by Warmington. Virtually unknown to the banks as well as to the general public, Hutton had moved up into the big league of Orange County property companies. Betty, without wanting or intending such an outcome, was the largest single developer in the Inland Empire, as Riverside County described itself, as well as the owner and manager of a 2.5-million-square-foot plaza in Orange County.

⁕ ⁕ ⁕ ⁕ ⁕

The challenge now was to wait out the recession, which in the case of office buildings did not ease in Orange County until the mid-1990s, and in the meantime to rescue the plaza from the negative image it had acquired under the Warmington label. Chris Felix took on the job. With nearly one-third of the Plaza completed and construction moving ahead swiftly, there were commitments to occupy less than 30 percent of its space. The leasing agents were becoming nervous. Felix was quick to realize that a change of name was essential to overcome the Plaza's "white elephant" reputation. He moved one step at a time. First, he persuaded Betty to move Hutton's corporate offices to a 10,000 square foot suite on the ground floor of the North Tower.

Soon afterwards, he proposed that the plaza's name must be changed to reflect its new and more creditworthy ownership. His idea was to rename it Hutton Centre.

Betty did not like this. By assuming the name, she inevitably would become a far more visible figure in southern California. Neither Betty nor her family had any wish to surrender any more of their privacy. If the project still proved to be a failure, their good name would be compromised. But Hutton Associates had no choice, Felix argued. The company needed to trade on Betty's credibility to foster confidence in the developer and hence the project.

Arlene Craig recalled a later meeting at which all Betty's executives joined forces to press the recommendation that the Hutton name be used to rescue Warmington Plaza. "I was sitting in her office with George Browning, Chris Felix, and Chester. Chris explained that a forty-five-acre project was a very large undertaking and that the plaza was by far the largest financial project Hutton had owned, developed, and managed. Betty was clearly uneasy, but finally, she relented." Drivers traveling along the Costa Mesa Freeway, one of southern California's busiest, were soon to see a sign reading Hutton Centre at the junction of Main and MacArthur. More than anything else, this sign put Betty Hutton Williams' name on the map in Orange County. Neither she nor her family ever liked it. Two years later she told a reporter, "Overseas we were very low key. We were always contracted to someone else, either a larger corporation, or the Thai government, or the Indonesian government. All of the publicity went to them. Back here in the property business I discovered that you have to come out in front. This really is not my style."

There was no turning back though. "We [had] become recognized as a major player in the real estate market," Chris Felix commented in the late summer of 1981. By the time the Hutton staff joined Betty and Chester for that year's "Trim the Tree" Christmas party, the company's property division had become involved in twenty-four joint ventures and four corporate entities.

Hutton properties were to continue growing. Despite the recession, construction continued in 1982 on Mission Square, the first high-rise building in Riverside; the University Heights project in Reno, Nevada; and on several of the projects taken over from Warmington. By 1983, Hutton Associates owned more than 750,000 square feet of completed commercial, industrial, or residential properties, in addition to Hutton Centre. The staff had grown to nearly forty employees, among them two of Betty's nieces, Jessica and Sally. The staff worked in three large offices, two in Hutton Centre, one in Reno. Betty was generous to her staff. The board approved an executive equity plan giving departmental heads and key employees partnership equities in the projects they were most closely engaged in. Everyone on the payroll could count on handsome Christmas presents and invitations to Betty's parties, the best and brightest on offer in Orange County or the desert resorts.

By letting it be known that she and her company were in the property market, Betty, as she feared, had opened Hutton Associates to a further round of offers from other investors and real estate peddlers. Felix was approached by agents looking to sell for less than $20 million the Oakland Athletics baseball team, whose market value shot up in the 1990s to $150 million. Within twelve months of his turning this opportunity down, the famed Mar-A-Lago home of the (*Saturday Evening*) Post family was also offered to Hutton Associates; it was later purchased and renovated at a huge cost by Donald Trump. Both these and dozens of other potentially profitable offers were rejected by Betty's advisors on grounds that Hutton Associates had no further wish to diversify. This strategy was unarguably correct, yet the company's real-life performance was soon, again, to compromise it.

The biggest problem was the economy. The early eighties was a time when many business activities in southern California were visibly in decline. Between 1980 and 1985, manufacturing in Orange County increased by only 1 percent. The county's inventory of unsold or unleased office space and shopping malls rose to 23 percent of the total available. Rents fell. Developers went bankrupt. The banks refused to lend more money for commercial real estate projects. The Hutton companies felt the cold blast of this second and deeper recession. Less than 25 percent of the 300,000 square feet in the Hutton Centre's two towers was leased by spring 1983. Chris Felix was forced to offer such loss-leader concessions as free rent, tenant improvement dollars, and discounts to small-space users. With construction due to begin on the third tower block, Hutton Centre's problems began to exert the same kind of pressures as Logical Business Machines, draining the rest of the company of its revenues.

Happily for Betty personally, none of these problems as yet affected her own and her family's stature. Hutton Associates in the early '80s enjoyed a public image as one of Orange County's most respectable and profitable firms. Yet behind the scenes, her company had problems.

Both its major operations—computer technology in Northern California and property in the south—simultaneously were sliding into trouble. The initial $3 million investment in Logical had quadrupled and offered no prospect of early return. George Browning still forecast improvements without being able to deliver. To fund its computer investment, Hutton not only was having to divert money from its now-faltering real estate division but was piling up corporate debt. According to Chris Felix, "We were slowly being bled to death."

Did Betty and Chester understand this? As the danger signals multiplied, Betty, with her attention to detail and ability to size up balance sheets, saw clearly that Logical was burning up cash at a rate that could not be sustained when Hutton Centre was also in trouble and the prolonged recession was undermining her other property interests. Chester, however, retained his confidence in George Browning. He urged Betty not to worry. In the summer of 1983, the couple took off on a cruise to the Guadeloupe Islands on the Norwegian liner, *Sagafjord*. The brochure called this " A Cruise to Nowhere."

By the time Betty got home, tensions among the Hutton company's top management were generating problems among its office staff. The bankers continued to be nervous. Betty, now seventy years old, faced serious challenges, personal as well as financial. Edna, her beloved ninety-four-year-old mother had not recovered from a fall. From now on, she would require twenty-four-hour assistance. Betty's husband of only four years was also grappling with the physical and mental traumas that accompany devastating illness. No longer could Chester summon up the drive and leadership skills that Betty might have hoped to find in the man at her side. Hutton Associates on the surface still seemed to be advancing, and Betty was becoming known as one of Orange County's leading philanthropists. Yet as the midpoint of the '80s approached, Betty was ill at ease. She had successfully reinvented herself in the years following Harold's death; now her company seemed in danger of losing in California the fortune that he and she had earned in Indonesia. Betty needed protection. No longer was she confident of overcoming the challenges of the new world into which she had precipitated herself.

Betty with Tom Parker

Betty Hutton's White Knight

It was still warm and slightly humid at 10:30 P.M. on June 11, 1984, as Tom and Sue Parker sat together on a sofa in their small hillside home in the beach community of Summerland, five miles south of Santa Barbara, California. Their chief preoccupation was coaxing their second baby son to go to sleep. Tom Parker, an ex–high school teacher still not yet forty, had already semi-retired from an active second career in purchasing and rehabilitating apartment buildings. Married to Susan Struck, the third daughter of Betty Hutton Williams's sister Mary, Parker was comfortably well off. He could indulge his passion for surfing and sailing his boat in the deep blue water and occasional squalls of the channel between Santa Barbara and central California's offshore islands. Tom and Sue were children of the 1960s. As students, they engaged in angry protests against the Vietnam War and toured Europe as near-hippies. Since then the Parkers, like millions of their contemporaries, had settled down to earn their living, buy their own home, and raise a family.

Sue, before she married, had spent close to three months at the Pierce Road home in Singapore. There Sue had come close to hero-worshipping Harold, who took her cruising along the coast of Malaysia and across the straits to Sumatra and Java in the *Destination*. Betty had found useful jobs for the visiting Struck girls to do, such as helping in Refican's offices in Tokyo and Singapore, and took them out on sightseeing trips to mountains, lakes, temples, and museums.

Sue Parker doted on her maternal aunt. She especially admired Betty's style, her lack of fuss and ostentation, and the aura of privacy and inner serenity that she projected to those around her. And Tom Parker concurred, though he had never known the Huttons well.

Nevertheless, it came as a complete surprise when, just as the Parkers had succeeded in quieting their baby and were preparing to go to bed, the telephone jangled. The voice on the other end turned out to be Betty's. Tom was amazed. "Here's a woman who had everything, who didn't need and never asked for favors, calling at 10:30 at night," he recalled. "Nobody calls you at that time, except your kids when they're in trouble."

Betty's voice betrayed no hint of trouble. As always, she was calm and, despite the late hour, unobtrusive. Yet inwardly, as Tom Parker was soon to recognize, Betty was at her wit's end. She was worried about the mounting debts of Hutton Associates and the potential exposure of funds held in the Hutton and Spennetta family trusts. Perplexed by the often conflicting advice of her CEO, George Browning, and her most dynamic vice president, Chris Felix, Betty over recent weeks had studied the company's profit and loss accounts. She had read and reread the reports of each of the partnerships in which Hutton Associates had invested. Some of these had been set up by her own executives using funds or credit from the company and her trusts. The executives would share the profits, but Betty could be responsible if they incurred bad debts and losses. She had discussed the deteriorating situation of the company with her husband, Chester, who continued to be optimistic. Despite the toll that frequent bouts of illness were taking on his energy and judgment, he was confident that his nominee, George Browning, would pull the company through the recession that had settled on all but a few of its businesses in the mid-1980s. But Betty was not persuaded. She sensed a crisis boiling up. Sylvia Law, one of her closest confidants, characterized Betty's state of mind in spring 1984:

> She was always so serious. She showed visible signs of distress. On top of her mother not being well, I knew she was not happy with the way business was going. Many meetings were held with upper management behind closed doors. I was aware of the unrest that was taking place.

With Hutton Associates headed towards an $8 million loss in 1984, Chris Felix in January had confided to Betty his deep concern about the financial hemorrhage stemming from the cash demands of Logical Business Machines and Byte Industries. Not only were George Browning's pet projects draining the company, his absence from the company to manage them had compromised his effectiveness with other operations, Felix complained. The rate of loss appeared to be accelerating. Even its real estate developments had compromised the company's position. The speed of Hutton's acquisitions had added to its cash-flow problems. Monthly expenses on many projects exceeded revenues.

Not all the news was bad. Browning as CEO had cleaned up most of the corporate mess inherited from others. He and Felix had tried hard to bring focus and structure to the organization. Felix had developed the Riverside properties. Mission Square near the spectacular Mission Inn was attracting good-quality tenants. In Orange County, Hutton Centre had shrugged off the poor image of Warmington Plaza. Leasing of its two completed towers had begun to improve, and the Doubletree Hotel chain had signed to develop a new 173-room hotel in the third block of the center. Interest rates, too, were declining. Hutton's developments were receiving favorable publicity.

There was still the alarmingly negative cash flow. Betty knew in her bones that any further adverse development in the economy could quickly exhaust her reserves and put her trusts at risk. She didn't show it, but Betty felt frightened and vulnerable.

None of this was apparent when she placed that late-night phone call to her nephew-in-law. Instead, she politely enquired if Tom would consider becoming a trustee for the Betty L. Hutton Trust. He would only need to commit one day a month to attend trustee meetings.

"I was initially surprised, more like shocked, but I accepted without hesitation," said Parker. He asked, "When would you like me to start?"

"As soon as possible," said Betty.

"I didn't really have a feel for what she was asking or why," Parker commented later. "Regardless, I made plans to go down the following month [July]." He and Sue knew something was wrong. Aunt Betty must be in trouble.

In fact, it was not the first time that Betty had sought Tom Parker's advice. In 1980, after Hutton Associates acquired a condominium in Calabasas, Betty casually mentioned a problem created by one of her partners' failure to put up his share of the cash. The Parkers lived close by. Tom had therefore assumed the management of the condominium and soon generated a positive cash flow. He ran the property for the next two and a half years until values appreciated enough for it to be sold at a profit. But Betty would never accept the proceeds from his success. To return something to her, Parker would buy her "toys" she couldn't send back—a video camera, a tape recorder, or other such items. Betty had little interest in these gadgets. She nonetheless recognized that Tom had taken on the Calabasas condominium, not because he needed a job or income, but because of two strong commitments that were to cement their relationship. One was his strong sense of duty. As Betty's nephew by marriage, Tom Parker felt an obligation to safeguard her interests. The other was that he had conceived, like his wife, a strong personal admiration and respect for Betty. "I had never met a person I cared more about, that I've respected more," he said.

Betty's late-night call to Summerland was the beginning of a new and exciting chapter in the life of Tom Parker. He and Sue had no need and no desire to change the lifestyle they were enjoying in Santa Barbara; yet once Betty called, Parker put aside everything except his own wife and children in order to respond to her appeal. Why? "Because she was family," he said. "Because she talked up the trust and its ability to do good. I was a child of the '60s. As a businessman I could go out there and make money for her, but I needed to do it for some greater cause. Maybe that was a conceit or a game in my mind; but that was Betty's carrot." She seldom was manipulative, but Betty knew exactly what kind of incentive to dangle before the young man she was soon to rely on.

Tom Parker presented himself at Betty's elegant offices on the ground floor of building number 9, Hutton Centre in mid-July 1984. He had a premonition that this would be the start of far more than a series of meetings of the Betty L. Hutton Trust. "I could tell there was some uncertainty as to why I was there. I had the same feeling myself. I asked for balance sheets, tax records, and cash flows. I needed to understand the whole picture of the corporation and of exactly what was going on, what was owned, and how the cash was being generated and expended."

Allotted a small cubicle not far from Betty's own office, it took Parker much longer than he anticipated to get to the bottom of the Hutton company's problems. He and Betty spent a lot of time together over lunch or in the office. She spoke very little but held nothing back. The company was in trouble. She was getting conflicting advice. She didn't know which way to turn. Betty's self-analysis was equally cool and professionally objective. As a trained accountant, she knew that the cash injections Hutton Associates was making into Logical Business Machines and Byte Industries could not be sustained, that some of her properties were seriously overleveraged, and that her own track record of picking advisors was unsatisfactory. Too often she had allowed Hutton Associates to invest in projects she barely understood. More than likely, she had given too much authority to her advisors without evaluating their personal agendas or monitoring their performance. Had she also spent too much time traveling the world with Chester and not enough on her business? Parker did not ask this question and Betty offered no comment. The probability is that both reflected on it silently.

After spending most of the summer at the Hutton office, Parker still had more questions than answers. "Looking back, I don't think anyone had a true feel for the overall corporate assets and how all the various pieces were impacting the core business. The more I learned, the more alarmed I became. Part of my worry stemmed from my own background. Coming from a smaller town and having done real estate development on a much smaller scale, I was always concerned with cash flow first and appreciation second. Risk was something I wanted to minimize."

By the early fall of 1984, Parker had reached two firm conclusions. First, Hutton Associates could not continue on its present path without exposing Betty to unacceptable risk. "This was no one's fault. The employees were honorable and worked hard. The company's way of operating was a tried-and-true way to make money during periods of inflation. But Betty was uncomfortable. She had built up a sizable fortune, and it just didn't make sense to put that at risk at this point of her life. She deserved to live the later part of her life without the worry of losing everything."

Parker's second conclusion was that "Betty must have protection. Someone had to help her get a grip on her business and finances." Parker consulted his wife. The former beach boy did not fancy himself a white knight. Yet Tom and Sue agreed that Betty was special. "She never felt the need to put down others in order to pump herself up. She really wanted to help other people. The more you were around her, the more you realized that."

Sue Parker urged her husband to go to Betty's aid. Betty's own preoccupation was less self-regarding. "We'll just build up the company and create the foundation out of it," she would say in her quiet but determined way.

"This created a rationalization for me," Tom recalled. "The foundation was her child. Creating it forged our bond together."

*****

Tom Parker devised a new corporate plan for the Hutton company. Its essence was simple, "Sell assets." Even if this meant not generating profits, Parker wanted to get rid of all investments that were adversely affecting Hutton's cash flow. Funds from disposals would be used to pay down or eliminate loans. For Parker, this was crucial. Betty herself had underwritten most of these corporate debts.

Under Parker's plan, Hutton Associates henceforth would stick to property management and development but on a more limited scale. The company's future policy would be to generate revenue for only three main purposes: to provide Betty with all the income she needed to cover her own and Chester's lifestyle, to protect her family and employees for whom she felt responsible, and to build up the Hutton Foundation to enable Betty to spend freely on the charities that gave her satisfaction and pleasure. As proof of his commitment to these aims and to underscore to others in the company his concern over the cash-flow problem, Parker undertook to accept no salary until conditions had changed.

This strategy did not commend itself to Hutton's existing management. George Browning as group president was working on other plans to rescue the company from its cash-flow problems. Browning proposed to form a real estate equity investment trust and sell stock. This, he thought, would solve the cash-flow problem by infusing revenue from stock sales into the company. Tom Parker disagreed. Selling stock posed two major problems, he said. If the shares failed to sell, Betty would still be at risk. Even if they did sell, Betty's assets were still compromised. Second, a stock offer would take too long. The company could sustain its current losses given the immediate economic climate, but were current growth conditions to change, as well they might, Hutton Associates could experience catastrophic losses; Betty's fortune could be wiped out.

Betty preferred Parker's strategy. "When I presented it to her, I could tell she was receptive. We didn't have to say a lot to each other. Once she saw that I was going in a direction she approved of, she gave me the latitude to continue."

George Browning, however, was still president and group chief executive. He was more widely experienced than Parker and he had come to Hutton Associates on Chester's recommendation. And Chester remained committed to Browning's leadership even though Chester's own management role was nominal because of his frail health. For Betty to reject Browning in favor of Tom Parker was therefore to act against Chester. It was not in her character to overrule her husband's judgment. Confrontation would be inevitable, and Betty disliked confrontation.

Betty finally decided that Browning had to be released. Hutton Associates needed to retrench. But how was she to put this to Chester? Betty's solution was to arrange a lunch with Tom and Chester at Coco's, a nearby restaurant. Before they left, Betty told Tom that he would have to give Chester the bad news. Tom accepted the responsibility. He did not expect the response he received. Chester exploded. "George has more ability in one little finger than you have in your entire body," he shouted. Betty remained silent. The atmosphere became tense as both men awaited her decision. Betty finally spoke. Recognizing both the necessity of the decision and the pain this was causing Chester, she turned to her husband and said in a whisper, "It doesn't work."

Her meaning was clear. The computer venture had to end. The company had to be downsized. Browning had to go. Betty needed someone by her who would manage her company for her benefit and the foundation's, and if this meant moving away from Chester's business judgment, so be it.

George Browning resigned as director of Hutton Associates in September 1984. As part of his severance package, he was given all Hutton's stock in Logical Business Machines. In October, Parker was appointed a director of Hutton Associates. Chris Felix was elected president. By the end of the year, Byte Industries had been sold. University Heights, the Reno project, was sold, and the Nevada office was closed. Harry Thompson resigned as an officer of Hutton Associates. Soon Felix and Parker were heavily involved in negotiations to sell Hutton Centre along with the operating company. Parker's plan already had begun to place Betty in a more secure position.

His emphasis on "protecting Betty" would soon make her company less of an independent business and more of a family operation. That was how Betty preferred it. Having treated her employees as family members and having employed each of her nieces at one time or another, she had already surrounded herself with those most important to her. The Parkers, too, were family. It made Betty feel more comfortable to have her business and her family as one.

Her Christmas letter for 1984 summarized her sense of relief. "We are reorganizing and have high hopes of an easier 1985," she wrote. With Parker at the helm of Hutton Associates, Betty felt a greater peace of mind than at any time since Harold was her champion. Chester had won her love, but as she aged, she felt more comfortable with someone younger and fitter at her side, someone to protect her.

By the end of 1984, negotiations were under way to sell Hutton Centre to two prospective buyers. Chris Felix was in charge of the deal. Parker recalled the process: "Chris had a real knack for keeping a lot of deals open. My job was to stand beside him, to work out numbers, give him input, and then once a decision was made, to clean up the mess." At the eleventh hour, a third potential buyer stepped in with the offer of a package deal that included purchase of Hutton Centre, the operating company Hutton Associates, plus two-year contracts for all the staff (with the exception of Betty's family, her secretary, Sylvia Law, and chauffeur, Tom Pooler).

The new bidder was Schneider of Pittsburg, Pennsylvania. In March 1985, Schneider bought all of Hutton Centre at a price that allowed Tom Parker to get all of Betty's money out. Schneider also took over Hutton's ongoing development and property management activities, including its twenty-five staff members and President Chris Felix, who was to head the new Schneider company. "The deal solved my problem with cash flow and corporate employees," said Tom. He described what happened next:

> The Hutton Company kept only the family employees and started again with a smaller, safer approach to real estate investing. The trust was insulated and secure. There was no recourse debt, in fact, there was very little debt on anything, except one building. So now Betty could not be hurt. We had the luxury of building a company in a safe, secure way with the foundation as its ultimate purpose.

Following the sale of Hutton Centre, Betty moved her office to a smaller and less pretentious building near her home. This was one of a group of single-story Cape Cod–style offices at The Orchard Complex at 2524 North Santiago Boulevard in Orange. Betty Hutton was more than relieved—she was reborn. Her choice of Tom Parker had been validated. Thirty years her junior, he was on the way to becoming both a surrogate for Harold as Betty's protector and a substitute for the son she never had. She had never lost her outward poise; now she started to enjoy the work of repositioning her business and preparing the way for its assets—and the profits it was soon to start generating—to be transferred to the foundation. This was the beginning of Betty's comeback. Surrounded by her family, she could stay busy, watch things grow, and not have to worry.

Chester, a generous spirit, meanwhile had put aside any chagrin he might have felt when Tom Parker was preferred to Browning. By April 1985, Betty felt comfortable enough—and Chester was well enough—to leave for a three-week cruise in the Caribbean. They flew from Los Angeles to Miami where they boarded the *Sagafjord* and returned via the Panama canal. "A great way to travel," Betty wrote. She had recovered the confidence and security that the 1984 "crisis" had taken temporarily from her.

PART XI "DOING GOOD"

Receiving Harold's posthumous award as Pioneer in Indonesia,
Betty, with Ibnu (seated), Japanese honoree (standing)

HONORS AND CHARITIES

Every seat was occupied in the cavernous Convention Hall of the Grand Hilton Hotel in Jakarta, Indonesia. The crowd, which had gathered for that evening's amphitheater ceremony on October 8, 1985, represented a unique mix of East and West, ancient and modern, business and politics, Asian and American commercial and cultural values. Two thousand people, mostly men in Nehru-style tunics, rose to their feet as a military band played the Indonesian national anthem to mark the arrival of Suharto, president of the Republic.

The diplomatic corps was led by the splendidly caparisoned envoys of Burma (now Myanmar). Representatives from China, India, Malaysia, the United Kingdom, the United States, and the USSR rose to their feet and applauded. The most important member of Suharto's government, the Minister of Mines and Energy, Subroto, then rose to his feet to introduce the guests of honor. They were sixteen "pioneers" who later that day were to receive gold medals to mark Indonesia's formal recognition of their contribution to the industry that provided more than half its national income—oil and gas. Among them were four Americans, one of them a woman, Betty Hutton Williams.

At the ceremony that followed, the minister called out the names of the honorees. Nearly all had been friends, partners, rivals, or business associates of Harold and Betty Hutton during the years when they pioneered the jungles of Sumatra. First among them was Lt. General Dr. Ibnu Sutowo, now retired as president of Indonesia's state oil industry, Pertamina. Ibnu and his wife had been at the airport to welcome their old friend Betty the previous evening. Next came Ir Anondo, 73, with whom Harold Hutton had negotiated many of Refican's earliest agreements, and Johannes Marcus Pattiasina, 73, whose troops had cleared a way through the jungles to enable oil to flow from Rantau field to the little harbor at Pangkalan Susu. Two Japanese pioneers were also waiting in line to receive their medals, both former colleagues of the Huttons: Shigetada Nishijima, 74, had brought in the Kobayashi Group that set up, with Harold's advice, the North Sumatra Oil Development Corporation Co., Ltd. (NOSODECO); and Sumio Higashi, 73, had helped Refican's initial shipments swell into the flood of Sumatran oil that Pertamina was later to ship to Japan.

The line of honorees grew shorter as four American oilmen stepped forward to receive their medals. Roy M. Huffington, 68, pioneered the development of liquefied natural gas in east Kalimantan. This laid the foundations of the huge fortune that enabled his son, Michael Huffington, to spend $26 million in an unsuccessful bid in 1994 to be elected a U.S. senator for California. Next in line was Don F. Todd, 60, who brought the first independent U.S. oil consortium to Indonesia after signing one of the early production-sharing agreements that Harold Hutton had helped General Ibnu devise. Then there was Arthur Brown Benson, 81, who first met the Huttons while serving as military attache at the U.S. Embassy in Jakarta in the late 1950s. With Benson, who went on to become president of Caltex, Pacific Indonesia, was his company's most admired leader, Julius Tahija, 69, another of the morning's honorees.

The ovation that greeted Betty Hutton Williams when she stepped up to the platform was easily the longest accorded to any of the foreigners present. Dressed in a gold lamé blouse and the long black skirt that protocol demanded, she was to receive a posthumous award for Harold. As the president of Indonesia placed the medal of honor suspended on green, white, and red ribbon around her neck, the oil minister read the citation:

> Harold Hutton, American
>
> Through his persistent efforts made at a great risk he successfully marketed crude oil from the oil fields taken over from Shell in north Sumatra . . . for the first time this crude export under full authority and management of PT Permina, was sold in the

international market. Proceeds earned from these transactions enabled PT Permina to carry out the rehabilitation of its oil fields.

The Indonesian Republic's acknowledgment of Harold's achievement was for Betty a transforming experience. Outwardly, she was cool, even diffident; inwardly, she was bursting with pride and filled with nostalgia. Her hosts made a point of emphasizing Betty's own contributions.

General Ibnu had driven her personally to the Hilton Hotel, now owned by the Ibnu family. She was accommodated in one of the presidential suites on the private penthouse floor, replete with batik tapestries, porcelain, paintings, and carvings. Chester had been too ill to accompany her so Betty had invited as her guest the same old friend, Brad Hovey, who years earlier had accompanied her on that first return journey to east Asia courtesy of Pan American Airways.

Brad wrote in his diary that during their journey to and from Jakarta, he and Betty consumed seven formal banquets, three airline meals, and two sandwiches over a period of ninety-six hours, without sleeping. Yet Betty, now in her seventies, stayed "fresh and exhilarated."

Following the ceremonies in Jakarta, Betty was flown in Pertamina's private jet to the Denpassar mountain resort, where the oil company's president and staff entertained the gold-medal honorees at a grand dinner with Ramayania dancers. The next day, Betty went shopping with Sally Sutowo before attending another smart dinner and cabaret performance hosted by the government's director general of oil and gas. As usual, Betty avoided the ubiquitous cameras, made light of her own role in Refican's early days in Sumatra, and deferred to her Indonesian hosts, especially oil minister Subroto and the two generals, Ibnu Sutowo and J. M. Pattiasina, to whom she was specially devoted. Yet everywhere she went Mrs. Hutton, as they still called her, was the center of attention. As the only woman ever to receive the Peloper Pioneer Award, albeit on Harold's behalf, she felt moved and deeply gratified.

Flying home, Betty told Brad Hovey that it was "very nice" of Pertamina to pay tribute to Harold thirty years after he had first set foot in Sumatra and ten years after his death. "She would not take a shred of credit for this," said Hovey, "but she did take pride in President Suharto's tributes to the contribution of a young man from California to the founding of the Indonesian oil industry."

"I liked that," Betty said.

She also liked the way in which her business and the role she was to play in it were being reshaped back home in Orange County. Tom Parker had worked quickly to restructure the Hutton corporate office. Together they now looked forward to implementing the commitment Betty had outlined to Tom when persuading him to come to her aid, "Build the company and create the foundation."

To build the company, a long list of nonperforming or underperforming assets had to be disposed of. By the end of 1986, three more risky real estate projects had been sold. Parker hit upon a novel method of securing Betty's interests in properties where it made sense to remain as owners: bring the tenants in as limited partners and build to suit. One of the first such tenant partners was a prestigious law firm, Best, Best & Krieger. In March 1986, they moved into a pioneering high-rise building in the Mission Square project in Riverside, which had been facing low-occupancy risks. Riverside by this time was one of the fastest-growing cities in California. In subsequent projects there, Parker signed the tenants first, committed them to a partnership, then built to suit tenant-partner needs. Both sides benefited from this arrangement.

By selling off risky properties without waiting for their values to appreciate, Parker steadily rebuilt Hutton's cash reserves. By 1990, the company had recovered its net operating losses from the mid-1980s. Betty was soon in a position to use her strengthened cash position to move back into the market. There were some attractive bargains available. Orange County's building frenzy over the previous decade had left dozens of high-rise offices, hotels, and science parks heavily underoccupied. Prime properties could be picked up in the still-distressed market of the early 1990s for thirty to fifty cents on the dollar.

The Hutton company now had the cash to afford these bargains. On April 1987, Parker bought the building in which Betty had been leasing her office space in the Orchard Complex in Orange. Other projects followed. In 1988, a building adjacent to the company's property in Cypress was purchased at a bargain-basement price. The Fairmount Venture Partnership was formed to construct a second two-story building in Riverside. An unused orchard and the land around Edna Spennetta's home in Villa Park was parcelized and sold for development to Chris Felix and a group of partners.

Once again, the company was growing but this time with a difference. The cash-flow problem had been resolved. Corporate debt had virtually been eliminated. All property loans were paid off with the exception of the Mission Square project, and even that posed a far lower risk because of the tenant partnership. As the 1990s opened, all litigation had been settled from the Hutton Centre days. There was also another name change. Under the terms of the sale of Hutton Centre, Betty could continue to use the name "Hutton Associates" for two years only; after that, the name was to become the property of its new owner. Betty was reluctant to give up the name of Hutton Associates, her first venture on her own. She liked its inference that her company was a team strongly focused on her extended family.

In the end, she agreed to switch to a new name, The Betty L. Hutton Company. Much had changed, and she now took pride in the Hutton name she was earlier reluctant to use. Before long, using its strong cash balance, the renamed firm owned nine large buildings completely. It was also responsible for managing 750,000 square feet of commercial rental space, roughly the same amount of space it had controlled a decade earlier in the Hutton Centre days. Then, however, the staff numbered thirty individuals and faced a cash-flow problem. Now there was a staff of nine.

Her company rebuilt, the early 1990s saw Betty with both the resources and peace of mind she needed to turn her attention to the goal that she and Tom Parker had come to regard as the primary purpose of making money—"to do some good." "Once we had agreed that I would stay and help guide the company," said Parker, "we made a pact. After the family was taken care of, all the assets would go into a foundation and the foundation would be Betty's legacy." Both were true to their word. By 1995, The Betty L. Hutton Company and the Betty L. Hutton Trust were able to move assets into the foundation on a large scale.

Already Betty was recognized as one of Orange County's leading philanthropists. Chapman University remained her favorite cause, but Betty's generosity now extended more widely, focusing on children and young adults, aging and hearing problems, and the World Affairs Council. In December 1981, concerned about her mother's hearing problem, Betty agreed to serve on the board of the House Ear Institute and confirmed her commitment with a gift of $1 million. Her interest in the welfare of children and young mothers led to other large gifts for the development at Martin Luther Hospital in Anaheim of "The Safe Place," a special area for emergency treatment of abused children. The hospital recognized her contributions with its second Ambrosia Vision Award. The first had gone to Disneyland.

Another of Betty's charities was the Discovery Science Center. Karen Johnson, director, recalled her initial contact. "Fourteen persons representing Orange County pioneer families were invited to an early morning breakfast. This was held in an unrestored, unheated 1899 farm house on eleven acres of land in Santa Ana, lacking even the barest hint of vegetation. Cold scrambled eggs and gray potatoes were served on cold china plates on a cold, drizzly day. Given such a paucity of creature comforts, I thought that if anyone present even opened a letter from us, it would be amazing; but that's not how it worked with Betty. Asked to join the Science Center board, Betty said yes so quickly I wondered if I had heard correctly. She was so wonderfully eager to do whatever she could to help children learn about science."

It was the same at St. Joseph's Ballet, created to provide low income children with a means to develop their self-esteem through dance. The ballet, like the Discovery Center, was little more than a concept when Betty became involved.

When space became available in a rehabilitated building in downtown Santa Ana, she walked silently through the facility and at the end of the tour turned to the ballet's director, Beth Burns. "So what you really need is a [dance] floor?" she asked.

"Yes, please," was the reply.

That evening as the director addressed an Orange County audience on what dance can do for kids, Betty walked over and whispered, "You have your floor." She handed her a check for $15,000.

The same kind of sensitivity led Betty to chair a fund-raiser for the YWCA Hotel for Homeless Women. She paid for a well-publicized dinner that attracted three hundred people at $200 a plate for the hotel. Following her mother's death, Betty took a keen interest in gerontology. Her contributions to the Gerontology Center at California State University at Fullerton led its director, Leo Shapiro, to write, "She was not only generous with her funds, she was generous of her time and effort. She arranged a luncheon and insisted on paying for it. The luncheon raised in excess of $20,000."

Many more substantial gifts were to follow, but Betty's contributions went well beyond money. Elected to dozens of charity boards, she never failed to attend committee meetings, including many that started at 7:30 A.M. To each board she brought good sense, fresh contacts, and wise advice. From each came special awards, new honors, and recognition for her philanthropy and service.

Three times the Boy Scouts of America honored her for her devotion. She received the Outstanding Individual Philanthropist Award from the Alzheimer's Association and a rare Certificate of Appreciation from the Salk Institute. In 1994, the World Affairs Council presented her with its Golden Orange Award at a dinner for 600 of its members, including four U.S. congressmen. Betty invited ten of her former employees to join her at one of the tables. "We all raised our glasses in a little toast to Harold," one of them recalls.

As she did so, Betty smiled and said, "Yes, he started it all."

Above: With George Argyros, chairman of Chapman University Board of Trustees,
Below: With Dr. James Doti, president of Chapman University

CHAPMAN UNIVERSITY—
"I HAVE NO DEARER CAUSE"

Betty Hutton's desire to "do something good whenever I can" stemmed in large measure from her Christian upbringing and the Spennetta family's belief that wealth carries with it a duty to share one's good fortune with others. During her marriage to Harold, she had lived alongside a man who, unlike Betty, had known what it was like to be poor but to whom generosity was second nature whenever he had funds to spare. Harold's giving tended to be personal—huge tips to waiters and parking valets, gifts of jewelry and clothes for his daughter and nieces. Betty's giving in her later years was better organized and institutional. She donated many millions of dollars to a long list of charities, but her favorite was Chapman University. Chapman was special to Betty not only because it occupied the campus and fine neo-classical buildings of her old high school, Orange Union High, but because on the Huttons' return from east Asia, the college provided the connections and sense of identity that helped them re-integrate with an Orange County to which, while overseas, they in many ways had ceased to belong.

Harold Hutton was introduced to Chapman by his rancher friend Edgar Pankey, whom he first met when Pankey and a delegation of American orange growers were drinking in the bar at the Raffles Hotel in Singapore (see "Retreating from the Far East"). Not long afterwards, Harold and Betty gave $10,000 worth of bunker fuel to assist World Campus Afloat, a program whereby hundreds of Chapman students spent "semesters at sea," sailing around the world while working on board ship for their credits under the supervision of Chapman faculty. Betty was an early supporter of this program.

She listened carefully as a group of the project's first students described their visits to the great port cities of the Mediterranean, their trip up the Nile River to Luxor, and their continuing journey via the Suez Canal to Bombay and Bangkok. Their first ship, the *Seven Seas,* soon to be followed by the *Rheindam,* was made available by the Holland America line. The line's Dutch owners opened the door for the American student voyagers to be received by government ministers and business leaders in each of the countries they visited. Later, C. Y. Tung, a wealthy Hong Kong shipowner, took over financial sponsorship of World Campus Afloat and provided the SS *Universe* as its campus afloat. Betty and Harold became friends of both C. Y. and his son, Tung Chee Hwa, who was subsequently named by the People's Republic as the first Chinese governor of Hong Kong when the former British crown colony was returned to the mainland's control in 1997.[25]

On his return home from Singapore in 1971, Harold Hutton was elected as a Chapman trustee. He joined several old friends on an illustrious board, among them Ross McClintock, in whose drilling barge Harold had explored for oil in the Sulu Sea, and Si Fluor, founder of the worldwide Fluor Daniel engineering corporation. It therefore came as no surprise when not long after Harold's death, Betty received a message from the Chapman authorities. Would she consider taking her husband's place as a member of its board of trustees?

The invitation gave Betty great pleasure. Her mind went back to the sunny days when as a schoolgirl she had studied, played games, and danced on the lawn in front of what had since become Chapman's administrative center, the handsome, pillared Memorial Hall. More recently, half a dozen of the daughters of the Huttons' business friends, "our Japanese and Chinese daughters," as she called them, had enrolled at Chapman with Betty's help.

---

25. The Tungs also purchased the superliner *Queen Elizabeth*, sister ship of the *Queen Mary* that now serves as a hotel and maritime museum in Long Beach, California. C.Y.'s intention was to turn the giant ship into a floating university for both Hong Kong and American students, but the *Queen Elizabeth* was set on fire and sunk in Hong Kong harbor, some say by pirates. More likely it was destroyed by members of the Communist seaman's trade union, angered by the Tung's employing Taiwanese crewmen on the great ship.

Chapman wisely chose the envoy sent to contact Betty. James Farley, another friend of Harold's, in the 1970s and 1980s was the college's best-liked and most successful fund-raiser. Farley and his wife Loa, like the Huttons and Spennettas, had moved to California from the Middle West. They spoke the same language and shared the same values as Betty. This was fortunate since Chapman, at the time of its invitation to Betty was running into a financial blizzard. Its problems stemmed from the mid-1970s recession that reduced enrollments and from Chapman's administrative problems, notably a pattern of uncertain leadership at the top.

Established by members of a group called the Disciples of Christ, the college traced its origins to the hectic decade that followed California's 1849 gold rush, when the state's population doubled and redoubled, but its government had no funds to provide schools. More than a decade elapsed before the first class opened at the exact hour of Abraham Lincoln's inauguration, March 4, 1861.

Inspired by the "great liberator's" ideals, the school accepted students of both sexes and all races, a radical concept in those days. Much later, the college, known for a while as Hesperian, transferred to a site in Los Angeles purchased with generous help from Charles Clark Chapman, a well-to-do native of Illinois. The Chapmans, like J. D. Spennetta, had moved west and made their business in the citrus industry. Enrollment at the small college rapidly expanded as veterans returning from World War II seized the opportunities opened up by the GI Bill.

When more room to expand was needed, once again the Chapman family stepped in with funds for the purchase of a bigger and better location outside Los Angeles—Betty Hutton's former high school on Glassell Street in Orange. Renamed Chapman in honor of its greatest benefactor, it became Orange County's first four-year accredited college.

Yet fitting as it was that Betty Hutton should join the Chapman board, at first she hesitated. Harold had once confided that the college's financial condition was deteriorating. No longer were ex-GIs enrolling in large numbers. Orange County, too, had experienced in the early 1970s a halt to its postwar expansion. With the ending of the Vietnam War, President Nixon cut defense spending and with it many of the aerospace contracts that underpinned the prosperity of local families whose children were most likely to enroll at Chapman. Orange County soon resumed its exuberant growth, but the college took far longer to recover.

Internal disputes marred the relationship between the president's office, the board of trustees, and the faculty. The college's expenses had risen above its income. The World Campus Afloat program, heavily undersubscribed, was draining scarce resources. The college was unable to meet its share of the payroll taxes. Chapman's bankers were uneasy. "Conditions in the campus became very volatile," wrote one of the college's historians. "Rumors circulated that Chapman might not survive."

It was James Farley who did most to overcome Betty's qualms about joining what one Chapman alumnus at the time called "a sinking ship." Farley persuaded her that a soon-to-be-elected new chairman of Chapman's board of trustees, himself a Chapman graduate, was exactly the kind of leader needed to shake up the college's administration and rebuild its shaky finances.

George Argyros, the new board chairman, was—and remained for decades to come—one of California's wealthiest and most dynamic entrepreneurs. Of Greek-American extraction, Argyros before he was forty had created a successful property empire that later was to embrace a wide range of nationwide commercial ventures. Argyros loved Chapman College, his alma mater. Moreover, he was determined to put his energy and strength of purpose, as well as his great wealth, to work to rescue his alma mater from its financial difficulties. His ambition was to set it on a course that would thrust Chapman into the top ranks of California's and America's smaller private universities. Betty had met and approved of George Argyros shortly before Harold died. She agreed to join the Chapman board when James Farley told her that Argyros's ambitious program to rehabilitate the college needed her support and wise counsel.

It was an exciting challenge. Together with Irvin Chapman, son of the college's first benefactor and other older friends like Pankey, Fluor, and McClintock, Betty participated in selecting a new administrative team to lead Chapman out of near-bankruptcy. Throughout November 1975, the board of trustees held emergency meetings. George Argyros gave the President, Donald Kleckner, forty-eight hours notice to resign or be dismissed. Kleckner was replaced by an acting president, Davis Chamberlin, one of Argyros's business associates (whose subsequent relationship with Betty Hutton is described in "The 'Widow Hutton' Re-invents Herself"). Chapman's overriding priority was to stem the tide of the red ink, buy time from its creditors, and recruit a new president. Betty backed George Argyros and the board in leading an aggressive new strategy with James Farley as a professional fund-raiser.

To win back public confidence and demonstrate that Chapman was moving forward, the new team launched an ambitious building program. No new buildings had been built since the late sixties when a music building, library, and science center had been added. Now, under Argyros's lead, Chapman was to relaunch itself, attracting gifts for operations and its endowment by a display of self-assertiveness and the "onward and upward" spirit that had made Orange County bloom. An early objective was to raise over a million dollars in only a few weeks to match a federal grant. Donations started pouring in, some as substantial as $150,000. One of the largest was a check for $350,000 with a note attached that began, "If we still need more . . ." The note was signed "Love, Betty."

That gift was only the first of more than a hundred Betty Hutton Williams made to Chapman. Harold's generosity already had led the group in charge of building a new athletics hall to name it posthumously the Harold Hutton Sports Center. Betty was deeply touched. In honoring the memory of her husband, she had begun her career as a major Orange County philanthropist and helped turn the tide for the school.

Betty attended the groundbreaking ceremony for the 44,000-square-foot, $1.6 million Harold Hutton Sports Center on March 22, 1977. Bad weather, labor strikes, and material shortages were to cause delays that risked the loss of the state's matching funds. Not until the fall semester of 1979 was the Harold Hutton Sports Center ready for its dedication at the annual Founder's Day celebration, November 10. Betty in a bright red suit and white orchids was the guest of honor. Acknowledging the Huttons' generosity, Chapman's current president G. T. ("Buck") Smith likened Harold's approach to that of the Greek hero, Alexander the Great, who once responded to a suppliant's request for help with the remark, "What you propose is enough for you to seek—but not enough for me to give."

Betty was greatly moved. She and Chester joined in the dinner dance in the new gymnasium that featured Les Brown and his Band of Renown. So successful was this event that Chapman later initiated an annual fall gala modeled after the Hutton Sports Center dedication evening to showcase its students' talents and acknowledge individuals who had made a contribution to the community. This "American Celebration" would evolve into annual dinner shows held in Orange County's best-known hotels and later, into spectacular annual displays staged on the floodlit campus. Both events proved to be successful fund-raisers.

Betty, an active member of the board of trustees, was to become a familiar face on the Chapman campus. Buck Smith recalled how shortly after he was appointed, one of his longtime friends, Poster McGaw, from Wooster College, Ohio, offered a $500,000 gift to Chapman if the board would commit $1.5 million by the time of Smith's inauguration, February 17, 1978. George Argyros immediately pledged $500,000. Betty pledged $100,000. The morning of Smith's inauguration, she called the president's office to find out if the board had met its challenge. Chapman lacked $243,000. She raised her commitment to meet this figure.

As the years went by and Chapman College not only recovered but went on to attain university status in September 1991, Betty's contributions never ceased. She funded an international student scholarship program, helped Chapman win a Steele Foundation grant, supported distance-learning activities at its resident education center (REC) in Palm Desert, later renamed the Betty Hutton Williams Academic Center. Valuable REC space for Chapman was also made available at Hutton Centre and furnished with the help of Betty's cash gifts and office furniture. When her mother died, Betty donated some six thousand books, a gift independently assessed to be worth over $35,000, with a provision for the library to sell or trade the books if that would improve its collection.

She also took risks to help Chapman. While her own business was in difficulties, though she never allowed the slightest hint of this to reach the ears of those who sought her help, Betty dipped into her trust funds to help develop Chapman's fine new Argyros Forum with a gift of $1 million. To acknowledge this gift, the administration wanted to name the forum's dining room in her honor. Students would daily be reminded of what she had done. Betty adamantly resisted. It was never her desire to be named for her donations and the Chapman sports center already carried Harold's name.

Despite her objections, Chapman's dining room was named for Betty Hutton Williams. Her picture hangs there as a reminder of the commitment she once summarized in a letter to President Smith, "There is no cause in which I have greater interest or which brings me more personal pleasure than Chapman College."

Betty Hutton's contributions to Chapman were far greater than the money she gave. She served on no fewer than six committees of the board and attended meetings faithfully. She also gave the wisdom of her advice. Each president during her tenure on the board met with Betty regularly. President James Doti, following his appointment in July 1991, met with her for breakfast at least once a month and, as he said, "went over everything." Betty would

Oil painting of Betty

rarely make suggestions. Instead, in the Socratic manner she would pose a series of questions: "Have you thought about this?" "What do you think about that?"

She also went on giving. When a campaign in the mid-1980s to raise $56 million for campus improvements and endowment stalled at only half that sum, George Argyros offered $2.5 million to rekindle interest. Learning of this gift at a lunch with President Smith, Betty volunteered to do the same. Smith recalls her comment: "I will not let this program fail."

Further gifts followed during the next president, Dr. James Doti's, administration—for rehabilitation of the athletic field and to help the $26 million project for Chapman's law school, despite the potential cash-flow problems that a newly established law school might create. "Move toward it now; you'll not do it in the future," Betty told Doti.

Chapman showed its gratitude on numerous occasions. On November 6, 1982, the college at its annual fund-raising gala presented her with an oil painting of herself. The faculty subsequently voted to award her an honorary degree. At first, the trustees overruled this. Like Betty herself, they felt it inappropriate to present an honorary degree to a current member of the board. The faculty persisted. An exception for Betty was made in 1988. At the commencement exercises that year, Betty Hutton Williams became an honorary doctor of humane letters in recognition of "her exceptional contributions and service." The standing ovation that followed moved Betty deeply as she accepted the award on the campus she had known for over seventy years.

Betty's achievements at Chapman were legion. She assisted in the college's rebirth in the '70s and its transformation in the late '80s and '90s into one of California's top-ranking regional universities. In Chapman, she could see many of the chapters of her own long life unrolling. It was a reminder of the Orange County of her youth, of the husband with whom she had spent nearly forty years of her life, and of the scores of friends and thousands of admirers earned through her service to the school. Through Chapman, Betty sought to do good whenever she could. No university ever had a closer or more dedicated friend.

THE HUTTON FOUNDATION

T he last years of Betty Hutton's life were among the happiest she had
known since childhood and the early decades of her marriage to Harold.
Betty was content. She lived alone, but she never felt lonely. The 1990s
were far more relaxed and confident years than the turbulent 1980s because her
business was in good hands and profitable, her family and the trusts no longer
were at risk, and Betty could start to move assets on a large scale into the
foundation she had dreamed of as a mechanism for "doing good."

Betty's contentment was contagious. She rarely spoke at length, but those
closest to her were struck by the aura of sweet-tempered benevolence that
inspired her comments and her actions. Even in times of tension, the air of
serenity that surrounded her would spread like a pool of light to her staff, her
family, and her friends. To be sure, there were occasions in the privacy of her
office when she and Tom Parker were in conference when Betty's eyes would
mist over. But her tears when they came were of relief that together they had
rescued Hutton Associates from its traumas. Sometimes, Betty would throw her
arms around his neck and silently hug Tom for a moment.

As she approached her eightieth birthday, all eight other buildings in
the Orchard Complex where Betty had her office had been acquired by her
company. All told, she had spent $4 million to acquire total control of the
Orchard, allowing her to do what she wanted, namely improve the landscaping
and maintenance of the entire block up to her own high standards. Each day she
would go to her office, arriving at 8:30 A.M. Sylvia Law recalls, "I always knew
it was Betty when I heard the tap-tap of her cane. She would sit down in the

chair beside my desk and ask, 'What's happening?' Tommy Pooler would bring her coffee, [and] we would sit and have a chat before the day got started."

Twice each month, Betty would meet Tom Parker and Arlene Craig. Now back working full time at the company after two months' transitional work with Schneider on the Hutton Centre sale, Arlene supervised the installation of new computers at the Orchard to speed up and consolidate the company's accounting. She and Tom developed a very precise and detailed reporting process so that everyone knew exactly what was going on within the company. "Betty was always on the ball," Tom recalled. In fact, as well as in name, she was chairman of the board.

In early 1990, a five-year corporate plan was devised for The Betty L. Hutton Company. This plan said:

> Our objectives are becoming more long term in nature. The last five years have been [a time] in which we often had to react to situations. Our planning was positioned towards twelve-month cycles. This last year we have fortunately solved the remaining problem areas and can now develop a realistically achievable long range plan. The basic goals remain the same, security, long term cash flow, and peace of mind.

Betty was now able to devote most of her time and resources to her other priorities—family, staff, and preparations for the Hutton Foundation. The company stuck to its strategy, which paid off handsomely. Cash flow turned sharply positive. Summarizing the progression, Parker noted:

> *1991–2.* During this time, we actually had more commercial square footage under management than in 1984 when we had 40 employees. We were using independent contractors within the real estate field who acted as brokers for the company. This kept the corporation much simpler.
>
> *1992–3.* We started to buy distressed properties. We had established good relationships with several brokers. They knew we were

responsive, worked quickly, and paid commissions. So we saw a lot of the deals. Our properties remained full. Yes, the rents we got were maybe 20 percent below earlier heights. But the cash flow was still good. Also, at this time, interest rates on bank deposits were now down to 6 percent. So our net income, adjusted after inflation, was actually better during the real estate decline. We were able to take advantage because we had great cash flow.

1994–5. This was the time when Betty and I decided we should start moving some serious assets into the foundation. We thought it was time she began donating more of the net profit of the corporation. Up until 1995 she would take out a half a million for donations. The other $2–$3 million in profits would be reinvested in our asset base. 1995 was a turning point. Betty could see our plan for the foundation take shape. We identified a niche in helping nonprofits own their own buildings. Working with Kidney Health Care Centers, the Visiting Nurses Association, the Girl Scouts, we saw how valuable it was to these organizations to have a fixed rent and/or equity in a building.

Legally, the Hutton Foundation had been set up in 1980. Originally, it was to be activated only after Betty's death. But Parker and Arlene Craig, advised by experts on charity law, now urged that it be funded and activated in time for Betty herself to make large donations from it during her lifetime. By spring 1995, more than $10 million had been moved into the foundation's accounts. Eventually, it was to take over the whole of Betty's estate. Arrangements to make this happen in the most tax-efficient manner required innumerable meetings with Betty's lawyers and accountants. She wanted to make the best use of the know-how as well as the funds her companies had accumulated for the foundation's benefit. Parker suggested and Betty enthusiastically agreed that they focus its activities on PRI (program-related investments), which were low-interest loans to nonprofits to help them acquire their own buildings. This entrepreneurial use of the foundation's resources attracted both Betty and Tom.

To honor her late husband, The Hutton Foundation helped the Passkeys Foundation, set up by Chester to "open doors to positive, successful living," to establish its Outstanding Youth Citizen Program. This program offers ten scholarships each year to graduating seniors from Orange County high schools and is administered, as Betty in her later years invariably preferred, by one of her own family members—in Passkeys' case the Reverend Russell Williams, the older son of Chester. Betty L. Hutton scholars receive annual $1,000 awards in recognition of their "active, productive involvement in their local community."

Late in 1995, Betty was approached by the same Jim Farley who had introduced her to Chapman, who came up with an unusual request. The World Affairs Council of Orange County, of which both Betty and he were trustees, was looking for support to conduct a day-long seminar entitled "United Nations: Reform or Wither Away." Thirty years earlier, Betty, a staunch Republican, would scarcely have entertained a plea for help for a U.N.-related venture, but since then, her experience in east Asia had made her far more internationally minded than most Orange County leaders.

At a meeting with the council's officers, she agreed that the end of the Cold War had ushered in a new era and a global economy in which fresh initiatives were needed to tackle such problems as Third World poverty and threats to the global environment. The United Nations must play a part—but the United Nations must be reformed.

Betty wrote a check for $10,000 to help produce a video recording of the council's program, which took place at Chapman University with ten hours of debate, led by the United Nation's undersecretary for peacekeeping and ambassadors from Australia, Japan, Liberia, and the European Union. Not long afterwards, when the video, which contained a long list of recommendations for reform of the United Nations, was ready to be presented, Secretary General Boutros Boutros-Ghali visited Los Angeles.

Betty was driven by a World Affairs Council representative to the downtown Hilton Hotel where the secretary general received her in a private room. Betty was constructive and animated. Boutros-Ghali was well briefed on her experiences in east Asia. He thanked her for her support for the reform proposals put forward by the World Affairs Council. Several of these were to be incorporated in his own plans for modernization of the United Nation's structure.

In February 1993, Betty's family threw a splendid party at Chapman University to celebrate her eightieth birthday. More than 150 friends and admirers gathered in the newly completed Argyros Forum. The toasts were warm and affectionate, but afterwards, Betty told Sylvia Law, "I hope they don't think I'm retiring." She never did.

Betty at eighty still served on no less than six committees of the Chapman board. To walk, she needed a cane to support her, but every day she was busy—on family, firm, and foundation business. The center of her life was her extended family—her sister, Mary, her nieces who worked with her in the business, and Chester's family, especially Doug, who painted her home at the beach and became a frequent companion. Unfortunately, Chester by the

Betty's family at her eightieth birthday party at Chapman University

early '90s had become too ill to remain at their Villa Park home. Needing twenty-four-hour-a-day care, he was moved into a Mission Viejo retirement home. Betty never failed to telephone him each morning and evening. Weekends she went to see him, though gradually Chester became less able to participate in the card games they would play or even, on occasion, to recognize her.

Betty bore her grief over Chester's decline with silent fortitude. When he died, April 10, 1993, Chester's sons arranged for his remains to be interned alongside his first wife's in Los Angeles. Betty was at the graveside as the older of his sons, the Reverend Russ Williams, who had officiated at their marriage, spoke for Betty as well as his family. "Chester Williams was a good man.," he said. "He meant well, lived well, and did good. He was a fine father, a fine husband, a great friend."

Chester's death threw Betty still more closely into the arms of her own family. She loved organizing family outings. With her niece Sally, she went antique shopping over weekends in Palm Springs or San Francisco. She drove frequently to Santa Barbara with Mary to visit the Parker family and vacationed in Maui with Mary and the Parkers in August 1989 and again in July 1995. She also hosted Christmas feasts in Villa Park and Easter weekends in the desert. At one such family celebration when four generations of Spennettas were present, they heated the swimming pool to ninety-five degrees and twenty family members crowded into the home. Only half that number slept that night in a bed.

Betty's office staff by now had become "family" too. Twice, she hosted all her employees and their families on all-expenses-paid vacations on the island of Maui. The group would meet each evening around the hotel swimming pool during the "happy hour" to sip exotic drinks and share the experiences of the day. Betty was in her element. "Nothing was too much trouble to make us feel comfortable," said Tom Pooler, her driver. "She didn't talk a lot, just smiled, and we loved her for it." Betty's kindnesses to her staff were legendary. When Sylvia Law needed surgery in 1993, Jack, her husband, was sitting in the hospital waiting room when he heard the click, click of a cane. In came Betty.

"She waited until my surgery was over before she left," said Sylvia. "She had a word with the doctor to make sure I would be all right. When I got back to work, I told her how special that was. 'Well, I always think of you as my daughter,' was Betty's reply. It was the nicest thing she ever said to me."

Jerry Baker, another of Betty's aides during the Refining Associates days, meanwhile had returned to the Orchard office after her husband died. Betty invited her to the 1995 Bob Hope Classic golf tournament in Indian Wells. The final day of the tournament coincided with Betty's eighty-second birthday on February 20. "I was thrilled to be in her home where President Eisenhower once lived," Jerry wrote. "We celebrated her birthday in our bathrobes, sitting around the breakfast table, just Sylvia and her husband, Jack, Tom Pooler, and me."

This was to be Betty's last party in Indian Wells. The California desert was always very special to her. There she had overcome the tuberculosis she suffered as an adolescent. There at that Palm Springs gas station, she had met the man who for forty years had been the light of her life, the partner with whom she had reached across the Pacific and built up a fortune. Now Betty was on her own, yet she was never lonesome. Her secret was to keep on working and giving of herself and her wealth.

She still had to face the realities of aging. She had symptoms of Parkinson's disease. The old hockey injury to her left knee made it difficult for her to walk more than a few yards. She needed help from her chauffeur to get in to and out of her car. Old age is often accompanied by irritability and self-pity, as aches and pains bring with them increased awareness of physical infirmities and fading mental powers, but Betty showed no evidence of either. She did not feel sorry for herself. She never got angry with others. There were no signs of her experiencing those "intimations of mortality" that afflicted both Harold and Chester in their declining years.

On June 11, 1991, Betty sustained a serious fall. Not until the following morning did she manage to telephone her office. All night, she laid on the floor of her Villa Park home, drifting in and out of consciousness. Rushed to St. Joseph's Hospital, Betty was treated for a badly broken hip and arm. She remained at home until early August then eased her way back to work and a full schedule.

Her fall, however, was a portent. Once Betty returned to her office, she was visibly frail and uncertain of her balance. Her voice was down to a whisper. Her family tried to convince her that she needed live-in help, but Betty scorned the idea. She valued her privacy more than her comfort. To the last, she was to maintain the independence and emotional self-sufficiency that since childhood she had guarded as her most precious asset.

On August 8, 1995, Tom Pooler arrived at her Villa Park home as usual at 8 A.M. Betty was nowhere to be seen. He tapped on her bedroom door. Betty had fallen again and had not regained consciousness. Pooler called for an ambulance. He alerted Tom Parker at his office. "Jessica was with me," says Parker, "We jumped into the car. On the way to Betty's house, an ambulance pulled right in front of me and my heart started beating very quickly. I followed the paramedics into the house and saw Betty on the floor. I didn't see any activity. I felt she was in such pain that she wasn't able to talk or open her eyes." Betty had come in from work, prepared her evening meal, stepped into the bedroom to change, and collapsed. Her dinner things were still neatly laid out and untouched.

The paramedics loaded her frail body into the ambulance. "I asked the driver to go to St. Joseph, her favorite hospital," said Parker. "They said there was no time, we had to go to the nearest hospital, Chapman Medical Center. There the doctors told us that Betty had suffered a massive stroke. There was little that could be done."

Betty remained in a coma for the next five weeks. All her family members gathered around her. They tried to insulate her from the crush of well-wishers who wanted to assist. At her office, the staff was devastated. Arlene Craig recalls, "It was difficult, in fact at times impossible, to concentrate on anything other than the fact that Betty was not with us, working alongside us until the last one left for home."

She never recovered consciousness. The left side of her brain, which controls speech and most mental processes, was destroyed. Betty Lee Spennetta Hutton Williams was moved to St. Joseph's Hospital and then home. Her sister, Mary, niece Jessica, and Doug Williams were at her side when she died at noon on September 16, 1995.

Betty was laid to rest next to Harold in the family's burial plot in Orange County's Fairhaven Memorial Park. At the private service for those closest to her, Chester's son Russ Williams officiated. The site of the grave is the one Betty herself had chosen eighteen years earlier. She and Harold are now buried together near a southern magnolia tree. Their plain stone markers reveal no message other than their names and dates: Harold Hutton 1904–1975 and Betty L. Hutton Williams 1913–1995. However, during the Christmas season of 1996, a basket filled with pine, red velvet ribbon, a silk poinsettia, and a gold-leafed palm was placed near their graves. The note attached to the basket read,

Betty—I miss you so much, but know you're with Harold. Love . . .

No one knows who wrote this, but it could have been from any number of the thousands of people in a dozen countries who remembered this dynamic pair.

Last photo taken of Betty

EPILOGUE

Two days after the mortal remains of Betty Hutton Williams were laid to rest, Chapman University offered its public tribute. Nearly a thousand people whose lives Betty had touched gathered on the morning of September 21, 1995, to remember her contributions to Orange County and the wider world as pioneer, philanthropist, and neighbor. Most of the faculty who attended wore their caps and gowns as a measure of their special regard for a woman who had earned the highest respect from the academic community.

James Doti, president of Chapman, had ordered the university's flags to be flown at half mast for two weeks over the campus where as a schoolgirl Betty had danced and as a trustee of Chapman she so often had lent a sympathetic ear to staff and students alike. In his eulogy Doti said:

> She was an extraordinary woman. Since the announcement of the stroke she suffered, I have noticed a more quiet and introspective attitude on campus. It seems as if many of us realized that losing Betty would diminish our own lives.
>
> When a major gift was needed to get our sports center constructed in 1977, Betty was there. When $5 million was needed to place us over the top in our Enterprise '86 campaign, Betty was there. When students needed additional funds to take part in a study abroad program or an international music tour, Betty was there. When our Palm Desert Academic Center needed financial support to stay afloat, Betty was there. When we needed a significant match to release other funds, Betty was there. And when we needed to completely renovate the Hutton Sports Center this summer, Betty was there.

At her death, the Hutton Foundation had been fully active for little more than a month. Yet Betty lived long enough and took uncommon pleasure in the fact that she could actually see the foundation "doing good." During the four weeks before her stroke, she wrote nearly $250,000 in checks on the foundation's account. On her desk when she left the office of The Betty L. Hutton Company for the last time was a check she had typed herself but left unsigned. Her estate therefore honored it for her.

So ended the earthly life of one of southern California's golden girls, whose horizons and accomplishments reached far beyond the small towns in which Betty Spenetta had grown up. But the Huttons' story has not ended.

Together, Harold and Betty wrote a chapter or two in the long and splendid story of American enterprise. They pushed their piece of the American dream far beyond the continent's edge. They assisted in the extension of the frontiers of the United States into international trade and investment, encapsulating in their business and their travels the early stages of the globalization of American industry and finance. Their story personifies the transformation of the United States from an inward-looking, farm-centered giant into the world's biggest trader and investor and history's greatest, and perhaps its last, superpower.

The Huttons were no less Americans for becoming global citizens. Their achievements and their legacy reflect a made-in-America combination of qualities that is to be found in few other countries—driving ambition and compulsive generosity; insatiable curiosity and innocence, even naiveté, in the face of external events they only vaguely understood; and most of all, an instinctive belief that every setback offers a stepping stone from which to spring forward to the future. Tomorrow, the Huttons believed, will always be better than today.

Harold, in particular, was one of nature's optimists. In his life he was a callow and rebellious schoolboy, a hard-drinking and romantic roughneck, a shrewdly calculating and risk-taking investor, a natural and successful trader, and a big-thinking and big-spending capitalist. Yet underneath his bluff, businesslike exterior was a warm heart, a razor-sharp brain, the infectious enthusiasm of a young man who never grew old, and a deep abiding love for his fellow human beings. Harold was a man of his times who saw the future more clearly than most of his contemporaries and backed his vision with cash.

Harold Hutton's central features were his love of life and family, his penchant for hard work and honest business, his lack of pomp, and his adherence to a code of conduct grounded in the Ten Commandments. Harold was not religious, and there were times when he cut corners, but his deepest instincts were to keep his promises, pay his debts, tell the truth, and stand by his friends. To many Americans who have watched the decline of such virtues in Washington, D.C., and in the media, these values may seem old-fashioned, but Harold took it for granted than any man not only pays his way and carries his share of the burden but also plays by the rules. Harold Hutton was a wheeler-dealer who became a multimillionaire in his lifetime, but he was always an honorable man, a man of his word.

Betty Hutton, too, lived as she was raised—by the book. She lived long enough to benefit more than Harold did from the fortune they had built up together. True, she came close to losing it, but by calling up her reserves of good sense and a sweet, strong character, she cut her losses, enlisted her white knight, made her comeback, and switched her emphasis from making money to caring for her family and doing good for others.

And that is why the Hutton Story, far from ending, goes on and on. It is the stuff that movies are made of—romance in the desert; hard slogging in the oil patch, the jungle, and the South Pacific; struggles with lawyers and bankers; high politics and intrigue in east Asia; and then, as the curtain falls, a happy ending. Harold Hutton and Betty Hutton Williams are still remembered by their families and hundreds of their friends, and their spirits and their achievements live on in the charitable foundation that Harold Hutton always dreamed of and

Betty created in his memory. Well endowed and strongly managed, the Hutton Foundation continues the saga that began with a chance meeting at a California gas station and leaped across the Pacific on the wings of luck and enterprise.

INDEX